Contents

Electronic News Gathering (ENG) and Electronic Field
1 Production (EFP) 1
ENG—CAPTURING THE EVENT 2
EFP—STUDIO PRODUCTION ON
    LOCATION 4
SUMMARIZING ENG AND EFP 5
FILM TO VIDEOTAPE: CHANGING
    TECHNOLOGY 6
    TV News 6
    Nonbroadcast Video 8
    Home Video 9
    Advantages of Video 9
STUDIO TV AND PORTABLE TV 9
    Electrical Power Needs 9
    Advantages of Indoor Studio 10
    Disadvantages of Indoor Studio 10
    Emergence of Videocassettes 10
KNOWING THE BASICS 11

Processing an Image to Video:
Lenses, Cameras and Videotape
2 Recorders 13
THEORY OF LIGHT 13
    Photons and Light Waves 13
    Spectrum 14
PRINCIPLES OF LENS OPERATION 15
    Human Eye 15
    Lens Elements 16
    Focal Length 16
    Focus 16
    Macrofocus 17
    Aspect Ratio 17
    Iris 18
    Zoom Lenses 19
    Light Quality Control 23
    Accessories 24
    Filters 24
    Interchangeable Lenses 26
    Care and Cleaning of Lenses 27

VIDEO CAMERAS 27
    Camera Basics 28
    Camera Functions 30
    Monitoring the Picture 31
VIDEOTAPE RECORDERS 33
    Low-end Professional: Hi8, S-VHS,
        3⁄4-Inch SP 33
    Standard Format: Beta SP, 1-Inch, and MII 34
    Time Code 35
    Typical Control Functions 36
    Typical Inputs 36
    Typical Outputs 36
    Onboard Decks 37
    Meters 37
    Warning Lights 38
    Time Base Correctors 38
    Maintenance 39
    Troubleshooting 39
BATTERIES 39
    Recharging 40
    Life Span 41
    Proper Care 42
TRIPODS AND CAMERA-MOUNTING
    DEVICES 42
    Fluid Heads 42
    Tripod Legs 42
    Dollies 43
    Cranes and Booms 43
    Steadi-Cam 44
    Car Mounts 44
    Aerial Mounts 45
    Special Mounts 45

Microphones and Audio-
3 Recording Techniques 47
STRUCTURE 47
    Dynamic Elements 47
    Condenser Elements 48
SENSITIVITY 49
    Directional Sensitivity 49

Frequency Response 51
Sound Sensitivity 51
IMPEDANCE AND OTHER FACTORS 51
Impedance 52
Other Factors 52
STYLE 52
Hand Mikes 53
Mounted Mikes 53
Lavaliere Mikes 54
SPECIAL APPLICATIONS 54
Performance Microphones 54
Multiple Application Microphones 55
Headset Microphones 55
Surface Mount and Pressure Zone
    Microphones 55
Wireless Microphones 56
Parabolic Microphones 57
Contact Microphones 57
ACCESSORIES 57
Mounts 57
Acoustic Filters and Windscreens 57
AUDIO CABLES AND CONNECTORS 58
Balanced and Unbalanced Lines 58
Connectors and Adapters 58
Signal Loss in Audio Cable 59
Phase 59
Filters and Pads 60
SELECTION AND PLACEMENT 60
Choosing a Mike 60
Placing a Mike 60
MIXING, MONITORING AND STEREO 64
Mixing 64
Monitoring 65
Stereo 66

4 Light, Lights and Lighting 67
PHYSICAL PROPERTIES OF LIGHT 67
Color Temperature 68
Intensity: The Inverse Square Law 69
Angle of Light 69
SOURCES OF LIGHT FOR PORTABLE
    VIDEO 72
Sun 72
Artificial Light 72
LIGHTING EQUIPMENT 74
Lamps 74
Light Housings 75
Mounts 77
Lighting Modulators 78
POWER REQUIREMENTS 82
Volts and Amps 83
EXPOSURE AND SHADOWS 83

Base Lighting 83
Lens Quality 84
Correct Exposure 84
Use of High Gain 84
Quality Lighting 84
Contrast Ratio 85
LIGHTING TECHNIQUES 86
Three-Point Lighting 86
Other Lights 90
Adding to Existing Light 91
Using Camera-Mounted Light 92
LIGHT AS AN AESTHETIC FORCE 94
Source Lighting 95
Portrait Lighting 95
BALANCING THE PICTURE 96
Force of Elements Within a Picture 96
Balancing an Interview Shot 97
Framing 97
PRINCIPLES AND TECHNIQUES FOR
    GOOD LIGHTING 98
Mood Lighting 100
Chiaroscuro Lighting 100
Zone Lighting 101
Lighting With Color 101
Correct Quantity of Light 102

5 The Basic Shots 103
IDENTIFYING THE STORY LINE 103
TYPES OF SHOTS 103
Varying Shots by Focal Length 104
Special Use Shots 109
Camera Action Shots 117
FOLLOWING THE ACTION 119
Breaking the Rules 119

6 Scriptwriting 121
ENG 121
EFP 122
Goals 122
Knowing the Audience 122
Format 123
Central Visual Theme 123
Research 124
Treatment 124
Outline 125
Storyboard 125
Script 125

7 Pre-Production 135
ENG 135

Portable
Video
ENG & EFP

2nd Edition

Norman J. Me
and Tom Tanq

Boston   Oxford

Focal Press is an imprint of Butterworth–Heinemann.

Copyright © 1997 by Butterworth–Heinemann

 A member of the Reed Elsevier group

 Recognizing the importance of preserving what has been written, Butterworth–Heinemann prints its books on acid-free paper whenever possible.

 Butterworth–Heinemann supports the efforts of American Forests and the Global ReLeaf program in its campaign for the betterment of trees, forests, and our environment.

© 1992 by Knowledge Industry Publications, Inc.

ISBN 0-240-80304-3

The publisher offers special discounts on bulk orders of this book.
For information, please contact:
Manager of Special Sales
Butterworth–Heinemann
225 Wildwood Avenue
Woburn, MA 01801-2014
Tel: 617-928-2500
Fax: 617-928-2620

For information on all Focal Press publications available, contact our World Wide Web home page at: http://www.bh.com/focalpress

10 9 8 7 6 5 4 3 2 1

Printed in the United States of America

EFP 136
PRODUCTION CREW 136
   Executive Producer 136
   Producer 136
   Director 138
   Videographer 138
   Audio Engineer 138
   Lighting Director 139
   Grip or Utility 139
   Talent 139
   Editor 139
SCHEDULING AND COORDINATING 140
   Factors to Consider 140
   Guidelines for Schedule-Making 141
LOCATION SELECTION AND SURVEY 141
GRAPHICS AND PROPS PREPARATION 143
CLEARANCE ON COPYRIGHT
      MATERIALS 143
TRAVEL PLANNING 144
   Transporting Equipment 144
   Equipment Cube 144
   Air Travel 146
   Travel Tips 146
   Foreign Travel 147

8 EFP Styles 149
CORPORATE AND PROFESSIONAL
      VIDEOS 150
   Corporate News Show 150
   Instruction, Training and Demonstration 151
   Sales, Promotion and Motivation 153
PUBLIC SERVICE ANNOUNCEMENTS
      (PSAS) AND COMMERCIALS 153
   Public Service Announcements 153
   Commercials 153
   Budgets 155
PERFORMANCE VIDEOS 155
   Entertainment 155
   Historical Archive 159
SPORTS VIDEO 160
   Competition Coverage 161
   Feature Coverage 163
MUSIC VIDEOS 164
   Variety of Settings 165
   Style and Technique 165
NATURE AND DOCUMENTARY VIDEOS ... 165
VIDEO ART 166

9 ENG Styles 169
SPOT NEWS 169
   Shooting in the Middle of the Action 169

Shooting in the Aftermath 171
Shooting on the Perimeter of the Action 172
Dealing with the Authorities 173
GENERAL NEWS 174
   Get a Good First Shot 174
   Avoid Long Sound Bites 174
   Cover Long Sound Bites with Video 175
   Keep the Story Moving 175
FEATURE NEWS 175
   Try Different Techniques 176
SPORTS NEWS 176
   Features 176
   Competition 176

10 Technical Editing Basics 179
VIDEOTAPE FORMATS 180
   Reel-to-Reel Format 180
   Videocassette Format 180
TYPES OF EDITS 185
   Assemble Edit 186
   Insert Edit 187
TECHNICAL CONCEPTS 187
   Scanning 187
   Fields, Frames and Segments 188
   Tracking 190
   Control Track Editing 190
   Time Code Editing 190
   Time Base Correction 190
EDITING MACHINES 191
   Video Controls 191
   Audio Controls 191
   Video Connections 193
   Synchronization 195
   Audio Connections 196
   VIDEO INPUT Switch 196
   Understanding the Editing System 196
   Performing an Insert Edit 196

11 Creative Editing Basics 199
SEQUENCING THE SHOTS 199
   Basic Sequence 199
   Sample Script 200
   Match-Action Cutting 201
MAINTAINING CONTINUITY 201
   The 180° Line Rule 201
   Crossing-the-Line Editing 204
   Continuity Within Sequences 204
ESTABLISHING A STORY LINE 205
   Beginning 205
   Middle 205
   End 205

Visualizing Paragraphs 206
Shooting Without a Script 206
PACING 206
Editing for Dynamics 207
Avoiding Predictability 207
Editing to Music 207
Varying Editing Speed 207
POST-PRODUCTION 208
Dissolve 208
Wipe 211
OnLine Edit 211
EDITING SOUND 211
Accurate Representation of the Event 211
Adding Sound for Effect 211
Avoid Abrupt Edits 212
Natural Sound 212
Laydowns and Laybacks 212
Editing Methods 213

12 Live TV From the Field 215
GETTING THE PICTURE OUT 215
Telephone Lines 216
Microwaves 216
Satellites 216
COMMUNICATIONS 217
INTERRUPTED FEED BACK (IFB) 218
Portable TV 218
Mix-Minus 219
FORM AND STYLE 219
Spot News 220
Scheduled Events 221
Live for the Sake of Live 222
EFP 222
WHAT CAN GO WRONG? 222
Know the System 222
Power in the Truck 223
Lighting 223
Cables 223
Batteries 224
Crowds 224
Permission 224
Timing 224

13 Budgeting and Pricing 225
ENG VERSUS EFP 226
ENG 226
EFP 226
IN-HOUSE VERSUS INDEPENDENT
PRODUCTION UNITS 227
In-House 227

Independent 227
CREATING AN ACCURATE BUDGET 228
Line Costs 228
Overhead Expenses 230
BUDGET TRACKING 230
Computer Assistance 231
EFP PRICING FORMULA 231

14 Copyright and Legal Issues 235
PRIVACY 235
News Productions 235
Non-News Productions 240
COPYRIGHTS 242
Violations 242
Piracy 243
Exclusivity 243
Bugs 244
Courtesies 244
Pool 244
Public Domain Materials 245
Protecting Your Work 245
Obtaining Protection 246
Alerting Others of Protection 246
Scope 246
INSURANCE 246
Comprehensive Liability 246
Equipment Loss or Damage 249
Rental Floaters 249
Restrictions 249
Other Coverages 249
Errors and Omissions 250
Workers' Compensation 250
Completion Guaranty Bond 250
Producers' Insurance Policies (PIPs) 250

15 New Trends and Technologies 251
DIGITAL TECHNOLOGY IN PORTABLE
VIDEO 251
CAMERAS 252
VIDEOTAPE RECORDERS 253
NONLINEAR EDITORS 253
EXHIBITION MONITORS 254
HIGH-DEFINITION TV (HDTV) 255
DESKTOP VIDEO 255

Glossary 257
Bibliography 267
Index 269
About the Authors 274

List of Tables and Figures

Figure 1.1: Shooting home video 2
Figure 1.2: Home video of raging fire 3
Figure 1.3: ENG on location.......................4
Figure 1.4: EFP shoot 5
Figure 1.5: ENG flowchart 6
Figure 1.6: EFP flowchart 7
Figure 1.7: News photographer in 1980 8

Table 2.1: Videographer's basic set
of gear 14
Figure 2.1: Interior of a production van 14
Figure 2.2: Differences in wavelength
determine color 15
Figure 2.3: Still camera depth of field 17
Figure 2.4: Standard macrofocusing
knob.......................................18
Figure 2.5: Typical zoom lens controls 20
Figure 2.6: Optical group for zoom lens ...21
Figure 2.7: Pistol grip on zoom lens 22
Figure 2.8: Large zoom lens 23
Figure 2.9: Effect of fog filter 25
Figure 2.10: Filter wheel 28
Figure 2.11: Professional video camera 30
Figure 2.12: Camera control switches 31
Figure 2.13: Waveform monitor color
bars 33
Figure 2.14: Vectorscope color bars............34
Figure 2.15: SONY color TV monitor 35
Figure 2.16: Beta SP recorder 36

Figure 2.17: Industrial U-Matic VCR 38
Figure 2.18: Common batteries 40
Figure 2.19: Anton Bauer Snap-on®
system 41
Figure 2.20: Fluid head tripod 42
Figure 2.21: Dolly with hard wheels 43
Figure 2.22: Portable boom 44
Figure 2.23: Lipstick-cam camera 44

Figure 3.1: Dynamic and condenser
microphones 48
Figure 3.2: Condenser mike 49
Figure 3.3: Pickup patterns of micro-
phones 49
Figure 3.4: Super-cardioid microphone 50
Figure 3.5: Frequency response chart 51
Table 3.1: Microphone impedance
levels 52
Figure 3.6: Dynamic omnidirectional
mike..53
Figure 3.7: Integral mount on mike 53
Figure 3.8: Boom or fishpole mike............54
Figure 3.9: Tram lavaliere microphone 54
Figure 3.10: Headset mikes 55
Figure 3.11: Boundary mike 56
Figure 3.12: RF wireless mikes 56
Figure 3.13: Vega Pro 33 wireless mike......56
Figure 3.14: Mike clasp 58
Figure 3.15: Desk stands for mikes 58

Figure 3.16:   Zeppelin system 58
Figure 3.17:   Male XLR connector 59
Figure 3.18:   Audio-balanced line
                connectors 59
Figure 3.19:   Audio adapters 59
Figure 3.20:   Unusual microphone
                placement 61
Figure 3.21:   Mike with shock mounting 62
Figure 3.22:   Cable of lavaliere mike 63
Figure 3.23:   Mixer inputs and outputs 65
Figure 3.24:   Headphones monitor audio 65

Figure 4.1:   Cameras respond to light 68
Figure 4.2:   Inverse Square Law 69
Figure 4.3:   Light meter 70
Figure 4.4:   Sun as light source 70
Figure 4.5:   Backlit subject.......................71
Figure 4.6:   Quartz-halogen versus
                tabular quartz lamp 72
Figure 4.7:   HMI light 73
Figure 4.8:   Scoop light 75
Figure 4.9:   Open-faced spotlight 76
Figure 4.10:   Lowel Softlight 2 76
Figure 4.11:   Portable light kit 77
Figure 4.12:   LTM Pepper 200 77
Figure 4.13:   Gaffers and C-clamp 78
Figure 4.14:   Light with wall mount
                and flag..................................78
Figure 4.15:   Two lights with barndoors 79
Figure 4.16:   Cucalorus throws mottled
                shadow pattern 80
Figure 4.17:   Reflector 81
Figure 4.18:   Light with umbrella................81
Figure 4.19:   Wire mesh screen 81
Figure 4.20:   Silk cuts light 82
Figure 4.21:   Light with daylight blue gel 82
Figure 4.22:   Portraiture style of lighting 86
Figure 4.23:   Lighting zones 87
Figure 4.24:   Light placement when
                subject faces camera 88
Figure 4.25:   Four lighting techniques 89
Figure 4.26:   Soft lighting 91
Figure 4.27:   Create a natural look 93
Figure 4.28:   Lighting with camera light 93
Figure 4.29:   Portable 12-volt light 94
Figure 4.30:   Battery-powered light 94
Figure 4.31:   Source lighting 95
Figure 4.32:   Portrait lighting 96
Figure 4.33:   Key light................................97

Figure 4.34:   Light placement with
                shadows 98
Figure 4.35:   Light placement for an
                interview................................99
Figure 4.36:   Chiaroscuro lighting 101

Figure 5.1:   Focal length and image
                size 104
Figure 5.2:   Wide angle and telephoto
                perspective 105
Figure 5.3:   Angle of view and distance
                to subject 106
Figure 5.4:   The wide shot 106
Figure 5.5:   Straight-on shot 107
Figure 5.6:   Use of the foreground 108
Figure 5.7:   Medium shots 109
Figure 5.8:   Vanishing points 110
Figure 5.9:   Rule of thirds........................111
Figure 5.10:   Close-up shot........................112
Figure 5.11:   Extreme close-up (XCU)
                shot 112
Figure 5.12:   Cutaway shot........................112
Figure 5.13:   Framing the picture 114
Figure 5.14:   Framing the center of
                attention 115
Figure 5.15:   Reporter stand-up shot 116
Figure 5.16:   Low-angle shot.....................116
Figure 5.17:   Interview shots 117
Figure 5.18:   Framing leads the subject.......120

Figure 6.1:   Objectives and outlines
                for a script 126
Figure 6.2:   Blanks used for a
                storyboard 127
Figure 6.3:   Completed storyboard 128
Table 6.1:   Terms used in scriptwriting ...130
Figure 6.4:   Storyboard without audio 130
Figure 6.5:   Scripts with revisions 131
Figure 6.6:   Computer program
                to format scriptwriting 132

Figure 7.1:   Pre-production checklist 137
Figure 7.2:   Location scouting report 142
Figure 7.3:   Equipment checklist..............145
Figure 7.4:   Protective cases 146

Figure 8.1:   Corporate-style news shots ...150
Figure 8.2:   Instructional video shot 151
Figure 8.3:   Instructional TV system 152

Figure 8.4:   Public service
                announcement 153
Figure 8.5:   Stand-up presentation
                commercials 154
Figure 8.6:   Three-camera remote shoot,
                live switching 156
Figure 8.7:   Three-camera remote shoot,
                with VCRs 158
Figure 8.8:   Two-camera remote shoot.....159
Figure 8.9:   An archive video 160
Figure 8.10:   Cameras for professional
                location video 161
Figure 8.11:   Sports interview, two
                cameras...................................161
Figure 8.12:   Vehicle for remote work 162
Figure 8.13:   Multi-camera remote
                professional sports shoot 163
Figure 8.14:   Line-of-scrimmage shot 164
Figure 8.15:   Experimental video 166

Figure 9.1:   ENG photographer
                shooting a story 170
Figure 9.2:   Shooting spot news 172

Figure 10.1:   ¾-inch U-Matic editing
                system, A/B roll editing
                system 181
Figure 10.2:   Video and audio track
                pattern on 2-inch quad-
                ruplex videotape....................182
Figure 10.3:   Video and audio track
                pattern on Type C
                videotape 182
Figure 10.4:   Video and audio track
                pattern on ¾-inch
                cassette tape..........................183
Figure 10.5:   Video and audio track
                pattern on ½-inch Betacam
                SP videotape.........................183
Figure 10.6:   Video and audio track
                pattern on digital videotape ... 184
Figure 10.7:   Digital video recorders 185

Figure 10.8:   Video and audio track
                pattern on 8mm
                videotape 185
Figure 10.9:   SONY EVO-9700 HI8
                edit system 186
Figure 10.10:   HI8 player-recorder 186
Figure 10.11:   Assemble editing....................187
Figure 10.12:   Edit control buttons 188
Figure 10.13:   Insert editing 189
Figure 10.14:   Electron beam scan 189
Figure 10.15:   Edit machine 192
Figure 10.16:   Standard editing system 192
Figure 10.17:   Audio VU meters 193
Figure 10.18:   Cables for two-machine
                editing 194
Figure 10.19:   SONY BVW-75
                inputs/outputs 195
Figure 10.20:   Player/recorder control 197

Figure 11.1:   Continuity in a simple
                action sequence 202
Figure 11.2:   Camera placement 203
Figure 11.3:   A/B reels 209
Figure 11.4:   Multi-machine edit system 210

Figure 12.1:   Microwave van 217
Figure 12.2:   Portable satellite
                transmitter 218
Figure 12.3:   Satellite news gathering
                (SNG) trucks 219
Figure 12.4:   Live TV news coverage 220

Table 13.1:   Budget tracking 231

Figure 13.1:   Computer program for
                video producers 232

Figure 14.1:   Model release forms 241
Figure 14.2:   Form PA for copyright
                protection 247

Figure 15.1:   Non-linear editing system 254
Figure 15.2:   Multifunction device 256

Preface

When we wrote the first edition of this book, video production was undergoing many profound changes. Cameras were becoming far more efficient, giving better images with less light. New formats of videotape were emerging and video practitioners had a growing array of choices of videotape recorders. Editing systems were being designed to allow users of portable formats to create sophisticated productions with network-quality look without having expensive equipment.

As we write the second edition, we find that many of these technological changes are still occurring. Cameras continue to shrink in price and size, but the images they produce are better. New videotape formats continue to appear and existing ones reappear in new and improved versions. Editing systems designed for portable video can do many wondrous things while still preserving the quality of the original image.

None of these changes were completely unexpected because technological changes have been proceeding so swiftly since the late 1970s. The change that is perhaps the most surprising is the pervasive use of portable video by so many different sectors of society. Broadcast and cable industry use of portable video continues to increase both in news coverage and general programming; both shoot the majority of their video outside the studio. Corporate use of video has increased dramatically with in-house video newsletters, information and motivational tapes and teleconferences common in thousands of corpo-

rations. Governmental agencies, medical facilities and educational institutions have found portable video to be indispensable in many everyday applications. Independent production houses have become abundant. The market for videotaping almost every kind of event is always expanding. Besides the bride and groom, the next most common sight at a wedding is the videographer. Home video users have voracious appetites for new equipment and continually find new and innovative uses for portable video.

This acceptance of video in our entertainment, businesses, schools and even our private lives has given video a heightened importance not only in American society but throughout the world. Not many would disagree that TV had a great deal to do with the awesome changes in Eastern Europe during 1989 and 1990. The technology and the power of video have truly made us one global village. The entire world now watches events take place in real or near real time. The power of video to communicate is being felt in every segment of society using video. The importance of video has never been greater and the importance of quality video has never been so crucial.

The convergence of video and computers is a significant factor with corporate, governmental, medical, educational and home video enthusiasts utilizing their desktop computers to provide titles, transitions and special video effects in their creations. While the camera, VCR and editing machine technology is in a second or third generation, the interface of personal computers with video is just beginning. New hardware devices and software to provide editing, character generation and special effects are appearing constantly.

All these changes present a difficult challenge to the aspiring professional. The world of portable video is a fast-paced and dynamic one that requires frequent updates about equipment, techniques and applications. This reality is the main reason for a second edition. *Portable Video: ENG and EFP* has been greatly expanded to cover more topics and techniques. By going into more depth and adding new areas, the authors have attempted to make this book a complete guide to almost any video application. Today's video-grapher should have an extensive working knowledge not only of the equipment but of the myriad techniques and styles that make up the craft. This book provides the knowledge necessary to gain, advance or enhance an understanding of today's and tomorrow's video needs.

The second edition is written for professionals who want to know more about the trends in both equipment and techniques in professional portable video. College and university students who intend to pursue careers in video will find that the information in this book will help them get and keep the crucial first job. The basic concepts and theory presented in the book will be useful not only to professionals and students, but also to the home video maker because good video is a goal shared by all. It no longer takes a $40,000 camera and a $100,000 edit system to tell a story or record a once-in-a-lifetime event on video. This book is written to help any video practitioner do the job properly.

Acknowledgements

Many people have helped at various stages of this project and all deserve recognition. Naming them all would be beyond our ability to remember, but most are included in the following list: Lynn Campbell, Manny Sotello, Louis Zapata, Peter Stone, Pete Garrow, Mike Barber, Joe Vitti, Charlie Beckner, Linda Douglass, Pete Noyes, Ray Farkas, Matt Stevens, Ken Preston, Con Keyes, John Warren, Lynn Medoff, Sarah Medoff, Natalie Medoff, the Helfords, the faculty and staff of the School of Communication at Northern Arizona University, Marty Sommerness, Manny Romero, Tim Huelsman, and Mara Alper. We thank you for your patience, time and kind assistance.

1 Electronic News Gathering (ENG) and Electronic Field Production (EFP)

In the mid-1970s broadcast news production exited the studio to capture news events in a new way—a way that would allow the instant replay characteristic of video production. Until that time, news events were shot on 16mm film, which needed to go to the TV studio or film lab for processing before being shown on the nightly news show. "Film at eleven" was a common announcement during the six o'clock news about a late-breaking news story because the film was still being processed.

In the early 1970s, portable video cameras smaller and lighter than existing studio cameras were introduced. In addition, these cameras were battery powered and designed to give acceptable video images with less lighting than studio cameras.

By the late 1970s, the use of portable video cameras became widespread for news coverage. Many TV stations gladly gave up the use of the film-processing lab and film-editing bench for the videotape editing bay. Videotape of a news event delivered to the station before 5 p.m. could easily be edited and aired at the edited and aired on the 6 p.m. news. This new method of covering and promptly airing the news became known as electronic news gathering (ENG). News coverage became electronic because videotape creates an image by an electronic rather than chemical process.

At about the same time that news operations began using portable video cameras, hospitals, government agencies, corporations, educational institutions and independent production houses began to use portable video as well. This became known as electronic field production (EFP). It was used for documenting and archiving healthcare procedures, disseminating information, promoting products and services, doing public relations and providing entertainment. The ease of recording images with instant playback or re-recording over previous footage was well suited to groups with less-experienced camera operators and smaller budgets.

The main thing that both ENG and EFP have in common is high-quality video production using portable equipment easily transported outside of the studio. This equipment has also become available to consumers. In fact, the largest group of users of portable video equipment is home video enthusiasts. Sales of video cameras for use in the home have grown rapidly since 1980. In fact, about 15 million **camcorders,** or combined video cameras/recorders, are currently in the hands of consumers in this country. Most home video work is personal event coverage, such as birthday parties and graduations. (See Figure 1.1.) But there is a growing segment of home video camera users who use their cameras for more sophisticated entertainment projects and electronic news gathering. Many local TV stations and even Cable News Network solicit videotapes of newsworthy events from amateurs who keep their camcorders handy

Figure 1.1: Shooting home videos

in case a big story occurs in their vicinity. Although the technical quality of the video shot by most amateurs cannot match local broadcast standards, amateur video sometimes shows events that professionals could not possibly know about in advance or could not get to soon enough after the event happened. Examples include explosions, plane crashes, fires and ship tragedies. (See Figure 1.2.)

Not only is some video shot by amateurs shown nationally, but like the police brutality video shot in the spring of 1991 in Los Angeles, some amateur video can cause changes in local government or even more far-reaching social change. An amateur video enthusiast shot some video of dolphins being slaughtered while fishing boats were attempting to catch tuna. The exhibition of this tape led to such strong sentiment against the corporations that canned and sold the fish that these corporations decided to promote "dolphin-safe tuna" to remain in the good graces of the buying public.

ENG—CAPTURING THE EVENT

ENG, or **electronic news gathering**, is just what the name implies—shooting videotape for TV news. The style of shooting evolved directly from the 16mm filming style of early TV news and the newsreel style developed since the early 1900s. The primary concern is capturing an event on film or videotape, regardless of how much quality must be sacrificed. This can mean everything from shooting from the shoulder instead of from a tripod to underexposed, off-color footage due to bad lighting conditions.

Quality is important, but the event being recorded can supersede any quality standards. To stop taping during a police shootout because the sun set and there was not enough light for a good picture would not make sense. Any image that can be recorded is better than no image at all. Sometimes the audio may save the story or even be the story if no image is visible. The sounds of gunfire and screaming over a black picture can tell a story better than someone describing it long after it has happened. The video photographer must decide when it is better to accept lower quality and get something on tape or save the tape and get shots in a different, more quality-controlled manner. When in doubt, it is wiser to do it both ways and decide which is better when editing.

Time is also a big factor in ENG taping. It would be nice to set up three or four lights to do an interview, but if the senator only has two minutes, the news photographer must use a **sungun** (a portable light on top of the camera) on the subject's face. The lighting may be hot and flat and produce bad shadows and no background, but watching the senator live on camera responding to charges is more important than appearance. On a different day when there is a half-hour allotted for a 10-minute interview, the time can be spent making the subject look as attractive as possible.

ENG is a style in which decisions are made on a case-by-case basis and sometimes on a shot-to-shot basis. Often the news photographer must make a split-second decision; the slightest hesitation could ruin the shot. There is little control available; action cannot be stopped or repeated. Most of the time the photographer has no idea what is going to happen next or which way participants will go. The key is to be prepared for anything at anytime.

Work in the ENG field revolves around two simple ideas: the script will be written later and everything that will visualize that script must be shot by edit time. An ENG photographer also functions as part field producer, director, reporter and writer. Many decisions need to be made so quickly that there is no time for discussion. The photographer must make these decisions without hesitation. This is, of course, only one extreme of ENG style.

For much of the daily work of a news photographer, there is a considerable amount of communication with the reporter and others regarding the

Figure 1.2: This shot was recorded by a home video enthusiast who arrived at the scene of a raging fire before the professional news crew. Dramatic shots like these are often purchased by local TV stations for use in their newscasts.

way things are done. The job and the end results are always better when several ideas are brought forth to find the best solution. The ENG photographer must be able to work as a member of a large team including reporters, a field producer, director and others. (See Figure 1.3.) At the other extreme is the ability to work completely alone with no one to help with decisions or equipment. In this situation, the entire story depends on the photographer.

EFP—STUDIO PRODUCTION ON LOCATION

EFP, or **electronic field production**, refers to moving studio production into the field, or on location. The biggest difference between ENG and EFP is the way they are scripted. In ENG the script is written after the story has been shot—scripting to the video. In EFP the script is written first and the video shot to fit the script. This difference can also be described as control; the EFP photographer has control over the subject where as the ENG photographer, in most cases, does not.

There is also a difference in the length of the story/project. ENG scripts average 1½ to 2 minutes. EFP projects (except commercials and public service announcements) are often much longer. Locations are scouted and conditions are planned for in EFP work. If the lighting is better in early morning, then the shooting is scheduled for that time. Lighting, microphones, tripods, dollies, props and any other special items can be arranged before the crew members leave the studio. They know in advance what the situation will be and what they will be required to do.

EFP work can also be done by a single person. A photographer with a basic set of gear can do many of the simpler types of jobs seen in the smaller markets. The mom-and-pop commercials, political ads, public service announcements and location shots can be done by a one-person crew. As the complexity of the spots and setups, lighting and props, for example, increases, the need for additional crew members increases. Most larger productions come from ad agencies or in-house writing staffs; they even provide a producer or

Figure 1. 3: An ENG crew shooting a standup on location during a breaking story.

Figure 1. 4: This EFP shoot involves people responsible for directing, videography, script, mike placement, audio levels, videotape machine operations and performers.

director to oversee the taping on location. Storyboard layouts determine the look and content of each shot. The bigger the production, the less that is left to chance once the crew is in the field. (See Figure 1.4.)

EFP work is often governed by the idea that time is money. The client is paying top dollar and does not want that money wasted. Planning is of the utmost importance. Unlike ENG, in which almost nothing is controlled, every aspect of EFP must be tightly controlled. Costs must constantly be assessed in EFP work: Is the project going over budget? Does the storyboard get the right effect or must it be changed in the field?

In contrast, time is the crucial element in ENG work and time also the critical factor. Is the story going to make airtime? Is it worth the time or should it be changed to a different angle?

SUMMARIZING ENG AND EFP

ENG can be summarized by these points:

1. The story is the most important thing.
2. The deadline must be met.
3. Time must always be considered.
4. The script must follow the video.
5. The photographer must be able to assume all responsibility for getting the story.

EFP, in turn, can be summarized by these points:

1. The client's goal is the most important thing.
2. The budget must be met.
3. Planning and storyboarding are essential.
4. The shots must match the script.
5. The producer must be able to assume all responsibility for getting the project done.

Figure 1. 5: ENG flowchart.

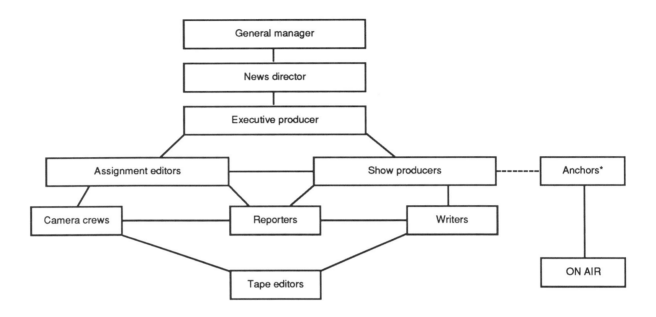

*While anchors are downstream from the rest of the organization, they often have a say in the operation of the newsroom, even without any designated power.

See Figures 1.5 and 1.6 for visualizations of the hierarchy of people involved in ENG and EFP work.

FILM TO VIDEOTAPE: CHANGING TECHNOLOGY

The evolution of portable video is closely related to the overall changeover from film to videotape. At the time of this transition, there was a great need for low-cost, portable equipment in the broadcast as well as the nonbroadcast television industries. The easy-to-use video camera and recorder filled this need, enabling TV production to come out of the studio and into the field.

Before the 1970s film was the medium used to visually reproduce events with movement in situations ranging from network TV to home movies. Since the early days of the newsreel, news events had been recorded solely on 16mm black-and-white film. With the development of color posi-

tive films, TV news stories took on a more realistic look. At the same time, 8mm and Super-8mm film cameras were the only formats economically feasible for home users. These film cameras were generally inexpensive and light, making them very attractive to those interested in work with portable equipment.

In the short period of time since the 1970s, videotape has almost totally replaced film. As the video technology has become more sophisticated, both the cost and size of video equipment have decreased while the quality and variety of applications have greatly increased. (See Figure 1.7.)

TV News

News departments of innovative TV stations first started switching to videotape to gain an edge over competing stations. By eliminating film processing time, videotape could be broadcast almost as soon as the tape came in from the field; more stories could be done and late-breaking stories

Figure 1.6: EFP flowchart.

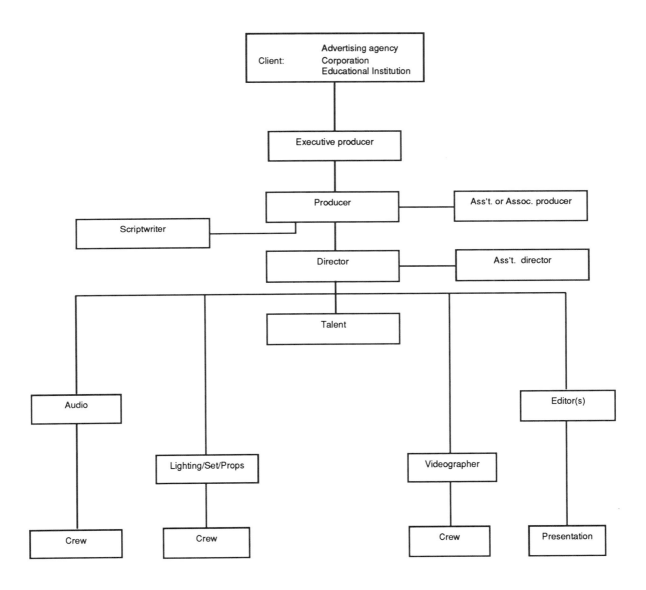

Figure 1. 7: News photographer in 1980. Each full set of gear weighed about 80 pounds. Photo by Joe Vitti.

could still be aired in some form. In addition, as the cost of video declined and the cost of film rose, the economic advantages of videotape over film became undeniable. With the development of portable microwave transmitters to transmit videotape live from the field, film became a thing of the past for everyday TV news.

Nonbroadcast Video

The enormous change in the TV news industry had some counterparts in the non-news areas of production as well. Large corporations, educational institutions, government agencies and independent production houses became aware of the

low operating costs and improved quality of portable video. In some non-news applications, video production had started to leave the studio with the introduction of the black-and-white **porta-pack video** system in the late 1960s. This system was used in some educational, governmental, medical and home applications. The format was limited because of the low quality of the image, the difficulty in editing and the black-and-white picture. In addition, the tape was wound on an open reel that was susceptible to exposure to heat, moisture and handling, which could physically damage the tape and further downgrade the video image. Most uses were for acquiring information and training where quality was not an issue.

The appearance of the U-Matic videocassette format in 1971, coupled with the introduction of color portable cameras, signaled the true beginning of professional video shot in the field for uses other than news or sports coverage. Commercials, instructional programs and medical films formerly shot on 16mm movie film or 35mm slide film could now be shot on ¾-inch videocassette and have broadcast quality. That is, they could be shown on a color TV monitor and appear similar to the videotape shown on a broadcast station. Thus these applications attracted more attention by those interested in high-quality professional work.

Superb quality video can now be shot in the field in a variety of tape formats for commercials, in-house corporate video newsletters, sales and promotional programs, demonstration and instructional programs, sports coverage, features production (for video magazine shows) and general entertainment uses. This segment of the video industry, with numerous applications, has outgrown news applications.

ENG operations can be found in all local broadcast and cable TV stations, the TV and cable networks (for example, NBC and CNN) and various regional and national news services. The total number of these news operations is probably less than 2000. EFP operations can be found in virtually all hospitals, educational institutions (universities, community colleges, many high schools and even elementary schools), governmental agencies and associations (for example, the American Association of Retired Persons) and corporations of all types and sizes. The total of these types of EFP operations is somewhere around 10,000.

Home Video

The technology of professional portable video has filtered down to the consumer or home video level. Millions of people now own their own videocassette recorders, video cameras or camcorders. There are various formats available for home use: the capabilities of some have even surpassed the U-Matic (self-threading cassette) and the newer, higher-quality U-Matic **SP** (superior performance) formats. Numerous magazines are published for enthusiasts that discuss every aspect of prerecorded videotapes for purchase or rental and many aspects of video production for home use. These magazines feature consumer versions of professional type equipment such as camcorders, home video editors, tripods, special lenses, video processors, lighting kits and other accessories. Now it is even possible to make a sophisticated TV program with consumer equipment readily available at many appliance or department stores. For computer-oriented consumers there are computers with software specially designed to interface with video equipment and allow the home video enthusiast to perform edits, titling and even create dazzling special effects in their home videos.

Advantages of Video

Although some people still record home movies on film, this practice has become rare because costs for film and processing are very high: more than $10 for about 3 minutes of film compared with about 5 cents for video. Film stock is expensive because of its silver content as compared with iron oxide (similar to rust) in videotape. Film stock is also not reusable; videotape can be reused many times. In addition to low operating costs, video's strongest selling points continue to be instant playback capability and the ease of monitoring what the camera sees. An out-of-focus shot is not discovered in film production until the processed stock is returned from the lab. These video capabilities benefit both the novice and professional. Directors of major motion pictures and commercials are using more video in their productions because of the ability to monitor. Some 35mm- and 70mm-film cameras have built-in video cameras that allow the director (sometimes in a distant production trailer) to see and direct each shot the photographer shoots. The control of a studio TV director has now become available to the Hollywood movie director, on location as well as on the studio set.

STUDIO TV AND PORTABLE TV

Ever since TV programs began to light up the screens of home sets in the late 1940s, the making of TV programs has been a struggle with difficult-to-control variables.

Electrical Power Needs

Unlike film cameras that have long been self-contained and therefore portable, TV cameras have required a dependable source of electrical power and a method of transferring the image. These requirements resulted in cameras that were tied to the studios with umbilical cords (also known as camera cables).

In addition to the need for power and signal transfer, TV cameras have almost always required more light than their film counterparts. This need for sufficient lighting has usually resulted in the use of many high-powered, carefully placed lighting instruments.

Electrical power needs are increased when the additional TV cameras, tape decks, switchers, camera control units and monitors are included—equipment necessary for traditional TV work. Therefore, it is not surprising that the overwhelming majority of professional TV work has been done indoors where there is plenty of electrical power. When TV work had to be done outdoors, for example, the Thanksgiving Day parade or a baseball game, the large studio-type cameras were taken on location and connected to camera cables. This method works and is similar to today's procedures for large, predictably scheduled remote shooting sessions, or shoots. However, sudden rainstorms have created potentially dangerous situations for crew members near electrical power. In England, where the weather is often damp, most outdoor production is still shot on film, whether or not the rest of the production is done on film or video.

Advantages of Indoor Studio

The indoor studio provides protection from the elements, a lighting grid to supply proper location and power for the necessary lighting instruments and, if properly wired, plenty of safe power for all the equipment. Studios provide control over other variables also. The clear empty space of the studios floor allows large cameras to be mounted on large heavy studio pedestal mounts, which help the camera operator get the smooth and steady camera movement shots needed for high-quality production.

A less obvious advantage of studio production comes to light when a celebrity, politician or busy executive comes to the studio because the producer or director has more control and gets more cooperation. There probably will not be any interrupting phone calls, visitors or frantic assistants demanding attention. In the studio, the director is in charge of all elements of the production, including the talent. But there are some negative aspects to studio production as well.

Disadvantages of Indoor Studio

The equipment used in a TV studio is often large and quite heavy. A large amount of floor space is needed for three cameras, lighting panel and control, video switcher, audio console, tape machines, telecine, camera control units and time base cor-

rectors found in almost all studios of industrial quality or better. Obviously, floor space is quite expensive to buy or rent, especially when the ceiling may be 20 feet high and, special soundproofing material needed. Walls must have an acceptable appearance and floors must be specially designed to allow easy access to wiring.

TV studios, when properly designed and built, are sophisticated and expensive workspaces. This reality has never bothered the broadcast networks or very large corporations, but for many organizations that have a need or desire to produce high-quality TV on a limited budget, space and financial considerations have often kept them out of TV production. Even local TV stations have been denied large, well-equipped studios because of the financial and space requirements.

In the past, corporations were forced to rent studios. Smaller TV stations were limited to their available space. This often meant that commercials requiring a great deal of space, such as those for automobiles or large appliances, simply could not be done in the studio or the products had to be shown on slides instead of videotape. Dramatic productions were nearly impossible with a small studio facility.

Before the mid-1970s professional-quality TV production was limited to those organizations that could afford to build a studio and supply the accompanying paraphernalia such as lights, dimmer panels, sophisticated switchers and synchronization generators or those that could afford to rent a properly equipped one.

Emergence of Videocassettes

The emergence of the ¾-inch videocassette format has provided a simple means of playing professional-quality TV to an audience. Unlike earlier industrial and educational formats that required threading and were difficult to edit, the U-Matic and all videocassette formats allow high-quality recording and easy editing and enable less sophisticated users (such as corporate media specialists and educators) to get more directly involved in creating and showing TV to their audiences.

The most important feature of the videocassette format is that it allows the camera and videocassette recorder to be self-contained. The cameras and videorecorders developed for portable use do not require an external source of synchronization or electrical power. One person with a camera, videorecorder, camcorder and batteries can create professional-quality TV. Since this initial change, the adoption of portable TV cameras has spread to corporations, educational institutions, governmental agencies, local organizations and home users. TV production has, by virtue of videocassettes, become a portable medium—one that can leave the studio and enter the rest of the world at will. TV has become a mass medium not just because of the audience but also because of the large number of people involved in the creation process.

KNOWING THE BASICS

Although video technology continues to evolve and increase in complexity, the fundamental principles of video remain the same. The home videotape user, the educational TV technologist, the industrial video specialist and the aspiring TV news photographer all need to learn the same basic video skills because they share a common objective: to tell a story, to get a reaction. The common problem lies in communicating an idea while working within the limitations of time and budget.

Students or beginning videographers/photographers can quickly learn to provide a certain level of quality in their work by learning the recipes for success in video. Even TV news has certain rules and formulas that can be applied to many situations and yield satisfactory results. By-the-book photography may have some creative drawbacks, but it can convey the basics of telling a story. Later, after the basics have been learned, a photographer can seek an individual style. That style is what creates those truly unique views that make video photography an art.

A video photographer may know nothing about a story at the beginning of a shoot or the story may be completely scripted in advance. In either case, the goal is the same: turning out a top-notch, complete and well-photographed product. Often the photographer also does the sound, lighting, directing, writing and editing. More often than not, most decisions in each of these areas must be made on the spot. The necessary elements must come together in a controlled fashion to produce a quality video product, often without the benefit of scripting, rehearsing or sufficient time for lighting.

Understanding every aspect of the job and the equipment involved is essential for achieving personal satisfaction and producing a coherent product. The photographer must be master not only of style and technique but also of the equipment—the tools of the profession. Knowing the basics of motion photography and having an awareness of the total operation of the videotaping system are what enable a good video photographer to produce good video.

2 Processing an Image into Video: Lenses, Cameras and Videotape Recorders

Like any craftsperson or artist, a successful videographer wants the most information possible on the tools of the trade. Knowing how a piece of equipment works reveals its limitations and its possibilities. To become truly proficient at creating video, a TV photographer sooner or later has to learn the technical things too often left just to the engineers and maintenance staff.

The medium of TV involves three basic forms of communication: sight, sound and motion. The basic tools for creating these for TV are a camera, a tape machine, a microphone and a source of illumination. In Chapters 2, 3 and 4, the basic elements of each piece of video equipment are introduced. This chapter discusses the camera and the tape machine—the two most important elements in capturing sight and motion. Chapter 3 deals with microphones and recording technique—the sound element. Chapter 4 presents light sources and their control—the final part of the sight component.

There is no end to the machines, gadgets and accessories that any videographer can consider prized possessions on a shoot. There is a big difference, however, between a basic set of gear and the ideal set of gear. While budgets will determine the type and quantity of equipment, there will always be several items that simply cannot be left out. These may be of the lowest or highest quality, but they constitute the minimum needed to do the job.

Today's TV photographers have a wide range of equipment available; therefore, it is hard to give a definitive list. The list in Table 2.1 will satisfy job requirements at the minimum standards of quality almost anywhere. (See Figure 2.1.)

THEORY OF LIGHT

Without light there would be no picture. Therefore, some knowledge of the physical and artistic characteristics of light is a prerequisite of understanding TV photography.

Photons and Light Waves

Light is just one part of the total electromagnetic radiation spectrum but, unlike other forms of this type of energy, light is visible radiant energy. Actually made up of very small energy particles called **photons**, light follows the common rules associated with all wave physics. The big difference between light and x-rays and radio waves is its inability to penetrate solid objects. Light is easily reflected. In fact, except for the light source itself, reflection is the only way light can be seen. Shining a bright light into a dark night sky produces no evidence of that light from the side or below unless some dust, fog or other material crosses the path of the light and reflects it.

The photons released by the light source travel in a straight line away from the source at the same speed. The sun is the best example of a light source. Points at the same distance away from any side of the sun receive the same amount of light.

Table 2.1: Videographer's basic set of gear.

Camera with lens	Omnidirectional hand mike
Video cassette recorder, or VCR, either mounted on the camera (on board) or separate (stand alone)	Shotgun mike
Tripod with fluid head	Two lavalier mikes
Set of three AC-powered (120V) location lights and AC extension cords	Four-to-six hours of battery power
Camera mounted light, 30V or 12V with batteries and cables	Several audio and video cables of varying lengths

Figure 2.1: The rear interior of a production van is outfitted with custom shelves to store equipment. A BVW-35 in a protective carrying bag is in a ready-to-go configuration on the van floor.

Light also decreases in brightness by a predictable amount the further from the source; the inverse square law describes this relationship, which is discussed in Chapter 4. The sunlight on Venus is much more intense than the sunlight on Earth. Much like the fragments of an exploding bomb, as photons leaving the source of light at the same time get further and further away, they also get farther from each other; this decreases the intensity of the light.

Photons travel in a straight line until they encounter something. In space that may be quite a long time but once they reach Earth, it does not take much to start blocking them. Our atmosphere, which is actually very thin by physics standards, blocks a great deal of sunlight striking the Earth. Some of the light is absorbed by the air and converted into heat; some is reflected by the air, which is the source of our beautiful blue skies. The same is true as light strikes the surface of the planet. Everyone notices that a black car sitting in the sun gets a lot hotter than a white car. The black car is absorbing the light and its energy while the white car is reflecting most of it. Photography concerns itself with both the reflected light and the absorbed light. Knowing that light always travels in straight lines and how light is absorbed or reflected is the key to understanding so much of what is modern photography and how today's video equipment works.

Spectrum

Like all electromagnetic radiation, light can be classified by its wavelength or frequency. In addition to its speed (186,282 miles per second), light waves can be measured in units called **nanometers (nm)**. Visible light, or white light, contains all the wavelengths between 400nm and 700nm. Wavelengths shorter than 400nm go from ultra-violet and x-ray to gamma and cosmic (the shortest). Wavelengths longer than 700nm go from infrared and radar to broadcast signals such as TV and radio transmissions—the longest).

Shining a white light through a prism reveals the various frequencies that make up that light; these frequencies will be bent at different rates according to their wave lengths. The resulting light on the other side of the prism appears as a rainbow. This represents the spectrum of frequencies contained in that light. In nanometers the colors in the rainbow range from violet (400nm–430nm) to green (492nm–550nm) to red (647nm–700nm). Lights that have a continuous spectrum have all the wavelengths between 400nm and 700nm present. (See Figure 2.2.) Not all light sources have continuous spectrums and not all wavelengths within any spectrum are present in equal amounts. Sunlight has much more energy in the shorter wavelengths, (blue, indigos and violets) whereas filament light has more energy in the longer wavelengths (oranges and reds).

The brain is color adaptive to what the eyes see. We tend not to notice the difference in the relative colors of light sources. The light in our homes at night seems to be the same color as light in our yards at noon. To the optical prism or the objective camera, the color of light in those two situations is very different. Taking still photos indoors at night using just the lamps in the room for light results in pictures tinged with orange. The film is

designed to see the true colors present. Our eyes and brain are so amazing that they adapt to and interpret different colors of light sources. The camera cannot perform nearly as well without help from us.

PRINCIPLES OF LENS OPERATION

The lens of the human eye is a truly amazing mechanism for directing and focusing light upon the light-sensitive rods and cones in the back of our eyes. In video cameras, the zoom lens tries to perform the same tasks. While our eyes have a single lens, video lenses are complicated devices with many individual pieces of glass that can be physically moved to direct, focus and magnify the light from images in front of it.

Human Eye

The human eye is one of the most perfect image processors in the world. Computer-controlled by the brain, the eye has an iris that controls the quantity of light and muscles that focus on objects at any distance; these work in synchronization to create perfect three-dimensional color pictures. The lens of the eye brings the image it sees into a form that the rest of the eye can use. It does not utilize the energy of the light to do work but simply acts to conserve the energy information so that the brain may have the most accurate image possible. The function of the lens is to focus the image on the surface of the cones and rods that make up the interface with the optic nerve, which

Figure 2.2: Although the visible light band is narrow, within this band are differences in wavelength that determine the color of light. *Graphic courtesy Manny Romero.*

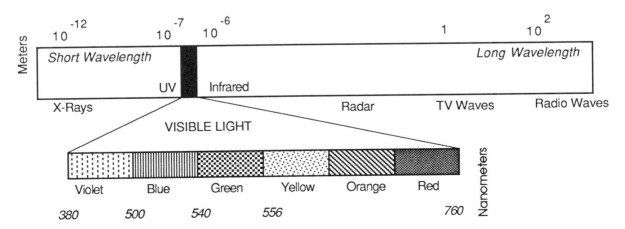

then sends the picture to the brain. If the lens cannot focus properly, the picture is fuzzy; if it cannot transmit light efficiently, then the picture is dark or distorted.

Lens Elements

No less valuable than the eye's lens is the lens on a camera. While most discussions on video equipment center on the camera and tape machines, the lens is a crucial part of the image-gathering process. A high-quality lens can make the best camera the best performer and a poor-quality lens can leave the camera's picture out of focus and distorted. The eye has one simple lens that does amazing things. The camera needs several lenses called **elements** to duplicate the complex workings of the eye. Non-zoom lenses used in photography are made up of as many as five elements in two groups that properly place an image on the recording or focal plane. A zoom lens, which is used on most TV cameras, has 13 or more elements.

A lens is basically two prisms joined together. If joined at their apexes, they form a **concave lens** that refracts light out from the center. If joined at the base, they form a **convex lens** that converges the light to a single point. Light refracted through a prism can be broken down into areas of different wavelengths. Even after prisms are joined to make lenses, small defects can cause aberrations in the sharpness and color of the image by not transmitting all frequencies evenly. By combining groups of concave and convex lenses and using special coatings, almost all the defects of any single lens can be overcome. Such defects as chromatic and spherical aberrations, curvature of the field, distortion, flare and astigmatism are all corrected by the many elements contained in the average TV lens. Each of the many elements in the lens serves a specific purpose in controlling the quality and quantity of the visual information.

Focal Length

The distance from the optical center of the primary lens to the point where the light converges (the principal focus) is the **focal length.** On TV lenses the focal length can be read off the lens itself. The focal length determines the field of view that the lens has. A lens with a very short focal length has a very wide field of view—a **wide angle lens.** A lens with a long focal length has a narrow field of view—a **telephoto lens.** Focal

lengths are measured in millimeters (mm). The average TV zoom lens starts at about 9mm and goes to over 100mm. Focal lengths between 5.5mm and 25mm are considered to be wide angle fields of view. From 25mm to 75mm a lens is said to have a normal field of view, meaning that the lens sees things in a way similar to how your eye does. From 75mm to the longest focal lengths available, the lens has a narrow field of view and is referred to as telephoto.

The field of view of a lens is often expressed as the horizontal angle of view and measured in degrees. The widest setting on the most common lens is about 9mm. This focal length represents an angle of view of about 52 degrees, which would have a view 6 feet wide at 6 feet from the camera. The widest lenses available, 5.5mm, have an angle of view of about 75 degrees, which covers a picture 10 feet wide 6 feet from the camera. Similarly a lens of 300mm would have an angle of view of less than 2 degrees and would cover only a span of about 1 foot 50 feet from the camera.

The advantage of a zoom lens over lenses of fixed focal lengths is that the focal length can be set at any point from 9mm all the way to 100mm or whatever the parameters happen to be on that lens. While fixed focal length lenses, sometimes called **prime lenses,** are generally of a higher quality than zoom lenses, they are simply not practical for most TV shooting styles.

Focus

Another set of elements in the lens determines the sharpness of the image sent to the principle focus or focal plane. These elements are usually at the front of the lens. By moving these elements further away or closer to the remaining elements, objects at different distances to the focal plane can be brought into sharp focus. The point of focus in front of the camera determines an area called the plane of focus. Almost all lenses have focusing marks on the barrel that read in feet and meters. If the focus barrel is turned so as to line up the number 10 on the focus mark, then the plane of focus is at 10 feet from the camera (actually from the focal plane of the camera). Often objects at other distances are also in focus with the barrel set at 10 feet. The range of acceptable focus in front of and behind the plane of focus is called the **depth of field**; this can be read on 35mm still cameras right off the lens for any plane of focus. Video lenses do not have this convenience; the eye must judge what the range is. (See Figure 2.3.)

Figure 2.3: This still camera lens has its focus set at 10 feet and its f-stop at f5.6. The middle scale on the lens lets us read off the depth of field for those settings. At f 5.6 everything from 30 feet to approximately 7 feet will be in focus.

Three factors have an effect on the depth of field for any chosen plane of focus: the focal length, the iris opening and the distance from the camera. As the focal length increases, the depth of field decreases; as the iris is opened up, the depth of field decreases. As the lens is focused on objects closer and closer to the camera, the depth of field also decreases. The greatest depth of field occurs at wide angles with the iris opening very small and the lens focused at infinity. The shortest depth of field comes at telephoto settings with the iris wide open and the lens focused at its minimum focus point.

Use a 35mm still camera to learn about the effects of depth of field. On a bright day, focus on an object a medium distance from the camera; then hold the depth-of-field preview lever down to see what is in focus and what is not. Hold the lever down again, and adjust the iris of the camera to see how it affects the depth of field. (Otherwise, refer to the depth-of-field measurements on the lens to see what will be in focus.) Also try different focal lengths if you have a zoom lens on the still camera. As you begin to use a video camera, you will get used to combining the effects of focal length, focus and iris to achieve the results you want.

The **hyperfocal distance** of a lens is the distance from the lens to the first point where an object is in focus when the lens is focused at infinity. In shooting news or any uncontrolled action where there is little time or ability to focus properly, this number comes in handy. The number will vary depending on the iris setting and focal length, but at full wide angle the iris settings will not have much effect on the hyperfocal distance. This translates into the ability to focus the lens at infinity and keep everything at the hyperfocal distance or beyond in focus with the lens at its widest setting.

Macrofocus

Although every lens can focus on infinity, each lens has a limit on how close it can focus. This varies from one type of lens to another. The minimum distance minimum object distance for the Canon J14X8B lens is 27.5 inches. Most typical TV lenses have a minimum distance similar to this. A very valuable feature to have on any lens is a macrofocusing ring. The **macrofocus** is usually a pull-out knob on the rear area of the lens barrel that allows the shifting of positions of the rear elements inside the lens. (See Figure 2.4.) Sliding these elements by rotating the macroring can bring objects closer than the minimum object distance into focus. It is possible to macrofocus as close as the very surface of the front element of the lens itself at wide angle. The macrofocus can be used with the lens focused at any point and set at any focal length. However, with the macrofocus engaged, the front focus or the focal length cannot be adjusted without disturbing the focus of the picture. In macro, a zoom lens in effect becomes a fixed focal length lens.

Creative photographers have found an unlimited use for the macrofocus. The macro's effect on the front focus and zoom means they will not perform as they normally do. With a lens set in macro, any change of the focal length changes the point of focus. This abnormal behavior can lead to some very unusual shots with intricate changes in planes of focus. Shots can be made where the focus automatically changes when zooming from one object to another. An understanding of the relationships among the various elements that make up a TV lens can lead to interesting shots that enhance quality.

Aspect Ratio

Even though lenses are round, the pictures they make are rectangular. The ratio between the width and the height of the TV picture is always the same. All standard TV cameras have an **aspect ratio** of 4:3 (or 1.33:1 in cinema terms): for every

Figure 2.4: This Fujinon 14X8.5 CCD zoom lens has the standard macrofocusing knob at the back of the 2X housing and just above the 2X changing lever.

4 units of width in the picture, its height will be 3 units. It is like the picture frame of a photograph. This limitation becomes most noticeable when, for instance, a producer asks for a still picture of a military officer in a book. The still photographer turns the camera on its side to get the portrait of the general head to toe. Next, extra space is needed on either side of the photo because the aspect ratios do not match. The full shot of the general from the book will probably be just head and shoulders or a tilt up from boots to face to avoid the empty or undesirable space on either side of the photo. Learning to see things as the video camera sees them means getting used to seeing everything in this 4:3 aspect.

Iris

Every lens has an aperture for controlling the amount of light passed on to the focal plane. Just like the mechanism in the eye that controls the amount of light, the aperture is referred to as an **iris.** This control over the amount of light is done by a series of overlapping metal leaves or fins that can be rotated one way to make the hole very small or rotated the other way to make the hole very large. The efficiency of a lens to pass light is referred to as its **speed.** A fast lens can transmit a large amount of light whereas a slow lens transmits a much smaller amount of light. The speed is measured in f-stops. An **f-stop** is the ratio between the size of the aperture and the focal length of the lens. F-stops are a standardized way of measuring the passage of light on every lens; the numbers refer to a specific amount of light. Any lens set at f8 gives the same amount of light no matter which camera or format of recording. The differences in lens speeds come in how wide the lens can be opened. The smaller the f-stop number, the more light the lens transmits. A lens that can go to f2 in not as fast as a lens that can go to f1.4.

Most lenses range from f16 to f1.8 in f-stops. Each f-stop shown on the lens represents twice as much light as the one before it or half as much as the one after it. The f-stops would normally be f16, f11, f8, f5.6, f4, f2.8, f2 and f1.4. An iris at f8 lets in twice the amount of light as a setting of f11 but only half as much light as f5.6. If the exposure is increased by one stop you are allowing in twice as much light. The smallest f-stop number tells you how fast a lens is. The typical lens mentioned above can only go to f1.8, which is only one quarter of a stop faster than f2 and three-quarters of a stop, or 75%, darker than the next full stop of f1.4. A small increase in the fastest f-stop can greatly affect the lens's ability to gather light, particularly in low-light situations. For most cameras, a lens faster than f1.4 would not show any improvement in gathering light. Each camera has an internal optical system; most of them are rated at f1.4. New news cameras coming onto the market have internal speeds of around f1.2. Lens makers are making lenses with speeds to match this, but both cameras and lenses of this type are very expensive. It does no good to place an expensive fast lens like an f1.2 on a camera that can only receive an f1.4 amount of light.

Video lenses allow the increase or decrease of exposures by fractions of stops because the iris is free moving (unlike a still camera) and can be set at any point within the range of the lens. At the stopped-down end of the iris (the smallest aperture), there is always a position labeled "C" for **cap.** When the iris is in this position, no light at all is being sent to the camera. This feature protects certain workings of the camera when not in use and also shows the camera true black (see "black balance" later in this chapter).

Most lenses operate best at the middle range of their f-stops. The optimum is usually f5.6 and one stop up or down from there. Only in very controlled situations is it possible to always operate at optimum. At f5.6 the flaws that may be inherent in the lens will be at their minimum and all the lens elements will be performing at the best degree possible. The iris has an effect not only on the exposure but on the look of the shot as well. The f-stop setting is only one factor in setting up a shot and does not have to be dictated by lighting conditions.

All video lenses have servos that control the iris setting. A **servo** is an electronically powered gear that is touch sensitive: press hard, fast zoom, press lightly, slow zoom. (See Figure 2.5.) A switch can easily change the iris from manual to auto to allow the camera to set the proper exposure for you. This can be as big a minus as it is a plus to the photographer. Another small button on the lens allows

the operator to briefly put the lens into auto iris only for the time the button is depressed. This method is generally the choice of most photographers because it can set an exposure quickly but not stay in auto all the time where it is likely to roam. **Roaming** is where the iris reacts to everything that comes into the frame. In a scene with much action or many camera moves, an auto iris can fluctuate wildly as dark-clothed subjects and bright light sources pass through the frame. The result is an amateurish scene with a picture that fluctuates from dark to light with very movement in the frame. Most scenes require only one exposure.

Zoom Lenses

Lenses used by still photographers and a great many cinematographers generally have a fixed focal length. Video cameras almost without exception have a zoom lens: a lens that can change focal lengths through a series of sliding elements within the lens. Zoom lenses permit changing the field of view without changing the point of focus or the aperture. Unlike the two optical groups that make up a fixed focal length lens, four different optical groups make up a zoom lens.

1. The **focusing group** gathers the light into a sharp, clear image.
2. The **variator group** moves inside the lens to change the image size from wide angle to telephoto.
3. The **compensator group** moves with the variator group to keep the image in focus and reduce aberrations caused by the first two groups.
4. The **prime lens group** focuses the image on the recording surface, such as film or a TV camera chip.

This complex system of optics permits zooming in or out without changing the focus point. When setting up a shot for proper focus it is customary to zoom all the way into the object that is the center of the focusing plane and then zoom out to the desired focal length for shooting. (See Figure 2.6.)

TV zoom lenses also come with a box of electronic servos formed into a hand grip and attached to the side of the lens. The servos drive a series of gears that turn the zoom barrel as well as the iris ring. A rocker-style switch on top of the hand grip controls the zoom servo, which allows you to move the elements continuously at speeds from a mere crawl to a fast snap zoom. The zoom and the

Figure 2.5: The typical TV zoom lens has a hand grip like this one with a rocker-style zoom control, a button labeled "RET" to see return video from the deck (either from confidence heads or on playback), a switch to select auto/manual/remote control for the iris and a button to set camera exposure if the iris is in manual control.

iris can be operated electrically from any remote location if properly wired into the lens control unit. The most popular remote zoom is the pistol-grip handle. (See Figure 2.7.) With an extension cable, the zoom control can be operated from anywhere the operator wants. On all lenses the power zoom can be turned off, or the servo disengaged, and returned to manual control by simply twisting the zoom portion of the lens tube. This method of zooming generally cannot be done as smoothly as the power zoom but can be done faster than most servos can operate. Zooms that are this fast are generally not used except as special effects or in certain types of sports coverage. An adjustment within the zoom-control housing can change the speed range of the power zoom. For most uses, the factory-preset speed range is by far the best choice for TV work.

The range of the zoom can vary greatly from one lens type to another. Most consumer camcorders have a 6:1 or 8:1 zoom ratio. If the widest focal length is 9mm, then the longest is either 54mm or 72mm. The zoom ratios for professional lenses are more often 12:1 or as high as 18:1. Lenses are often listed as simply a 10X or a 14X or whatever the multiplier is for the maximum focal length. Sometimes the multiplier is followed by the minimum focal length such as the standard TV zoom lens, the 14X8.5 lens, which has a minimum focal length of 8.5mm and a maximum length of 119mm (14 times 8.5). Currently an 18:1 zoom ratio is the maximum made for handheld cameras, such as the ones used for portable video work. Longer focal lengths would require lenses too heavy to carry; also, at such extreme focal lengths, it becomes very hard to maintain a steady picture on a light-weight camera. Lenses are made with zoom ratios as high as 40:1, but they are made for studio-type cameras. The widest focal length available on a zoom lens right

Figure 2.6: Optical groups for a typical TV zoom lens.

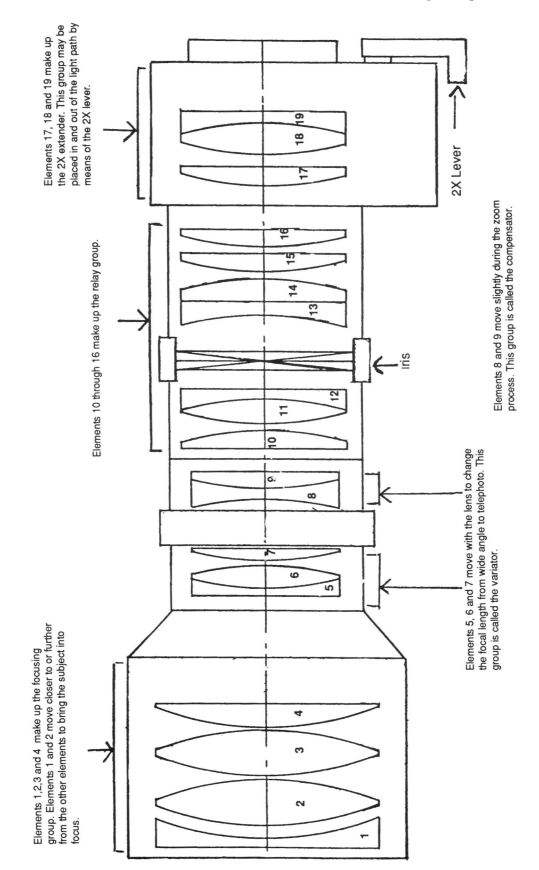

Elements 1,2,3 and 4 make up the focusing group. Elements 1 and 2 move closer to or further from the other elements to bring the subject into focus.

Elements 17, 18 and 19 make up the 2X extender. This group may be placed in and out of the light path by means of the 2X lever.

Elements 10 through 16 make up the relay group.

Elements 8 and 9 move slightly during the zoom process. This group is called the compensator.

Elements 5, 6 and 7 move with the lens to change the focal length from wide angle to telephoto. This group is called the variator.

2X Lever

Iris

Figure 2.7: Many photographers prefer to use a pistol grip attachment on their zoom lens. This handle offers more control, even when the camera is on a tripod and contains a rocker-style zoom control, a VCR record switch and a return video button.

now is about 5.5mm, which is considered an ultra-wide angle lens, but this lens does not have a large zoom ratio. Most wide angle lens zoom ratios are about 8:1. (See Figure 2.8.)

A common feature on TV zoom lenses is the **2X range extender**. This small device, which is part of the last elements at the rear of the lens, has a lever that can be moved to a 2X position; this drops an optical system into the light path, effectively doubling whatever focal length the lens is set at. The zoom can continue to be used with the extender in place but all focal lengths will be doubled. In effect, a lens that ranges from 10mm to 100mm would become a 20mm-to-200mm lens with the extender in place. In the highly competitive news business, this addition to the lens is an absolute must. It is less important for field production because the 2X range extender slightly degrades the quality of light passing through it. Whenever the 2X range extender is engaged, the amount of light passing though it is reduced by about one-half (the equivalent of losing one f-stop) and the sharpness of the image is reduced by a sometimes noticeable amount. This makes the extender of limited use in low-light situations. If the highest technical quality is required, use of the 2X range extender is not recommended but should be considered if it would enhance the value of the shot.

The best thing about a TV zoom lens is that it can be the one lens that fills all your photographic needs. A video camera generally has less maneuverability than a still camera. A newspaper photographer can duck, squeeze, crawl and climb to wherever necessary snap a picture. The average TV camera is much larger and heavier than a still camera; generally it must be shoulder- or tripod-mounted and therefore cannot be maneuvered to get the best framing possible. The zoom lens allows the TV photographer an added ability to compose in the viewfinder by instantly changing focal lengths to get the desired image size without moving the camera.

The worst thing about a zoom lens is its needless over-use by photographers and editors. The use of the zoom on the air or in the finished product should serve some artistic or journalistic purpose. Another minor drawback is that many zoom lenses lose some light at the very end of their focal length range. For example, the Canon J13X9B zoom lens has a maximum relative aperture of f1.6 from 9mm to 99mm, but at 117mm the maximum aperture is only f1.9. In low-light situations this sudden darkening of the picture at the very end of the zoom can be noticeable. Therefore, for high-quality work it is best not to use a zoom at the end of its range. Using the auto-iris can make up for this effect as long as there is enough light to set the exposure in the middle range of f-stops.

When the lens is zoomed all the way in, it is nearly impossible to get a steady picture. Any small movement of the camera will be greatly exaggerated by the long focal length; this makes shooting off the shoulder next to impossible. A special type of zoom lens made popular by Schwem is called the **Gyrozoom.** This lens uses a special motion control device within the lens to take the shake out of the picture. It is highly desirable for use in helicopters or aboard boats. The zoom range is on the order of 60mm to 300mm, but the lens is slow so it may not be the best choice in low-light situations. Because the lens is always trying to hold the picture steady, it is difficult to **pan** (move the camera to point left or right) or **tilt** (move the

camera to point up or down) the shot. It must be done slowly or the special motion control device will over-compensate for any movement. Nevertheless the gyro lens can produce spectacular results when compared to ordinary zoom lenses.

Light Quality Control

The elements of the lens combine to make the sharpest image possible with the smallest loss of brightness at the focal plane where the image will be recorded onto a light-sensitive medium. As lenses are sealed units, the operator has no control over how well the lens works inside. The last layer of quality that the manufacturer puts on the lens is a special coating on the glass used for the elements. This coating helps with color reproduction and aids in correcting many minor flaws in the glass's ability to transmit a sharp image. Special care must be taken when cleaning a lens so as not to harm this coating.

The best way to insure against damage to the front element of your lens is to always keep a clear filter or a **UV (ultra-violet) haze filter** on the lens. Most TV stations prescribe that a camera never leaves the lot without one of these filters on the lens. Neither filter has any noticeable effect on the picture quality or amount of light transmission but only serves to protect the front element from scratches, dirt and other problems that could cause costly repairs or lower the quality of the lens.

One of the most common problems in maintaining image quality is glare on the lens from light sources. At certain angles to a light source, light rays reflect off the front element causing a glare across the lens surface. This glare reduces the contrast of the picture as well as its sharpness. Just as our hands often function as a sunshade for our eyes when we look in the general direction of the sun or any bright light, the camera lens needs the same protection to work at its optimum. The sunshade that comes with the lens is an absolute must to protect the front element from direct light striking it. As the light source comes closer and closer to the camera's field of view, it becomes increasingly difficult to protect the lens. You may indeed find yourself using your hand to shade the light from the lens. Once the light source is in the shot itself, there is little that can be done. Glare is actually the worst when the light is just outside the shot. When light is in the shot the glare is reduced, but other effects called **flares** (circular patterns of reflections in the lens) can be just as objectionable if not used in an artistic fashion.

Figure 2.8: This large zoom lens has a 17X multiplier and an 8.5mm minimum focal length. The maximum focal length is 17X8.5mm, or 144.5mm.

Accessories

There are many attachments for a lens that will enhance its performance. Many photographers like to take shots at more than the 9mm focal length that their standard lens allows. While changing to a wide-angle zoom lens is probably the best way to get a wider angle, it is also time consuming to change the lens not to mention inconvenient and expensive to have a second lens available. A **retrozoom** is another set of optical elements that can be mounted on the front of most normal zoom lenses. This attachment works like the 2X extender only it decreases the focal length by multiplying the focal length of the lens by 0.8X. This would make a normal lens 7.2mm instead of 9mm and allows zooming and focusing as normal. The other way to get a quick wide-angle shot is to attach a **single-element wide-angle lens.** This curved lens either clamps or screws onto the front element of your normal zoom lens much like a filter. The drawback here is that the picture can be focused only with the macro focusing device, thus preventing the use of the zoom: the lens becomes a fixed focal-length instrument.

There are teleconverters that look and work like retrozooms to make objects even larger than with a normal lens. **Teleconverters** multiply the image size by about 2.8X but unlike the 2X extender, they do not cut the amount of light down by any noticeable degree. One drawback of both the retrozoom and the teleconverter is the added weight on the camera and lens itself. This can put added stress on the camera body at the point where the lens is attached.

Close-up lenses or **diopters** are single-element attachments that work at fixed focal lengths. Placed over the front element, diopters increase the image size by allowing a focus on objects closer to the camera. Like the single element wide-angle attachment, diopters must be refocused at each focal length change so the zoom cannot be used with them in place. New lenses in the early stages of development will zoom from very wide angles to long telephotos and permit focusing from the front element to infinity without being in macro focus; unfortunately, none are currently on the market. It should be only a matter of time until they become available for TV work.

Filters

The clear glass and UV filters mentioned above are but just a few of the many types of filters available for a video camera's lens. Most lenses have a threaded lip on the front element that a round filter or filter adaptor can be screwed into. The most common size diameter is the 77mm filter, although filter size may vary from one type of lens to another. Some lenses have no threads on the front element and require an adapting ring that clamps to the outside of the lens barrel. Most filters are threaded on both sides so that they can be stacked onto or combined with another. Generally, no more than two filters can be used at one time without the filters showing in the corners of the picture. This is called **vignetting** and may also be caused by other factors such as a poorly aligned lens. Many photographers leave the clear filter on all the time and add any other filters on top of it to make sure that the front element stays protected at all times.

Two other types of filter mounts are available for professional use: the round nonthreaded filters such as the popular Series 9 from Tiffen and the film-style square filters such as the 4-by-4 inch and the 6-by-6 inch. These filters require special adaptors, which are made for every lens. With the larger unthreaded filters it may be necessary to obtain a larger sunshade for the lens to avoid a vignetting problem and still shade the front of the filter from light sources. The square filters are generally used with a matte box. A **matte box** is a rectangular tapered box that looks like a bellows and attaches to the front of the lens in a way that allows the lens to be focused without rotating the matte box. A series of slots at the back of the box permits the use of up to three square filters. This slotted portion of the matte box may be rotated independently of the lens to orient the filter as desired. (See the discussion of star and graduated filters below.) The rest of the box acts as a sunshade for the filters. In film use the box can also be used to create a split screen and other matte effects, but these effects are better done in postproduction when shooting with video. Nevertheless, the matte box is the most versatile and effective system of using filters with the lens, although it may be too cumbersome for most ENG work and some EFP shooting where weight and maneuverability are important considerations.

Filters fall into three broad categories: color enhancement, diffusion and special effects. **Color enhancement filters** can be used to change the perceived color of light used in a particular shot so objects appear natural to the camera. This type of use is generally unnecessary because of the white balance circuit in the video camera. The other use of color filters is to enhance or alter the color of a scene after the camera has been balanced for true-color representation. **Diffusion filters** reduce the sharpness and/or contrast of the picture. They are often used to give an artistic or film look to the video. **Special effects filters** do everything from multiple images to split-screen fields of focus. Many of the effects of filters can also be done electronically in post-production. It is a good idea to shoot a scene calling for filters at least once without filters so that the producer or editor has the choice of using or not using the effect.

The following is a partial list of the more popular filters used in TV work. Most are used for EFP shooting or feature stories in ENG. They are not recommended for general news use. Most of these filters come in different degrees of effect rated from 1 to 5. A number 1 filter has only a slight effect and a number 5 has the maximum effect.

Sepia Effect Filter This filter gives the scene a warm brown tone similar to that of old photos from the turn of the century. It can be used to imply a look back in time, such as a ghost town.

Enhancing Filter This filter creates a warm look by selectively improving saturation of reds and oranges with little effect on other colors. It is used to bring out better skin tones on light-complexion subjects and give dark-skinned subjects a deeper, richer color. It is also good for the fall-color shots of autumn.

Polarizing Filter This filter reduces glare and reflections on surfaces, such as glass or water in the picture, while saturating colors and darkening in the blue of the sky. The polarized filter is

free to turn in its housing to achieve the correct angle to the reflections. As you turn the polarizer, watch the effect in the viewfinder to find the optimum orientation. It can make white clouds really stand out from the blue sky or take away annoying reflections from car windows.

Fog Effect Filter This filter creates the look of real fog in the scene. The effect is most noticeable in overexposed areas of the picture or around light sources in the shot. It can add a dream-like quality to scenes or give atmosphere to interior scenes. (See Figure 2.9.)

Low-Contrast Filter This filter lowers the contrast in the picture and mutes the colors. It allows black areas to become lighter and reduces the density of shadows, allowing more detail to be seen while not affecting the white areas of the picture. It is a good for scenes where shadows are particularly dark and can help give video a film look.

Double-Fog Effect Filter This filter combines a soft fog with a heavy low-contrast effect that allows a sharper image than fog alone. It is particularly good to reduce the effects of overexposed windows in interior shots without adding a dense fog look to the picture.

Diffusion Effect Filter This filter uses a slight ripple effect in the filter glass to reduce the sharpness of the picture without creating a fog-like effect. It is often used to hide skin blemishes or wrinkles from the camera and looks good in backlit situations. It also causes a halo effect around light sources in the shot.

Softnet Filter This filter uses a net material between laminated glass that creates a soft diffu-

Figure 2.9: This with/without fog filter scene shows the effect of a number 4 fog filter, which adds the look of atmospheric fog and lowers the contrast in the scene.

sion without the halation, or blurring, of highlights in the shot. The net comes in several colors allowing multiple effects from one filter: black net leaves the dark areas dark; white net lowers the contrast as it diffuses; red net warms the colors of the scene; skin tone net enhances skin color.

Dot Filter Instead of a net to cause the diffusion in the picture, this filter glass is covered by thousands of dots in varying sizes (similar to a paint sprayer mist). It comes in white, black and skin-tone. The filter is similar in effect to the net filters but without the slight star effect on highlights.

Star Filter This filter has engraved lines forming a grid on the glass surface that causes highlights, such as the sun, candles and headlights, to appear star-like. The grid comes in different sizes from 1mm- to 4mm-spacing; a 1mm grid has the longest rays and a 4mm grid, the shortest. Star filters also come in varying numbers of points; stars with 4, 6, 8 or 12 points can be created. The filters can give a glamorous quality to pictures with highlights in them, making them sparkle or helping reduce the sharpness of light sources (by using a 12-point 4mm star) without affecting anything else in the picture. They are also free-spinning without their housings to allow the points of the star to be rotated to any angle.

Split-Field Effect Filte This filter is basically a close-up lens cut in two. It allows you to have a close object in the bottom half of the picture and a faraway object in the top half of the picture all in sharp focus. The one-half close-up lens is a fixed-focus element; this means that the lens must be focused first on the background and then the foreground object or camera must be moved in or out until that object is in focus also. This filter creates the ultimate depth-of-field lens where everything from just in front of the lens to infinity is in focus.

Graduated Filter This filter contains the effect only in one-half of the filter, while creating a smooth transition from that effect to clear near the middle of the filter. Graduated filters come as sepias, corals, oranges and neutral densities. They are generally used over the sky portion of the picture to change the color of the sky without changing the color of subjects on the ground. They can create the look of a sunset sky without turning the ground pink too. The neutral density filter can be used to gain an even exposure on the sky as well as the ground on overcast days. The filters work best in a matte box set-up where they can be

positioned at just the right place in the frame without adjusting the shot.

A problem of some filters with nets and dots is that the diffusion material can sometimes be visible in the picture. This can easily happen when the lens is wide and at maximum aperture. The net or screen can be faintly visible across the entire picture. A good way to avoid this is to get filters that fit behind the lens. For video cameras this would mean having them in the filter wheel of the camera. If this is not possible, it may limit the use of some filters to smaller apertures or longer focal lengths so that they will not be seen.

A homemade way of getting around this is making your own diffusion filters. By taking a small piece of hosiery and stretching it across the back of the lens, holding it there with a rubber band, cutting off the excess and reseating the lens into the camera mount, you can create a very good behind-the-lens net filter. Try different colors and textures of hosiery to see what effects are possible.

Interchangeable Lenses

Most cameras on the market cannot use just any lens. A lens for a Sony camera cannot be put on an Ikegami camera without being modified at the factory. Some models of cameras may share the same lens specifications but they are the exceptions. One factor that causes this lack of interchangeability is the back focus setting of the lens. Each lens has an adjustable ring at the rear of the lens that contains the macro focusing adjustment. The back focus sets the distance of the prime lens to the focal plane. Even a small change in the proper distance can make the picture fuzzy and unacceptable. A camera with a maladjusted back focus may look in focus on tight shots but out of focus on wide shots. The back focus can only be adjusted when the lens is at its widest setting.

Each camera manufacturer has a different design for the prism block used to channel the incoming light from the lens to the chips, or in older cameras, the tubes. The differences in prism design from one camera company to another can be so great that the small back focus adjustments possible on the lens are not enough to overcome these differences. The problem is particularly acute when it comes to changing from tube cameras to CCD chip cameras. A lens made to work with tubes has to have a major overhaul at the factory to be used with chips. Since the chips are attached directly to the surface of the prism (unlike tubes where each tube can be moved individually to help the back focus), all the focusing must be done at the lens. As the red, green and blue wavelengths pass through the prism, they have different focal points. For the chip camera, the lens must be corrected for the longitudinal and lateral chromatic aberrations to produce a sharp picture on each of the three chip surfaces. It is always wise to check with the manufacturer to one see if one lens will work on more than one model of camera.

Care and Cleaning of Lenses

The greatest enemy a lens has is dirt, and it does not take much to get a lens dirty. Besides the huge amount of dust in the air, there is always the chance that something will come in contact with the lens and smudge it, for example, your hand or fingers. For the lens to work at its optimum, it must be free of all dirt and smudges. Loose dirt or dust can be blown or brushed away but not wiped away. Touching the lens with dry cloth or tissue may actually grind the dirt into the glass. For loose dirt a soft photo brush and an air blower can be used. Simple squeeze-style blowers or air-in-a-can can be purchased at any photo store.

Do not blow air from your mouth. If the lens is still not clean, switch to a liquid cleaner. Always try to use a cleaner made to be used on high-quality glass. Lenses and even some filters can be very expensive. A deep scratch or other blemish can require an equally expensive trip to the factory for regrinding or replacement. Most photo stores sell lens-cleaning solutions along with tissues to wipe the lens clean. A homemade solution of half alcohol and distilled water works well as do some commercial products from the grocery store. A very clean, soft lint-free cloth can also be used instead of the photo tissues. There are also products on the market that have premoistened towlettes in individual packets for cleaning lenses on location. No matter what you use, the method should be the same. Never use more fluid than you need and never grind the pickup material (such as a tissue) into the lens. Always use a circular motion and try not to go over the same place more than once if you can help it. A good cleaner used sparingly will do the job and any excess will evaporate quickly. Never use plain water; it has too many mineral deposits in it and does not evaporate quickly enough.

Keep a cap on the lens at all times the camera is not in use, such as when it is in transit, storage or any hazardous environment (a desert, beach or windy conditions). Often the dirt on your lens will not be visible in the viewfinder. Visually inspect the cleanliness of the lens often. The time when dirt really stands out is when there is any glare on the lens or a highlight, such as the sun, in the shot. While a little glare and the sun may be part of the shot, any dirt on the lens will stand out like a huge sore thumb. The time not to find out that you have a dirty lens is in the middle of a shot where you pan past the sun. It may have been the only chance to get that shot.

Modern TV lenses are made to work in the harshest environments. This does not mean that the nonglass parts never need cleaning. The rotating barrels of the focus, zoom and iris all must be kept clean. Wipe the lens free of any dust and dirt as often as possible. Use a compressed air blower to get in the small places, possibly with the help of a soft brush such as a tooth brush. Never use water to clean the lens. Never use any cleaner that has an oil in it. All the moving parts of the lens and servos are on sealed bearings and need no further lubrication. If they are stiff to use, they are dirty, not in need of an oiling. Make sure the gears and teeth of the lens barrel are always clean and free of dirt and dust. Most lens units are considered waterproof but are really just water resistant. If exposed to excessive dampness, they may short out or dirt may collect in the condensation and foul the servos at a later time. If the lens does get a bad drenching, allow it to dry out completely by putting it in a sealed plastic bag with silica gel or another desiccant (a substance that absorbs moisture).

Check the tightness of all the accessible screws on the lens (including the back of the lens) as well as the lens control unit on a weekly basis. Like most TV equipment, any repair work or extensive servicing should be done by experienced people. If you wish to do more than the very basic care, have someone with more experience show you the right way to do it. The final word on lens care is to know the lens's factory service center near you. Most offer overnight service or even loaner lenses; they can certainly help you over the phone with small problems. Keep a heavily used lens in top-notch shape by having a factory overhaul every two years.

VIDEO CAMERAS

A current model portable video camera barely resembles the huge, heavy studio camera of TV's early years because of the numerous design changes made over the years. But the color video cameras of the earlier days of TV had to perform the same basic functions as today's cameras: light filtering; the separation of white light into red, blue and green; image sensing and signal processing. Today's cameras are simply smaller, lighter and more accurate.

Camera Basics

We have now taken the light that makes up a real image, traced its progression though the lens, and seen how the lens may manipulate it. It is now time to transform that image into a form we can record.

In a film camera, this would be as simple as having a light-sensitive material on a celluloid backing exposed to the image. The camera would simply be a means to move and position the film. For a video camera, recording the image is a more involved and complicated process. The inside of a TV camera is filled with circuit boards and other wiring with at least a dozen places to make adjustments. Since making a change in any one of the adjustments causes a change in the remaining unadjusted areas of the camera, the proper equipment as well as the proper training is required to touch anything on the inside. Unless you have been shown by a qualified maintenance person how to make adjustments inside your camera, do not try it.

Filter Wheel   The first thing an image passes through as it comes from the lens is a filter wheel in any broadcast-quality camera. This wheel (sometimes two wheels) contains typical photographic filters just like those on the front of a film camera lens. It is much more convenient for the video camera, as well as the operator, to have them behind the lens. Normally there are four types of filters in the wheel: clear, color correction, light reduction and cap. The electronics of any camera is just like a roll of film: it has a specific speed or **ASA** (level of sensitivity to light) and is balanced for a specific color of light. All TV cameras are made to work their best with light at 3200 degrees Kelvin, the color temperature of typical TV lights. (See Figure 2.10.) Shooting a scene lit by TV lights is done with the filter wheel dialed to the clear (3200-degree or indoors) position. If the shoot is outdoors in sunlight, then the filter wheel is turned to the daylight or 5600-degree position. This filter is nothing more than an orange-colored filter designed to convert daylight color temperatures to that of tungsten (TV lights). A similar

Figure 2.10: The filter wheel on this camera is set to 3200°K, which will allow the camera to shoot accurate colors when video lights are used.

filter in film is the 85B. The camera can be balanced to any light temperature, but for now we will assume it is operating at its factory-designed optimum (or preset) of 3200 degrees. As the amount of sunlight increases, a video camera cannot increase shutter speeds (except for special effects) to regulate the amount of light it receives if the range of the iris has been exhausted. The most effective way for a video camera to handle high-brightness levels is to simply dial in a **neutral density (ND) filter** on the filter wheel. These filters, often called NDs, are usually combined with a daylight filter in the same wheel position. The other typical item on a filter wheel is the cap position, which is just like a lens cap: a solid covering with no light coming through.

The standard one-wheel camera has four positions on its wheel.

1.   Clear is used for interior shoots, or exterior shoots when the amount of sunlight is very small, or at night.
2.   Daylight is used outdoors in moderate amounts of sunlight intensity or in shaded areas.
3.   Daylight + ¼ ND is used for open sunlit areas on clear days.
4.   Daylight + ⅛ ND is used for very bright daylight scenes, such as a sunny day at the beach or the ski slopes.

A ¼ ND allows 25% of the light to pass through it without affecting it in any other way. A ⅛ ND allows 12.5% of the light to pass through. While each camera model has different nomenclature or different combinations in their filter wheel, they all operate on the basic principles stated above. These filters allow a camera to shoot in any lighting conditions above the minimum required to make a picture.

Prism The light forming the image passes through a prism after going through the filter wheel. Unlike most consumer and low-end industrial cameras that have only one pick-up device, a professional camera will split the beam of light into its three primary TV colors: red, blue and green. These are not the primary colors of art classes, and they should not be equated in any way. The way a TV camera arrives at all colors of the rainbow is considerably different from the way an artist would on a canvas or even as film would in making a color print. The camera prism delivers a very pure blue, green and red picture to three targets or light-sensitive surfaces. These three colors can be recombined later to represent the true colors of the object being photographed. It is the intensity of each TV primary color that determines the true color when the information is recombined into a video picture.

Chips or Tubes There have been two methods for converting the light coming from the prism of the camera to electronic impulses and thus to video signals: tubes and chips.

Video pick-up tubes were examples of one of these methods. A Saticon tube used a light-sensitive mixture of selenium, antimony and telerium on the surface of its target. This type of tube was commonly used in lower-priced cameras. A better material was used to make up the target surface of Plumbicon tubes. The Plumbicon's lead-based surface allowed the camera better low-light sensitivity and a sharper image.

In the 1980s cameras were switched to using **charged coupled devices (CCDs),** which became known simply as **chips.** After about 1990 camera manufactures stopped making cameras with tubes because the chip technology far surpassed tubes. Many problems that were inherent in tubes such as smear, lag and burn-in were eliminated by the use of chips.

It is always possible to tell a tube camera by noticing when a bright light source comes into the shot. The tube camera will leave a comet tail or smear as it moves past the hot spot. A chip camera will not do this although many of the early types of chips create a long, vertical line of color through the hot spot. This line will only be present as long

as the hot spot is on camera, but the smear created on the tube camera may be burned into the tube and last seconds, minutes or days depending on the brightness of the hot spot. Shooting highlights with a tube camera can therefore be a risky business. Shooting the sun can be fatal for a tube camera but have no effect on a chip camera.

Most chips are rated by the number of pixels that each chip has. Each **pixel** is like a grain of emulsion on a film; the greater the number of them present, the sharper the image. Unlike film however, the more pixels, the more sensitive a chip is to light. The latest cameras can almost see in the dark. They are capable of making good pictures in no more light than that of a single candle. This is something a tube camera could never do.

Video Signal Electronic impulses from the chips or tubes are sent on to the rest of the camera called the processor. Much of the camera's insides makes up the video processing unit of the camera. This complex series of boards and circuits shapes the video image into its many parts. The information that makes up a video signal is the breakdown of the image into many components: mainly chroma and luminance. Before that information leaves the camera, it can be recombined into one composite signal or left separate in its component state to be recombined later.

Fields and Frames The images of the video signal are relayed in a similar manner to that of film. Each video image is just like a frame from motion picture film. Video is recorded at a rate of 30 frames per second instead of 24 frames like the movies. Each video frame is made up of two fields, sometimes called odd and even.

NTSC, PAL and SECAM Whether a video signal is component or composite, it is based on a reference system. In the United States the reference system is called the **National Television Standards Committee (NTSC),** which was set up by the federal government. Only a few other countries use the NTSC system, most notably, Canada, Mexico and Japan. NTSC has 525 lines of resolution and scans at 59.85 fields (29.97 frames) per second. One drawback to the NTSC system is that it allows the viewer at home to adjust the color on their TV set. This led NTSC to be jokingly referred to as "Never Twice the Same Color." Having no guarantee that the viewer's set is properly adjusted can mean a great deal of loss for the artistry of video.

The other two reference systems in the world are the PAL and SECAM standards. **Phase Alter-**

ation by Line (PAL) was developed by Germany, England and Holland in 1966. PAL has 625 lines of resolution and scans at 50 fields (25 frames) per second but does not have color controls on the TV receivers like NTSC. Consequently, PAL has less color distortion than NTSC, but because of the slower scan rate, many NTSC viewers see PAL pictures as flickering too much. In 1962 France introduced the **Sequential Couleur a Memoire (SECAM)** system, which was later adopted by the Soviet Union and several other European countries. SECAM has 625 scanning lines at 50 fields (25 frames) per second like PAL.

These three systems are not compatible with each other. A special box is necessary to translate one system to another when making dubs.

Camera Functions

On the outside of every professional quality camera are the operational controls. These switches and buttons are the only means of controlling the electronics inside the camera. While there are generally few controls on the camera, just one switch in the wrong position can affect the quality of the video or even prevent the camera from operating. (See Figure 2.11.)

Power Switch There is always a main power switch on the camera, usually in the rear, that sends energy to all parts of the camera or camcorder. A group of switches near the front of the camera contains another power switch. This switch is usually a three-position switch: Stand-by, Save On, and On. **Stand-by** is when you do not need to operate the camera but want to start up the camera suddenly. A trickle current from the power source keeps the circuits warm and allows the camera to be ready to shoot in just a couple of seconds when it is turned on from the stand-by position. **Save-On** gives you a picture in the viewfinder, but if the camera is hooked up to a VCR in any way, it prevents the VCR's tape servo from coming up to speed thus saving deck battery power. If you try to record when the camera is in this mode, it will take about five seconds for the VCR servo to come up to speed before the recording can begin. In a news situation this is clearly a disadvantage, but if you are spending quite a lot of time lining up a shot, this function lets you work with the camera without running the deck battery (or camcorder battery) down until you need to roll. The **On** position is when everything is up and ready for instantaneous recording as soon as the button is pushed.

Figure 2.11: Professional video cameras have a large array of switches, input and outputs to allow maximum versatility and control over the video and audio signals.

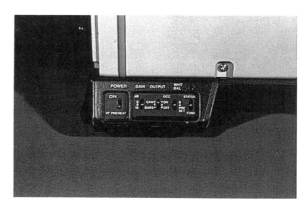

Camera/Bars Switch This switch makes the output of the camera either the picture it is making or the color bar generator contained within the camera.

Gain Switch Most cameras offer the user two choices of gain in the sensitivity of the chips. **Gain,** which is measured in decibels (dBs), is usually left at zero or normal for most shooting. To raise the level of exposure if the lens is already wide open, you may elect to move the switch to a +9 dB position. Under extreme low light, you can go to the last position of +18 dB. Each of these gains doubles the sensitivity of the chips. They also increase the **picture noise** (graininess). A +18 dB picture is not considered to be of broadcast quality unless it is a news tape shot under terrible conditions. Even +9 dB can be objectionable in most news and almost all EFP situations. Use them only when you absolutely have to.

White Balance Channels Many modern cameras have three channels of white balance circuits to choose from. The first two are normally called "A" and "B." They both work the same way and allow you to balance for two scenes. If a shot requires you to follow a subject from a sunlit to a room lit with only incandescent light, you can set the white balance on A for daylight and the balance for B for incandescent. As you follow the subject from one room to the other, only a quick flip of the switch is needed to maintain the proper colors. The third position is Preset. This setting puts the camera in its factory-preset white balance of 3200 degrees Kelvin, the normal TV light's color temperature. The camera now acts like a film camera with constant color reference (such as in daylight film); any correction for color temperature has to be done by means of filters on the lens or on the lights themselves. (See Figure 2.12.)

White Balance Button To allow the camera to work under any type of light, each professional camera has a white balance circuit. By showing the camera something white (zooming in on a white card, wall or paper) and pressing a button or flipping a switch, the camera sets the reference volts on each chip to make a white picture with that color of light. An indicator in the viewfinder tells the operator when the white balance is done (usually in two or three seconds or less). Some new cameras also tell what the color temperature is on the scene you white balanced for. Some cameras also have a **black balance** switch to set the black reference in the camera. This is done automatically in most cameras but heat can affect

Figure 2.12: The camera control switches on an Ikegami; HL-55. The white balance button is covered by a protective door labeled "W. BAL" to prevent an accidental touch of the switch while recording.

the black balance. If your camera has a black balance, it is good to use it every time you white balance or anytime the atmospheric (hot/cold) temperature changes even if the light does not. A good camera should white balance under any color of light (with any filter dialed in from the filter wheel) and give true color reproduction in the video.

Shutter Selection Many cameras now have variable shutter speeds much like film cameras. The normal shutter speed of a video camera (usually an electronic shutter) is 1/60 of a second. Speeds of 1/125, 1/500 and 1/1000 of a second are available. These additional shutter speeds allow the camera to do certain special effects or let the operator shoot at low f-stops in bright light, but they are not useful in most situations. The most common use is in sports photography on an isolated camera. The faster shutter speeds allow for brilliantly clear and sharp slow-motion pictures and freeze frames of fast-moving objects. The trouble is that when these pictures are played at normal speed, they appear to stutter or jerk on the screen. Only use the faster shutter speeds for shots to be played in slow motion or frozen or on shots with little movement.

Monitoring the Picture

Up to this point we have only discussed the inner workings of the camera and the means of controlling those functions. Now it is time to see the results of what the camera is doing, starting with what the camera sees up through analyzing the quality of the video output.

Viewfinder In some early video cameras, the viewfinder was simply a glass window with some cross hairs in it. The operator never even looked through the lens. Today's cameras have high-resolution video mini-monitors as viewfinders. Since the picture appears after it has been processed, the operator sees just what the tape machine or any output destination of the camera sees. The only difference is that the picture is in black and white. The viewfinder has brightness and contrast controls that need to be set at proper levels. The contrast control should be turned up all the way and the picture quality adjusted by the brightness knob only. A good picture should show whites as white and any deep shadows as rich black in the black-and-white viewfinder.

Most cameras have a considerable amount of information available to the operator in the viewfinder. Some information is contained in the picture itself, such as the zebra striping. The **zebra**

bars that appear over parts of the picture are a graphic display of the exposure level. Most cameras come from the factory with the zebra bars set at 70 **IREs** (Institute of Radio Engineers) of video; this means that any portion of the picture with an exposure of 70 units, as measured on a waveform monitor, will have these stripes. This measure of 70 units corresponds to the exposure of skin tones on a subject with a light complexion. If a person's face is the part of the picture that needs proper exposure, then the zebra bars should appear over the brightest highlights on the face. Many photographers prefer that skin tones be more in the 55-to-65 unit range and back the iris off (reduce the lighting) to just remove the zebra bars from a face; other photographers prefer to set them at 100 units to better see overexposed portions of the picture, especially when people are not in the shot. Zebra bars can be set at any level by a service person.

Other warning lights or indicators show low battery power, end of tape, low-light levels, the filter in use and the shutter speed in use. The RET button on the lens control unit can be held down to show return video in the viewfinder. This return video may be the confidence playback function of the deck in use while the actual recording is being made or the tape playing back from the deck just like a normal monitor.

Color Bars   The color bars are the most common reference point in any TV work. Any professional camera has a switch that turns on a color bar generator within itself and feeds it to the camera output. This internal color bar system is essential to track down any problems in the video system because it is such a known reference. If the color bars do not look right, nothing else will.

Waveform Monitor   The waveform monitor is needed to make adjustments on the electronics of a camera. Generally only camera maintenance people use this device, but the data it provides are needed for any high-quality work with cameras, tape recorders, microwave or satellite transmitters or time base correctors. This monitor, sometimes just called a **scope,** is the window to the inner parts of the video signal. Any problem with the video signal can be found by analyzing the different information available from it. A photographer wishing to truly master a video camera should learn to read and use the waveform monitor. (See Figure 2.13.) Hooking a camera up to a monitor and experimenting with exposure should give some information on how a video signal works and how to recognize problems in the camera.

Vectorscope   The vectorscope also checks the video signal parts but only for the color or chroma of the TV signal. If reds in the picture do not look right, this scope can identify whether it is the operator's eye, the TV set or the camera that is wrong. (See Figure 2.14.) The waveform monitor and vectorscope are the two most important means of analyzing the quality of your video signal.

Color TV Monitor   The most common but technically weakest form of monitoring the video picture is the color TV monitor: a plain TV set. (See Figure 2.15.) It is good for showing composition to others such as the director or reporter. Unless the monitor has been carefully set up and adjusted and viewing conditions are optimal (no glares or low room light, for example), any other information such as true color reproduction or even exposure cannot be judged from the picture on the screen. The viewfinder and the waveform and vector monitors are the most accurate indicators.

Maintenance   To maintain your camera, protect it from shock and keep it clean. There is virtually nothing inside a camera that the typical operator can repair or adjust. Take good care of the camera, and notify qualified maintenance personnel if there is a problem. It is the operator's job to keep the outside of the camera in the best possible shape. Screws holding the side panels in place or any other screws must be checked for tightness on a regular basis. Protect the camera from the elements as well as from bumps, jolts and drops. While most cameras are water resistant, none of them are waterproof. A rain jacket is an absolute must.

Troubleshooting   You must be able to tell when something is not right with your camera. More important, you should also be able to accurately diagnose the problem with the camera. Many times the correct diagnosis can lead to a very simple operator-capable fix. A switch in the wrong position is the most common error. Know where all switches should be set and check them first in case of trouble. Check your power source. Put up color bars and see how they look. If the bars look good, then you know the problem is not the output of the camera but in the input before the image gets to the video processor section of the camera. Unfortunately, there are not many problems that can be fixed in the field. Identify a good maintenance person or factory service center if you do not have an in-house repair facility or you are out of town.

Figure 2.13: The waveform monitor shows what color bars look like when everything is working properly. This picture looks at both fields of one frame of video and shows both chroma and luminance.

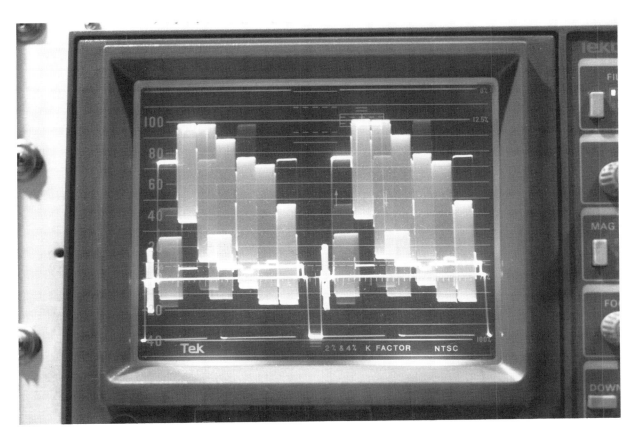

VIDEOTAPE RECORDERS

Videotape recorders are used in a wide variety of applications. New videotape recorders can be purchased for less than $200 for a VHS consumer deck to well over $30,000 for a professional-quality digital format deck. The major differences among the various decks stem from the format of the videotape and the application for the deck. Portable decks must be constructed to be light, to run on batteries and to have the ability to withstand temperature variations and be somewhat protected from dirt, dust and water. Professional-quality decks feature high resolution, good picture stability and color and the ability to encode or record a number of different types of information like time code onto the tape.

Low-end Professional: Hi8, S-VHS, ¾-Inch SP

The biggest revolution in the video world came when broadcast-quality equipment became available to the average consumer. Because of the 35mm format anyone can take a still picture of the technical quality needed for publishing. Now the average citizen can make TV of technical broadcast quality. The Hi8 and Super-VHS (S-VHS) formats have the minimum 425 lines of resolution necessary to be considered broadcast quality. Even network news turned to these formats during the Persian Gulf War because of their small size, light weight and high quality. Parts of one episode of the popular TV sitcom *Growing Pains* were shot on Hi8 without any consciously noticeable dip in quality. Both Hi8 and S-VHS come in models that feature all the options of a professional format in a slightly larger package than the regular consumer models and both make dockable decks that will go on camera heads designed to be used with higher-quality formats.

The ¾-inch U-Matic format was the standard of the portable video world for over a decade but has been quickly replaced and is no longer being manufactured. For users who still have consider-

Figure 2.14: This vectorscope shows how color bars are represented when the video signal is at optimum.

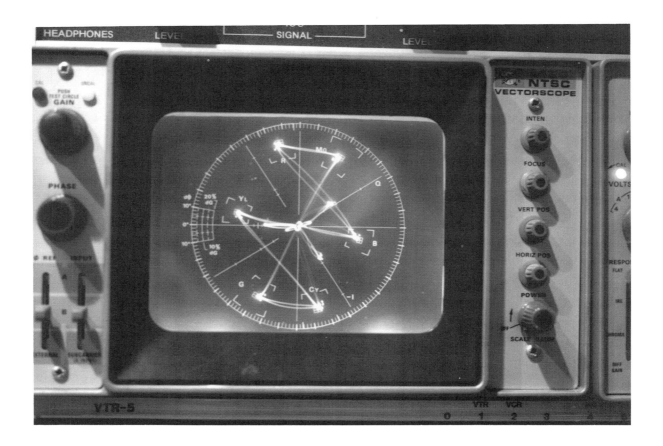

able ¾-inch libraries and those who want an inexpensive broadcast format just a notch below the new broadcast forms, Sony offers the ¾-inch SP format. This format makes use of that great number of ¾-inch tape machines already out there but allows users to upgrade to metal tape and much higher quality without junking the old machines. Because of the vast libraries of ¾-inch tapes in the world, this format will be around for a long time as a playback system but should disappear quickly as a portable record format.

Standard Format: Beta SP, 1-Inch, and MII

In the early 1980s Sony developed a ½-inch format for broadcast use out of their consumer format called Beta or Betamax. The new format was introduced as part of a one-piece camera recorder unit they called a **"Betacam."** The term went on to mean the Beta format for professional use as opposed to home-use Beta tapes. Many people still mistakenly refer to any professional camcorder as a "Betacam" whether it is made by Sony or not. The original Betacam format is no longer made and has been replaced by Beta SP. Like ¾-inch SP, this format allows the use of the older format but greatly improves the quality of the video when metal particle tape is used. (See Figure 2.16.)

The standard for studio tape, the 1-inch C format, has had very limited use in the field. While there are portable 1-inch decks made, they are just barely portable and certainly not dockable with a camera. They are usually mounted on a cart and cannot be subjected to any movement such as being carried while recording.

The M format was introduced in the mid-1980s about the same time as Beta. It was an offshoot of VHS but never developed a professional following. In 1987 the MII format was introduced to compete with Beta SP. MII also makes use of metal particle tape but uses a cassette shell unique to the format unlike Beta, which still uses the original Beta cassette shell. Blank Beta tapes purchased at the local discount store will work in any professional Beta machine. No other format can do this with a consumer tape.

Time Code

As the electronics of the tape machines became more and more accurate, more and more information could be stored and retrieved within the video signal. The first bit of extra information to be added to the video signal was an identity device called time code. Similar to edge numbers in film, time code allowed each frame of the video to be numbered. Wherever the tape was played, scenes or shots could be referred to and found by their time code number.

Most time code is recorded like a third channel of audio on the video tape. It has a separate track and its own space on the tape. This type of encoding is called **linear time code.** On the SP and MII formats there is also a form of time code recorded in the picture portion of video signal. The numerical information is added to the vertical interval space left as the tracing beam shuts off to return to the top of the picture. This channel of time code is simply called **vertical interval time code (VITC).**

User bits can store characters of the alphabet as well as numbers. Whatever is entered into the user bit channel will be recorded within every frame of video just like time code. Once set, user bits do not advance or change as the recording takes place. Each frame has the same information. That makes user bits a good way to label tapes. The operator's name, initials, date or unit number can be placed in this channel to aid in cataloging later on. The limit is only eight characters, however.

Figure 2.15: This Sony color TV monitor is in a protective carrying bag that has a built-in hood to cover the screen from sun glare. This monitor has two inputs and can be run from several types of batteries or plugged into a normal 110V outlet.

One of the more popular uses for vertical interval time code is that of a clock. While linear time code is usually set on Record Run so the numbers only advance when the tape does, VITC can be set on Free Run so the numbers continue to advance no matter what the VCR is doing. The VITC can be set in sync with any clock just like a wristwatch. Many news photographers set the VITC in sync with their reporter's watch. In this way, reporters can take time code notes using the time of day while the photographer is shooting. During a long interview, sound bites can be noted easily without looking at the tape machine. Later in editing the reporters can simply have the editor switch the playback machine to VITC and search quickly for the sound or shots referred to in their notes. This can save valuable minutes when editing under deadline pressure.

Typical Control Functions

The standard video recorder operates in the same manner as any audiotape recorder. There are positions for play, record, stop, fast forward, rewind and pause. More up-to-date models have a search function that allows the operator to scan the pictures on the tape at a fast rate with the machine in the pause or play mode. Some older models of video recorders have an audio dub function that allows the recording of audio on only one of the audio channels (usually channel 2) as long as there is video already recorded on the tape.

Figure 2.16: This BVW-35 Beta SP recorder is set up for ENG or EFP with a protective carrying bag, cable ties and headphones.

The small video recorders or decks that fit on the back of a camera have fewer functions than the stand-alone models. While many of these onboard decks have a complete function panel, it is usually covered by a panel or door and rarely used by the operator. These types of decks are generally thought of as record-only decks because of their limited functions for other uses. The play function on the typical onboard broadcast-quality deck does not play the tape back in color but only in black and white; sometimes the tape must be viewed through the viewfinder of the camera. Onboard decks cannot record a video signal from any source other than the camera. Its light weight makes the onboard deck the more popular model to use, but its limitations usually mean that a second deck may be needed.

Typical Inputs

Dockable decks have a very limited range to their functions and thus have few input points. They accept video only from the camera to which they are attached, but they do permit audio to be recorded either through the connectors in the back or from the camera's own mike. The best of the professional onboard decks have input/output points for time code to allow one deck to be slaved to another deck or source to share common time code. A switch usually tells the machine where to look for time code: internal or external (another source). There are two ways a typical stand-alone videocassette recorder (VCR) can receive a video signal: the BNC connector or the multipin cable connector. The origin of the acronym **BNC** is often debated, but one popular thesis is that it stands for **"Baby N Connector."** This name comes from a similar connector used during World War II by the Navy.

Typical Outputs

There are two types of VCRs in professional use today: the standard record/playback decks and the newer style of record-only decks, some of which have limited playback. The standard record/playback deck can play back recorded video in color at the highest quality the tape has to offer. A record-only deck may have rewind as its only other function. Newer record-only decks can rewind, fast forward and play, but not in color. They need a special adapter to play the video back in color in a form necessary for broadcast or editing/dubbing. This is why these decks are used only for recording the video, while others are used to play it back. By reducing the functions available, the record-only decks are smaller and lighter than the full service decks and are therefore capable of docking with the camera to form one-piece camcorder units, such as the very popular Sony Betacam.

The video output of a VCR usually comes from three types of connections and forms. Component format decks have a multipin connector that allows the video signal to stay in its separated state as it leaves the deck for another source that can handle component video. The next output is the National TV Standards Committee (NTSC) composite signal that comes out of a BNC connector. On lower-quality machines, this signal may come out of an RCA-style plug. On all professional decks, there will be two of these composite video outputs. The other possible output path is through an F connector that carries a standard TV signal on either channel 3 or 4. This may be hooked to any TV set as an antenna so that an actual monitor is not needed.

The standard male XLR connector provides the audio outputs of any professional deck. Switches on some decks allow the mixing of the output of both audio channels into just one connector for more flexible uses. The audio output levels can be controlled on each channel separately and the signal always comes out at line level impedance. (See Chapter 3.) Less expensive decks may have RCA or miniplug connectors to get audio from the deck. There is always a socket for a headphone or ear piece to monitor the sound recording and playback. This connector is usually a female ¼-inch phone plug but can also be a ⅛-inch miniplug. Some decks have sockets for both.

There is also an output for the time code, which works both as the video is being recorded and on playback, and a BNC (video connector) output for a **TBC** (time base connector used to correct minor playback problems) if one is used. A switch called **confidence playback** on most professional decks permits the audio and video to be monitored while it is being recorded. The audio confidence, delayed by about one second, can be heard on the headphone output only. The video confidence can be seen on any of the video outputs of the deck or in the return position through the camera's viewfinder. Only meant to serve as a quick check on whether something is indeed being recorded on the tape, the video confidence picture is black and white and of poor quality in appearance. The same is true of the audio confidence: the quality is poor

but it shows that something is being recorded. Confidence playback is often used to spot-check the recording in progress. It makes no sense to waste time shooting if the machine is not working properly. (See Figure 2.17.)

Onboard Decks

Many new camera systems come as one-piece camcorders. These machines make it easy for one person to shoot from the shoulder and eliminate one cable and battery. These decks are not made to playback video for any other reason than to check to see if something was recorded or to see what exactly was recorded. Because of this, there are no real output connectors on these decks except for a headphone, a time code BNC (for jamming time code to another deck) and perhaps a video BNC out. While this video out on a record-only deck passes the video from the camera while recording, the best place to get a video signal for monitoring or transmission is the BNC port directly on the camera. Onboard decks do not have as many functions as the stand-alone VCRs but they record with the same level of quality. With an added adapter, any record-only deck can be converted into a stand-alone deck and used with a multipin cable or BNC coax cable to record from the camera or any video source.

Meters

The audio record levels are always visible on analog **VU (volume units)** meters on the deck. The meters, calibrated from -20 decibels to 0 decibels in the green and 0 to +3 decibels in the red, indicate the strength of the audio signal. A good recording should have the loudest passages or sounds peaking at 0dB with most of the signal around −10dB. If the meter needle goes above 0dB into the red, it may mean that the audio is distorted. The ability of a deck to record audio over the 0dB level is called **head room.** Some machines have little or no head room and distort any sound hotter than 0dB. Others can handle signals up to nearly +3dB without distortion although the sound may be somewhat compressed. On one of the meters there is usually a scale to read off video signal strength as well. This is usually a short green line. When the meter select switch is in the video position, the needle should be somewhere on that green line. A dark picture can give the needle a low reading and a very bright picture, a high reading. If no video is present, the needle does not register. A third scale is there to measure VCR battery strength. A Batt

Check button shows the relative strength of the battery. Most battery scales are not calibrated; the needle position means something only if you know what a fresh battery reading looks like on that particular machine.

Warning Lights

Every deck has warning lights that tell the operator that something has gone wrong or needs checking. The most common of these is the **tape end warning.** When the tape is in the last two minutes of record time, this light flashes and an audio warning can be heard over the headsets but nowhere else. This method of alert is the same for all the warning functions. Other warnings usually include **RF** or **Clog** (no video being recorded), **Servo**

(VCR receiving poor video quality), **Dew** (excess moisture inside the machine) and **Battery** (battery's power nearing end).

Time Base Correctors

The complicated electronics of TV operates on very precise timing for the various functions involved in creating the TV signal. Anytime two or more signals are mixed, such as videotape mixed with live pictures from the studio during a live newscast, the timing of their electronic functions must be in sync. The **Time Base Corrector (TBC)** is one way to bring the video in sync with the broadcast signal of the TV station. It also improves the stability of the picture by replacing the control track of the video with a newly generated

Figure 2.17: The top photo shows the array of inputs and outputs of a standard industrial U-Matic VCR. The bottom photo shows the much larger array on a professional Beta SP VCR.

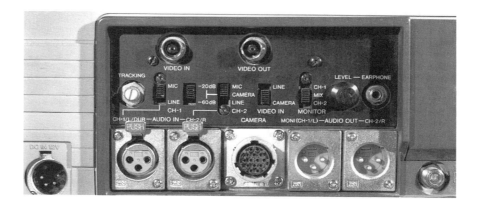

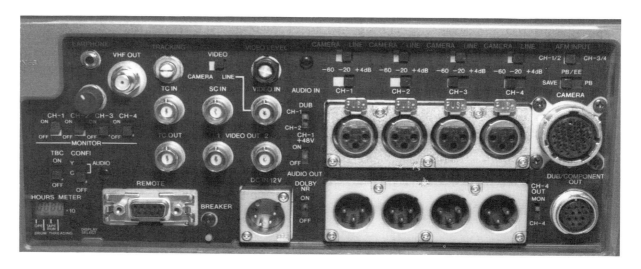

one, thus illuminating any errors or defects in the original information.

Maintenance

As with a camera, there is very little you can do to fix a VCR unless you have been trained in a factory-sponsored school or by experienced technicians. As any other piece of equipment, the VCR must be treated with respect. Do not let it get dirty; if it does, clean it as soon as possible. Do not let it get wet, and keep it away from harmful environments, such as cigarette smoke. For news use, the deck will go into some of the worst imaginable conditions. If the deck is not at its top performance level, it is not likely to bring home good-quality video. The best professional decks are made to take abuse but to a limit. The best protection for stand-alone decks is a cloth carry bag custom made to fit the deck. This offers not only protection from dust, dirt, water and shock but also a good shoulder strap and plenty of pockets for carrying extra equipment, such as a spare battery, tapes or audio gear.

Most VCR manufacturers recommend using a cleaning tape either once a day or once a week. This tape cleans the machine's video and audio heads of any dirt particles that may interfere with the recording process.

Troubleshooting

There is always a time when things simply do not work. One of the most likely things to fail for the portable video photographer is the tape machine. Because of the highly accurate moving parts and their exposure to the environment when tapes are changed, the tape deck is subject to more wear and tear than the other equipment. A mental check list should be second nature to anyone using a portable VCR in the field. On such a complex machine, the solution to a problem can be easy if you know where to look for the cause of the trouble.

The most common reason a deck will not work is also the simplest: no power. It is often easy to tell when there is no power present but a drained battery can sometimes work some functions but not others. Check the battery first. The next most common is the tape itself: Is the record tab in place? (If not, the machine does not go into record.) Is the tape being treaded? (If not, it may not be seated properly in the tape carriage.) Is the tape rewound? Once these things are checked out, the problem may be in the circuits that control the mechanics, sometimes called the

machine's logic. Shutting the power off to the deck for a minute or two may clear the logic circuits and allow them to reset.

You should know the position of every switch on the deck for every function you wish to use. There may be switches that you will never use in your type of work, but if they are in the wrong position for some reason, they may prevent the correct operation of the machine. Study the manuals for your equipment carefully. It is not uncommon to have just the playback function of a deck fail, so in certain circumstances you may want to play the tape back on another machine just to be sure. There is very little field repair work that can be done on a VCR. The video heads can be easily clogged but can be just as easily unclogged without a trip to the shop. If a head-cleaning tape is not available on location, a new unused tape can be played or fast searched in the clogged deck. The rougher oxide on the new tape can often break the clog loose.

BATTERIES

More power-efficient cameras and decks with higher-capacity battery technology have made power worries considerably less in recent years. Most people are familiar with lead-based batteries like those in our cars or flashlights. This type of battery is rarely used to power a large piece of equipment because it does not pack enough punch per ounce of battery weight; also it generally cannot be recharged. The most popular source of battery power today comes from the **nickle-cadmium (nicad) cell.** This battery gives quite a bit of power for its size and weight and can be recharged up to a 100 times or more before wearing out. The most power from a cell of the same size comes from a silver-based battery cell that can deliver about twice the power of a similar weight nicad, but a silver battery is more difficult to care for and costs considerably more than a nicad.

The battery's power output must match the power requirements of the equipment it is hooked up to. A 30-volt power belt made for portable lights would fry a 12-volt system camera. Batteries made to run the 12-volt VCR may not be the best choice to run to the 12-volt camera system because decks use less power. In today's world of camcorders there is generally one battery that powers both units. The most popular is the **clip-on brick battery.** The 13.2 volt or 14.4-volt capacity of these batteries gives them the reserve power to operate the equipment at its

Figure 2.18: The three most common batteries in video production. Starting clockwise from upper left: (1) a BP-90-type battery used primarily in VCRs; (2) a snap-on-type battery or "brick" commonly used on cameras and camcorders; (3) an NP-1-type battery used in both VCRs and cameras as well as monitors.

rated volts (12 volts) for the maximum amount of time without harming them.

Battery capacity is rated by **ampere hours (amps, or Ah).** The typical brick battery has a rating of 4Ah, that is, it can deliver one amp of power for four hours. The manual with your camcorder's power consumption tells you how many watts the camcorder uses, say 18w. Amps are watts divided by volts. In this case 18 watts ÷ 12 volts = 1.5 amps; this means that a 4Ah battery should run the camcorder a little over 2½ hours (4 hrs. ÷ 1.5 amps = 2.7 hrs.) Of course the exact time will always vary depending on the age of the battery and the operating conditions.

Generally there are three types of packaging for the batteries used in today's video productions. (See Figure 2.18.) The small thin NP-1 battery and the larger flat BP-90 style battery, both originally developed for Sony, were primarily designed to be used as deck batteries although both can power cameras and camcorders. The larger square brick batteries are designed primarily for use as on-board sources of long-lasting power. The brick concept was developed by Anton/Bauer using a patented three-point attaching plate. These plates can be easily mounted on cameras, camcorders, decks, monitors and belts to provide power in any configuration. (See Figure 2.19.)

Recharging

The first step in proper battery care starts with proper recharging. A battery should always be fully drained before it is recharged. Many new charging systems on the market finish draining half-used batteries before recharging them. If the charger does not do this, try to discharge the battery fully without overdraining the battery to avoid what is called a memory. A battery will memorize the amount of power it is accustomed to giving. If the battery is always only half drained when recharged, the battery will learn to have only that amount of power because of the memory.

There are two types of battery charging: fast and slow (trickle). A fast charger works only on batteries designed to be fast charged and takes about one hour. Because fast chargers are very hard on batteries, they are not recommended for average use but only in emergencies. The slow charger usually takes about 12 to 14 hours to fully charge a battery. Most chargers will prevent overcharging and automatically switch to a maintenance cycle once the battery is charged. At 14 hours per charge, one charger is needed for every battery in use every day. The charger must also match the battery. While many types of batteries are made to fit the same brackets, they do not work on the same chargers. You cannot charge a nicad battery on a silver cell recharger.

Life Span

The order of battery use needs to be rotated so that no battery gets more use than the others. This makes the batteries reliable to the same degree; one should not wear one out while others go without any usage, which can also be harmful. A professional battery should be able to undergo 100 recharges before the drop in capacity becomes too impractical. The life of the battery may be extended by regular checks on the condition of the individual cells within the battery. A bad or weak cell can hasten the demise of the other good cells by shifting too much of the load over to them. The single bad cell can easily be replaced to extend the life of the battery.

Figure 2.19: The standardized Anton Bauer Snap-on ® system is patented and has become the most common way of providing power to professional video cameras.

Proper Care

Batteries are very susceptible to temperature, both hot and cold. The ideal temperature for a battery is about 75 degrees Fahrenheit but as temperatures drop below freezing or go above 100 degrees Fahrenheit, the ability of the battery to deliver power starts to fall off rather quickly. In very hot climates or when batteries are left in the car for long periods of time, a cooler with a no-leak ice pack is a good way to ensure fresh batteries. The reverse is true for very cold weather: keep the batteries as warm as possible. Temperature also comes into play when recharging the battery. Never try to recharge a frozen or a blazing hot battery. Always allow the battery to reach a normal temperature before putting it through the rigors of charging. Once charged, the typical battery has a shelf life of about two days at full capacity. After that it will start to lose about 5% of its power every day; the decay accelerates as time goes by. If the batteries cannot be left on a trickle charger, their shelf life should be kept in mind.

TRIPODS AND CAMERA-MOUNTING DEVICES

Portable cameras are made so they can be used off the operator's shoulder for hand-held photography. While this is essential, it is not the optimum way to use the equipment. Most professional uses of portable cameras and camcorders involve a tripod mount because the tripod raises the production values of photography more than any other element except lighting. (See Figure 2.20.)

Fluid Heads

Any professional tripod head involves a combination spring/fluid mechanism for giving pans and tilts smooth motion. The fluid acts as a dampening agent to resist movement so that the camera does not simply jerk up and down or to the side. There are two adjustments for the fluid (one for tilt and one for pan) that can make the resistance as heavy or as light as the operator likes. There are also locks for the pan and tilt to keep the camera in one place without drifting. To make a fluid head work, the camera must be perfectly balanced on the head without tipping forward or back. The head must be leveled (indicated by a plumb bubble bullseye), the pan and tilt locks off and the pan and tilt friction at the lightest setting. A good tripod should permit you to tilt the camera forward and back under these same conditions, take your hand off

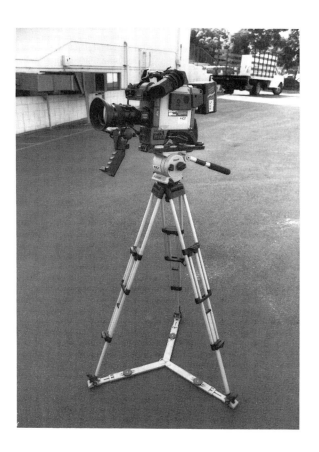

Figure 2.20: The single most important aid in shooting quality video is the tripod. This Vinten Vision 10 fluid head and two-stage legs with a spreader is a lightweight and versatile professional tripod.

the camera at any angle and have the camera stay in that position without drifting. If it does drift, it means the spring portion of the head is not adjusted properly. There should be an adjustment for the spring as well as one to slide the camera back and forth to get the center of gravity over the center of the head. The head must be rated for the weight of the camera. If the camera is too heavy for the head, all the functions of the head will be of little value. Trying different levels of friction helps find the point where the camera can make very smooth movements with little effort.

Tripod Legs

The days of the wooden tripod or sticks are long gone. Most tripods today are made of alloys, graphite or aluminum and are very light weight. The lightness is a great asset for the news crews, but weight can be helpful to stabilize the camera, particularly on windy days. Never trust a tripod to hold your camera up in a strong wind or in any situation where things are likely to bump into it. Lightweight tripods are made to help the operator not to take the responsibility for holding the camera. If you walk away from the camera, make sure that the camera cannot fall or take it off the tripod and set it on the ground until you return.

The best tripods have a two-stage leg deployment that can go from a height of about 16 inches up to around 6 feet. The length of each leg can be set separately so the tripod can be used on uneven surfaces with minimum leveling at the head. Most leg designs make use of the spreader, or spider, to keep the legs from sliding out from under the camera on slick floors. These spreaders have an adjustable span to bring the legs in closer or spread them further apart or be removed entirely in difficult situations.

Dollies

The simplest form of a dolly has wheels on the tripod legs. While this type of dolly may be good for some of basic moves, it is hard to control and almost impossible to steer once movement starts. Many dolly platforms are made on which to mount the tripod. The most common dolly, a **doorway dolly,** accommodates any tripod but is small enough to fit through most doors. This dolly has large inflated tires that give a smooth ride over fairly flat surfaces. For uneven or rough surfaces, the tires can be replaced with special wheels that run along rails laid on the ground. (See Figure 2.21.) This type of dolly obviously takes time to set up, while any dolly usually requires a second person to push it. On larger dollies, like the **crab dolly,** the operator sits on the dolly itself while the built-in tripods raise or lower the camera hydraulically.

It is possible to use homemade items to make a dolly without the cost or hassle. The most popular is the wheelchair. While the operator sits in the chair with a shoulder-mounted camera, another person can easily roll the chair. Another possibility is the grocery cart. Just about anything with wheels can be made to work in certain situations.

Cranes and Booms

The crane shot is a favorite of the movie industry. The shot starts out high and wide as the camera slowly descends to eye level in the middle of the action. On a **crane** the operator sits on a platform that is raised or lowered at the end of a long arm. A

Figure 2.21: Dollies can be used with rubber wheels on a smooth surface or with hard wheels on specially laid tracks like this one. This type of dolly provides a very solid base for the camera and incredibly steady pictures while the dolly is moving. Because the operator rides on the dolly, one or two extra persons are required to execute the move. The camera in this photo is also equipped with a video prompting device. A remote sending unit relays the text to the TV monitor and is reflected in the two-way mirror in front of the lens. *Photo by Tony Burke.*

boom is an arm on whose end the camera is remotely mounted. All camera functions such as pan, tilt, zoom and focus are are done at the base of the boom arm. The smaller versions of these booms are very popular in video field production and can be operated by one person. (See Figure 2.22.) They can also add an incredible amount of production value to the shoot by moving the camera through a space where no person could go, such as sweeping over the heads of the crowd.

Figure 2.22: A portable boom that can be remotely operated by one person. *Courtesy Stanton Video Services, Inc.*

Steadi-Cam

The **steadi-cam** is a revolutionary way of stabilizing the hand-held camera. This complex system of counterbalanced arms is worn by the photographer with the camera mounted at the end of the armature. While it is rather strenuous to operate, the steadi-cam combines many of the effects of the dolly and crane to achieve an incredibly stable picture even with the operator running over obstacles or down stairs. A video screen mounted in the arm near the hand grip allows the operator to see the picture from the camera no matter which way the camera is pointed. A new smaller version is made specifically for EFP. It is lighter and easier to use but still takes quite some practice to learn.

Car Mounts

Shooting in or into cars can be very troublesome. For the time when the camera must be mounted outside the car, a suction device with a camera attached grips the hood or door. This mount can provide some dramatic angles, but safety lines should always be used to insure that the suction holds. There are also sets of bars and clamps that fit almost every car and allow a camera to be placed almost anywhere.

Figure 2.23: This tiny camera, sometimes referred to as a lipstick-cam because of its small size, is actually only the bottom third of what is shown here. The lens makes up the rest of its size. This camea is connected to a small camera control unit (CCU) by means of a thin cable. The CCU in turn sends video to any recorder hooked up to it. There are several interchangeable lenses including a fiber optic lens that can be run up the operator's back under clothes and placed through the front of a baseball cap to appear as a decorative button to create a totally hidden body camera.

Aerial Mounts

Shooting from an aircraft can be very limiting because of the air turbulence and the vibration of the engines. Even in a helicopter, the picture really only looks steady on the wide shots. As soon as the photographer zooms in, the viewer can see the chop of the ride. The Tyler Mount acts like a steadi-cam of the air. Attached to the frame of the aircraft, this mount removes the vibrations and minor bumps of the ride and produces a steady picture even at long focal lengths. The aircraft must be approved for using it but the Tyler Mount offers excellent aerial photography.

Special Mounts

Many types of mounts can be made with a little ingenuity. The key is making them strong enough to hold the camera and withstand other forces. If you can think of a place to put the camera, then someone can surely devise a way to get the camera there. Anything attached to an aircraft would have to have FAA approval. With the advent of new color cameras called lipstick-cams that are the size of a lipstick it is possible to put a camera just about anywhere. A lipstick-cam can be placed at the end of an audio fishpole boom to get shots from odd places, such as holding the fishpole camera out of one moving car to shoot another car. You can move the camera from the wheels, up the side, over the hood and then raise the camera to let the car speed on past under the camera. (See Figure 2.23)

3 Microphones and Audio-Recording Techniques

Microphones are the first link in the technical chain that forms an audio production. The choice and placement of the mike along with its quality help determine how strong this link will be.

Microphones (mikes) have existed for more than 100 years. The first was used in Alexander Graham Bell's telephone to change audible voice signals into electrical energy. It was a simple and inexpensive carbon microphone sensitive to the frequencies of sound typically generated by the human voice. Carbon microphones are still used in many telephones today.

STRUCTURE

A **microphone** is a transducer, a device that changes energy from one form to another. Microphones change sound or acoustical energy into electrical energy, or more specifically, sound waves into electrical signals. The microphone **diaphragm** catches the sound waves while the microphone **element** translates that mechanical energy into electrical energy.

Four basic designs have been used for microphone elements over the years: carbon, ceramic, dynamic and condenser. The first two, carbon and ceramic, were the elements used in early mikes but are rarely used now in professional audio work. The latter two, dynamic and condenser, are the mikes of choice for almost all professionals. Since each element has a unique electrical and sonic property, knowing the differences among them helps in choosing the right mike for the right job.

Dynamic Elements

Dynamic elements have parts inside them that physically move when struck by sound waves. This movement creates an electrical current, which becomes the audio signal. Although there are many different variations of dynamic elements that have been manufactured by various companies, there are two general classifications: the moving coil type and the ribbon, or velocity, type.

Moving Coil Most moving-coil microphones are made up of a Mylar diaphragm attached to a coil of wire called a voice coil, which is suspended within a magnetic field. As the term dynamic implies, dynamic elements are designed to allow movement. In a moving-coil element a finely wrapped coil of wire moves when the diaphragm is struck by sound waves. This movement within the magnetic field induces a very small voltage in the coil, which becomes the output signal.

A moving-coil microphone is the most widely used in professional audio applications for several reasons.

1. They have a very good frequency response close to what our ears hear and can gather audio from many different kinds of sources. A common frequency range of a professional dynamic mike is 40 Hz to 15,000 Hz.

2. Generally the most ruggedly designed mikes available, they are shock-resistant, unimpaired by most temperature extremes and insensitive to extremes in humidity.

3. They are generally inexpensive.

Ribbon, or Velocity   Another dynamic microphone similar to the moving-coil mike is the ribbon, or velocity, mike, in which a thin ribbon-like piece of corrugated metal is positioned between the poles of a magnet. When struck by sound waves, the ribbon vibrates between the magnetic poles, causing a small voltage in the ribbon that becomes the audio signal. Since ribbon is flat, it is sensitive to sound pressure striking it directly from either the front or the back. Ribbon mikes were used extensively in the 1930s and 1940s in studio-produced radio. While they are very sensitive and have a very good high-frequency response, their drawbacks include shock sensitivity, fragility and noncompact size.

Condenser Elements

Condenser microphones have a light diaphragm that serves as one plate of a two-plate capacitor. Capable of storing electrical charges, a **capacitor** is an electrical component with two electrodes (+ and -) separated by a small distance. Unlike the dynamic element that makes use of electromagnetism to generate electrical impulses, it operates on a principle known as **variable capacitance.** The diaphragm and the backplate act as the electrodes of a capacitor. (See Figure 3.1.) When sound waves strike the diaphragm, the distance between the two electrodes changes, producing a change in its capacitance, or ability to store an electrical charge.

This results in a very small signal voltage that becomes the start of the audio signal.

The quality of a condenser mike depends on the design of its capsule, which is the condenser element and its acoustic system or housing. The capsule plays a major role in how the mike responds not only to different frequencies but different directions of sounds.

A condenser mike requires two additional features to produce its audio signal. One is an impedance-converting preamplifier that converts the signal immediately to low impedance to enhance signal quality. The other feature is a power supply of DC voltage to the capacitor element to polarize the two plates and provide power for the preamplifier. In electret condenser microphones, the voltage needs of the mike are smaller because the diaphragm is capable of holding a permanent charge; the power supply is needed only for the preamplifier. A good electret mike should hold its internal charge for 10 years or more but will eventually wear out. A disadvantage is its inability to respond to the higher frequencies as well as the externally polarized condenser mike.

In condenser microphones, the power supply can be located in the microphone itself or at the end of a short cable to the capsule. In a configuration referred to as phantom power, the power may also come from the console, mixer or VCR to which the mike is connected. (See Figure 3.2.)

Considered the mike of choice for accurate sound recording in professional work, condenser microphones are sensitive and have excellent frequency response. One drawback is that it is more expensive than its dynamic counterpart, a second is that it requires a battery or power supply. Al-

Figure 3.1: Diagrams of dynamic and condenser microphones. *Courtesy Shure Brothers, Inc.*

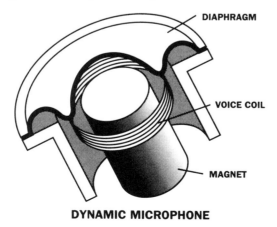

DYNAMIC MICROPHONE

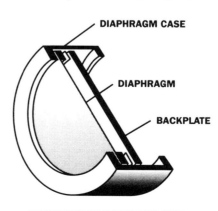

CONDENSER MICROPHONE

Figure 3.2: Condenser mike with phantom power. *Photo Courtesy Electro-Voice, Inc.*

though a single small battery does not at first seem like a serious drawback, a condenser microphone battery is quite small and sometimes difficult to install properly because of polarity; beginners often install the battery upside down. This type of battery may be hard to find at local stores, thereby making replacement more difficult. Finally, condenser microphones are sometimes too sensitive for extremely noisy situations or sudden loud noises and are sometimes inappropriate for outdoor use.

SENSITIVITY

Microphones can also be categorized by their sensitivity—their ability to reproduce sound in several different ways. **Directional sensitivity** is the mike's ability to pick up sound from various directions. **Frequency response** is the mike's ability to pick up sounds of differing pitch or wavelength. **Sound sensitivity** refers to a mike's

ability to generate a signal from a second source. The more sensitive a mike is, the more signal it will produce.

Directional Sensitivity

Microphones have different abilities to pick up sound from varying directions. A **polar response chart** shows the pickup or polar pattern where sounds can originate and still be transduced into an electric signal. Manufacturers usually provide polar response charts to provide technically accurate information about the pickup characteristics of individual microphones. These standardized charts depict the angle of sound sensitivity relative to the element of the microphone and sound pressure levels. In effect, they show how a mike will respond to sounds that come from various angles and at various levels of sound pressure. The head of the mike is at the center of the chart and its base is at the bottom. Sounds coming from the top, or 0 degrees, are called **on axis** and those from the bottom, or 180 degrees, **off axis**.

A microphone's ability to gather sounds at various degrees off axis is what determines how directional the mike is. The further the distance from the tip of a mike, the less sound level is transduced. On the chart this is shown by the concentric circles around the tip of a microphone, which represent sound levels that decrease in intensity as you go away from the mike. These charts are especially helpful because there are many variations of the general pickup patterns. Also, many mikes have slightly different patterns at different frequencies. In addition, there are some hybrid and altered versions of the standard patterns. (See Figure 3.3.) Two major polar patterns describe professional mikes: omnidirectional and directional.

Omnidirectional Omnidirectional mikes have patterns that pickup sounds equally from all

Figure 3.3: Pickup patterns of microphones.

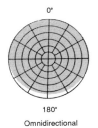
Omnidirectional

Unidirectional Cardiod

Supercardiod

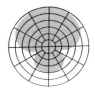
Hypercardiod

Bidirectional

directions. The pickup pattern is three-dimensional and almost spherical. If you place an omnidirectional mike in the center of a circle of people, the sound level coming from any of those people should be almost identical to the others, assuming that they are all equidistant from the mike and all persons are speaking at about the same level. The design of this type of mike is based on the mike's response to acoustic sound pressure, which is nondirectional. The mike's diaphragm can react to sound pressure changes equally from any direction. However, a pressure-type mike does tend to be more directional at higher sound frequencies; it is best to point the mike in the direction of the primary sound source to be recorded. In other words, even for an omnidirectional mike, sounds on axis will tend to sound better in quality than sounds off axis.

Directional   A **directional mike** uses a pressure-gradient device to achieve its polar pattern and achieve directionality in one of two ways. It can respond to differences in audio pressure between the two faces of its diaphragm (the pressure-gradient device) or achieve directionality by the use of reflectors. Directional mikes are good at reducing background noise from two sources: 1) off axis and 2) excessive reverberation (usually found inside small rooms). They can also be placed at a greater distance from the sound source while maintaining their frequency response and sensitivity. These are the mikes of choice in stereo recording because of their ability to give a sense of sound location.

Bidirectional   A **bidirectional microphone** picks up sound equally from only two directions. Resembling a figure eight, its pickup pattern is achieved in mikes that are purely pressure-gradient devices (no reflectors used). The most common of these mikes is the ribbon mike. One of the oldest mike designs around, the ribbon mike is still widely used today in radio and studio work. Larry King has made the ribbon mike familiar to a new generation of TV viewers by using it as his desk mike and logo on *The Larry King Live* show on CNN. If you interview someone who is at the same but opposite distance as you are from the mike and who speaks at about the same volume, a bidirectional mike will be equally sensitive to both voices and eliminate any side audio. This assumes that your locations are at the correct angles relative to the mike.

Unidirectional/Cardioid   By combining pressure and pressure-gradient designs into one mike, the resulting pattern variation is called a cardioid.

Cardioid microphones are unidirectional and pick up sound primarily from one direction. The word cardioid comes from the shape of its response chart, roughly an inverted heart-shaped pattern. Cardioid microphones pickup sounds almost entirely from the area directly in front of the mike and almost nothing from the far sides or rear, which makes them very desirable in noisy situations. By varying the ratio of pressure versus pressure-gradient in the mike design, several types of cardioid patterns can be found. The three basic patterns are cardioid, supercardioid and hypercardioid. (See Figure 3.4.)

Ultradirectional   More directional than the hypercardioid, the **ultradirectional** or **shotgun microphone** uses an entirely different capsule design to achieve its special purpose. The shotgun mike allows even greater distance between mike and source and greater rejection of off-axis sounds. Shotguns are usually more sensitive over the entire frequency range than other directional mikes. The design is simply a tube with the diaphragm at one end. The tube has slits in it covered by a audio-dampening material to assure the full frequency response of the on-axis sounds. This allows sound to enter the tube from straight on (parallel to the tube or on axis) while reflecting off-axis sound through the slits. The longer the tube, the more directional the shotgun mike is. Because its polar pattern is more sensitive to a wide range of frequencies, it is more directional for higher frequencies than for lower ones. Many shotgun systems have audio filters that cut out lower sound frequencies to make the mike more

Figure 3.4: An Electro-Voice® RE-10 dynamic super-cardioid microphone. The ribbed shaft aids in the directionality of the microphone.

directional, which makes the sound received more tinny in quality with a lack of bass.

The shotgun is the workhorse microphone of ENG and EFP work. For the stand-alone newsperson, a shotgun mounted on the camera is the primary source of natural sound and sometimes even interview sound. A two-person news crew uses the shotgun for almost all sound gathering. In production the shotgun is often boom-mounted for precise sound gathering in the studio and on location where hidden mikes are not possible.

Frequency Response

The goal of a sound technician is to accurately capture the sound source for reproduction. This requires a microphone capable of picking up the entire frequency spectrum of the sound waves that strike the mike's transducing element. A mike used for picking up conversation needs to be sensitive to the frequencies of the human voice, a range of about 100 Hz to 10,000 Hz. A mike used in a sound studio for picking up the sounds of piccolo must accurately transduce frequencies as low as 500 Hz and as high as 15,000 Hz. Although the construction and pickup pattern of a mike may qualify it for a particular application, it should not be used unless it has the appropriate frequency response capabilities.

Most professional-quality microphones can reproduce sounds within the frequency range of about 500 Hz to 15,000 Hz. A chart can show a mike's frequency response, or sensitivity to various frequencies of sound. (See Figure 3.5.) Ideally, the microphone will have a flat response curve, which implies that the mike is equally sensitive to all frequencies in its range. The most common fault of microphone frequency response appears at the upper end of its frequency range where the response curve drops off considerably, demonstrating an inability to reproduce sound waves at high frequencies. This drop off is present at low frequencies but is not quite as common and often less important. Many mikes are designed with special characteristics to slightly alter their frequency response.

It is common to have a mike with a **bass rolloff switch** of some sort, allowing the user to purposefully de-emphasize frequencies at the low end of the audio spectrum. This helps correct the proximity effect, or the tendency of unidirectional and bidirectional mikes to emphasize the bass or low-frequency response when the sound source is close to the mike. Other mikes used in vocal work sometimes have a **presence boost** in the upper midrange

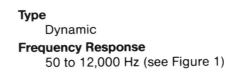

Type
　Dynamic
Frequency Response
　50 to 12,000 Hz (see Figure 1)

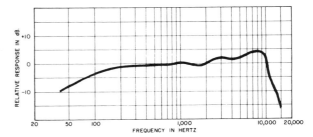

to enhance the voice. These features also help add brilliance, clarity and general intelligibility to the sounds recorded.

Sound Sensitivity

Microphone sensitivity refers to the amount of signal a given microphone produces from a given input sound source. Different mikes have various sensitivities; some mikes simply put out a stronger signal than others. Sensitivity is determined by measuring the mike's output power when the microphone is placed by a sound source of a known sound intensity or pressure. At first it may seem that the more sensitive a mike is the better, but experienced audio production practitioners realize that good audio production consists of an absence of the sounds you do not want to hear as well as the presence of the sounds that you do want to hear. Overly sensitive mikes can be just as much a problem as those that are insensitive.

Overload　Dynamic mikes are very hard to overload. They have very low distortion across their entire 140 dB dynamic range. The same cannot be said for condenser mikes. At high acoustic levels the output signal of the capsule can overload the impedance converter circuit in the microphone. Some mikes have built-in pads that can reduce that signal but at the cost of adding noise to the sound quality.

IMPEDANCE AND OTHER FACTORS

Microphones can also be differentiated by several technical factors. One factor, impedance, is very important because selecting the wrong impedance mike can cause immediate and sometimes serious problems. Other factors like output noise and maximum sound pressure are important only in very specific situations where the production requires specific sound pickup other than typical voice or music or in situations that have quite a bit of interfering signals or sounds.

Impedance

Microphone impedance refers to the amount of resistance a signal encounters in a microphone circuit. The more impedance in a circuit, the less signal will flow out of it. Therefore, all other things being equal, low impedance microphones produce more signal than high impedance microphones.

Most professional mikes have low impedance, which allows long audio cable runs without significant loss of signal. Their higher level of signal relative to high impedance mikes gives better rejection of hum and other types of interference. Also, low impedance mikes are compatible with almost all professional audio and video equipment.

Although impedance levels are rated as either high or low (corresponding to the designations high Z or low Z), mikes can be found that are somewhere in between. Table 3.1 lists typical microphone impedance levels and their corresponding measurement in ohms, the unit of electrical resistance.

The impedence of a professional mike is usually 150 ohms; it is measured as -60 dB, which is referred to as **mike level.** After an audio signal has been passed through a mixer, VCR, microwave transmitter or any other processing device, the signal coming from that device is usually sent at a medium impedance of 600 ohms and is measured as +4 dB, which is referred to as **line level.** When audio signals are called high or low in professional situations, what that usually means is that the line level is high and the mike level is

low, since truly high-level impedance (9600 ohms) is never used.

Other Factors

Besides the major considerations of element construction, pickup pattern, frequency range, sensitivity and impedance, there are several other factors to consider when selecting a microphone. Hum and radio frequency interference, signal to noise ratio, output noise, clipping level and maximum sound pressure are often specified by the manufacturer. Some of these factors are critical for broadcasting applications but are not as important for less exacting applications.

STYLE

Of all the equipment manufactured for the reproduction of sound, microphones display the widest range of appearance and design. Although there are many different brands of compact disc players or reel-to-reel audiotape recorders, they vary only slightly in appearance. Microphones can range in size from a lavaliere smaller than a dime to a shotgun mike over two feet long to a studio overhead mike the size of a large grapefruit. Because microphones vary extensively in size, weight, appearance and application, knowledge of these factors provides a better understanding of how to use microphones and select the one appropriate to the task.

There is a direct relationship between microphone size and weight; obviously, the larger the microphone, the heavier it is. Size is a concern only some of the time. When a microphone is seen by an audience, such as in TV work, the mike must be unobtrusive.

Since a variety of mike styles can achieve the same sound, other factors determine which mike is used and where it will be placed. After considering polar patterns, frequency response and sensitivity, you can choose a style.

Table 3.1: Microphone impedance levels.

Rating in Ohms	Impedance Level
38 to 150	low
600 to 2400	medium
9600 and above	high

Hand Mikes

The hand mike category is the broadest of the style categories. It is not a question of which mikes are in it but which are not. A typical hand mike found throughout the world today is the Electro-Voice 635A. (See Figure 3.6.) This omnidirectional dynamic mike is so rugged, it could be used as a hammer. Built to last a lifetime, it is virtually the generic mike. The mike is small enough to fit in a hand and light enough not to be a strain. It is the general purpose hand mike. Almost all hand mikes are similar to the 635A in appearance. They have a relatively small head or capsule for the diaphragm at the end of a 4- or 5-inch staff. Some mike shafts are even contoured to fit the hand more naturally. Hand mikes can have any polar pattern, be dynamic or condenser and have various quality levels.

A hand mike is generally held by a person, such as a singer or someone addressing the camera. As it is easily manipulated, it is good for gathering sound quickly from multiple sources, such as a reporter doing an interview who can point the mike at the person talking with little effort or even walk the mike closer to the source. Almost all hand mikes are made with a pleasing appearance so that they will not be distracting on camera. Hand mikes can be mounted on a deck or a floor mike stand. In ENG work, where speed can be the overriding factor in getting the job done, the hand mike is indispensable because of its versatility despite any limitations. However, there are a couple of disadvantages: 1) limited range and 2) not the highest quality.

Mounted Mikes

Designed to be supported by a mechanical system such as a desk stand or overhead boom, a mounted mike can be one of two types: studio or shotgun.

Studio mikes are designed purely for the highest-quality sound reproduction. Because appearance is not important, these mikes may be larger than those that appear on-camera or on a speaker's podium. The on-camera or podium mikes are sometimes referred to as desk mikes but are still designed for studio use only. Studio mikes are not moved often, especially not when sound is being recorded. Many have solid or integral mike-attachment devices for use on mike booms and floor stands. (See Figure 3.7.) The ribbon mike is a classic example of a studio mike. Another famous example is the one Johnny Carson uses on *The Tonight Show*. The disadvantages of these mikes are that they have little use outside the studio and they cannot be hand-held.

Figure 3.7: Integral mount on mike. *Photo courtesy Electro-Voice, Inc.*

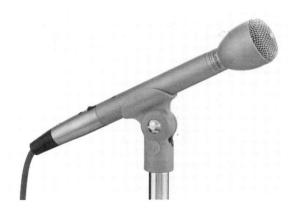

Figure 3.6: EV-635A, a rugged dynamic omnidirectional mike. *Photo courtesy Electro-Voice, Inc.*

Shotgun mikes are also not meant to be hand held. There are three primary ways a shotgun mike is mounted: 1) on a camera, 2) on a studio boom or stand or 3) on a portable boom called a **fishpole.** Both studio and shotgun mikes require a fair degree of isolation from mechanical noise, that is, noise caused by handling or brushing up against something. A good camera mount for a shotgun has a rubber pad in the holder surrounding the mike to cushion it from shock. A boom usually has a suspension system of heavy-duty rubber bands so that the shotgun literally floats within the holding bracket. Generally, shotguns are not meant to be seen by the camera so their appearance does not matter. They can gather quality audio at a good distance from the sound source. Because they are so directional, a boom allows the operator to position them at the best possible angle to get only the desired sound while keeping them out of the shot.

The disadvantage of mounted mikes is their need to be fixed to a certain location. The most widely used mike system in professional production, the fishpole shotgun, is fixed to the fishpole and also requires a full-time operator. (See Figure 3.8.) If the shotgun is fixed to a camera, it cannot always be at the right angle to cut out unwanted background noise; it will gather any and all sounds in front of it.

Lavaliere Mikes

Lavaliere or mini-microphones became quite popular when TV presented new problems for audio production professionals. The mikes used on TV

Figure 3.8: A boom or fishpole mike can get close to the sound source and not be in the shot.

Figure 3.9: A Tram Lavaliere microphone without a tie clip. The condenser element lies behind the screen. The mike is small enough to hide just about anywhere.

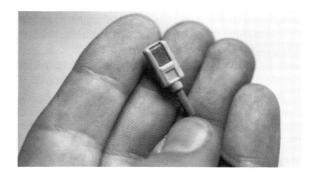

had to sound good and they also had to have an acceptable appearance on camera. The lavaliere mike was one answer to this appearance problem. Designed to be worn by the person whose voice is to be recorded, lavaliere mikes, or lavs, are quite small and unobtrusive.

Often used as tie-clip mikes, lavs usually have a condenser element. (See Figure 3.9.) Two of these mikes are often placed on the same tie clip in a technique known as **dual redundancy** to provide a backup if one fails.

Lavaliere mikes are almost always constructed with an omnidirectional pickup pattern because the sound of the human voice emanates from the mouth in an omnidirectional pattern. Designed to be worn either against the clothing of the person or beneath a clothing article, such as a tie, scarf or shirt, lavaliere mikes are designed with a built-in boost in the high frequency range because the sound reaching the mike may be filtered by the cloth and cause higher frequencies to be missed.

SPECIAL APPLICATIONS

In addition to the considerations of structure, sensitivity, impedance and style, the type of application for the mike may influence which mike is best for your audio needs. Special application microphones have been developed to meet the needs of some atypical applications.

Performance Microphones

Microphones designed for performances will usually have special characteristics or devices built into them to suit the needs of audio performers. Consider the needs of a performer like Mick Jagger. Because of his bouncing, swinging and jolting style of singing, he needs a mike that will take some abuse. First, his mike should have a shock mounting that dampens the noise created from rough handling. He would also need a mike that would withstand the explosive wind and breath sounds generated from his movement and style of singing. Mikes designed for this purpose have a special filter called a pop or blast filter that will stabilize the diaphragm and thereby minimize the distortion and allow truer sound reproduction. Performance mikes are often used at very close range. Any viewer of rock stars on TV will see that they practically swallow the mike as they sing. Mikes used for this purpose must have the characteristics that enhance the singer's vocal qualities that include a bass roll-off feature to minimize a booming low frequency sound or a boost of the upper midrange frequencies. Another common design feature of performance mikes is the ability to reject background noise to permit higher amplifier level of the desired sound before getting audio feedback in the system. For performers who prefer handheld performances, lightweight mikes are necessary.

Multiple Application Microphones

Some microphones are now designed and marketed to be used in a wide variety of applications. These mikes are designed so that they are able to provide different pickup patterns in different situations. The mikes designed in this way are also known as **convertible or system mikes.** These mikes often come with a standard power module and several attachments that allow different configurations for various applications. Some mikes change configuration by the flip of a switch. Essentially, this type of mike can function as a handheld omnidirectional, unidirectional mike or even one or more variation of the special cardioid patterns to provide the pickup abilities of various type of shotgun mikes. As with any multiple-purpose tool, this type of mike may not be as good in any one configuration as the best mike of its type. However, this slight trade-off of some excellence for versatility is a worthwhile one for many users with limited budgets but a wide range of audio pickup responsibilities.

Headset Microphones

Headset microphones are mounted on a bracket with one or two earphones attached. This headset is worn on the head of announcers in both radio and TV. Their TV use is usually restricted to announcers who are usually not seen on camera.

Figure 3.10: Headset mikes typical of those used by sportscasters. *Courtesy Shure Brothers, Inc.*

(See Figure 3.10.) The headset mike has a miniboom that holds the mike in place very close to the announcer's mouth. This is especially important in situations where the announcer may have to turn his head to follow action or receive information from another person.

This mike can have either a dynamic or condenser element. Its pickup pattern is cardioid because the important sounds are coming from one source, the announcer's mouth, which is located an inch or two in front of the mike.

Surface Mount and Pressure Zone Microphones

Surface mount and pressure zone microphones, also called **boundary mikes,** are usually used in situations where two or more people are the sources for audio to be recorded or broadcast and these people are positioned in front of a flat surface such as the floor or a table. (See Figure 3.11.) The polar pickup patterns of these mikes are somewhat different than conventional mikes. The mikes come with both omni- and unidirectional patterns, but only one hemisphere of the omnidirectional sphere or unidirectional heart shape is available.

When this type of mike is unidirectional, it can be used to isolate a particular vocalist or part of a musical group. It can also function as a single instrument mike, for example, for a bass drum, by placing the mike on the floor directly in front of the instrument.

It is possible to create your own boundary mike with mikes you already have. By taking a hand mike or lav and laying it parallel to the floor or boundary surface, pointing it to the center of the sound source, and raising it just slightly (1mm or 2mm) off that surface with a bit of tape or some-

Figure 3.11: This boundary mike by Crown called a PZM® can be mounted on any surface such as a tabletop or a floor. The power supply with this mike has controls to change the sensitivity and filters to shape the frequency response to get the best sound from varying conditions.

thing else small, you can achieve a close approximation of an actual boundary mike.

Wireless Microphones

There are numerous situations where a standard microphone is appropriate for the audio needs of a production situation, but the use of audio cable is not. The wireless microphone, often referred to as a Radio Frequency (RF) mike, frees the person being miked from the tether of an audio cable, which is often aesthetically undesirable in film or TV shots. (See Figure 3.12.) In some situations where sound recording is the only goal, the required cable lengths may be too long or the person being miked may move around too quickly or too often to avoid getting tangled in the cable, for example, an energetic rock singer who does not stand still or a referee at a football game.

A wireless microphone system can consist of any standard mike connected to a small portable radio transmitter. (See Figure 3.13.) The radio transmitter is concealed on the person being miked and sends the radio signal encoded with the audio information to a receiver at a location which may be up to one-quarter mile away although the standard receiving distance is no more than 300 feet. Some wireless microphones have the transmitter built into the mike handle itself.

Although wireless mikes are essential in location TV work, they should not be the first choice for standard audio production. When the audio signal is transmitted via radio frequencies, usually

Figure 3.12: RF wireless mikes. *Courtesy Shure Brothers, Inc.*

Figure 3.13: A Vega Pro 33 wireless mike system. The transmitter on the right can use a variety of mikes such as the Tram lavaliere shown. The Tram has a LEMO connector to plug into the transmitter; three types of mike clips for the mike itself are shown. *Courtesy Shure Brothers, Inc.*

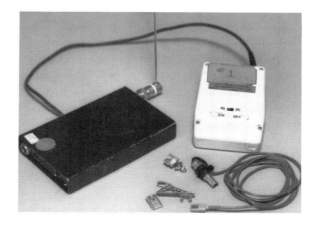

on a VHF frequency of 174 MHz to 216 MHz, some noise interference occurs. This is particularly true in urban environments where machinery, x-rays, automobiles and other RF signals from standard broadcasting and point-to-point communications generate radio frequency interference.

When you buy a wireless mike, you will be asked where the mike will be used and then assigned a VHF frequency. Since mike frequencies are the same as those used for TV transmitters, you should not have one on the same frequency as a local station's transmitter. A mike bought for use in Boston may not work well in Chicago. Production crews traveling around the country try to have wireless systems that can change frequencies to adapt to the local airwaves.

One of the biggest causes of interference is reflected radio waves from the transmitter striking the receiver at different times, just like reflected audio waves cause echo. The path between transmitter and receiver must be as clear of obstructions as possible, especially anything made of metal. To further improve your chances of getting a good signal, make sure the receive and transmit antennas are parallel; in other words one cannot be horizontal while the other is vertical. Also be sure that they are not curled or bunched up if they are the soft type.

Parabolic Microphones

A parabolic microphone is highly directional but not convenient to use. Its name is somewhat misleading because it implies that the microphone is in the shape of a parabola. The parabolic or **dish mike** is simply an omnidirectional microphone placed at the focal point inside a parabola-shaped dish reflector. The principle upon which the parabolic mike works is identical to that of a satellite TV dish: distant or weak signals strike the parabolic dish and are automatically reflected to the transducer at the center or focal point. This reflection process results in a much stronger signal than if the microphone was pointed directly at the sound source. The dish mike is very directional because sound waves not coming straight into the dish are not reflected to its focal point and therefore not recorded.

A parabolic mike is used on the sidelines of football games to give the director close-in sound of the players on the field. It is also used in surveillance and nature situations, such as recording bird calls. Because of its design it tends to pick up high-frequency sounds better than low-frequency sounds. The reason for this is that low-frequency

sounds have long wavelengths and sometimes miss the dish. Another problem is that they are somewhat large and clumsy. This is not the mike you would want to use for an interview.

Contact Microphones

Although most microphones are designed to be sensitive to sound waves propagated through the air, some are designed to pick up sound waves through another medium such as wood, metal or other dense materials. Contact microphones are attached to a hard surface, for example, the top surface of a violin or guitar. The mike vibrates with the movement of the surface on which it is mounted. This vibration generates the output signal. Contact mikes are often constructed with ceramic elements.

ACCESSORIES

Differing applications and locations demand that microphones be flexible enough to be positioned in various places under numerous conditions. To get acceptable sound, many accessories are available to the audio technician for mounting the mike and insuring that quality sound can be gathered under adverse conditions.

Mounts

Microphones are not free-standing instruments and require a device or mounting system to keep them secured in place. For interviewing or sound collection on location, this is most often accomplished by simply hand-holding the mike. In most studio work mikes are almost always attached to something. Although some microphones have an integral mounting system that allows them to be easily and directly attached to mountings, most do not. Mikes without a built-on feature for mounting require a bracket or most commonly a mike clasp. (See Figure 3.14.) After a clasp is put on the hand mike, the mike is adaptable to the vast majority of mike-mounting devices, including studio booms, floor stands, desk stands, gooseneck stands and a variety of stands for special applications (See Figure 3.15.)

Acoustic Filters and Windscreens

Some microphones are designed to cope with problems inherent in close miking. Inexperienced announcers and people who are being interviewed may pop their p's speak too loudly or forcefully or blast the microphone with too much sound. Many mikes now have pop-and-blast filters built into

Figure 3.14: Mike clasp for attaching mike to stand. *Courtesy Shure Brothers, Inc.*

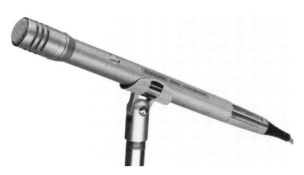

them to correct these problems. These filters are contained inside the mike housing; the sound must pass through them before striking the diaphragm. Some filters are designed for use in front of the mike rather than inside it. These filters, made of a mesh material, also reduce pops and blasts from vocalists.

Windscreens are foam-rubber-like casings designed to fit over the tip of a microphone. Almost all hand mikes, lavalieres and headset microphones can be used with windscreens to reduce the sound made by the air currents or wind. The effectiveness of this type of wind screen can vary greatly depending on the nature of the mike. In general, the more directional a mike is, the more susceptible it is to wind noise and the harder it is to protect. Because shotgun mikes are the most affected by wind, a simple foam windscreen is not enough to achieve quality audio under windy conditions. For optimum sound a shotgun is used in a basket-type windscreen called a **zeppelin.** (See Figure 3.16.) This device surrounds the mike with a space of dead air while allowing most audible frequencies to pass through.

Figure 3.15: Various desk stands for mikes. *Photo courtesy Electro-Voice, Inc.*

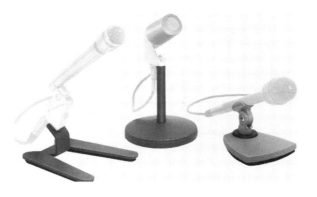

Figure 3.16: A zeppelin system is used for cutting down wind noise. *Courtesy Light Wave Systems, Van Nuys, CA.*

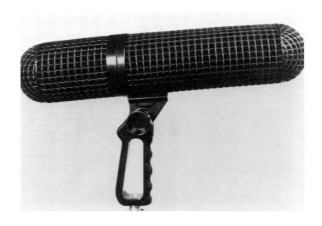

AUDIO CABLES AND CONNECTORS

To complete the technical chain of an audio system, the signal must get to a recording device through an electrical interface: a cable and its connectors.

Balanced and Unbalanced Lines

An unbalanced line is the type of audio line found in most consumer-level audio products, such as home camcorders and cassette recorders. The cable consists of a single conductor carrying the positive signal and a shield carrying the negative signal of a circuit. While this type of line is fine for most consumer needs, it is limited to cable lengths of less than 10 feet and can be susceptible to outside electrical interference, especially in cable lengths over 10 feet. This type of line is not recommended for any professional use.

In a balanced audio line, the mike signal is carried by two leads instead of one. The shield is the ground so that the conductor leads are completely isolated from other electrical components. A balanced line is far less susceptible to RF interference and ground loop hum found in unbalanced lines. If you must connect a balanced line to an unbalanced line, it is best to have a one-to-one isolation transformer between the two. This device keeps the ground loop of the unbalanced line from inducing hum or noise in the balanced line.

Connectors and Adapters

The standard connector for balanced audio lines is the three-contact XLR-type sometimes referred to as a **canon connector.** (See Figure 3.17.) The input end of an XLR cable is always a female connector (receptacles for the connector pins) and the output end is always a male connector (the connector pins). A microphone always has a male connector. The XLR connectors are the only type used in professional audio recording buy may not be the only types encountered in field production or news gathering. (See Figure 3.18.)

It is typical in ENG work to be asked to record audio sources from a wide variety of systems in the field. A good audio kit should include adapters to tap into any of these systems. (See Figure 3.19.) The most common is the ¼-inch phone plug. This plug comes in a balanced (stereo) and unbalanced (mono) versions. In most cases you will not need a stereo signal. This ¼-inch connector is the most common way to tap into a house PA system or audio mixing board not designed for video production. The output of such systems is usually labeled "monitor out" and is typically mono at mike level. Many video supply companies sell adapters that are ¼-inch phone (stereo or mono) at one end and XLR at the other.

Other connectors that you are likely to encounter in the field are the ⅛-inch or mini-plug, the RCA-type connector that your stereo uses, the micro-plug, such as those found in those miniature tape recorders and a modular telephone line plug. While adapters are available to convert these plugs to XLR, it is quite easy to make up short cables

Figure 3.17: High-quality microphones used for portable video have a male XLR connector at the end. *Courtesy Comprehensive Video Supply Corp., Northvale, NJ.*

Figure 3.18: Audio-balanced line (XLR) connectors. *Courtesy Comprehensive Video Supply Corp., Northvale, NJ.*

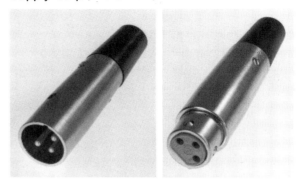

with the different types of connectors at each input end and an XLR at the other.

Signal Loss in Audio Cable

One advantage of using low-impedance mikes is the ability to use cable runs over 10 feet in length. A mike level signal is able to travel up to 200 feet or more with insignificant loss of signal strength. On very long runs, there may be a loss of some audio frequencies and an increased susceptibility to hum or electrical interference. For long distances, it may be necessary to amplify the audio with a mixer near the source end to deliver enough signal strength to the cable destination. By amplifying the signal to line level from mike level, a higher-quality signal with less hum can be transferred over a greater distance.

Phase

If the polarity of the audio cables or mikes used in a single system does not match, the signal may be out of phase and cause the cancellation of some

Figure 3.19: Various audio adapters to provide flexibility for working with audio signals.

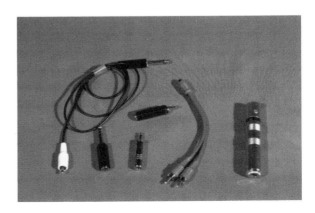

frequencies or the entire signal itself. This can be a very tricky problem to track down without the use of a volt-ohm meter or a cable tester. While this problem is not common, it is possible. If you find a cable or source that is out of phase, a small in-line adapter can reverse the phase (polarity) of the audio line, or you can rewire the cable or mike.

Filters and Pads

There is a variety of in-line filters and pads in barrel style that aid the audio-gathering process. These items can be invaluable in getting the most out of your mikes and overcoming weak points in your audio system. The barrel style allows you to put the filter or pad in the audio line at any point where there is a connection.

Switchable Attenuator Pad   A switchable attenuator pad reduces impedance by 15 dB, 20 dB or 25 dB to avoid overload distortion at the recorder from too strong a signal.

Line Adapter   A line adapter is a 50 dB attenuator that reduces line level to mike level. While the output level of many mixers, VCRs and amplifiers is at line level, most recorders only accept mike level input.

High Pass Filter   A high pass filter reduces bass and rumble by rolling off the low frequencies. This filter is good for reducing air conditioner noise and wind rumble.

Low Pass Filter   A low pass filter reduces hiss by rolling off the high frequencies.

Presence Adapter   A presence adapter gives a slight boost in the upper midrange of frequencies to enhance the quality of the human voice.

Response Shaper   A response shaper puts a slight dip in the upper midrange of frequencies to reduce sibilance that can sometimes be present in certain mikes or miking situations.

SELECTION AND PLACEMENT

Now that the numerous characteristics of microphones have been explained, it is appropriate to discuss how to use this information to complete the processes of mike selection and mike placement.

Choosing a Mike

Mikes have varying elements, pickup patterns, frequency responses, impedance, appearance, application and special accessories, such as built-in filters. In addition, some mikes even have a type of personality, a sound different from other similarly constructed or designed microphones. Because of the variety of choices, it seems that the

selection process could be lengthy and complicated. Fortunately, this is not usually the case. Most audio production facilities have a finite selection of mikes available for production work. This selection consists of representatives of the different types of mikes available: omnidirectional, unidirectional, dynamic, condenser and so on. Not many production houses would stay in business if they decided to buy an additional microphone whenever the producer or production manager decided that a new mike might be somewhat better than those already owned. High-quality microphones are expensive. Good-quality microphones can often yield high-quality sound in a variety of situations, and many good mikes often overlap each other in what they can do well. For example, a cardioid mike is best for many interview situations, but an omnidirectional mike might work just as well if you can keep the extraneous noise in the room low and get the omnidirectional mike close to the source.

There are five factors to consider when selecting the best mike for any production.

1. General production goals concern what the end product is supposed to be—how it will be distributed, who the audience will be and what quality level should be obtained.
2. Environment of the production means how much control there will be over the sound environment.
3. Sound sources involve the nature and number of sound-generating entities that are part of the production.
4. Type of sound concerns the technical aspects of the sound sources like frequency and volume.
5. Detailed production goals involve the specific goals for the overall sound of the production as well as the individual sources.

Placing a Mike

Not only must you choose a mike based on its design characteristics but also based on where the mike must or can be placed. Limitations such as personnel, budget, time, boom shadows and environmental concerns can dictate which mikes you can use. Knowing how to place a particular mike lets you know if that mike is right for the job you have to do. (See Figure 3.20.)

Hand Mikes   A hand-mike is often the easiest to use. You simply pick it up and point it at the source of the sound. Singers, TV evangelists, used car salespeople and TV reporters often use hand mikes, which are made for gathering audio close-in to the source. Meant to be seen on camera most of the time, hand mikes do not require a boom person or as much time and hassle to be put in place as a hidden lavaliere would require. There is just one hard and fast rule: they must be within about one to two feet from the source of audio. Some hand mikes are shock-mounted within their outer shell to withstand rough handling without creating excessive mechanical noise. The Electro-Voice Re-50 is a shock-mounted mike well suited for ENG work. (See Figure 3.21) A news photographer working without a soundperson may have no choice but to give the reporter a hand mike to gather almost all the audio, especially for interviews and stand-ups. The hand mike allows the reporter to place the mike where it can get the best sound. If the news crew is talking to a gathering of steel workers outside a closed factory, the reporter can maneuver the mike to whichever person is talking while being able to bring the

mike back to record the questions as well. The biggest problem is, if you are using a shock-mounted mike, the sound of fidgeting fingers on the mike can be very distracting.

In EFP work the hand mike is used more often as a prop and not out of necessity as in ENG. Since the quality of the audio is more important in EFP, it is not a good idea to leave the handling and placement of the mike in the hands of the talent. That is why most EFP crews have a soundperson. Some talent, such as a used car salesperson, like to have the mike to hold onto like a security blanket. It may in fact be just a prop with the actual sound being recorded by an unseen mike. If you have time, budget or personnel, there are usually better ways to get that audio. The best exception to this rule is in the case of singers but even they are now going to the new micro-headset mikes (such as Madonna has used) to free their hands for dancing.

Even when a hand mike is used on a floor or desk stand, it still must be within the two-foot range to obtain quality sound. As the mike is placed further from the sound source, there is an

Figure 3.20: Sometimes good sound pickup requires unusual microphone placement.

Figure 3.21: IEV RE50 omnidirectional dynamic mike with shock mounting. *Photo courtesy Electro-Voice, Inc.*

increased risk of the audio sounding hollow or having an echo. For a news conference where several people seated at a long table are to speak, using more than one mike is a good alternative. It is best to follow the **rule of three to one** in the placement of the mikes, however many there are. This principle says that for every unit of distance between the mike and the audio source, the distance between mikes should be at least three times greater. The greater the directionality of the mike, the less chance there is of phase problems from reflected sounds or multiple mikes.

Camera-Mounted Mikes   The best mike to mount on a camera is the ultradirectional type, although any type of mike can be used. A shotgun microphone will pick up audio mostly from the camera's field of vision. Distant sounds that come from the sides (outside of the picture) are not picked up nearly as well. Even in highly directional mikes, there are still flanges (off-axis lobes) of sound pick-up to the side and rear areas of the mike. While those flanges are not as sensitive as the on-axis lobes of the polar response chart, they may still pick up some unwanted sounds, such as the reporter whispering in your ear next to the side of the mike while you are shooting.

This type of audio is called **background (BG) audio.** Most producers refer to it as natural sound, or the sound the camera naturally hears. It is the most valuable sound an ENG person can get. Natural sound is what makes many pictures come alive. Having it can mean the difference in keeping your job or losing it. Some news photographers try to

use their camera mike to do reporterless interviews. While under certain time pressures or acoustic conditions this may be acceptable, most of the time it is not. The photographer places the camera (and therefore the mike) as close to the subject as possible to reduce the amount of background noise from this interview so the person sounds more on-mike. The net effect here is okay sound but a picture that has its perspective (and therefore its subject) distorted. It makes people's heads and their features seem enlarged or out of proportion.

Boom Mikes   While any microphone can be placed on a boom, the most common one is the shotgun. The portable boom or fishpole allows its operator to place the mike in the optimum position to gather the best audio. This is a common way for production crews and larger news organizations to gather audio in the field. Good team work between the photographer and the soundperson can keep the mike out of the picture but in the right place to get the best audio. The task of the boom operator is to keep the desired sound source on-axis while aiming the mike away from other distracting sounds. In the case of the reporter interviewing people on the street, a fishpole can be used by an audio person to do what a hand mike does without the mike being seen. This gives a more natural, realistic look. The audio person lines the mike up with the person's mouth at an angle to avoid having it also pointed at the street or an idling car at the curb. Most of the time the mike is at waist level as close to the person as possible and pointed up. The fishpole can also be held above and pointed down to the audio source, but this increases the possibility of reflected sound being gathered if the ground is a hard surface, such as concrete.

Mini-Mikes   Lavs or mini-mikes can be the best sounding but most frustrating mikes to use in field productions. They are by far the most susceptible to mechanical noise caused by rubbing against not only the capsule but the cable as well. Extra care is needed when using this type of mike. The most common use of a lav is on someone's tie, jacket or shirt. The most common lav clasp is the alligator clip. You simply clip on to any edge or fold of material. The two most common mistakes in using lavs are not hiding the mike cable and not properly securing it. (See Figure 3.22.) It is a major distraction to see people being interviewed on TV using a lav simply hanging from the front of their clothes. It just looks sloppy. This leads us to another problem. It is natural for everyone to move somewhat during a conversation. If the mike is placed wrong or the cable is not secured, a little movement is transferred into a horrendous scratching sound called mike rustle.

You must use considerable care in choosing where to attach the mike to a person. Look for a spot that is nondistracting to the camera and will not be brushed against by any part of the person's clothing or jewelry. Next, make sure the cable is fastened down so that it cannot pull on the mike. The easiest way is to loop the cord to the back of the alligator clip and pinch it with the material used to hold the mike. The other way is to use a fabric tape or similar product to tape the cable to the inside of the clothing. For an active wearer of a lav both procedures are recommended.

Because this mike is so small, most EFP users like to hide it in the person's clothing. This is not an easy job, but the results are well worth the effort. This mike placement can make everyone wearing one sound right in any kind of production without any hint of a mike being present. There are many ways to hide a lav mike that is often no

bigger than a small pea. The dangers are clothing russle and muffling. The mike capsule must be as unobstructed as possible even if it is already under the clothing. The mike must be completely taped down between clothing layers with the capsule taped on both sides and only the grill area of the capsule left exposed. If the mike goes between clothing and skin, the mike must be taped directly to the skin using medical tape or the equivalent. Sometimes a little funnel made of tape or even very soft leather can be fashioned to shield a hidden mike from russle. This process is tricky and may take some trial and error to perfect.

Wireless Mikes The distinguishing factor about a wireless mike is not the mike, but the means of transmitting the audio from a mike to a receiver at the recorder. Of all the types of mikes, using a wireless is the most dramatic in its results. There is nothing like hearing perfect up-close audio without a lot of background sounds around a subject who is obviously some distance from the camera or who is moving about the set or location.

Figure 3.22: The cable of a lavaliere mike should be looped to the back of the clip. This hides the cable and lets the clip stop the noise that can result from mechanical or rubbing sounds that travel up the cable. The clip prevents the sound from reaching the mike.

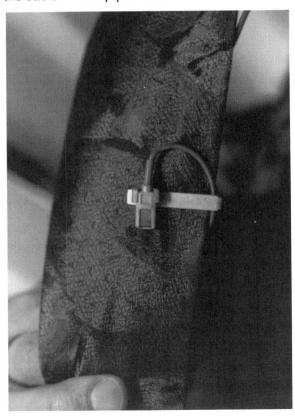
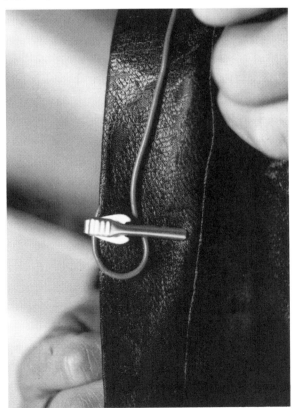

Combining the use of the wireless with the hidden mike can truly free up your subjects to be as natural as they can be. Wireless mikes have become so popular in all forms of EFP that most producers simply will not work without them. They have become as important (if not more than) as boom mikes to get high-quality audio without the mike being on camera. A wireless allows the talent to roam the location cable-free, to turn backwards to the camera while still being on-mike, and to have close-in mike sound. With extensive use of wirelesses, any production can take on a natural feel by focusing the viewer's attention on the sound picked up from the subject as it would sound if the viewer were actually there.

The use of wireless mikes has also made quite a difference in news gathering. Veteran news producer Ray Farkas has made extensive use of wireless mikes on stories for the networks and other news outlets. Farkas has been the pioneer in using wireless sound to lead photojournalism into a new era. By eliminating the boom mike and placing the camera and crew a great distance from the subject, Farkas is able to relax the video subjects so completely that they forget they are wearing a mike *and* being videotaped. The results have commonly become known as the "Farkas Interview," an interview that is not only more conversational in tone but actually looks like the viewer is eavesdropping on a private conversation. This technique can make a simple news story more compelling to watch and more convincing. Although no staging is allowed in journalism, the obvious presence of camera, lights and mikes can make an interview look more like a TV show than a slice of real life.

Even without the more complex uses that Farkas has developed, the wireless is an invaluable tool for any everyday news crew. Besides wiring a subject for better natural sound or walking interviews, the wireless can be plugged into PA systems or placed on podiums at meetings, gatherings and concerts so that the camera can go anywhere within the location and still have a house audio feed. The wireless can be quickly and easily placed anywhere within a scene to get a close-in presence to the sound.

Even if you cannot plug in directly or put the mike at the source of the audio at an event that has a PA system (**house sound**), you may be able to place the wireless directly in front of the PA speaker. The audio is not as good as a direct feed, but if the sound system does not have excessive buzz or hum, you can still get house sound. The small size of wireless transmitters allows you to place the mikes just about anywhere. If you are shooting a long line of Super Bowl ticket buyers, you might simply set the wireless on the counter at one of the ticket windows. You could then make a shot from anywhere around the window and still have great audio from the activity there. One shot may be from the end of the line with the window in the background as the viewer hears the conversation at the window. This helps focus the viewer on what is taking place. The technique may also be as simple as putting the mike at the stream's edge for a wide shot of a beautiful valley as canoers pass through it. The camera is up on the side of a small hill but the audio is of the water flowing in the stream below and the sounds of the canoers as they pass through the shot. Synchronous sound that you could not get with the mike at the camera position can now be gathered with creative use of the wireless. It is this simple and subtle use of close-in sound that can make a good video story into a great one.

MIXING, MONITORING AND STEREO

After you have selected the appropriate mike, mount, filter and screen and achieved proper placement, you need to consider other aspects of the sound-recording process. Multiple microphones for any given sound situation require combining signals, called **mixing.** To insure that your sound is appropriate for your situation, you must also learn to monitor the sound. A brief mention is also made here about stereo sound recording.

Mixing

The last stage that audio is likely to go through is some form of mixing before it is recorded at the VCR. To mix audio it first needs to be monitored. Whenever more than one mike is being recorded on a single audio channel, it is best to use a mixer to make sure each mike can be separately controlled to insure the best performance. The popular portable mixer by Shure, the FP-31 (see Figure 3.23), has three input lines, a low-cut filter on each line, a tone generator, two bridged output lines and a master output volume control. It can take line or mike level impedance and feed phantom power to condenser-type mikes on any line. This type of mixer gives you more flexibility when combining several sources of audio together before recording. It is very popular for use with camcorders for the audio person needs to carry only one of these portable mixers. Two record

Figure 3.23: This Shure FP31 mixer has three inputs and two outputs. The mixer is battery-powered, can both line- and mike-level inputs and outputs, contains a tone generator and can provide phantom power for certain types of condenser microphones. *Courtesy Shure Brothers, Inc.*

channels on the VCR can be set up with a tone signal from the mixer; the input volume adjustments can be made at the mixer. In some cases the sound person will use a wireless mike to send the output of the mixer to the camcorder, thus allowing the photographer to roam freely while the audio person can go wherever the best sound gathering location is.

Monitoring

While the performance of your equipment may be well known, you cannot really know if everything is working fine unless you actually hear what you are getting. (See Figure 3.24.) A good pair of headphones is absolutely mandatory for any audio person and a good earpiece essential for a one-person operation. Without hearing what you are getting, an unheard problem can make all your

Figure 3.24: Even when there is a one-person crew, it is necessary to use headphones to constantly monitor the audio and its quality. *Photo by John Lebya.*

efforts worthless. Most professional VCRs offer a confidence playback head in the audio recording circuit. This system allows you to actually hear the sound on the tape after it has been recorded while you are still recording. The playback head passes over the tape about one second after the record head lays down the audio. Because of this delay, confidence audio sounds weird because it is out of sync with what you are seeing. Most photographers and audio persons only spot-check the confidence circuit occasionally during the recording process because of the distraction.

Stereo

At the time of this writing and for the foreseeable future, stereo audio in most field productions and news gathering is not practical. True stereo needs to be recorded on the FM tracks of the VCR; only the newer models of recorders are capable of receiving stereo. Such factors as the mikes used and critical mixing techniques make stereo recording a very demanding job in the field. There is more effort required at that time than most productions can afford. Because of these factors, this book does not address stereo recording.

4 Light, Lights and Lighting

Lighting is probably the most overlooked and misunderstood aspect of ENG and EFP. Very often light kits are low-priority items in budgets for field gear and subsequently, especially in these days of lean budgets, the light kits are never purchased. Existing kits often go for months without replacement bulbs, again a result of the low priority assigned to remote lighting. Because of the limitations of trunk space, crew members and setup time, the portable light kits are often left at the station, in the studio or in the vehicle.

It seems odd that lighting equipment gets such casual treatment; after all, it is the manipulation of light that is the key to all photography. When using relatively inexact video cameras, you must pay constant attention to the light factor to produce a realistic image.

Portable video practitioners may treat lighting casually because much of their work is done outdoors. Under most daytime circumstances, available sunlight provides enough light to allow the video cameras to see the desired scene and record the action. But seeing is not always good enough. With some additional lighting effort and consideration, the camera will not only see the scene and action, but it will also detect additional mood, dimension and interest in a good video segment.

This chapter looks at some technical aspects of light and lighting requirements for video; basic lighting objectives and sources of light for portable video; and finally, lighting equipment and successful techniques for ENG and EFP.

PHYSICAL PROPERTIES OF LIGHT

Light waves constitute part of the electromagnetic spectrum. Besides having different frequencies than other types of waves in the spectrum, light waves differ because they can be seen when transmitted. (See Figure 2.2.) Light of differing frequencies appears different to the eye. Lower-frequency light waves appear red; higher-frequency light waves appear blue; medium-frequency light waves appear green. This variable color appearance is referred to as hue or tint. Red, blue and green are known as the **primary additive colors.** Combinations of these three colors can be made to create all other visible colors. This gives a very basic explanation of why three-chip (and formerly three-tube) cameras give off red, green and blue light information. Mixtures of the information from these chips can generate the full-color image seen on a color monitor. If all the primary colors of light in the visible spectrum are combined, the result is white light.

The primary colors for paint and similar substances are magenta (reddish blue), cyan (blue green) and yellow. These three primary colors are called the **subtractive primary colors.** Mixing materials of these colors will yield different results than the mixing the colors of light.

The amount of a particular color is called **saturation.** A heavily saturated green color on a monitor is bright green; a less saturated color is a pale green. Color is called **hue, tint** or **chrominance** in TV production. On a TV monitor, the level of color can be somewhat manipulated by a control, usually labeled "color."

In video production the amount of light differs from the type of light. Stated in another way, the **quantity** (brightness, intensity or luminance) **of light** is different from the **quality** (hue, tine or chrominance) **of light.**

Color Temperature

Color temperature is a scale for measuring the hue, or tint, of light. Although our eyes generally perceive light as being white most light has a tint of some kind. Since white light is a combination of the three primary TV colors (red, blue and green), it is not surprising that one of the three primary colors slightly dominates most light sources. Color temperature, measured in degrees Kelvin (°K), helps assign a quantity to qualitative color changes. (See Figure 4.1.)

The sun displays varying color temperatures at different times of the day. In the morning when sunlight strikes objects, it tends to make them appear reddish-orange. These same objects at noon might appear slightly bluish, while the late afternoon sun makes them appear reddish-orange again. Video cameras tend to exaggerate these predominant colors, giving the objects an unnatural appearance. In early morning, sunlight measures about 2500°K to 3000°K. Noontime sunlight is 5600°K or higher, and in the late afternoon the color temperature is similar to early morning, again about 2500°K to 3000°K.

Despite the fact that early morning and late afternoon color temperatures are lower in degrees Kelvin, it is incorrect to call the reddish-orange color at 3000°K cooler than the noontime blue of 5600°K. Although videographers refer to blue and green as cooler colors and gold, red, yellow and pink as warmer, the technical concept of color temperature needs to be separated from emotional response to colors.

Color temperature changes occur throughout the day: If you shoot the first half of a story at 8:00 a.m. and the second half at noon and do not compensate for the change in color temperature, the reporter in the scene will probably have a skin tone change from reddish-orange to blue as the story progresses from the first half to the second. You need to white balance every time anything changes, including the time of day.

Like sunlight, lamps also have varying degrees of color temperature. For example, ordi-

Figure 4.1: This chart represents how video cameras respond to different kinds of light. *Graphic by Manny Romero.*

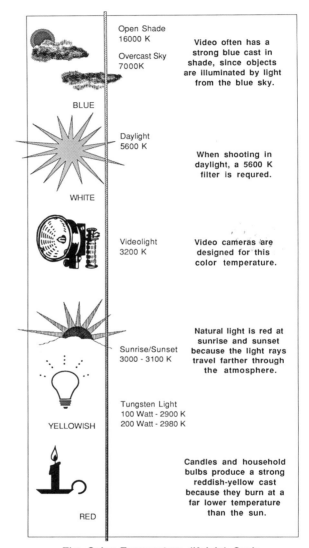

The Color Temperature (Kelvin) Scale

nary household incandescent bulbs are around 2800°K and tungsten-halogen bulbs designed for use with video cameras are 3200°K. Fluorescent bulbs are trickier if they are the consumer type most often found in offices and homes. Their color temperatures vary from brand to brand, but most are around 4200°K. Other types of bulbs are made to give off light at 5600°K.

Situations with mixed sources of light can cause problems. Imagine the face of a subject whose right side is lit by a tungsten-halogen lamp and whose left side is lit by a fluorescent bulb. If the camera is set for 3200°K, the right side would look normal and the other side could be a sickly greenish blue. Since the video camera compensates for only one color temperature at a time, it is best to avoid mixed lighting situations. In the above example it would be best to turn off the fluorescent and add tungsten-halogen light to the left side of the face. This may not always be possible, however, because some lights must stay on to prevent disruption of others.

The biggest advantage of modern video cameras regarding color temperature is that they white balance under any light if the lights are evenly blended. As long as the scene has a consistently even mix of any number of light sources that are within a limited range, the picture should be close to the true colors. When the mix changes regarding distance from any of the light sources, the ratio of relative intensities changes. Mixed-light white balancing works best when each light source is about the same intensity and close in relative color temperature. It is hard to mix tungsten and daylight (3200°K to 5600°K), but tungsten and household incandescent or fluorescent are much closer in temperature (3200°K to 2800°K or 4400°K).

When working with other ENG crews in changing light conditions, it is good etiquette to discuss the light to be added or used. If one crew chooses to use a tungsten light when all others are shooting available light, it can create some bad feelings and bad video. To avoid problems, work out lighting logistics with others before the actual shooting begins and work cooperatively with other crews.

Intensity: The Inverse Square Law

A lamp placed near us gives off a certain amount of light. If the lamp is moved closer, there is more light; if the lamp is moved away, there is less light. The actual relationship between distance and illumination is often critical in location video work because of the amount of light falling on a subject.

This relationship is described by a law of physics known as the **inverse square law,** which states that the amount of light diminishes by a factor equal to the inverse square of the distance change. When the distance between a light and the subject is doubled, the amount of light falling on the subject is reduced by a quarter of the original amount. In other words, increasing the distance by a factor of two reduces the amount of light falling on the subject to $1/2^2$ or 1/4 the original amount. Keep in mind that this law applies to unfocused rather than focused light sources. It helps explain

Figure 4.2: Inverse Square Law. The amount of light striking an object (as measured by a light meter) is equal to the inverse square of the distance from the light to the object. When the distance is 1, the amount of light is $1/1^2$ or 1. When the distance is 1 + 1, the amount of light stricking the object is $1/(1 + 1)^2$ or 1/4.

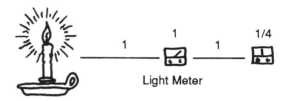

Light Meter

light placement and its relationship to f-stop and base illumination. (See Figure 4.2.)

The intensity of light is measured in units of footcandles. One **footcandle** is the amount of light given off by one candle one foot away. Light meters are indispensable in film work but are rarely seen on a video shoot because of such factors as auto iris and seeing what the picture looks like with respect to exposure in the viewfinder.

However, one way to judge your camera and lights is to measure their performance with a light meter. Try all the different lights in your kit one by one and measure the footcandles at various distances and angles to the light. You will quickly see how much light is given off and how the lights may be aimed or manipulated to suit the camera's needs. This experiment is particularly good for adjustable lights.

The meter can check the ASA rating of your camera or show how many footcandles it takes to get a good exposure at different f-stops. The advanced professional uses a light meter to light a scene without the camera present, to light by a certain formula without a lot of trial and error, or to create a certain amount of light to work the lens at a specific f-stop. The light meter can be invaluable in doing site surveys when looking at the available light. (See Figure 4.3.)

Angle of Light

As Edison and other early film-makers quickly discovered, the sun is one of the best sources of illumination for making pictures. Unfortunately, this cheap and easy source of natural light has

Figure 4.3: A Sekonic light meter that measures the amount of light reaching the subject.

some annoying qualities in addition to the beneficial ones. First, it is not always visible in the daytime. Clouds, smog, mist, trees, buildings, mountains, billboards and even large people can prevent sunlight from reaching the lens of the video camera. The sun also changes position in the sky continuously throughout the day. At early morning the sun rising in the east strikes the subject in a scene at a low angle. This low-angle sunlight yields less light than the higher-angle sunlight characteristic of slightly later in the day. Also, the quality of the light is somewhat different as well—it casts a reddish-orange glow as opposed to the bluish glow of the noonday sun.

Because of these differences in the angle of the sun and the quality of light at different times of the day, when more than one shoot is required to complete a particular scene, it is best to shoot the scene at the same time of day with similar amounts of cloudiness. Many directors of TV commercials favor the early morning light because of its reddish-orange glow and will shoot the entire commercial with that type of light. This may require several shoots at that location on successive days. The different light characteristics can also be used to show a progression of time. The portrayal of a farmer going through a day's activities would include the reddish-orange light of the morning, the near-shadowless stark light of noon and the long shadows and pinkness of the evening. Some photographers attempt to manipulate the overall light appearance by performing the white balance procedure while the camera is aimed at a light blue card. This procedure tends to give the video a golden hue. The color of the scene can also be

manipulated by filters on the lens just as in film photography.

Traditional standards of photography contend that sunlight reflected off objects yields the most natural (and hence most eye-pleasing) light. Therefore, objects or subjects need to be placed in such a way that sunlight is reflected from them into the lens. This can be accomplished most easily by positioning the camera between the sun and what is to be shot. If the subject gets between the camera and the sun, there are two possible results: a strongly backlit shot or direct sunlight shining into the lens. Both effects can be undesirable if handled incorrectly by a novice camera operator; however, they can be used to great advantage by a skilled operator. (See Figure 4.4.)

Backlight and Lens Flares   In a strongly backlit shot, the background is much brighter than the subject. This type of shot creates a difficult problem for most cameras. The automatic iris control would adjust for the brightest part of the picture and thus close the aperture. The subject, compared to the background, reflects much less light and appears darker than normal. Often a strongly backlit scene must be reshot because facial features are not discernible. (See Figure 4.5.) A backlit scene may be done with the manual iris to achieve the proper exposure on the subject, but the results might not be what you want for the overall scene.

A second effect of the sun behind the subject is direct sunlight shining into the lens and onto the face of the camera's chips or pickup tubes. This can result in an optical effect called **flares** (a line of pentagonal shapes emanating from the sun), which may be undesirable. CCDs (charged coupled devices) in older cameras can be very susceptible

Figure 4.4: When using the sun as your light source, try to get the camera between the sun and your subject.

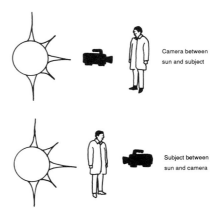

Figure 4.5: A backlit subject can lead to a picture that is exposed for the brighter background, resulting in an underexposed subject.

to a chip overload where a long vertical line cuts through the image of the sun or any other intense hot spot. Newer technology chips and electronics have eliminated this problem. For users of the older tube technology, the sun can be a great danger. The sunlight may cause permanent damage to pickup tubes. Direct sun burns in its image on the sensitive tube face, which will remain visible in the picture and videotape until the costly pickup tube is replaced or fixed.

Once you have mastered the use of light that directly reflects from the subject, you can use backlit and lens flare shots to your advantage. Both play an integral part in photography, especially in commercials and movies.

In movies and TV commercials, the sun is often used as the backlight in the overall lighting of a scene. If you study these shots carefully, you will find that two things are generally taking place: (1) additional light is being put on the subjects in the form of high-intensity arc lamps or reflector; and (2) the backgrounds are also backlit. When using this style, very little of the picture should be brighter than the subject. Even in ENG and EFP applications, a backlit shot can produce warm or pastel colors and good textures as long as the background is also shaded and little or no portion of the sky is in the shot. This effect may be desirable for many reasons, for example, to soften the features of a subject's face.

A backlit scene is said to be lit with ambient or reflected light: nature's soft light. This reflected sunlight tends to be more blue than direct sunlight, but white balancing in this reflected light offsets

the problem. In effect, by using this reflected light you are getting the best qualities of sunlight without the drawbacks. You can get great skin tones without the horrible dark shadows caused by harsh, direct sunshine.

At certain angles sunlight can reflect off a subject's surface creating a glare. This is when backlighting can be troublesome. Paved surfaces such as concrete can be very hard to use in backlit shots. That is why in backlit TV commercials they wet the streets down with water to darken the surface. Wet concrete actually reflects less light as long as there are no puddles.

Lens flares, caused by direct light striking the lens, can also be desirable. The rows of flares created can be used to add dynamics to the shot and help emphasize the sun or light source. A story on solar power practically requires a shot of the sun. Any chip camera should be able to shoot the sun with no damage to the camera. A tube camera, however, is an entirely different matter. With a little care and caution, you can shoot the sun without harming the pickup tubes. Using the iris in the automatic mode helps to prevent damage, but careful setup of the shot is critical. Keep the camera moving. This is when the difference between various kinds of pickup tubes becomes quite noticeable. Some tubes burn very quickly and may not be able to deliver the shot without damage. Others are far more forgiving and can be pointed at the sun for several seconds with no damage. You can pan across the sun to see if the sun leaves a comet tail or smear behind it. Slow the pan down until it just begins to smear or until you come to a static picture. Never leave it pointed at a bright object like the sun for more than few seconds.

By using the automatic iris feature and a camera with good tubes and electronics, you should find that a shot of the sun can last up to 10 seconds with no damage to the tube. Work your way slowly up to that point. The first sign of a comet tail or smear means that damage can occur. Keep the camera moving until you are sure about what you are doing. Some beautiful shots can be taken that include the sun. A pan across the sun can produce a series of flares that may actually add to the movement or aesthetics of the shot.

An integral part of the quality of light is the angle by which it strikes the subject in relationship to the camera. It not only makes a different in the way the camera perceives the subject's color but also in the way the subject appears artistically, emotionally and editorially. The angle of light creates the shadows necessary for depth. It can be reflected onto the subject to create soft, warm colors. The angle can also suggest time of day.

SOURCES OF LIGHT FOR PORTABLE VIDEO

Even though today's cameras can shoot in nearly any type of light, not all light sources will produce the quality of light you desire. With an understanding of each type of light source, you will be better able to judge the performance of your camera, particularly when it comes to reproducing realistic colors.

Sun

The single best source of light for portable video, the sun, is also the cheapest and, in many locations, the most readily available as well. The sun can be the hardest light source to manipulate but usually helps make the subject's skin tone appear natural. This is not surprising because the sun is our natural supplier of light—the light by which we judge reality. Almost everyone has bought clothing in an artificially lit store only to perceive its color quite differently in the sunlight. Mismatched sock wearers often realize the color disparity only after the sun reflects off the socks. This usually occurs at a sufficient distance from home to prevent a return and quick change. Since the sun follows its own schedule, it is necessary to go to great lengths to control it.

Artificial Light

Common artificial lights come in two categories: incandescent and fluorescent. The common screw-in household incandescent bulb is generally too dim and too low in color temperature to be of much use for video. People tend to appear orange-yellowish in this type of light. Fluorescent lamps give more even light and are of a higher color temperature. These lights can give subjects a blue-green skin tone. The light from typical office ceiling fluorescents is highly diffused, eliminating the shadows necessary to give subjects the appearance of depth and yielding a flat or washed-out appearance. For these reasons, common incandescents and fluorescents are usually avoided in portable video, if at all possible.

Today's low-light cameras work in almost any light level and under almost any type of light. While these capabilities allow the photographer to shoot anywhere without the need for additional lighting, they still do not satisfy some of the basic needs of photography. For a news photographer, shooting available light is a major blessing, but it is of only some help for a discriminating photographer in EFP and stylized ENG work. It comes back to the definition of photography: manipulating light, shadow and color to achieve a specific artistic or editorial result. Professional video practitioners use specially designed lights that give a better color temperature for natural skin tones (either 3200°K or 5600°K) enable them to have control over light direction and intensity.

Tungsten/Quartz. Tungsten or quartz lights are the most common light source used in video production. While using a filament within a sealed globe to produce light, they are quite different from common household light bulbs. These professional lights are often called tungstens, tungsten-halogens, quartz or just incandescents. In video production all these names refer to the same type of light. Tungsten filaments give off a very constant 3200°K over their lifespan, which may only be around 75 hours of use. Most tungsten bulbs are used in some sort of housing that enables the user to control the light. (See Figure 4.6.) One

Figure 4.6: Quartz-halogen versus tubular quartz lamp. *Photo courtesy GTE Products Corp.*

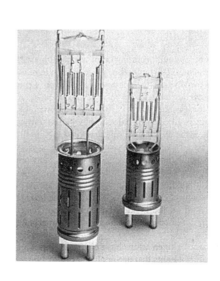

form of the tungsten bulb comes with its own reflector and focusing lens. This type is called a **Parabolic Aluminized Reflector (PAR).** It is similar to the headlights in a car and is often referred to as a **sealed beam light.** Unlike the bare bulb tungsten lights, the PAR lights can come in different color temperatures such as 5600°K (called a PAR 64) for use outdoors.

Fluorescent Unlike filament bulbs, fluorescent bulbs emit light when a gas within the bulb is excited by an electric current and then strikes the phosphor coating of the glass. The typical fluorescents found in the home and office can vary greatly in color temperature. Some are as low as 3000°K while others are 6500°K. Professional lighting handbooks have long charts and tables to deal with the wide variety of these lamps in correcting them to different film stocks. The white balance function in video cameras allows the camera to adjust to these lights as long as they are the same. If you are mixing colors of light (different types of sources), you must correct the sources so that they are all the same color. If you do not, you can end up with subjects that appear odd in color on the tape. Since the primary colors in fluorescent light are blue-green, you should avoid using them in conjunction with other lights. Several manufacturers now make fluorescent lighting units and bulbs designed to be used for video production. They can be purchased in either 3200°K or 5600°K.

Carbon Arcs The most famous light in Hollywood is the big carbon arc light that has been used on movie sets ever since film-making was invented. These large round lights, called **studio arcs,** are intensely bright and use two carbon electrodes and high, direct current voltage to create an arc between them. The optimum word here is large. The arc lights still used today are very big in size and weight and not only produce large amounts of light but large amounts of heat as well. They are mostly used outdoors in movie productions and seldom used in video production.

HMIs Another type of arc lamp uses alternating current instead of direct. The most common arc of this type is the hydrargyum medium arc-length iodide (HMI) light. The light is created by a mercury arc between two tungsten electrodes sealed in a glass bulb or globe. HMIs are a daylight temperature light. As they are used, the temperature tends to decrease, however. A new light may be as high as 6000°K, but a very old bulb may be as low as 4800°K. HMI lights have been very popular in film-making and are becoming very popular in video as well. Unlike tungsten lights, HMIs involve more in their operation.

It takes a very large amount of power to start the arc in the bulb, up to 60,000 volts for the one-second starting surge. After the surge, it takes about three minutes for the light to come up to operating strength and color temperature. HMIs operate using a 220-volt AC circuit and require a ballast not only for the starting surge but to regulate the voltage to the lamp. Each light runs at a specific voltage and no two bulbs operate at the exact some voltage. The ballast for most small HMIs, such as the kind you would use for a video production, runs on a normal 110- to 120-volt power supply and increases the voltage up to 220. Even though HMI lights can be small enough to use on top of the camera, the ballast must be attached to the light by a cable. Today's small, light HMI ballasts are still more bulky than a tungsten light. (See Figure 4.7.)

Figure 4.7: HMI light. *Courtesy Arriflex Corp.*

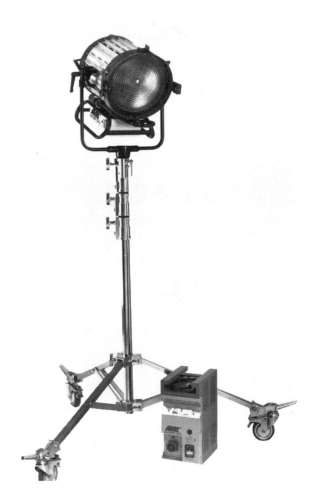

The advantages of an HMI are many. Since the light is at sunlight temperatures, color perception is at its best. They come in sizes from 200 watts to 12,000 watts. You get much more light from an HMI lamp than from a tungsten lamp of the same wattage: five times as much, in fact. A 1200-watt HMI puts out the equivalent of 6000 watts of incandescent light. The lights may cost more to buy, but they are cheaper to run per footcandle of light output, a major consideration if only a limited amount of power is available. HMIs also come in a DC-battery version for portable use. A simple battery belt operates a light of about 200 watts for around 20 to 30 minutes. That's like having a portable 1K (battery-powered 1000-watt light) with you, if you were using tungsten. HMIs come in almost any type of housing so there are few situations where they cannot be used.

Industrial HID High-Intensity Discharge (HID) refers to another type of arc-discharge that produces light through vapor or gas pressure in a glass globe. The three most common types of HIDs are mercury vapor, metal halide and sodium vapor. For video use the metal halide is the only one of interest. Metal halide lights are used in sports stadiums, parks, airports and malls to light large areas at night. The color temperature is closest to daylight and similar to HMIs. Metal halides tend to be yellow-green but the camera can be easily white-balanced in their light. The other two types of HIDs are also used primarily for industrial night lighting or city street lighting. Because of their strange line spectra, it is difficult to white-balance these two lights. Mercury vapor has no blue or red wavelengths, and sodium vapor has almost no blue or green. They have no value for video production and make it very hard for the camera to reproduce colors accurately.

Artificial light is, for the most part, a necessary evil in portable video. There are many disadvantages to using artificial lights:

1. Expense
2. Cumbersome
3. AC power requirements necessitating extension cords
4. Excess heat
5. Artificiality or sickliness of subject's appearance if not properly placed and balanced

It seems that there are enough reasons to justify leaving the light kits in the studio, but there is one compelling reason to bring them: If you do not, you will miss quite a few important shots.

Even today's video cameras are not sensitive or accurate enough to allow us to always use available light.

There are also more subtle reasons for using artificial light.

1. You must often add light to maintain a realistic appearance—existing light may create an unrealistic appearance to the camera and you must compensate with added light to make the subject appear more normal on tape.
2. The existing light may be undesirable—too harsh in some areas, too dim in others. Added light can give the proper balance.
3. Added light can enhance the shot aesthetically. You can highlight important visual elements and de-emphasize the less important ones.
4. You may sometimes *want* to create an artificial environment to achieve the mood of the story. This is particularly true in EFP work, especially when making commercials. Though less common in ENG, the practice of creating the environment with the addition of artificial light sources is not at all rare.

To put it bluntly, the artificial light kit helps the portable video cameraperson maintain the necessary control over the environment. Artificial lights are tools that a good ENG or EFP practitioner uses to help get the shot that will make the video piece a professional product both for exposure and for creative reasons.

LIGHTING EQUIPMENT

Lighting equipment comes in four categories: lamps, housings, mounting equipment and light-modulating equipment.

Lamps

Although a beginner may assume that the remedy for a very dark scene is the addition of as many ordinary light bulbs as possible, TV field lighting requires a special type of light bulb. This special type of bulb, called a lamp or globe, was developed to suit the specific needs of TV production. The **tungsten-halogen lamp** provides a bright light at a fairly constant level for a reasonably long period of time. This lamp is an improvement over the ordinary **incandescent** (household) **tungsten filament bulb** because it provides more light and does not become appreciably dimmer as the lamp ages, as do common tungsten bulbs.

The common bulbs dim because small amounts of tungsten burn off the filament and deposit themselves on the inside of the glass envelope, causing the glass to become darker and allowing less light to pass through. The tungsten-halogen lamps are designed so that the tungsten particles that are burned off the filament tend to reattach to the filament, thus preventing early filament burnout or attachment of the tungsten particles to the outer glass envelope. Another reason that standard household lamps are not used for TV production is because the color temperature of the light they give off tends to make human skin tones appear too orange-reddish.

Lamp handling requires a note of caution. Lamps can become extremely hot during use and remain hot for some period of time after operation. They should not be handled when hot; not only can they cause severe burns, but the lamps are also extremely fragile when hot and the filaments break easily. Lamp handling, even after a cool-down period, must be done with care. Handling a lamp with bare hands can leave a slight oil deposit on the glass that will hasten the lamp's burnout. The area of glass that was touched can be weakened, leading to a possible bulb explosion when the lamp is turned on. If lamps must be handled, do so with cloth or plastic gloves, but only when the lamp is cool. It is wise to carry some heat-proof gloves along with your lighting kit to avoid any possibility of burns or lamp-glass contamination from the oil on your skin. Some companies will supply you with small plier-type tongs designed for lamp removal and installation.

Spare lamps are necessary. Every light kit should have them. Even though most lamps are rated for about 75 hours of use, a burned-out lamp after fewer hours is not uncommon—often occurring in the middle of a story or production shoot. Make sure the replacement lamp is designed and rated for the housing you are putting it into. If you replace a burned-out lamp with one that has a higher wattage rating, you may damage the housing or even start a fire. Using a replacement lamp with a lower voltage rating than is required can cause a nearly instantaneous burnout of the new lamp.

Light Housings

To gain control over artificial light sources, it is necessary that the bulb be in something more than a simple socket. The light housing or fitting is the primary control over how the light reaches the subject or scene. The housing can direct, focus or limit the illumination coming from the bulb. The housing can also dissipate the heat a bulb produces. Almost every year new and improved housings are developed. The lights available in 1980 seem old and outdated when compared with the lights available in 1990. Like cameras and VCRs, lighting is a fast-changing part of video production. However, the basics have not changed in decades. Light housings fall into two broad categories: floods and spots. While there are dozens of variations within these two groups, a few simple types usually account for most lights available in a typical video production.

Floodlights Floodlights are the simplest of all lights. While they provide even illumination of wide areas, they are not easy to control. The flood's primary use is to provide base illumination for a scene or to fill shadows created by other lights. Shadows cast by floodlights are usually soft in character and not very dense. Lighting produced by floods is usually referred to as **flat lighting.** The housings are simple with little means of controlling the light.

Scoops The most basic floodlight is the scoop. (See Figure 4.8.) As its name implies, it is simply a large bowl, 14 inches to 18 inches in diameter, with a bulb in the bottom of it. Because of its size, although it weighs practically nothing, a floodlight is mostly used in studios. The lights just take up too much space in a vehicle and on location.

Broads Broad lights have a small reflector behind a linear-filament (or tubular) bulb. They

Figure 4.8: Scoop light. *Photo Courtesy Colortran, Inc.*

are usually quartz and between 500 watts and 1000 watts. Broads are easier to control than scoops. Most have small **barndoors** to regulate the light spread. The light from a broad is fairly hard, producing well-defined but low-density shadows. Because of their small size, broads can be easily placed anywhere in a room as long as there is no danger of heat damage to the surroundings. Small broads are often called **nook lights** and are used to light backgrounds or flood hard to get at spaces.

Floodlight Bank   This light is made up of several sealed-beam-type lights in a rectangular housing. The overlapping of the lights creates the soft effect of a floodlight. Sometimes called **modules**, they can contain from four to twelve lamps, usually laid out in banks that can be switched on individually. They are also referred to by the number of lights in the module, such as a nine-light. Only one version of this type of light is used in most video productions because the size and power requirements are too great for small-scale location shooting.

Internal Reflector Soft Lights   Usually referred to as just soft lights or sometimes **zip lights,** these instruments shield the bulb(s) from lighting the scene directly but reflect their light into a curved plate at the back of the housing. This white or silver plate reflects the light onto the scene. While reflected light cannot be focused,

Figure 4.9: Open-faced spotlight shown with flip-on filters and adjustable deflector. *Courtesy Lowell-Light Manufacturing, Inc.*

Figure 4.10: A Lowel Softlight 2. This light uses a heat-resistant cloth reflector and two independently switched 1000-watt bulbs. The light folds down for easy carrying and storage.

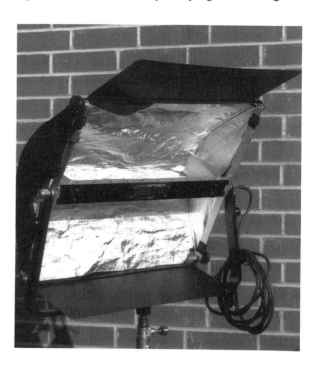

the light from a soft light is the easiest flood light to control. The degree of softness in a light source is determined by the size of that source, that is, the size of the bulb and any reflector used. For scoops and broads the bulb shines directly onto the scene softened only by the small reflector areas behind the bulbs. A soft light uses only the reflected light from the large backplate of the housing making that plate the source of light. (See Figure 4.9.) The shadows created are very soft and fall off quickly. Soft lights are always quartz and come in strengths from 200 watts to 2000 watts. Reflecting the light in this way reduces the efficiency of the bulbs. The output of a 1000-watt bulb is 40% to 60% less in a soft light than in a broad light.

Spotlights   Spotlights are used to light specific areas of a scene. These lights can be easily controlled and focused. The main source of illumination in most scenes is provided by a spotlight of some sort. The sun is the best example of a spotlight. The opposite of floodlights, spots need a very compact source of illumination to produce well-defined, dense shadows. A spot is made up of a small bulb and some form of parabolic-shaped reflector to concentrate the radiant light into a direct beam. (See Figure 4.10.)

Open-face Spot   The open-face spot is the most commonly used light in all of video production because it is the most economical and efficient light to use. Almost all open-face spots have the ability to focus from a spot position (called "pinned") to a flood position. While the flood position is not as even and uniform as that of a broad or other floodlight, this housing allows most users to get double duty out of one light housing. The disadvantage of this type of light is the quality of its light pattern. The light beam is uneven in intensity and the lack of a focusing lens can prevent getting distinct, hard-edge shadows. For most work in EFP and almost all work in ENG, these drawbacks are minimal.

Fresnel Spot   The fresnel spot has the same structure as the open-face light but has a focusing glass lens that the light passes through. Most fresnels can also be adjusted from spot to flood like the open-face lights. This system is designed for maximum light control. Unlike the open-face light where changing from spot to flood is achieved by moving the bulb closer or further from the reflector, the fresnel light moves the bulb and reflector together closer or further from the lens. A fresnel also allows a much narrower spot (around 10 degrees). The focus of the lens gives shadows a hard, well-defined edge but leaves a soft edge to the pattern of the beam so that the blending of several lights to cover a large area is possible without unevenly lit spaces. Fresnels come in tungsten and HMI sources and range from 100 watts to 10,000 watts. The one disadvantage is the loss of

Figure 4.11: Portable light kit with Fresnel spot lights. *Courtesy Arriflex Corp.*

Figure 4.12: This LTM Pepper 200 has a fresnel lens to focus its 200-watt light into a concentrated beam.

light with the lens. A 1000-watt fresnel only puts out light equivalent to a 650-watt open-face light. (See Figures 4.11 and 4.12.)

Ellipsoidal Spot   The ellipsoidal spot (sometimes called a **focal spot**) is the most specialized in its application. Here, the lens moves back and forth in front of a fixed bulb and ellipsoid-shaded reflector to focus the edges of the light pattern on a particular surface. Often stencils are inserted in the light housing to throw a well-defined pattern (such as venetian blinds, prison bars or tree limbs) on the surface of a wall. Generally, this type of light is too expensive, big and limiting to use for portable video. It is usually used in theater productions and dramatic applications in the studio. If you have the time and budget, it can add greatly to the look of your field productions.

Mounts

Most TV studios have a system of cross-hatched pipes (called a **lighting grid**) on which lights are hung. Lights designed for studio use ordinarily have a C-clamp for this application. In the field, lights are most often attached to tripod stands, some of which have small wheels to allow for easy repositioning.

Small lights are more flexible than large lights to mount, since their weight does not require a sturdy tripod. Small lights, such as lensless spotlights, are often attached to poles, cameras or light tripods, or shelves by means of a large clamp called a **gaffer grip**. (See Figure 4.13.) Some

Figure 4.13: Various size gaffers and a C-clamp.

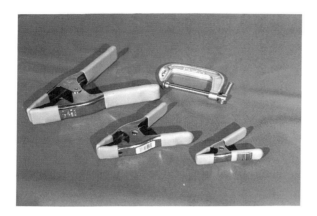

companies offer wide varieties of clamps, mounts and special poles for securing lights in the field. (See Figure 4.14.) Many ENG situations allow camera-mounted lights only because camera movement is unpredictable and available light insufficient.

The most popular methods of mounting lights are quite common and inexpensive: **gaffer tape** and **grips.** Lights can sometimes be taped to poles, trees or equipment cases with gaffer tape. Gaffer tape is usually silver and, although it is sometimes referred to as duct tape, it is not the same thing. Gaffer tape is expensive and has a cloth backing, and while it has good bonding strength, it is much easier to remove than duct tape. It is strong, but not nearly as reliable as the gaffer grip. Exercise a

Figure 4.14: Light with wall mount and flag.

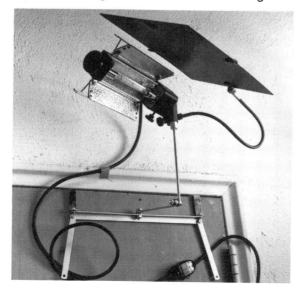

considerable amount of caution when using tape to mount lights. Do not forget that lights generate heat on all sides. They can scorch paint and material and cause a fire. Falling lights break and often explode. If you stick tape to anything, you better be able to remove it. Good tape may stick too well to most surfaces. Removing it may also remove paint, wallpaper, floor tiles or even wood veneer. Removal may leave tape gum deposits on the surface. The owners of the property may not take kindly to your ruining the decor.

In a situation in which there are excess crew members, it may be possible to have a crew member, a **grip,** hold a light for you while you are shooting. It is not recommended because the lights get hot and the holder often moves the light, but if all else fails, have a steady crew member don the heat-proof gloves, avoid puddles of water and stand as still as possible.

Lighting Modulators

Although some lights have built-in adjustments to allow for focusing the light beam, many that are used for field production do not. When using remote lighting, you must have control over both the amount and direction of the light. You must also control where the light does and does not fall on the scene you are lighting. In addition to selecting the appropriate lamp for size and function, you must often use additional equipment to maximize light control.

Barndoors are rectangular pieces of metal (both two- and four-door) attached to the front of lights that direct the light beam more carefully. (See Figure 4.15.) Barndoors give you control over light falling on areas that do not require it or areas that simply should remain in shadow. **Flags** are similar to barndoors in that they shade or deflect light away from areas that should not be lit. They are commonly rectangular pieces of metal or black cloth that may be attached to a light mount, but are not attached to the light itself.

Flags (or **gobos**) come in a wide variety of shapes and sizes: round ones are called **dots** and **targets,** narrow ones are called **cutters, fingers,** and **sticks.** As they increase to a size large enough to control soft lights, they are referred to as **teasers.** They are also referred to by where they are placed, such as **toppers, bottomers** and **siders.** Flags are the most effective way of controlling light in the cramped spaces of location-shooting but usually require more time to set up than the videographer has to spend in ENG situations. (See Figure 4.16.)

Figure 4.15: Two lights, one with a full scrim and one with a half-scrim, both of which have barndoors attached.

Reflectors have light-colored surface that, unlike flags, reflect light onto desired areas rather than block it from certain areas. (See Figure 4.17.) Reflectors can be stiff cardboard, metal or even light-colored cloth. Umbrellas are common in many portable lighting kits. They are attached to the housing itself with the light in a flooded position and aimed directly into the umbrella. (See Figure 4.18.) The reflective surface than returns the light past the housing onto the subject.

Umbrella lighting produces a very soft quality light at a reduced intensity. Soft lighting reproduces colors at a lower intensity and the level of chroma is less saturated than under hard-light sources.

It may be desirable sometimes to reduce the amount of light from a lighting instrument. Although **faders** (lighting controls that electronically reduce light output) are common in studios, they are rare in most ENG and EFP situations. A square wire mesh screen called a **scrim** can be used on the front of a light on location to effectively reduce the amount of light from that instrument. (See Figure 4.19.)

One way to reduce the amount of light coming from a fixture is placing a **neutral-density (ND) gel** in front of the light. This greyish gel is calibrated to show exactly how much light is being cut. The three most popular grades are referred to as N3, N6 and N9. N3 (½ ND) has 50% transmission, which is one stop less light: N6 (¼ ND) has 25% transmission or two stops less light; N9 (⅛ ND) has 12.5% transmission or three stops less light. These gels do not diffuse or color the light in any way. ND gel also comes in large sheets and rolls for covering windows to allow interior shooting.

Figure 4.16: This Cucalorus, or cookie, throws a mottled shadow pattern. The pattern becomes less defined the closer the cookie is to the light source. For outdoor use it can be combined with a diffusion material to soften the pattern.

To diffuse or soften the light from an instrument, you can use a **diffuser,** which is a square piece of material often framed in metal that spreads out the light beam so that it produces a less harsh shadow. The actual diffuser material is usually some type of flameproof spun glass or frosted glass. The amount of diffusion is dependent on two factors: the density of the diffusing material and its size. Frosted glass is usually placed on the front of the light housing; small sheets of diffusing material in frames are placed just in front of the housing, and large areas of materials such as silk are placed several feet in front of the light. The latter produces the softest light of all. (See Figure 4.20.) Several companies make a wide variety of diffusing materials that are often referred to by such names as **102, tracing paper, soft frost** and **shower curtain.**

In addition to changing the *amount* of light that comes from an instrument, it is also possible to manipulate the *color* of light by placing a colored, heat-proof, cellophane-like material over the front of the lighting instrument. This modulator is called a gel and is somewhat common in EFP work. Many lights have **gel frames** that attach to the housing.

Color gels can be divided into two categories: color correction and color elimination. The most famous gel or filter of all is the **85B.** This is the manufacturer's name for a certain type of orange gel that corrects daylight temperature to tungsten temperature. In film shooting almost all film stock is rated for tungsten light. This lens filter allows the film to be used outdoors. The filter wheel in a video camera has a daylight position on it. That filter is the 85B. Since video cameras can white-balance for any color of light, it is more important to correct the light sources than to put a filter on the lens.

The most common gel used in video production is the **daylight-blue** that converts tungsten light to a daylight temperature. (See Figure 4.21.) It is

Figure 4.17: A reflector should be at eye level and at an angle to the subject.

Figure 4.18: Light with umbrella.

often called **color temperature blue (CTB)** and comes in several strengths: full, half, quarter and eighth. Another use for this gel is matching the color temperature of a TV screen. Most color TVs have a temperature of nearly 9000°K. You could change the hue on the TV screen to dial out all the

Figure 4.19: A wire mesh screen fits in front of an open-faced spot to reduce light output.

Figure 4.20: Two-foot-by-three-foot silk attached by a gobo head on an extension arm held by a grip head atop a C-stand. A full silk cuts the amount of light by one stop.

Figure 4.21: Light with daylight blue gel in a gel frame.

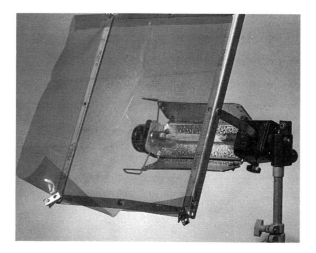

blue but this is not always possible. By using a full-blue plus a half-blue daylight gel together on your tungsten lights, the TV screen will be reproduced on your tape with the right color.

Like the 85B, the other popular color correction is in the orange (or warm) areas. A **color temperature orange (CTO)** can be used to bring HMI lights down to match tungsten lights or can be used on tungsten lights to give a warm early morning sunlight look. A good trick is to use a quarter- or half-CTO on a tungsten light that is being used to simulate sunlight through a window. If the other lights are unfiltered, the one with the CTO reads just like daylight to the viewer. Another good use for this gel is for photographing dark-skinned people. By balancing for tungsten and then putting a ¼ CTO over the light that is on the dark-skinned subject, the blue is taken out of their skin tone thereby lightening the color enough to read well on the camera. Several other filters, such as cosmetic rouge or chocolate, do the same thing for dark skin but the effect on any light-skinned subjects in the same shot is minimal. To be very precise at correcting color temperatures would require the use of a color temperature meter to get all the light sources to match perfectly. This is a luxury only the wealthiest productions can afford. Your best bet is to use a good color monitor and experiment with different gels to see how they perform.

Color elimination gels are sometimes call **party colors.** They are not meant to correct light temperature but to change a light to a single hue by filtering out the other colors. Colors like red, green, pure blue and almost any color you can think of are used for special effects, certain moods or to recreate the light from a bar sign or similar natural source. These colors are used on background lights and almost never for lighting a subject. Gel-makers offer a sample booklet of all their gels and diffusers, usually free of charge. You must keep in mind the emotional effects of the colors you use. Colors based on reds and yellows are warm and soothing to the eye, while colors made of blues and greens are perceived as cold and harsh.

POWER REQUIREMENTS

The last thing to consider before starting to learn how and where to set up lights is the amount of electricity it takes to operate them. Too often a photographer simply starts setting up lights, with or without a plan, thinking only of the look of the shot or area to be lit. No sooner are the lights in place than the circuit breaker blows. Before you attempt any location lighting, you must have a thorough understanding of the amount of power required and if you have it available for use.

Volts and Amps

All the lights you will be using out in the field run on 110 volts to 120 volts AC: normal household current. Only battery-powered lights use direct current (DC), which is why the two types of bulbs are not interchangeable. The amount of current available measured in amperes (amps) and multiplied by volts gives you the power expressed in watts. The equation would therefore be *watts = volts x amps*. Since each of your lights has a watt rating, you can figure the amps needed for each light. This equation would be *amps = watts ÷ volts*. To build in a safety factor it is a good practice to use 100 as the voltage even though it may really be 120. Any long extension cable runs can cut down the amount of volts and put you in danger of an overload. If you wish to put up two 600-watt lights in a room, you would divide 1200 watts by 100 volts to find that 12 amps of power are needed to safely run the two lights.

Most homes and offices have electrical outlets divided into many separate circuits. In an older house each circuit may be only 15 amps yet have several outlets (in different rooms) on that circuit. Most modern homes and offices have more circuits with fewer outlets per circuit and each circuit has 20 amps. This means you should never have more than 2000 watts on any one circuit. Finding more than one circuit may be difficult. The first place to start is by finding the circuit breaker box for the area you are working in. The circuits may be labeled in the box. If they are not and you need more than 20 amps, try to find outlets as far from each other as possible to increase your chances of getting two separate circuits. The other obvious thing is to see if anything else is being used on the circuit you are using. A coffee maker can limit the amps available to you. Locate the circuit box before shooting begins just in case something does blow. If you know you will be working in an older home where fuses may still be in use, have spare fuses available.

On locations requiring a lot of power either have a professional gaffer tap into the electrical system or simply rent a generator. There are many types of generators made for TV and movie work that can supply power with little or no noise. Electricity is dangerous and should be dealt with accordingly. Make sure all fixtures are grounded,

do not stand in water while touching anything connected to the power, and do not overload any system you are using. Some lights are only meant to be used with bulbs under a certain wattage. Many extension cords are made to carry only a certain number of amps. The length of the cable also determines how much of a load can be carried. A 2000-watt light with 200 feet of cable would need an 8-gauge wire (sometimes just called #8). The lower the number, the more amps it can carry. A 500-watt light could use a 16-gauge cable to go 100 feet. The more wattage you use, the smaller the gauge number should be; the longer the cable run, the smaller the gauge number. All the cables should be three-wire cables. An overheated cable or light housing can easily start a fire. An ungrounded cable could lead to an electrocution.

EXPOSURE AND SHADOWS

The two basic objectives of lighting for video are the quantity of light and the quality of light. As just discussed, not all light sources are the same. In every shooting situation, indoors or outdoors, the first thing a good photographer looks at is the amount of light available. The next step is to judge the quality of that light. This section shows you some basic techniques for determining these two factors.

Base Lighting

One of the early drawbacks to video photography was that the video camera required a large amount of light to record a good image. Unlike film cameras that can use extremely light-sensitive film stock or developing procedures that maximize a small amount of light, the light sensitivity of video cameras was limited by the quality and sensitivity of the pickup tube, a component not subject to easy replacement or change. Therefore, the first requirement in video lighting was to provide the camera's pickup tube with a quantity of light large enough to enable the camera to function properly. This minimum level is the base light.

Today's chip cameras require very little base light to make a good picture. Very little does not mean no light, however. Base light should be thought of as the minimum light required for shooting. The scene always looks better, especially in EFP work, if the light levels are somewhat above the base. The first requirement in lighting a scene is to make sure you have enough base light on every area of the scene for which you wish to see detail. Areas with less than base light appear muddy or go black in the picture (which you may want to happen). By knowing your camera's contrast ratio, you can determine the base-light level in foot-candles for any f-stop you use.

Lens Quality

The lens on the camera can also make a difference in the quantity and quality of light falling on the face of the pickup device. A **fast** (good light-gathering ability) **lens** with high-quality glass components can make a camera perform better than a **slow** (poor light-gathering ability) or lesser-quality **lens** at the same light level. This becomes particularly noticeable at lower-light levels. By using a higher-quality lens, the required base light for any camera can be lowered. If the base light, or minimum level of light, is not reached, the video image will be too dark.

Correct Exposure

These problems are easy enough for most beginners to notice. The solution is simply to add more light (quantity) to the scene. Most of the newer portable cameras have a signal of some kind that alerts the camera operator to a potential low-light problem. This indicator is sometimes an **light emitting diode** (**LED**) that glows when there is insufficient signal level output from the camera. A slightly different version of this type of indicator is a white line that indicates either too much signal (which requires a reduction in iris opening), a proper operating range requiring no iris setting change or too little signal (necessitating an increase in iris opening or a general increase of light on the scene). There are many other aids visible in the viewfinder of different cameras that help find the right exposure.

A typical professional camera available for ENG/EFP applications, the Sony BVP-70, requires 15 lux (f1.4 + 8dB gain) for a minimum picture and 2000 lux at f5.6 for an acceptable image. **Lux** is a measure of light quantity used in countries that use the metric system: 10.74 lux is equal to 1 footcandle. In a controlled situation, you should try to achieve that light level when setting up. The use of a light meter at this light level might be a good practice to ensure a technically acceptable video image. Since each camera and lens is different, you need to know what the lowest acceptable light level is for your camera. In general, the main subject of the shot should be at least at that light level, and no other portion of the picture should be brighter than the level of the main subject.

Use of High Gain

Use of the high gain circuit increases the sensitivity of the pickup device, thus increasing the range of light in which the video camera can supply an image. However, use of this additional amplification enhances the noise, or graininess, in the video as well. The resulting picture often appears somewhat grainy and darker areas of the frame are muddy and have confetti-like specks of color. Scenes or stories shot in high gain that require editing or duplication will suffer noticeably.

Obviously, some stories must be shown despite minor video flaws. Unfortunately, too many important news stories occur at night. Shooting these stories requires as much boost to the lighting situation as possible. The often used 12-volt or 30-volt battery-powered portable light gives acceptable illumination only on subjects 6 to 10 feet from the camera. When shooting outdoors at night, these battery-powered lights offer only a little help on large scenes but they are still necessary. The +6 dB or +9 dB gain is quite often used when more light is needed but cannot be added. The +12 dB or +18 dB gain should be used only on very important stories because of the graininess of the resulting video image.

These large gain enhancements may be used at night to record objects at a distance or in special situations, for example, when the lights would interfere with the actions of a SWAT team's operation. The resulting video will be noisy and the video level (the amount of video signal) will probably be low, but there is a common procedure to improve the picture quality. When the tape is played or transferred through a time base corrector or video processing unit, the chroma level can be lowered on the shots done at low light and high gain. Lowering this level causes the colored, confetti-like speckles in the darker areas of the picture to lose their color. This technique produces a nearly black-and-white picture, but since our eyes see very little color at night the loss of some chroma is not objectionable. However, the brighter areas of the picture retain some chroma, and the perception of overall noise in the picture is greatly reduced.

Quality Lighting

Through experience and the right blend of journalistic necessity and common sense, the video camera operator eventually develops expertise in knowing the quantity of light needed for good video images. In addition to light quantities, the video camera requires light with certain qualities.

To reproduce objects in a realistic way, the lights must show the texture and shape of objects accurately. Good lighting allows you to show objects in the three dimensions of height, width and depth, despite the fact that the TV screen has only height and width dimensions. Skillful use of lighting can enhance the mood of a particular scene and heighten its desired effect. Even in ENG, appropriate lighting can re-create a mood to tell a story more effectively and accurately.

Contrast Ratio

Unlike the human eye, video cameras are severely restricted in their ability to perceive large variations of brightness within a given scene. When extremely bright objects are framed with very dark objects, many video cameras do not reproduce details well in either the light or dark areas. Excessively bright areas, such as a pure white shirt, may tend to glow and appear otherworldly. Very dark portions of the screen may be muddy and lack detail, resulting in an unappealing, two-dimensional image.

Most video cameras can tolerate bright areas that are no more than 20 times brighter than the darkest areas of a scene. The newest chip cameras have contrast ratios of 30:1 or 40:1. The typical film used in motion pictures has a contrast range of about 200:1 and our eye sees at about 1000:1. This is primarily why film looks better than tape and why our eyes see the best of all. As technology improves the contrast range of video, the quality of the look will increase dramatically. But for the present, it is still a good rule of thumb to stick with the 20:1 rule. For example, if you measure the reflected light from the brightest area of the picture and it is equal to 200 footcandles (FCs), then any area of the picture reflecting less than 10 FCs of light is beyond your camera's contrast range.

A piece of white paper reflects 60% of the light that strikes it, while black paint reflects only 3%. White plaster, however, reflects 90%. If you have 200 FCs of light falling on a white plaster wall in a scene, it will reflect 180 FCs. A black chair in that scene reflects only 6 FCs, which is beyond your 20:1 contrast range. If you expose for the wall, the chair becomes underexposed even though the same amount of light is striking it. Therefore, you must keep in mind not only the amount of light striking the objects, but also their ability to reflect that light.

These considerations demonstrate why it can be very difficult to expose for two subjects in the same scene when one is in the shade and one is in the sun. When using a TV camera, you must expose for the brightest area, but the difference in reflectiveness between objects in both sun and shade can be well over 200:1.

In a practical sense, videographers and photographers must watch out for bright/dark combinations in every shot. The contrast ratio problem becomes more apparent when the brightest and darkest areas of the scene are right next to each other or where one is much larger than the other. If your subject is wearing a bright white shirt and dark trousers, suggest lighter trousers or a pastel shirt. White blouses can be less harmful to the contrast ratio if partially covered by a scarf, handkerchief or jacket.

A dark-skinned subject can present problems to a video camera operator. A light-colored shirt and light background can make a proper exposure difficult. In daytime shooting, extra light is often necessary to brighten the subject's facial features. You must pay close attention to lighting and background to avoid losing the dark-skinned face in the background.

Do not forget that an extremely dark or extremely light portion of the screen can often be compensated for by an iris adjustment. The problem arises when two extremes appear in the same shot. When in doubt about your contrast ratio, use a light meter to measure the amount of light (in footcandles) that is reflected from the dark and bright areas of your scene. If it seems that the ratio will be over 20:1, *do not shoot it* until you have made the appropriate changes, such as altering camera angles or focal lengths or adding light to the dark areas to reduce the ratio.

In ENG work, you are often forced to work with shots that have more than a 20:1 contrast ratio. An example might be an interview with a tall plane-crash eyewitness wearing a hat on a heavily overcast and rainy day. The white sky reflects large quantities of light, but the shaded face of the subject reflects very little light. The contrast ratio between sky and face will be far in excess of 20:1. The iris must be pushed, or opened, beyond what the overall picture requires, to get the face to show on tape with some detail. In this case, the background will be overexposed. If the background is overexposed, the edges of the subject's face will be undefined.

There are some possible solutions, however:

1. Try to find a dark background, for example, against a wall, firetruck or tree.

2. Frame the subject's face as tightly as possible to reduce the amount of background in the shot.

3. Anticipate these conditions and use a camera-mounted battery light with a dichroic filter to boost the color temperature of the light to a daylight temperature. Without the filter, the light on the subject's face will be too red, but even so, a reddish face is certainly better than no face at all.

In ENG, if you do not get the shot, a competitor probably will. It is your job to find a way to make the shot work with few distractions and without damage to your equipment. In some ENG situations, you may have to shoot despite adverse lighting conditions because the story is too important to miss. The audio may be usable, even if the video is not. Always make sure, however, that you are *not damaging your equipment:* If you do, you may get a part of the story but miss all others until the necessary repair is done.

In the better chip cameras, it is possible to drive the exposure to greater extremes and not have the picture look bad. In fact, in many EFP projects over-exposure of certain areas of the frame is a specific style. Unless you are using a tube camera, over-exposure can be used as a creative force if done with purpose. A shaft of sunlight coming through a window can blow out part of the picture or even part of the subject to show the intensity of that light or draw the viewer's attention to the daylight and thus to the subject.

LIGHTING TECHNIQUES

During a shoot, you will need to light many different scenes indoors and outdoors. Although each lighting situation is unique, there are some fundamental guidelines you can follow that will help you light any scene. Figure 4.22 shows some traditional portraiture lighting techniques for key and backlight positions.

Three-Point Lighting

The technique of three-point lighting has been used for years in both professional TV and photography studios. This method of lighting is simple but effective for many situations that call for lighting a particular subject or object. Three carefully placed directional lights—the key light, the fill light and the backlight—can light a subject in a way that provides an appropriate level of base light for the video camera; gives sufficient shadow

Figure 4.22: Quick lighting setups that maintain the portraiture style of lighting. Only one light is used in the top shot; one diffused or flooded light is used in the center shot; in the bottom photo, two lights are used for a quick formal look.

Figure 4.23: Use these lighting zones as general guidelines. They may not apply to recreating natural lighting, special effects or creative lighting but deal with formal portraiture lighting.

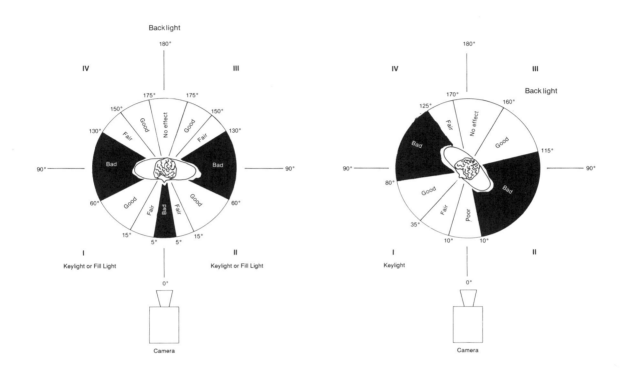

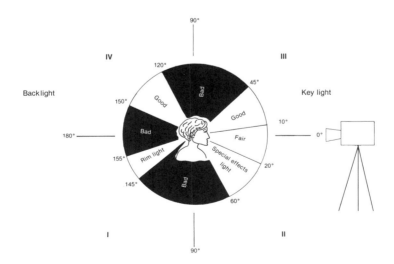

Figure 4.24: Light placement when subject faces camera.

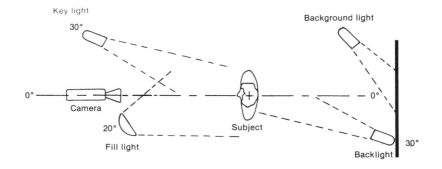

The standard three-point lighting setup with an added background light.

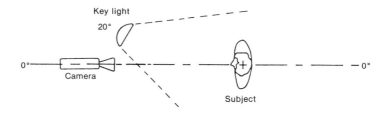

A single light source should be near the camera and flooded as much as possible.

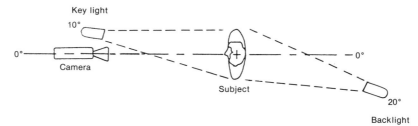

When only two lights are used, the combination of the key and back is effective.

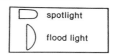

Figure 4.25: These four photographs represent four lighting techniques.

Key Light

Fill Light

Back Light

Key, Fill and Back Light

for definition of shape, size and texture; and separates the subject from surrounding objects and the background. (See Figure 4.23.) The three-point technique is appropriate for most ENG or EFP situations in which only a small area needs lighting. Figure 4.24 gives guidelines for light placement in a situation in which the subject is facing the camera. Figure 4.25 displays the same shot under four different lighting conditions.

Key Light   As the name implies, the key light is the most important light and is, therefore, placed first. The key light should be the brightest and most directional. A key light placed on the camera-subject axis produces a very flat, shadowless picture. In most cases, this is not flattering to the subject.

Follow these guidelines for the key light.

1. Place it off the camera-subject axis anywhere from 10° to 90°, depending on the effect or look you are creating.
2. For a subject not facing directly toward the camera, focus the key light on the short side of the subject's face from a point about 30° to 50° from the camera.
3. Make an effort to elevate the light above the subject's head at about a 45° angle above camera level.

The key light creates a strong shadow, sometimes called the **draw**, on the subject's face. This is called the **modeling effect.** The photographer is responsible for bringing the viewer's attention to the most important aspect(s) of the screen. Since the audience is naturally drawn to the brightest part of the screen and since the key light illuminates an area so brightly, the key light is used to focus the viewer's attention. The key light should be the light that the subject looks into—thus the short side of the face is lit by the key. Focusing the key light on the long side of your subject makes it seem like the subject is looking away from the light. This gives the appearance of subject discomfort or avoidance which can be misleading, distracting or unpleasant for the viewer. It also casts the draw, or shadow, out of view for the camera thus losing the three-dimensional effect.

Fill Light The next light to set when using the three-point lighting technique is the fill light, located at an angle about 10° to 45° from the camera on the opposite side of the camera from the key. Again the light should be placed above the subject to give a more normal appearance to the subject. In studio TV the fill light is often a scoop or a Fresnel spot adjusted to give a wide or flooded-out beam. These types of lights are preferable because they are less harsh and soften shadows created by the key light without eliminating them. Unfortunately, portable kits rarely contain scoops or other diffused lights. Typically, portable kits have small spotlights without lenses. Since the key and fill lights are usually of equal strength in portable kits, the fill is often placed at a slightly greater distance from the subject, resulting in a softer, less intense light for fill.

Many portable kits have adjustable lights that allow the light to be **pinned** to a narrow beam that gives sharp, bright light or flooded to give a softer, less bright light. For example, the fill light could be set at a distance from the subject equal to the key light and set in the **flooded** or wide position and the key could be pinned. *As a general rule, your key light should be twice as bright as your fill (a 2:1 ratio), but a key that is four times as bright as the fill (a 4:1 ratio) is not uncommon.* The combination of properly set key and fill lights should give enough base light for the video camera to operate at an acceptable level and create a perception of depth, giving your subject a three-dimensional quality.

Backlight The third light in the three-point lighting technique is the backlight. The backlight is most often a spot, both in the studio and in the field. It is usually as powerful as the key, but most of its light is focused on the back of the subject and is not reflected into the camera lens. The light is placed directly opposite the key light, behind and above the subject at an angle of about 45°.

It is not unusual for a backlight to be up to four times as bright as the key light for a key its to-fill-to-back ratio of 2:1:8. A ratio of 2:1:3 is, however, more common for bright backlight set-ups. A more subtle 2:1:1 is the most common choice. Barndoors are usually on backlights so that the light falls on the subject only, not on the camera. The backlight highlights or frames the subject with a rim of light. The primary purpose of this light is to separate the subject from the background. This separation effect can be heightened and better defined if you have the budget and trunk space for a fourth light called the background light.

Other Lights

With a minimum of setup time, you can properly light most ENG and EFP assignments using the complete lighting kit. Three lights are more than adequate to light any medium-sized meeting room. With the addition of extra light and some accessories, creativity need not take a back seat to expediency. Using some of the techniques mentioned below, you can create a pleasing natural light with soft shadows that meets your lighting requirements without disturbing the natural look of your location shoot.

Background Light The background, or fourth, light is often used to locate the subject in the set, that is, to show the relationship of the subject to the background. The placement of this light can vary, but the idea is to illuminate part of the background to show its texture, shape and location in space relative to the subject. It may be extra trouble to purchase, carry and set a fourth light, but it becomes very important when you must videotape a subject with dark hair or a dark shirt against a dark background. The fourth light can prevent you from losing parts of the subject in the background.

If the background light can be focused, then the area directly behind the subject (if the subject is centered or on the empty side of the frame if the subject is not centered) should be **hotter** (have more light) than the rest of the background. This is also the light that can add special effects to the scene. For example, you can make the background interesting by using a cookie or another shadow-forming device placed in front of a narrow-beam background light. A very common technique in movies is the venetian blinds effect. A slotted pattern on the background light gives the effect of window light coming through blinds. The light serves its purpose by giving highlight and detail to the background while also making it seem natural.

Experiment with background lights using different patterns and also directions.

Kicker Light   An additional light often used in EFP is the kicker light. It is a light set from a low angle to the side of the subject and slightly behind. Its purpose is to highlight the subject's hair or face. The kicker is often used in hair product commercials to add a glamorous look.

Eye Light   In some dramatic EFP presentations you can use a small, highly directional light to illuminate a subject's eyes. The eye light is usually a lower-wattage lamp aimed at the eyes, but not from a 0° angle (the camera position). The next time you watch a *Star Trek* rerun, watch for the eye light used in close-ups when Commander Kirk plays a highly dramatic or love scene.

Adding to Existing Light

Although some videographers shoot on location just to get out in the sun and others may be sent out by assignment editors or producers just to get the videographers or photographers out of the station or studio, the main reason for shooting on location should be to capture a scene *and* preserve its realistic setting.

Too often hundreds of pounds of delicate equipment is bounced around in a truck only to result in a scene that looks as if it could have been shot in the studio. The addition of artificial lighting often gives an artificial look to a remote scene and destroys the natural appearance of a location setting. If the subjects can easily perform or be interviewed in the studio, why bother hauling out the remote equipment? One reason for a remote shot is to preserve the natural environment of the subject.

Sometimes there is the need for minimum base-level lighting. Some situations simply demand additional light. The best way to fulfill the technical requirements of the video camera is to *add* to the existing light without overpowering it. Unlike studio scenes in which three-point lighting is the standard, many locations need only the existing light levels raised to produce a pleasing, well-lit scene.

Preserving Color Temperature   It is possible to add artificial light to daylight without significantly changing the color temperature. You can alter the temperature of the light from the artificial lights to approximate the temperature of daylight. For example, you can use a daylight-blue gel or a dichroic filter to change tungsten light to daylight with no noticeable difference in color temperature.

Preserving a Natural Look   To preserve the natural look of the location, keep the *direction* of the light the same or as it was without enhancement. Add your light source near to or in line with the existing light source. If your additional lighting produces shadows that are too dark, fill light may be necessary. The fill light should be as subtle as possible, but bright enough to fill the shadows. Many times natural light is nondirectional, so the additional lighting you provide should also lack directionality, that is, have no shadows.

Soft Lighting   The effect created by this type of additional lighting is often referred to as soft lighting. Shadows are undefined or have very hazy, soft edges. It is hard to re-create this type of light with standard lighting equipment alone. A soft light is designed to provide even, highly diffused

Figure 4.26: One light from the camera position, unmodulated (left), and one light from the camera position, using an umbrella (right).

light to fill in darker areas of a scene. Because of its design, it does not yield harsh shadows or create an artificial look. You can create soft light effects using hard lights but you must use umbrellas or a diffusing material, such as spun glass, placed in front of them. Diffusing material, such as a large piece of silk, can be stretched across frames or even hung from the ceiling in front of the lights to produce a wall of light. Any of these methods will yield a natural soft light on the subject or scene, but you must remember that the amount of light reaching the subject will be greatly reduced by the diffusing material. Light from an umbrella source is only one-half to one-third of what it would be if the light came directly from the light source. (See Figure 4.26.)

Bounced Light From Above The technique of bouncing light can also make a scene lighter without creating harsh or artificial shadows. Bouncing light is the best method of adding light in situations where the room is small and direct light would disturb the subject. If a room's ceiling is light colored, relatively smooth and no higher than 8 or 10 feet from the floor, you can aim a light at the ceiling and the reflected light will enhance the base illumination level. Almost any type of light can be used for this purpose, but very weak lights will lose much of their lighting power before reaching the subject. The best ceiling for bouncing is smooth and white. Highly textured ceilings will not reflect the light in a predictable or efficient way, while dark or non-white paint will change the color of the light.

Direct Light You can also achieve a natural look with direct lights by putting the key light at eye level at an 80° angle to the 180° line. A fill light 45° above the horizontal eye line and at the key light side of the camera position usually fills in the shadows to give a natural look. By adjusting distance and focus, you can obtain a pleasing ratio with no harsh shadows.

Reflecting Surfaces There is another simple technique to allow bounced light to illuminate your scene when ceilings are too high, dark or irregular and reflected or bounced light from the ceiling will not work creatively. Mount a light-colored, smooth, flat surface where you need a light source to reflect off that surface. White cardboard, polystyrene sheets called **foam core** available at art supplies stores or even cardboard with aluminum foil attached smoothly to the reflecting side will reflect light onto your subject. (See Figure 4.27.) Bounce cards are light enough and flat enough to put almost anywhere. This technique is especially useful in small rooms or offices. Some-

times the card can be placed on the floor of the room and the light reflected up to the subject to compensate for too much ceiling light.

Be careful of the shadows created by this type of lighting. A shadow on a wall cast by a subject from a low-angle light can be very objectionable. If the low-angle light is too bright, it can give the subject a horror movie look. The goal in this type of lighting is to provide enough base light for the camera to record the scene properly. Too much fill light will make your subject look washed out and two-dimensional. Even bounced light has some directional quality. The surface you use to bounce the light becomes the source. If the bounced light is set up using the principles of three-point lighting, then you can avoid most problems of flat, two-dimensional lighting. The proper use of bounced light can often provide an adequate base light level without the undesirable artificial or washed-out appearance.

Using Camera-Mounted Light

News photographers will often use a small spotlight mounted on the video camera to provide enough light to properly expose the subject or scene being shot. This method is usually used outdoors at night when no other light source is available. However, it can also be used when the subject is moving in low-light situations and the photographer must keep the subject lit, in crowded situations when stationary light placement is impossible and in rushed situations in which the photographer has only enough time to shoot the scene and move on to the next location or get back to the station.

Speed is very important in many ENG situations. The run-and-gun method of news coverage requires a news photographer to have that headlight or sun gun in place at all times so that subjects can be grabbed at a moment's notice for a quick off-the-shoulder interview or "bite". If there is no light or if existing light is poor, the camera light or sun gun is the best chance for a proper amount of illumination. If your camera light is strong enough, you may be able to bounce the camera light off the ceiling or another reflecting surface and still obtain a usable exposure.

Although the camera-mounted light is expedient, it has both practical and aesthetic drawbacks and is therefore not recommended for general field production.

1. Any light mounted close to the lens of the camera will shine almost directly into the eyes of the person being interviewed, caus-

Figure 4.27: To create a natural look, this interview set-up was done with two lights. The key light was a three-by-three-foot foam core with a 1000-watt broad light bounced off of it and the back light was a 100-watt fresnel. The window light was blocked by a duvetyn curtain to allow the use of uncorrected tungsten lights and to allow the camera to use a larger f-stop. The slower lens setting allowed better use of the practicle, or incandescent, light on the table and a more out-of-focus background.

ing that person to squint or be uncomfortable. Often, the subject will turn away from the camera because of this.

2. The light may be reflected off the subject's eyes or glasses, causing a hot spot in the picture.

3. A camera-mounted light aimed directly at a subject will yield a flat, washed-out image that prevents the desirable depth effect that can be obtained from three-point lighting. (See Figure 4.28.)

Figure 4.28: Lighting a subject with a camera light makes features appear harsh, puts a shadow on the background and produces a reflective shine.

4. Finally, a subject close to a background (such as a person against a wall) may cast an undesirable shadow on the background surface.

The average 30-volt power belt for a portable light lasts only about 15 to 20 minutes. If you do much shooting early in your workday using that light, it will not be available for later shots. A photographer working a night shift may have only one or two power belts, so it is important to conserve them and use AC lights whenever possible.

If a dichroic filter is available for your battery light, daytime shots can be filled with that light if the subject is close enough. A reporter standing in the shade, or backlit, can be helped out with a battery light and dichroic filter. The effective distance for this application is only about four feet in open shade so its use in this way is limited. And since most 30-volt lamps are 250 watts, they are ineffectual compared with direct sunlight.

Because of the excellent low-light capabilities of the new chip cameras, portable light can be smaller and less powerful than previously. New 12-volt lights are very small and can be run straight from the camera's own battery eliminating the need for additional batteries or battery belts. The lights come in 25- to 75-watt sizes and provide adequate light for most close-in shooting. (See Figure 4.29.) Using one of these lights off the camera battery will put extra drain on the battery and greatly reduce its running time. These low-wattage lights are good for filling in the eye socket

Figure 4.29: A portable 12-volt light like this 75-watt camera light with a swing-away dichroic filter can be powered by the same battery the camera is using.

shadows created by overhead lighting (such as fluorescents) without overpowering the subject with too much light and making the background too dark. In these situations overall color correction will be impossible, but a mixed-light white balance should yield acceptable results for ENG work.

Camcorder Light Many manufacturers of consumer camcorders are now packaging them with a small DC-powered light mounted on top. (See Figure 4.30.) This small light, often 10 watts to 30 watts, gives enough light to raise the base

Figure 4.30: The small battery-powered light mounted on this consumer camcorder helps provide enough light to properly expose faces without being too bright.

illumination to an acceptable level for many shots. The light is also good for lighting faces in a typical interview situation. The low wattage of the light prevents some of the harsh effects like skin glare from occurring and the light is soft enough to act more like a fill light than a harsh key light.

LIGHT AS AN AESTHETIC FORCE

It is helpful to divide lighting into two categories: source lighting and portrait lighting, provided you have some time to set up lights and position subjects. When shooting on the run, you may not have time to do any more than get enough light for a good exposure. If you do have any time at all, however, it is worth making your video look the best it can. Bringing up the light level on a person's face is not enough to give the viewer the maximum perception of the shot. But a combination of framing, background *and* lighting can bring the viewer more in touch with the subject and make the subject more watchable.

The flat lighting of the camera at the same location as the light puts no shadows on a subject's face nor does it show tone differences on a subject's face. After a tape with this type of lighting is dubbed (copied), the resolution begins to decrease and because there is no contrast to the subject's features, the face begins to disappear completely. The face washes out and has no texture or features. A news station often airs third- or fourth-generation dubs. The quality of these is already low, but if the lighting is very flat the picture will have almost no detail.

The very best cameras can see up to a 30:1 contrast ratio but the videotape can record only about a 20:1 contrast ratio. Most home TV sets have only a 10:1 ratio because of high levels of room light. Therefore, it is a good idea of keep the lighting ratios within about 10:1 and never over 20:1 for the overall scene and even less for the subject itself—but a contrast is always necessary. There should be light and dark areas in the picture and the surface of the subject's face must be clearly distinguishable. This modeling effect adds texture and more of a three-dimensional feeling to a picture, which makes it is easier to see on the home screen and easier to watch.

You can maximize the impact of your work by maximizing the information in the shot and capturing the feeling that you perceive in the subject. The camera is very objective, often too objective because of its limitations. It does not have the eyes of a human, and it cannot have the same depth perception, contrast ratio or freedom of movement that your eyes have. But by subjective camera placement and focal length, choice of subject, editing and lighting. you can create an image with the camera that reflects what you see. The ability to create this type of image makes a good photographer.

There are some things you can control so that the picture showing at home is as close as possible to the way things are. For example, you may think you are changing the picture too much by setting up several lights. You probably are not, however, if the end result is a picture with light levels high enough to properly expose the picture, a contrast ratio in the proper range, and a picture that looks natural and pleasing to the viewer. Because the camera does not see things in the same way you do, you must help it see that way.

Source Lighting

Source lighting is the best possible natural lighting; you see it most often in the movies. All the artificial light sources are cleverly placed so the viewer is unaware that any are used. The scene looks as though it is lit only by the natural light sources in the picture; this is why it is called source lighting.

It may actually take many lights to make a scene appear as though it has no added light. A room with windows should look as though the only light comes from those windows. To make a scene look like this, you can use artificial lights to

Figure 4.31: Use of a single light can make it appear as though the lighting source is coming from a window or a door.

fill in the shadows or accent certain highlights (thereby controlling the contrast ratio). You can also use artificial lights to make the lighting appear as though it is coming from regular lamps in a room, the light from a fireplace or candles, or any natural light source that happens to be there. (See Figure 4.31.) It is helpful to the viewer if the light source is incorporated into the shot or shown in a setup shot so that there is at least a subliminal awareness of where the light is coming from.

Balancing the lighting contrast ratio of the subject in the room to the daylight in the windows can be very difficult in source lighting. In EFP work as in the movies, large sheets of neutral density gels can be taped to the outside of the window to cut down on the amount of light coming in. These can also be combined with color correction gels to bring the color temperature down to the temperature of tungsten if it is easier than changing all of your artificial sources to daylight temperatures. It will take some practice to become proficient at balancing contrast ratios, but you can follow these rules to start:

1. Choose a natural light source and make it your key light.
2. Color correct so all light sources match.
3. If the key is too weak, add light from the same direction as the key and light only the areas originally lit by the natural key.
4. Add fill light to bring the contrast ratios down.
5. Make sure the shadows caused by the fill lights are not evident in the shot; only the key light and effects lights should produce any noticeable shadows.

Portrait Lighting

Portrait lighting is basically three-point lighting that does not try to hide itself. The subject of portrait lighting can look, and usually does look, as though lit in a studio. This type of lighting adds credibility and formality to the subject. If the subject is making a statement on a serious topic or trying to air a viewpoint, portrait lighting produces a serious look. The mayor or corporate president behind a desk can be lit in this formal way because the viewer expects it. Formal lighting is for formal situations.

However, if you are shooting a feature story, or your intent is simply to show someone working, portrait lighting would be very inappropriate. The lighting should be informal (and thus natural) if your look at the subject is informal. (See Figure

Figure 4.32: Umbrellas can give the light on the subject an informal look.

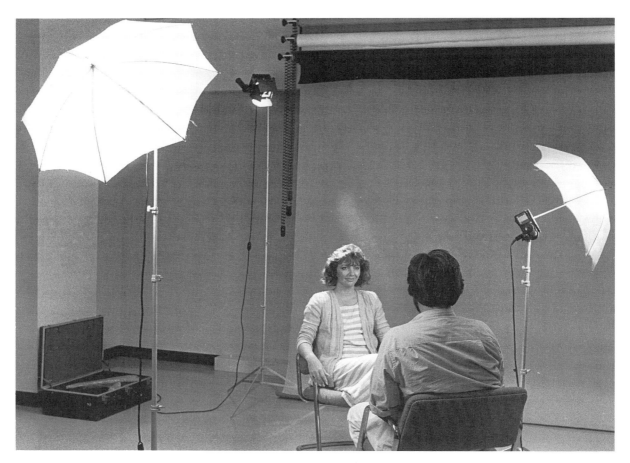

4.32.) The situation and the character of the subject determine the type of lighting.

BALANCING THE PICTURE

Any good picture has movement in it—not only the movement caused by the elements in the picture changing position, but also the movement of your eye looking at the picture. Your eye should be drawn to the subject but also must see the total picture in a non-disturbing way. A viewer's eye should be able to flow around the picture effortlessly, take it all in and settle on the subject in a very short time.

You have probably heard people refer to a painting or photo as balanced. This is a subjective term meaning that the picture is pleasing to the eye. The forces at work move your eye around the picture simply and comfortably, and the subject is the center of attention (not necessarily the center of the picture). Each line, curve, shape, color and

bright spot helps lead your eye around the picture. Horizontal lines represent things at rest, vertical lines things of strength, diagonal lines things in conflict and curved lines things in transition. These are the tools of framing with which you build good composition.

Force of Elements Within a Picture

Light and the shadows it creates can help define those lines as well as add color and contrast to move your eye around the picture. Think of all these elements as having direction and, therefore, force. Large dominates small, vertical dominates horizontal, bright dominates dark and diagonal dominates all. Assign a unit of force to each of these elements. The amount or prominence of these elements in the picture can add to or subtract from the amount of force. For example, bright has more force than dark unless there are more dark areas than bright areas. It is possible to vary the amount of each element to reach an equilibrium—a balance.

The subject should always have the most force of any single element in the picture. If the picture is balanced, the force of the subject equals the sum of all the other elements. The net effect is one of cancellation—the picture is in balance. If you are using natural or source lighting, you must choose your camera position carefully. Since you do not control the placement of the natural lights in this situation., you must control the placement of the camera, the focal length and the framing to balance your picture within the frame.

Balancing an Interview Shot

For an interview shot or on-camera talent, the basic framing and subject placement are not always flexible. By setting up lights, you can balance the picture after the framing and background have been chosen. The largest force in the picture is the subject—in this case, the face of the interviewee or talent.

Framing

Remember, the rules for framing the head of the subject talking are:

1. Always keep the eyes above the midpoint of the screen.
2. Keep the tip of the subject's nose on the vertical centerline.

If you follow these basic rules, the picture is well on its way to being balanced. The person's face, angled so that it is looking just past the camera (at the unseen interviewer), creates a movement or force in the direction the person is looking. This force is met by the open space between the person's face and the edge of the screen. This space should be larger than the space between the back of the person's head and the other side of the screen. The larger the space, the larger the force. The more at an angle a person is to the camera, the more space is needed to balance the picture. A profile shot should have all of the subject's head on one-half of the screen, leaving the other half empty.

Lighting To add light to this interview shot and keep the picture balanced, you must keep in mind that (1) the light creates still another force to balance and (2) you must maintain the modeling effect by light and dark areas within a certain ratio. The key light has the most force so it must go against the strongest opposition—the direction of the face. (See Figures 4.33, 4.34 and 4.35.)

A key light from the side of the camera the person is not facing pushes the face out of the

Figure 4.33: In the top shot, an umbrella light set off to the side creates a relaxed, comfortable feeling. Next, a harsh key light off to the side produces a serious, or private, mood in the middle shot; in the last shot, a light from below eye level creates a horror-movie look.

Figure 4.34: Light placement for a live interview with shadows.

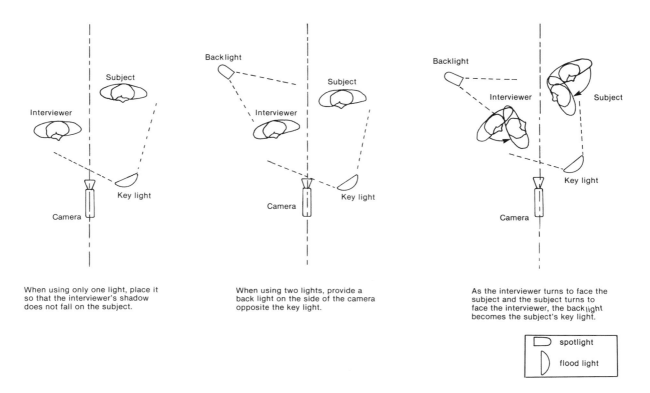

When using only one light, place it so that the interviewer's shadow does not fall on the subject.

When using two lights, provide a back light on the side of the camera opposite the key light.

As the interviewer turns to face the subject and the subject turns to face the interviewer, the backlight becomes the subject's key light.

spotlight	
flood light	

picture. If the key light comes from this direction, there are two major forces (the key light and the face) going in the same direction on the screen. You can compensate for this by adding more space in front of the head or adding other elements to block these forces.

When the key light opposes the direction of the person's face, it begins to balance the picture. A fill light can oppose the key to bring down the contrast level (fill in the shadows) and help complete the balance. Lighting the dark side of the face helps balance the force of the key so that there will not be too much bright area seen. You can achieve a balance between the small bright areas and the larger but darker areas by filling the larger side (camera side) until the desired balance is achieved.

The backlight can also help in this balancing act. If the backlight is placed opposite the key, the bright rim created on the shoulder and hair will be on the opposite side of the face as the key, helping push the head toward the force of the key light. A fourth light, a background light, can also be part of the balance. By creating light and dark areas or shapes with its shadows, a picture can have added interest and still maintain an equilibrium.

The concept of balance should apply to any scene you may shoot. If you do the head of a person talking with natural light, then position yourself and the subject so that the light falls as described above. Subjects should always try to look toward the light source. Even if a picture is balanced with the subject facing away from the light, it has a negative feeling to it as if the subject is turning away from something, but this may be the correct effect for certain situations.

Use the light to your advantage. Make it draw a viewer to the subject or direct the viewer's eye around the picture. Controlling light is what photography is about. Before any of us can be news camera operators, production videographers or corporate video makers, we must first be photographers. The road to photojournalist, artist or news gatherer must start with the ability to control light so that the camera can do its job.

PRINCIPLES AND TECHNIQUES FOR GOOD LIGHTING

Regardless of the lighting style you choose, approach the setup with the following principles in mind:

1.   Survey the available light, subjects to be lit and lighting equipment on hand.

Figure 4.35: Light placement for a typical interview.

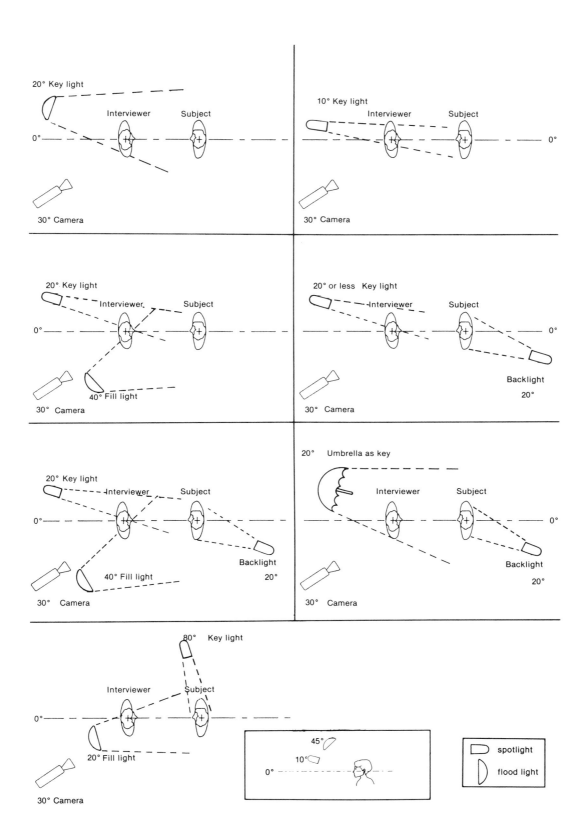

2. Decide on the appropriate color temperature.
3. Consider light direction and balance.
4. Light for your wide shot first, then your tight shots.
5. Build your lighting by setting one light at a time:
   a. Start with your key light. Place and adjust it with no other lights on until you are satisfied with the results.
   b. Place and adjust your fill light. Make sure that its placement and intensity are acceptable for the situation.
   c. Complete the basic setup with a backlight.
   d. If necessary, add background light and/or kicker, eye or special-effects lights.

By building your lighting setup one light at a time, problems surface early and can be more easily corrected without the confusion of other lights in wrong positions.

Mood Lighting

Once your basic lighting setup is completed, use the remaining time before the actual shooting to experiment with mood lighting. By simply modifying the setup, you can easily manipulate the mood of the shot. You can use bright lighting, often referred to as **high key lighting,** to suggest an open, cheerful environment, or subdued lighting (**low key lighting**) to enhance the drama of the shot. When lighting in the field do not forget that adding light to a scene starts to change the mood of the scene. The more subtle and indirect the lighting, the more natural people tend to appear *and* behave.

The mood you are trying to convey should dictate the type of lighting for a particular shot. Let the mood come through in the lighting already at the scene. Imagine that you must shoot an interview with a welfare mother in a darkly lit ghetto apartment. The easiest way to bring up the base light level would be to use the camera-mounted light. But a sun gun interview with bright light shining in the woman's eyes would look like a harsh, uncaring invasion by the media into the woman's life. You can shoot this interview using just one light, but its placement is crucial.

One possible solution might be a diffused light placed at a 90° side angle to the camera. Attach barndoors to the light and allow the background behind the woman to remain dark. The dreary apartment remains dark and the woman is lit, but

she is probably not distracted by the light. Your audience will focus on the woman and her story, rather than the bright lights in her eyes or a distracting background flatly illuminated by the camera-mounted light. The subtle lighting allows the woman to be the most important element in the story, not the expensive equipment that has intruded into her life. Good lighting is lighting that is not noticed. Good lighting techniques enhance the mood and bring out the subject for the audience. Good lighting does not challenge or distort the existing mood of the scene or direct attention from the subject.

There are several formal styles to creative lighting. Most are derived from master painters whose work can be seen in good art museums anywhere. If you want to be more than just a basic photographer, you need to study the styles that make up the creative world of lighting.

Chiaroscuro Lighting

Derived from the style of post-Renaissance painters who emphasized high contrast lighting in their works, **chiaroscuro** is an Italian word meaning light-dark. This style was perfected by the Dutch painter Rembrandt van Rijn (1606-1669). Chiaroscuro lighting involves selectively lighting certain areas of a scene while letting the shadow areas, especially the background, fall off to near black. The basic forms of chiaroscuro lighting are cameo and Rembrandt. **Cameo lighting** is similar to that of a cameo stone where the subject is sharply set off from the dark background. Only a few dense shadows on the subject are present; there is no background illumination at all. **Rembrandt lighting** is a highly stylized natural look where light appears to be coming from a natural source such as a window or candle but only illuminates very select areas of the scene. Unlike cameo lighting, Rembrandt lighting allows the shadows to be less dense (more transparent) so that some background is visible but at a much lower light level than the subject. The structure of the frame eliminates the need for the backlight unless there is a light source somewhere behind the subject. Each and every light used in Rembrandt lighting must appear to come from a natural source in the scene. The frame is constructed so that light areas of the subject are against the darkest areas of the background and vice versa. To study mood or emotional lighting, review a book of Rembrandt's paintings. Notice how light sources move the viewer's eye and how most of the light seems to come from one source. (See Figure 4.36.)

Figure 4.36: Two lights were used to give a chiaroscuro quality to the light in this scene. A single key light is positioned to look as though it is the light from the desk lamp. A backlight gives just enough highlights to the subject's hair to separate it from the background. By making use of the cramped and crowded desk, the subject is also framed in a Ray Farkas style.

Chiaroscuro lighting can convey both high and low emotional intensity. The quantity of dark and light areas helps determine what the perception will be. This type of lighting uses a low key, usually a fresnel with barndoors, and very little fill. The background is usually lit with other very directional, narrow beam lights to control the amount of scene receiving light. Chiaroscuro lighting intensifies the three-dimensional properties of the subject, clarifies the space around them and gives an emotional quality to the scene. The particular emotional quality should be selected on the basis of the subject you are photographing in ENG work and by what the script calls for in EFP. Each lighting set-up should have a predetermined goal beyond making a good exposure for the camera. Chiaroscuro lighting is the basis for almost all the motivational lighting you will do.

Zone Lighting

Along the same lines as chiaroscuro lighting, **zone lighting** selectively lights only certain areas of the picture, which is divided into zones by distances from the camera. This is usually foreground, midground and background. The subject is usually in the midground. Each of these areas is lit separately with dark or shadow areas separating them. This technique helps to create a three-dimensional look and draw the eye to whatever you wish to emphasize in the frame.

Lighting With Color

For most work in EFP and ENG, keeping the color of light the same from all sources in a scene is the standard. However, for creative work you will find yourself mixing colors of light more and more. By knowing what color any particular light source is, you can predict how it will look on the screen when added to your shot. If you are doing an interview inside a room during the day but for some reason you wish it to look as though it were night, you may light the subject with tungsten, balance for that and let some daylight spill into the background. The area lit by sunlight will appear blue, similar to that of moonlight (as used in TV and movies) especially if the daylight is of a much lower intensity than your key light. You may use daylight from a large window as your key on a subject but tungsten as the backlight to give the hair a warm glow. Once you have mastered which lights are going to be what color when the camera is balanced for any one of these lights, you can start to use color differences to your creative advantage.

Correct Quantity of Light

In ENG work, you will repeatedly face the dilemma of mood preservation versus mood contamination. When do you forgo mood and turn on the lights? Only experience answers that question. Fortunately, new cameras and lenses are being introduced that require lower base light levels than their predecessors. Hopefully, news lighting in the future will continue to become easier and more subtle.

In the meantime, one good rule of thumb is to shoot when you see the whites of your subject's eyes. If there is not enough existing light to see the white areas of the eyes in the viewfinder, then you should add more light. Often the light is too direct or too backlit; you will be unable to see a subject's eyes clearly. You may be able to overexpose the scene but still not accomplish this. More light must be added to a scene to keep the subject from appearing corpse-like or as a silhouette—effects you do not want except in special situations. Decide what the subject of your shot is and then expose for it. If the rest of the scene is overexposed, add light to your subject or change the shot.

Adding a dB boost will increase the sensitivity of the pickup device, thereby increasing the range of light in which your camera is effective. This should only be done in the most extreme cases. If a dB boost gives that added detail to a shot to be able to see the subject, then do it. Remember that every dB boost increases the noise or graininess of the picture. At + 18 dB, the picture quality is quite poor. Any dB boost for EFP use is strictly out. Only in very desperate ENG situations should you use this gain switch for signal boosting. Choose to use it very carefully.

5 The Basic Shots

Before beginning any video shoot, you should have a goal in mind. In ENG work, the goal is to strive to represent the truth, or the reality of an event or story in an appropriate context. In EFP work, the goal is usually dictated by the client or manager. The videographer is directed to tell a particular story in a way that will be perceived and understood by the intended audience. In a corporate video setting, the goal may be to effectively communicate the advantages and disadvantages of a new health plan to the employees. In a music video created for entertainment, the goal may be to visually capture a mood or statement intended by the musician's composition or song. In either case, you must assemble all the elements of the story.

IDENTIFYING THE STORY LINE

Before you begin a shoot, ask yourself what you are trying to do. Reduce the task to its most basic description. If you can capsulize the story in one sentence, you are well on the way to reaching your goal. A typical ENG example might be students at a technical school coming from other careers to study microelectronics and enhance their employment prospects. Every aspect of this story is contained in this one sentence. By giving yourself this starting point, you can expand the sentence outward until you have covered all points in as much detail as practical. For an average TV news story,

length is the factor that determines how much you can put into that story. Since TV news is more of a headline service than an in-depth documentary service, a story such as the technical school would probably take 90 seconds.

This example can easily be translated into EFP terms. If the owners of the technical school want to make a one-minute commercial for the school, the basic ingredients of the story will be the same. In both cases, because of the limited time available to the videographer every shot must count. Once you have a goal and a relative time constraint, you need the means to reach that goal.

TYPES OF SHOTS

Just as a musician uses a finite number of notes to create a finished song, so too does a photographer use a finite set of shots to create a story. The musician can vary the ways each note is played and there are infinite ways to combine notes. Like the musician, the uniqueness of the photographer's art comes from the execution of camera shots and movements. There is a specific purpose and design behind each shot and movement. Each shot is examined regarding composition, length and position relative to other shots in a story. To a large degree, these factors determine whether or not the viewer understands the story.

A photographer/videographer has various types of shots available for use in a video project. The first type varies in focal length of the lens. The second type includes some type of physical move by the camera, or the camera action shots. The third type is a group of specialty shots used in special situations to serve specific functions in the production process.

Varying Shots by Focal Length

The focal length of a lens is the distance from the optical center of the lens to the point at which the light rays are focused. Early video cameras used in studios were equipped with a turret that had a selection of several lenses of different focal lengths. Each lens was capable of one focal length. The physical length of these lenses gave an indication of the focal length of the lens. Generally, the longer the lens, the longer the focal length.

Portable video cameras today usually come equipped with some type of zoom or variable focal-length lens. The focal lengths are marked on the barrel of the lens at regular intervals from the widest to the longest. As the zoom is used, you can read off the lens which focal length you are using.

(See Figure 5.1.) Zoom lenses usually range from wide angle to telephoto. As the lens range shifts, many things change in the resulting picture. The most basic change is the size of the subject: it gets larger as the focal length increases (zooming in). This magnification of the subject also has other effects in the overall picture. As the field of view narrows (focal length increasing), the quantity of background decreases but its size increases (less is seen but it is magnified). This visual effect is known as **compression**. Objects at different distances from the camera and in line with each other appear to become closer to one another as the field of view narrows.

This phenomenon can be used to great advantage by the photographer. In a movie where the hero is running down the street toward the camera while being chased by a truck, a telephoto lens (long focal length) makes not only the hero appear large but the truck as well. The compression of perspective in the shot can make it look as though the truck is only inches from the hero when in reality the truck could be 100 feet away. The same

Figure 5.1: Relationship between focal length and image size. © *by the Eastman Kodak Co. Reprinted courtesy the Eastman Kodak Co.*

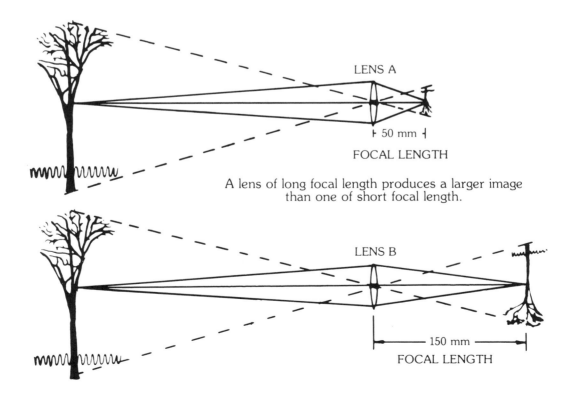

LENS A

⊢ 50 mm ⊣

FOCAL LENGTH

A lens of long focal length produces a larger image
than one of short focal length.

LENS B

— 150 mm —

FOCAL LENGTH

Figure 5.2: A wide angle perspective (left) with a large angle of view can have an open feeling. A telephoto perspective (right) has a narrower angle of view and objects appear closer because the perspective is compressed.

shot done with a wide field of view would show the truck's position more clearly and not have the same dramatic effect. At a very wide field of view, just the opposite effect could occur. In wide-angle shots, things in line with the camera tend to appear much farther apart than they really are. These effects can be used in any number of places to bring objects closer together or farther apart in a picture.

In place of focal-length change, you can substitute camera distance. By simply moving the camera closer to the subject, you increase its magnification. In the early days of photojournalism when each lens had one fixed focal length, the photographer had to walk to or from the subject to change the size of the image. Many people still refer to a wide shot as a long shot because you had to walk a long way back to get a wide shot with a fixed focal length lens.

With today's zoom lenses and wider angle of view, you need not walk as far or as much. The thing to keep in mind is the perspective of each type of focal length, especially when shooting medium or close-up shots. (See Figures 5.2 and 5.3.) Zooming in, creates less depth of field and three-dimensional view. When the photographer walks closer to the subject the perspective stays the same, the depth of field does not change as dramatically and much of the three-dimensional effect is still there.

In the following shots, the magnification of the subject and the framing make the shots what they are. While it is easiest to describe a close-up as

zooming in tight, you can also shoot a close-up by putting the camera very close to the subject. Therefore, the size of the subject in the frame is determined by either focal length or distance from the subject. For common photographic uses, these shots are best made by focal-length changes.

Wide Shot Sometimes called the establishing or master shot, the wide shot is generally the first a photographer should take when shooting begins. The wide shot has a short focal length and, therefore a wide angle of view. This shot should include all the visual elements of the story if possible. In the example of the technical school one-sentence story, the wide shot would be used to cover or visually explain that sentence. In fact, the wide shot might be used on a newscast in a bumper or tease, a preview that includes a shot of an upcoming story. In the technical school example, the wide shot would include the students, instructor, classroom and electronic equipment. Every key element should be there. The shot should show relationships and activities that yield information: the older-than-expected students, the instructor in an active teaching role and the equipment that is the subject of the lesson. These visual elements give the viewer the information that reinforces comments of the announcer or newscaster.

Usually each story contains more than one wide shot. As the writer expands a single sentence into several paragraphs to make a complete story, so the photographer must expand the idea into visual sentences and paragraphs. A story can be broken up into its component parts. It has a beginning, a

Figure 5.3: By changing the angle of view and distance to the subject, you can keep the plaza sign approximately the same size in the frame, but the background and perspective change dramatically.

middle and an end. These parts are a series of ideas or facts that combine to form the overall statement used to form your goal. Visually the story must be broken down into those same parts. Think of each part or sequence as a story unto itself. Again the idea of one shot telling the whole story comes into play and wide shots may be used throughout the story.

Establishing the Scene   The beginning of each sequence starts with a shot that establishes the idea of that sequence (or paragraph of the script). The wide shot begins a sequence by establishing what the viewer will be seeing and what the relationship is between all the elements to be

Figure 5.4: This wide shot establishes the setting and what the subject is doing; it is clear that he is a sculptor in a studio in an older building.

used in that sequence. (See Figure 5.4.) Within a typical sequence, the wide shot should contain every object or subject that will be videotaped in the remainder of the sequence. If we are to see a man using a lathe while the reporter talks about him and his current job, then the first shot should show the man, the lathe and his location. In that opening shot of the sequence, relate as much information as possible to the viewer. Questions that should be answered in this first shot include:

- How large is the setting or location of the story?
- What are the important objects?
- What is the main character doing in relation to the objects in the setting?
- What is the machinery or equipment doing?

The shots that follow in the sequence detail the answers to these questions.

Without the wide shot, those details could be unrelated and therefore seemingly irrelevant or even confusing to the viewer. Ideas that must be expressed in a story can often be said in a very short time thus leaving not enough time for a visual sequence. A wide shot most often takes care of this problem because it gives a maximum amount of information in a short period of time. Again this is the idea of one shot expressing a complete thought or idea.

Creating a Third Dimension   The information included in a wide shot is only one of several components required for a good wide shot. It the framing is off, or the shot is too busy or otherwise aesthetically unpleasant, you have not maximized the impact it can have on the viewer. Since the TV is a two-dimensional surface similar to a piece of paper or a canvas, the third dimension must be created. The illusion of depth is what makes a two-dimensional picture come alive. The term **flat** is often used to describe a shot that has failed to show any three-dimensional characteristics.

There are two ways to avoid a flat picture: use of the foreground and use of the vanishing point.

1. *Use of the Foreground.* Establish an area or object near the camera, place the subject in the mid-ground and line up a good background; the picture will have a feeling of depth because the objects are at very different distances from the camera. (See Figures 5.5 and 5.6.) Many times it helps to exaggerate this effect by placing the foreground object extremely close to the camera. (See Figure 5.7.) For this type of shot, the foreground object(s) are often in focus. Unlike backgrounds, if a foreground is out of focus, it should still be a recognizable form, such as a tree limb or a fence. If the foreground object is too out of focus, it may become more of a distraction than a help in framing. The *subject* must not be minimized by foreground or overpowered by background. Placement in the picture or lighting can make the subject stand out even with the other elements present. The subject should be the brightest area of the picture and the most visible, but not necessarily the largest part of the picture. Other elements can often serve to give the most emphasis to the subject, no matter how small it is.

2. *Use of the Vanishing Point.* In many shots in which a foreground is not practical or desirable, the use of angles can give the feeling of continuance in the picture. Break the picture down into horizontal, vertical and diagonal lines. The best examples of this occur when shooting buildings because the lines are easy to see. As your position and, therefore, perspective change, so do the lines. When you walk around a structure, notice that from some angles there are almost all horizontal and vertical lines and no diagonals. At a certain angle, however, there are many diagonal lines and almost no horizontal lines. At the point in which horizontal lines appear diagonal in the field of view, you can easily create depth in a two-dimensional picture.

In a drawing or on the screen, diagonal lines seem to converge at some point, implying a third dimension or movement to a distant point. For example, when you look down straight railroad tracks, you can see that, at some point, the two rails seem to come together. This is the vanishing point. (See Figure 5.8.) If you shoot from angles

Figure 5.5: The straight-on shot (left) is flat and uninteresting. All the architectual lines are horizontal and vertical with no foreground or background. Choosing a point of view with foreground (right) gives the picture depth because objects are both near to and far from the camera.

Figure 5.6: While the left shot shows the building clearly, the total picture area is not used to frame the subject. By moving under a nearby tree (right), you can use a branch to frame the picture. The branch not only adds interest and balance to the scene but also a foreground that increases the depth of the picture.

that produce diagonal lines moving toward vanishing points, then the shot will have a three-dimensional quality. Therefore, do not shoot objects straight on unless you have a good foreground; try to shoot from an angle.

Medium Shot The medium shot is the workhorse of most TV stories. It can be defined as a picture of the subject with little attention given to anything else. In most cases, depth and relationships within the frame are brought out with subtleties of lighting or just a portion of another subject or object in the shot. If a wide shot shows someone from head to toe, then a medium shot shows a person from the waist up. A subject is seen closely enough that the texture or surface features can give it the three-dimensional characteristics that a photographer desires. Lighting can play a major role in bringing out these features to enhance the feeling of three-dimensionality.

As with all shots, there is a need to maximize information when using the medium shot. In this type of shot, you do not need to show a subject's relationship to the surroundings, but you must show more detail of who or what the subject is or what the subject is doing. In the technical school story, one medium shot might be a student assembling a circuit board. The important elements of the shot are the subject's face, arms, hands and the circuit board. An important difference between the execution of the wide shot and the medium shot is the number of angles available for the medium shot that are not always available for the wide shot.

By keeping the same focal length and distance from the subject, the shot can be taken from the front, at a 45° angle from the front, at the side, over the shoulder, at low angles or at high angles. It may be helpful to divide the screen into thirds to aid in framing subjects in wide and medium shots. (See Figure 5.9.)

Where one wide shot will suffice to start off the story or segment of a story, many medium shots are needed to supply the bulk of the storytelling material. The key element in the medium shot is variety. If you can shoot the subject from several different angles, you can quickly make quite a few medium shots that will better prepare you when the material gets to the editing stage. The more angles and variety of shots you have available in editing, the more creative choices you have in assembling the finished story.

Close-Up Shot The close-up shot gives the intimate details of the subject. It shows the emotions in a person's eyes, the manipulations of the subject's fingers or the fine details of a craftsman's work. (See Figure 5.10.) If the medium shot shows a person from the waist up, the close-up would be a shot of the head only. It can be thought of as the final shot of a sequence or idea initiated in the wide shot. In our technical school example, the close-up might be a shot of the student's fingers positioning a chip or some other element on the circuit board. The elements in the shot are the fingers, the board and the part being fitted to the board.

Depth in a close-up is completely reduced to the texture of the objects being photographed.

Figure 5.7: These three angles are some of the possible medium shots of this sculptor at work.

There is little need for a foreground object or varying angle shot to show vanishing points. The detail of the close-up subject will usually give the depth necessary for a good picture. The number of angles from which a close-up can be shot is often more limited than either the wide or the medium shot. The variety lies in shooting the many different elements of a subject in close-ups. Other possible close-ups in the technical school example might also be of a face, a supply of parts or a book of instructions. In other words, you can shoot a detailed close-up of every element in the medium shot.

Extreme Close-Up (XCU) Shot The extreme close-up (XCU) adds drama or extra emphasis to a series of shots. In a photograph of a person, the XCU could be of the subject's eyes. For many story lines, this shot would be out of place, but when used correctly it can greatly improve the quality of the piece. This type of shot brings the viewer into a world not normally seen in such detail. The extreme close-up presents a larger-than-life image that may be extremely interesting for the viewer. (See Figure 5.11.) The subject should be chosen carefully and the purpose for this type of shot should be clear.

The XCU in the technical school example could show the tip of the soldering iron as it melts some solder onto the part just put in place during the close-up shot. Seeing the solder actually run and the smoke billow out from around it adds a sense of drama and visual excitement to a rather mundane classroom setting. An XCU of the student's eyes in a story like this would not be appropriate and would add little to the interest of the story unless you could see a reflection of the solder smoke rising in the glasses the student is wearing. The XCU need not be action-related but simply a detail shot, for example, a single stamp in a story about stamp collecting or a fruit fly in a story about crop damage. If used properly, this shot can be the most important in any piece, but it must be used at the correct time, have a good relationship to the surrounding shots and show an appropriate subject. By using the XCU, video pieces can demand a great deal of attention from the viewer.

Special Use Shots

This category of shots is defined by the function of the shot and not by the focal length or framing of the shot. These shots usually serve as some sort of transition from one part of the visual story to another or as an aid in the edit process to maintain continuity. The following shots allow the editor to take the viewer smoothly through the flow of the story while not affecting the visual style.

Cutaway As its name implies, the cutaway shot is used to cut away from the action. When an editor is putting together a series of shots and wants to avoid a **jump cut** (a break in continuity),

Figure 5.8: A camera at eye level (with a 0° tilt) shows a perspective with two horizontal vanishing points (the left one is shown here); these vanishing points are always on the horizon line. From any one viewing position (except at 90° to a plane), all parallel planes have the same vanishing point, while each nonparallel plane creates its own vanishing point.

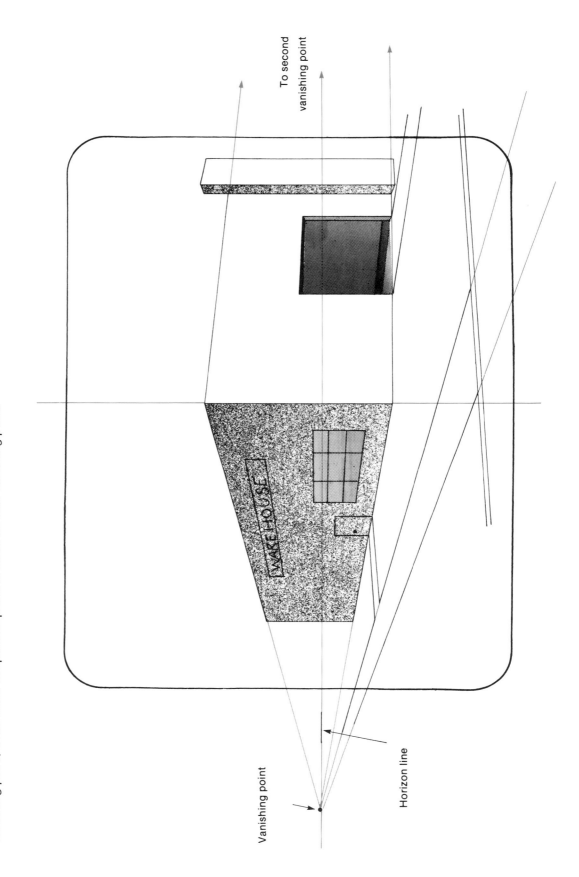

To second vanishing point

Vanishing point

Horizon line

WAREHOUSE

Figure 5.9: Use of the rule of thirds makes the sailboat and seacape a balanced picture. The sea is in the lower third of the picture, the boat is at B2 and the cloud is at A1.

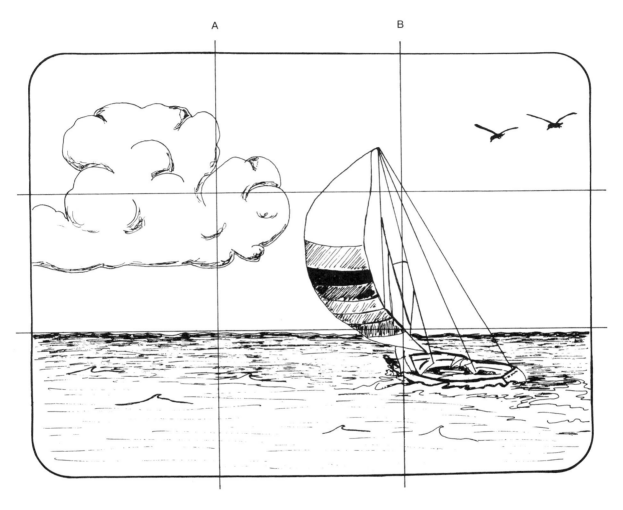

a cutaway is used to take the viewer away from the subject so that time or position can change without disturbing the continuity of the two shots. (See Figure 5.12.) The most basic example of this is during an interview in which two different sound bites will be **butted** (used back to back). The interviewee's head will not be in the same exact position from one shot to the next and therefore the edit can result in a basic jump cut in which the interviewee's head jumps instantly through space and time to another position. This is a break in continuity for the viewer who is used to having the illusion of real time within a story.

In TV news the solution to the problem is a cutaway shot to the reporter listening to the interviewee. This shot is inserted over the edit so that the audio is not disturbed and the bridge in time is not noticed by the viewer. This type of shot

is used many times in any action sequence where time compression is necessary, that is, where the subject must get from one part of the story to another in less time than it really took. In a sports story in which the beginning and end of one boxing round is to be shown, the editor must cut out most of the middle of that round. To avoid the appearance of the boxer jumping from one part of the ring to another, the editor uses a shot of the crowd for a few seconds between the first and second shots of the fight.

The cutaway is any shot away from the action or subject but related to it. It can be a wide shot, medium or close-up. A good cutaway should fit with the other shots, just as all shots in a story should blend together. In the two examples above, the cutaways are shots of people listening or watching. These usually make the best cutaways but

Figure 5.10: The left close-up shot shows the face of the artist clearly while maintaining his spacial relationship with the sculpture, and the right photo provides detail of his work as he shapes the clay.

sometimes they are not available to shoot. In these instances a close-up or extremely wide shot can often serve the same purpose.

The cutaway is used within a sequence of shots involving the same subject in the same location; it is *not* a transition shot . To go from a shot of the mayor in an office to a shot of the mayor at a fund raiser is not a jump cut. The audience knows there is a jump in time with this edit and perceives it as natural. If there two shots taken from about the same camera position and focal length of the president on the phone at his desk and of him signing a bill at his desk, then cutting to the second shot would be a **jump cut**, or cutaway shot. It would be

needed in the middle to bridge the two shots to avoid the break in continuity within that scene.

In the movies and higher-quality video productions, there are very few if any cutaways used and no one misses them. The reason is that the sequences are so well thought out that the action flows naturally from one shot to the next. Even in shooting news, with a little practice you can learn which shots to get and how to piece them together so that no cutaways are needed. In general, cutaways slow down the pace of a story without

Figure 5.11: This XCU of the sculptor's tool shaping the clay demonstrates the texture and pliability of the clay, which is not normally seen.

Figure 5.12: In the series of photos of the sculptor, this shot of his hands coming into the frame to exchange one tool for another is a cutaway from the main action of sculpting. It is still part of the story, but does not involve the main action of the subject.

adding any new information to the subject. In many instances the reporter cutaway can be eliminated by editing in shots of what is being talked about. If the president is talking about cutting spending, then why not show shots of the major items that are being cut? If you find creative ways not to use cutaways, your video pieces will generally look much better and be more interesting.

Transition Shot The transition shot is an editing tool that allows continuity while avoiding jump cuts. A subject moved from one location to another in an edit sometimes results in a jump cut if the shots are too similar. The simplest example of a transition shot is a scene where you allow the subject to move out of the frame. You are left with an empty picture and are now free to establish the character anywhere else you wish. The reverse of this is also true. Start with an empty frame for your next location and let your subject walk into the shot. In some cases it may be easier to pan to or away from the subject to get the subject in or out of the picture so that you can change location. One very common transition shot in broadcast TV is the building or room exterior shot. This is useful as a transition for a subject that is changing geographic locations and it also establishes the location for the next shot.

Close-ups make excellent transition shots. Because viewers see so little of the scene or subject, close-ups leave viewers at the end of an expression or thought. The close-up of a sculptor's hands shaping clay or even the XCU of the tool working the clay can be the end of one sequence. From there you could cut to a wide shot of the sculptor placing the sculpture on a shelf at the end of the day. This jump in time is blended into the story by causing the viewer to concentrate on only one small aspect of what the sculptor is doing before coming back to another time in the same location. Using this method makes it possible to maintain the level of action and information without wasting time on neutral transition shots, such as the subject leaving the frame. Each story has many ways of being told; the style and pacing often determine which type of transition shots work the best. It is a good idea to shoot for many different possibilities and make the final decision in the edit room.

Interview Shot This shot is commonly called the talking head. In most applications of ENG, interviews play a major role in the makeup of the piece. For a news story, the interview shot is an absolute necessity because an interview may constitute the entire story. While the shot is basically simple, the correct framing of the subject and correct focal length to get a good background can make the shot pleasing—not just a picture.

Framing The basic framing of the interview shot should be the head and shoulders of the subject. To place the subject in that framing, use the nose and eyes for reference. (See Figure 5.13.) There are two basic rules for framing the talking head:

1. *Never let the subject's eyes go below the horizontal midpoint of the screen.* If the focal length changes from waist up to a close-up of the face, the eyes of the subject should always be in the upper half of the screen. (See Figure 5.14.)
2. *Keep the tip of the subject's nose on the vertical centerline of the screen.* If the subject is talking to a reporter off camera, you will notice that this rule puts the subject's head slightly off center. Since the subject is not talking to the viewer directly, this type of framing leaves a space in front of the subject to imply that someone is there. If the situation calls for it, such as in a feature story where the reporter is very much a part of the story, it may be necessary to include the interviewer in the shot. If this is the case, it is best to show all of the reporter's head and shoulders in the frame along with the subject's. For most cases in general news and informational pieces, this reduces the importance of the interviewee, which may be something you do not want to do.

As mentioned above, the standard framing for the talking head should be tight enough to show the subject's face clearly on the average TV screen. In some cases, the framing may be tighter, as on a probing interview on "60 Minutes." The framing of an interview with a welfare mother who has had her food stamps stolen could be a close-up of her face to show the viewer her emotion. However, the same type of shot in an interview with a city official regarding an upcoming change in traffic lights would not have the same meaning. Reserve the close-up faces only for emotional or dramatic subjects. Children are the biggest exception to this rule—they almost always look good in close-ups.

It is possible to overdo the facial close-up. It is basic conditioning to zoom in for a tight face shot when the grieving mother of a dead child starts to cry. While some may argue that the emphasis is needed to convey the full impact of emotion on the viewer, there is also the argument that this type of

Figure 5.13: When a picture is framed widely, you must raise the subject's eyes in the frame to avoid excessive head room. As the shot becomes tighter, the head room will fall off sharply to keep the eyes above the midpoint. You are always framing for the face, not for the hair. The top two photos give too much headroom; the bottom two are framed correctly.

shot is an uncaring, vulgar invasion of the woman's privacy. It may indeed be more dramatic to zoom out from such a scene to give the subject some space, if only symbolically. In news photography especially, emotions are conveyed best by TV. While the emotions portrayed should be true to your subject, they should not be offensive to your viewing audience. Some subjects deserve more respect than to have their worst moments seen larger than life in every one's living room. The moral values or degree of good taste you express in your shooting should be the same as you would express anytime in your life. The tight shot can be a powerful tool both artistically and emotionally, but you must be careful how and when you use it.

Background and Focal Length   In some cases, the background can be of such importance that the framing or placement of the subject in the frame is dictated by that background. The best setup for an interview with a farmer about a flooded field may be a wide shot of the field that includes

the farmer. The farmer may be framed head to toe, but if you place the farmer on the edge of the flooded field, the impact is enhanced from both a visual and informational point of view. An interview background should add to *not distract from,* the interviewee. If an appropriate background cannot be found, then choose a neutral one or use a focal length that produces a depth of field shallow enough to make the background out of focus.

When setting up an interview shot with a specific background, first set up the shot with the background only. Add the subject to the shot. If the subject does not conform to the framing rules mentioned at the beginning of this section, do not bend the rules but move the camera location to satisfy both background and framing rules. A very common misuse of background and subject occurs when the photographer tries to put a sign over one shoulder or the other of the subject. If the sign is too high, many new photographers shoot the interview from a low angle or frame the shot so that the subject's eyes are below the middle of the screen. Both generally produce a very uncomfortable shot. Never let the eyes of the interviewee or the interviewer go below the horizontal midpoints of the screen. Simply move the camera and subject farther from the sign, so that the sign can be placed over the subject's shoulder while still maintaining good framing. Do not force bad framing on your subject just to get a good background. A little experimentation usually shows a way to make both satisfactory.

Reporter Stand-Up Shot This shot is a specialized version of the interview shot used especially in TV news. For EFP it can be used as any on-camera appearance by a narrator who is talking *directly* to the audience. Because of this direct link to the audience, the framing of the

stand-up is very important. A general rule for this shot is to never frame the subject looser than the waist up or tighter than the necktie knot. This allows the viewer to have good eye contact with the subject and feel a personal link, which helps establish credibility.

If the shot is framed too loosely, the importance of the subject is reduced or even lost in the background and the impact is greatly reduced. (See Figure 5.15.) The subject must be the focus of the shot. Background is important but very much a secondary part of the picture. The subject's monologue should help determine the type of background used. If the script is general, then the background should be as well. If the script deals with a power plant, however, the power plant should be in the background.

Figure 5.14: The framing on the two most common talking-head shots (top photos) is distracting to the viewer because the center of attention is in the bottom half of the frame in both cases. The framing in the bottom photos brings the center of attention to the central area of the picture, making the subject the dominant object in the scene.

Figure 5.15: Because the reporter is in the bottom half of the picture the background completely overpowers the scene. This de-emphasizes the presence of the reporter.

Many of the same rules that apply to the interview shot apply also to the stand-up shot, such as placing the subject correctly in relation to the background and keeping the subject's eyes above the middle of the screen. As in the interview, the best camera elevation is eye level. Any other angle tends to be either unflattering or can either add or subtract too much importance from the subject. (See Figure 5.16.) Sometimes, however, a slightly higher-than-eye-level shot does work. For example, if you are shooting a reporter in front of an open field and the camera is at eye level, the background is narrow and the horizon is low. If you raise the camera above eye level,

however, the viewer has a different perspective on the background. The horizon line is higher and there is more much more of the field visible behind the reporter.

The difference between the stand-up and the interview shot is that the subject is talking directly to the camera. The need for the implied second person, the listener, is gone. This allows you to frame the subject on or off center to fit the background in around the subject. For most stand-ups with a background, the subject should be off-center to properly balance the picture. The talent's inside shoulder should be angled slightly away from the camera to help add three-dimensional quality to the shot and visually direct the viewer to the background as part of the overall picture. Again, the subject is always in the foreground, never part of the background. A good rule of thumb is never let the talent be more than six feet from the camera if you are using wide or medium focal lengths. (See Figure 5.17.)

There are many variations on this type of shot. The most common is the walking stand-up. As with any shot, it should have a purpose. The reason for a walking stand-up shot can be as simple as adding a little movement to an otherwise static shot. The movement should be slow and comfortable. A relaxed walk not only provides the necessary movement but also adds to the conversational tone appropriate for a stand-up. The subject should already be walking when the shot starts and can either stop partially through it or continue to walk throughout the shot. The correct framing needs to be maintained on the walking subject, which requires zooming out as the subject approaches to maintain the waist-up framing.

Figure 5.16: The low-angle shot (left) is not flattering to the reporter and the sign running through her head is very distracting. Moving away from the sign and raising the camera to eye level (right) makes the reporter the focus of attention; the sign and the background fall into place.

Figure 5.17: At the distance in the top photo, the reporter's contact with the viewer is diminished as she becomes part of the midground. The reporter in the middle photo is a good distance from the camera but is obsuring the background. At the bottom, the reporter is close enough to have good eye contact with the viewer; the background gives added information without interfering.

As a general rule, the zoom-in is used much more frequently than the zoom-out in the stand-up shot. The zoom-in, or push, adds emphasis to a stationary subject, whereas the zoom out, or pull, usually de-emphasizes the subject. However, it is often necessary to zoom out on a walking stand-up to maintain the framing, and a zoom out can also be effective when there is some additional information to be imparted by expanding the shot. An example of this is a reporter doing a stand-up on an area very dry due to a recent drought. The shot starts as a waist-up shot; as the reporter talks, the camera zooms out to show the reporter at the end of a dock with no water in sight.

Another factor in stand-ups is direction. The audience is being spoken to, and therefore the direction of the stand-up should always be toward the camera or audience. If the talent is entering the frame from off camera, the direction should still be toward the camera and not at a right angle to it. This usually requires some camera movement to get the talent into the frame in the least amount of time, but the feeling of positive motion is worth the movement. Walking into a static shot is time-consuming and usually awkward. The only time a talent should have negative motion is when taking the viewer to another location or showing the viewer something behind the place where the stand-up starts. This can be very effective if the shot is well thought out in advance. The audience does not like to have subjects turn their backs to them without good reason. The main goal is always to communicate—every shot, every subject.

Camera Action Shots

This category of shots is defined by moving the camera or changing focal lengths as the shot is recorded. In general, these shots add dynamics, drama and interest to the story by having the perspective of the viewer change as the shot takes place.

Zoom Shot Probably the most overused and misused shot in the field of videography, the zoom is the ruin of TV news. The first thing any new photographer does is work the zoom switch until it is worn out. The best way to teach a new photographer to shoot is to tape the zoom switch to off. A zoom should be considered a link between two static shots. For example, start on a tight shot and end on a medium shot or vice versa. As in individual shots, the beginning and end of the zoom should contain different or at least more information.

The two most common appropriate uses of a zoom are (1) to show relationships and (2) to emphasize a subject within a larger picture. The first is a zoom out and the second a zoom in. While shooting a crowded unemployment office, start on a tight shot of one person waiting in line and then zoom out to a wide shot that reveals all the people waiting in line. This gives the viewer the perspective of an individual being buried in the mass of people. The relationship between the individual and the rest of the room is well established. You might want to emphasize that the individual is undergoing a tiring wait. A zoom in from a wide shot of that room to a tight shot of a very tired looking individual emphasizes this point. The shot draws the viewer's attention from the overall picture to the plight of one individual who is part of the situation.

The basic rules for the zoom shot are as follows.

1. Always zoom from something important to something else important.
2. Make sure the beginning and ending shots can stand alone as static shots.
3. Zoom out to show a spatial relationship.
4. Zoom in for emphasis.

Always keep in mind the time it takes to zoom. A zoom that is too slow may not be able to be used by an editor; a zoom that is too fast may not allow the viewer to perceive and understand what is taking place. If you have the time and tape, shoot a zoom at two or three speeds and choose the best speed when the piece is being edited.

When shooting for special effects or for an arty look, a slow zoom can give the feel of gentle movement and can add to the pace and flow of an edited piece. In a faster-moving piece, a snap zoom can be done by putting the auto-zoom servo on off and manually wrist-snapping the zoom ring from one extreme to the other. This produces a very dramatic result and should be used with that effect in mind. Too much of any one technique may be bad for the piece. The more noticeable or dramatic the technique, the easier it is to overuse.

Pan Shot   In many ways the pan is like the zoom in the way it is used, but it is harder to misuse. The two major uses of the pan are (1) to show relationships and (2) to show more information than is contained in just one static shot. A pan from a raging brush fire to a nearby house can show the danger the house is in by proximity. This type of shot does not work well if the pan lasts too long or if the angle is too great. If the pan lasts too long, it may not fit into the edited story; if the angle is too great, the relationship may be lost

because too much ground was covered between subjects. Panning too fast can blur the picture to the point where nothing is recognizable during the pan. Generally, this is not acceptable.

Try to pan slowly enough so that you can obtain a good freeze frame from your video at any point in the pan. There are tables available in cinematography manuals that show the maximum degrees per second of pan for varying focal lengths. As this may be too complex for most field work, just experiment to get a feel for what is too fast. There are, of course, many times when a long pan is desirable.

For a shot of an extremely long line of people, a long pan in place of several static shots or a zoom can be more effective. The same is true for long angles in pans. While about 30° to 90° is as far as you should normally pan, 180° or even 360° can be made to work in the right situation. For instance, when showing how a small town has decorated the entire main street for Christmas, a 180° pan from one end of the street to the other may be very effective. In the middle of a neighborhood totally destroyed by a tornado, a 360° pan could give a viewer a very dramatic overview of the destruction. Again, as with the zoom, the purpose of the pan should be to impart more information to the viewer in the least amount of time.

The **tilt** is just like a pan only in the vertical direction. The same basic rules apply for its length, speed and purpose. The shot must start on one properly framed picture and end on another, showing relationship to or more information about the overall subject.

Dolly Shot   In all the shots previously discussed, the camera is in a fixed position while shooting. The dolly shot requires the camera to move while the shot is being made. For EFP work, this type of shot should be done on a dolly or a wheeled tripod. On uneven surfaces, tracks or a platform can be put down for the dolly to move on. This could make the shot very time-consuming to execute, not to mention more expensive to the overall production. For ENG work, the use of such extra equipment is usually out of the question. Therefore, the dolly shot becomes a walking shot for most ENG work. Sometimes someone with a bit of ingenuity can improvise a dolly using a grocery cart, wheelchair, bicycle, golf cart or car if there are crew members to help.

The point to keep in mind when using the dolly shot is that the *perspective* of the shot constantly changes as the camera position changes. This is the purpose of a dolly shot. It is similar to a zoom because it is a transition from one shot to another in real time. The difference, of course, is the change in perspective. It can add a sense of drama by moving closer to the subject in a dolly-in shot or moving away in a dolly-out shot. The advantage of the dolly shot is that the focal length stays the same as the shot changes. If the focal length is short, the depth of field will be great; moving the camera in to a closer shot will not lessen that depth of field. In a zoom the depth of field would steadily decrease (increase focal length) as you zoom in. The results may be similar but the effects are quite different.

The dolly shot can also be a point-of-view shot. In ENG, the walking dolly shot gives the feel of a point of view, if not of a specific character, then certainly of the viewer as if actually present. This point-of-view idea can work in many stories. For example, in the earlier shot of the long line of people, a dolly shot along the line would give the viewer a first-hand look at what it would be like to be in that line.

Another use of the dolly shot is to replace a pan shot to maintain perspective. Instead of panning a long row of TV sets in a showroom, a dolly shot can keep each set in the same perspective (size in the picture). The desired feeling of such a shot is the vast number of sets and not so much the relationship of the sets to the room. As in shots, framing is important at all times. A dolly shot has a beginning and an end, and each must be a good shot. For a walking, on-camera subject, a dolly shot can keep the subject framed in the same way but let the background change to impart new information to the viewer.

To get a feel for the effect of a dolly shot, try doing a shot you would be zooming on as a dolly shot with a fixed focal length. Often you will notice that the dolly shot has a greater impact and is more pleasing than the zoom. The only drawback is that the shot requires more time and sometimes more skill than the zoom. A walking shot can be too shaky to look good in many stories because it looks out of place with all tripod shots in the rest of the story. While most ENG work should be done on a tripod, spot news is actually a good place to learn the effect and importance of a dolly shot.

FOLLOWING THE ACTION

Following the action combines all shots and camera moves. Spot news is the best example of this concept because of the severe time constraints on getting the visual story. As a story unfolds under the fast-paced conditions of spot news, the photographer tries to stay with the subject or the important aspects of the story. To do this, the photographer's position and camera zoom must be used to get and frame all the camera shots necessary to tell the story. Because of the fast pace the camera never stops rolling. Often a zoom is necessary or a camera position must change, but the important idea is that the action must always be followed. The action can be allowed to leave the frame (a transition shot) but it must be picked up again with a minimum of lost time.

Sports coverage is the easiest example of following the action (or staying with the ball). The action should determine how the shot is framed and what the camera must do. If the action involves more than one subject, such as in basketball, then frame for them all. If it only involves one subject, such as a football running back, then stay with that subject in the best framing to visually describe the action. In some cases it may be best to hold the same focal length and let the action take place while panning to keep it in the frame. Too much camera movement or zooming can ruin the visual presentation of an event.

All the rules in the previous sections apply to following the action, especially the rule that too much of anything is bad. A photographer needs to do what is necessary to get the shot, but if the piece overuses pans and zooms it may be too annoying to watch while yielding little information to the viewer. As for framing in following the action, it is always good to lead the action a little with the shot. For example, a runner on a track or an ice skater should not be framed in the center but slightly off center with the fat side of the picture in front. (See Figure 5.18.) By the use of the empty space in framing action, you give the impression that the subject has someplace to go. The subject should not be running into the side of the frame but space should be left for the subject to run into.

Breaking the Rules

Rules are simply guidelines to help understand the basics of portable video. Once you become proficient with the basics, you will begin to see the ways you can break the rules and still achieve truly great results. The talking head is a perfect example of this. By ignoring the basic rules of framing, it is possible to put the interviewee anywhere in the frame if you know what you are doing. Producer Ray Farkas has built a reputation in the TV news business by using unusual framing for interviews. At first look, you would think they

Figure 5.18: As the camera follows the skater, the framing leads the subject to give her room to skate into.

violate everything known about framing. On a closer examination, you discover that the frame is not only emphasizing the subject strongly but adding editorial content to the environment. The frame packs quite a punch. It is framing as well as content that sticks in the viewer's mind. They not only remember the subject's words but other things about the subject as well. The Farkas style is not easy to copy. Without the fundamentals of good photography, a novice attempt would simply look as though someone made a mistake or was trying to be arty and failed.

Stories can be told with nothing more than tight shots or wide shots. A popular term in today's television business is "cinéma verité." A character on a TV sitcom once described it as meaning something in France but shaky camera in America. Even though the description comes from a comedian, that is exactly what it has become. The true art of cinéma verité is rarely seen on today's TV. Simply having the camera on your shoulder does not mean that you are being artistic in a French way. Unless you are chasing a subject, it mostly means you are lazy or simply do not care to provide the audience with pictures that let the subject be the center of attention instead of drawing that attention to yourself.

Style is what separates the basic from the truly artistic but style can only come from the basic. If you are just learning to shoot video and tell stories with a camera, you need to concentrate on the fundamentals.

6 Scriptwriting

Many scriptwriters feel that writing for portable video is easier than writing for the studio. This opinion probably stems from the fact that the portable video scriptwriter can have natural settings and does not rely upon artificially created settings in the studio. Also, the nature of portable video includes shooting for the edit, where a specific look or effect can be created by doing a number of takes with slight variations and selecting the one that matches the script best during the post-production process.

Portable video projects can be long or short, dramatic or comical, fictional or factual, but they are all derived from a script. Scripts are necessary for ENG and EFP because they are blueprints or diagrams of the way stories are actually put together.

Regardless of style, intent or format, videoscripts have something in common: they are all written for the spoken word, that is for the ear. Writing for video is unlike writing for the print media. Readers of the print media can read at their own comfortable pace. They can reread words or sentences whenever necessary. This puts the burden of comprehension on the reader.

In video the script must be written in such a way that is is comprehensible to the audience the first time it is heard (unless it is a training tape that can be replayed). All viewers see and hear the video at the same rate. Even if viewers watch a videotape by themselves and are able to replay it, video scripts should be understandable at the outset.

Writing for any script requires both common sense and talent. A writer needs common sense to realize that writing for the ear requires relatively short sentences, words and phrases easy to pronounce and unambiguous in their meaning, and a conversational style. Writers demonstrate their talent by conveying precise meaning and selecting creative and interesting approaches to the material. This is not always easy—many scripts deal with mundane factual material, such as a piece explaining how a mowing device is connected to a tractor. A talented scriptwriter can take dull factual material and present it in an interesting way.

ENG

Scripts for ENG stories are generally written by reporters involved in covering the events shown in the video portion of the story. These people are often trained in broadcast journalism and have certain conventions that they must follow. It is beyond the scope of this book to attempt to explain this procedure. (See the Bibliography for several books on ENG scriptwriting.)

Essentially ENG stories are written to convey precise and understandable material in an informative yet interesting way. The written material should address the questions: who, what, where and when.

The biggest difference between ENG and EFP scriptwriting is the fact that ENG scripts are almost always written *after* the video has been shot. After an event has been covered, the ENG writer reviews the tape and writes a script so that the raw footage can be edited into a finished story. This procedure is necessary because the reporter is often unsure of what is going to happen at the event or what the usable footage will be until after the video recording has been made. (Keep in mind that a reshoot or second take of an event is often impossible in ENG.)

The ENG script is written between the time the event is shot and the time it is broadcast. This usually means that the script is written during the afternoon just before the evening newscast. The ENG scriptwriter has hours or sometimes just minutes to write the script. This is quite different from scriptwriting for EFP.

EFP

Generally, EFP scriptwriters have much more time for the process than scriptwriters in ENG. EFP scripts are often written with enough lead time to allow for a careful review and revision process. The process allows a script to be evaluated not just for its meaning and effectiveness but also for its adherence to the capabilities of the production unit that will shoot it and the budget for the project as well.

Scripts for commercials, training tapes, entertainment, etc., can be written and rewritten until the scriptwriter, producer, director and client are satisfied. The scripts usually do not have to reflect the reality of an event or issue as they do in ENG, but they must reflect the concept and intentions of the client and/or producer.

The procedure for EFP scriptwriting is often careful and lengthy.

1. Goals for the script must be set.
2. The audience must be carefully analyzed.
3. A format must be selected.
4. A central visual theme should be developed.
5. Research must be done to learn about the concepts to be shown or explained in the script.
6. A treatment should be written that conveys the essence of the script.
7. An outline is prepared that lists in proper order all important aspects of the script.
8. A storyboard is often necessary to help others visualize your ideas.
9. Writing the script is next and is often followed by reviews and revisions.

Goals

Once the process of initiating a video project has begun, set your goals at a reasonable and attainable level. Attempting to present the entire history of a large corporation in a comprehensive and detailed fashion may be unrealistic in a 3-minute portion of a 10-minute video presented to stockholders at their annual meeting. It may also destroy your budget.

The best way to avoid a problem like this is to set specific goals. Goal outlining should be done on two levels. First determine the overall purpose of your project. Is it to entertain, inform, demonstrate or persuade? Then set very specific goals.

An instructional videotape that attempts to familiarize sales managers of a farm implement company with a new model tractor might have the following goals.

1. Provide information about the new model: size, weight, performance, cost.
2. Increase motivation to sell the new model by explaining bonuses and incentives.
3. Introduce marketing and sales procedures that will enhance sales of the new model.

Any communication may have three different kinds of effects on an audience: cognitive, emotional and behavioral. **Cognitive effects** are those that occur when the audience gains knowledge or information. **Emotional effects** are those that cause an attitudinal or mode change in the audience. The third effect, **behavioral change,** occurs when the audience actually changes its behavior in some measurable way, such as buying a new brand of detergent or brushing teeth more frequently. In the planning stage, these potential effects can be viewed as obtainable goals or objectives.

Many video projects do not have all three types of desired objectives. Videos made for artistic or entertainment purposes may only strive for an emotional effect. It is appropriate, however, to consider that all three effects may take place in your intended audience.

Knowing the Audience

Once you have decided what the goals are for your video, it is time to pay more serious attention to your audience. Your video project can be tremendously exciting, visually creative and perfectly shot but a total failure if your script is not written for the intended audience. Consider the difference in a script for a feature that will appear on a local broadcast station's magazine show and a script for a video that will be shown only to volunteers for a charity at their organizational meeting. The topic may be the same, but the style would be quite different. The feature is scripted to heighted awareness about the good things being done by the charity and the need for volunteers or donors to help. The video shown at the organizational meeting would be written to raise the enthusiasm and energy level of the audience and demonstrate or suggest specific behaviors needed to help the charity.

This same charity might want to produce a video for use in elementary schools to inform children about the importance of the the charity efforts. Obviously the language of the script and the pacing and style of the shooting and editing would be different from either the magazine feature or the video made for committed volunteers.

The more you know about your audience, the better. Demographic factors such as age, income, sex and education level are perhaps the best starting points to help you become familiar with the audience. Information about these factors will help you to make some basic decisions about your script. You may also want to consider psychological factors such as lifestyle, attitudes, personal interests and hobbies. Writing for a small well-defined audience can be very different than writing for a large heterogenous audience.

The exhibition of the final product is also a consideration. Will 10 people see the video? 10,000? Tens of thousands? How will the video actually be shown? On broadcast TV? Cable? A private showing to a small audience using a small TV monitor? A showing to an audience of 100 or more using a projection TV?

After you have carefully considered the audience, you can move on to deciding on your format.

Format

Video projects can be categorized by their format, which refers to the overall organization of the project. Broadcast-TV programs conform to a limited number of standard formats that provide understanding of the type of entertainment and a time frame for viewers. In broadcast TV, most programs are written for 30- or 60-minute lengths. The most common formats include:

- drama
- situation comedy
- newscast
- talk show/interview
- game show
- documentary
- sports or event coverage
- highlight (sports)
- compilation/video clips
- magazine/features
- action/adventure

Many of these formats have been adapted to nonbroadcast situations to get attention and to increase viewer appreciation. For example, a new health benefit could be explained to employees of a large corporation by an executive talking to the camera and using an occasional chart or graphic. Another approach might have employees in a simulated game show, like *Jeopardy*, trying to give answers to questions about changes from old benefits to new. The parody of the game show format gives the writers the opportunity to inject humor into what might be very dull material. Another approach might be to have a TV talk show host interview the company executive rather than have the executive do a talking head. The show becomes more visually interesting; the question-and-answer format allows the host to represent the audience and their predictable questions.

Other formats are more appropriate for nonbroadcast TV projects or those that are not program-length projects. These include:

- demonstration/how-to
- instruction/classroom topics
- music video
- video art
- commercial
- public service announcement

Choosing one of these formats or a combination can give your project a structure and organization helpful to you as a writer and to your audience as viewers.

Central Visual Theme

Your central visual theme should be stated as a short phrase or sentence that conveys the essence of your visual goal and the look of your video project. The statement should include the major visual elements of your project.

If the project is a 30-second public service announcement for the local public library, an appropriate phrase might be "Books are your windows on the world." An appropriate phrase for a five-minute demonstration videotape of a new computer workstation could be "The new Plum III computer fits your desk, your hands and your mind." By stating your visual idea in a short, succinct central visual theme at the beginning, you prevent further levels of script and other production complexities from obscuring your original intent. Should problems arise during the pre-production phase of your project, it may be helpful to review your initial statement.

Research

Since producers of EFP video can provide their services to many different kinds of clients, it should not be surprising to learn that the product or service that is the central topic of the video project is one that may require a familiarity with technical terms or procedures beyond the realm of the video producer's experience. Since a complete video project requires a fluency in both the video and audio portions of the project, research is often necessary to attain this fluency.

This fluency can be achieved in several ways: (1) interviews with knowledgeable individuals, (2) reading, (3) viewing other information previously prepared either by or for the client.

Interviews   Interviews with experts may serve two purposes: you may better understand the topic area and you may be able to videotape the expert and use some of the footage for your project.

Reading Material   Reading material should be available in the form of trade journals or newspaper or newsletter articles that explain the area and provide background information. Books are often available to give in-depth information for longer projects or those involving highly technical subject matter.

Client Information   Information that originated from the client is potentially the most helpful, but it is often overlooked. Press releases, marketing information, previous advertising or sales brochures can give a quick and accurate overview of the client's goals, techniques or philosophy.

For example, a few years ago, a sugar manufacturing company needed a videotape that would give a brief history of the company and describe the steps taken to manufacture sugar from sugar beets. The tape was to be produced for elementary schools and libraries.

After checking numerous possible sources, it was found that an old brochure gave much of the historical information and a 20-year old film had animation sequences in it that helped show and explain the complex technical processes involved. In fact, the animation sequences were still accurate enough that some careful editing allowed them

to be transferred to video and used to explain that portion of the company's operation. Needless to say, much time and money was saved as a result of the research for related materials.

Treatment

Presentations involving drama, characters and a plot require a stated treatment, or brief summary of the project, written in the earliest stages of pre-production to allow the creator (or scriptwriter) to tell the story and better orient the production team (even the scriptwriter). The treatment is a short capsulization of the setting, characters, points of view and the plot. Major events or changes in characters or characterizations should be mentioned in the treatment. While this step is required in fiction, it is strongly recommended for nonfiction. The treatment tells the story in narrative form (without dialogue) so that the client or financial backers have a good feeling for what the finished product will look like.

The treatment not only keeps the scriptwriter on track, but it also keeps other members of the creative team *and the client* on track. The treatment provides firm guidelines for everyone to remember throughout the creative process.

For informational projects that have a nonfiction style, the treatment may be quite brief—two or three pages for a short video. This type of treatment should contain three elements: goal, strategy and content.

Goal   The goal of the project should accurately reflect what the originator wants: training, promotion, publicity, or whatever. This should be accomplished in a few sentences or a single paragraph.

Strategy   The strategy of the production explains what method will be used to accomplish the goal of the production. If the goal is to teach salespeople how to use a new lap-top computer to enter sales data, then the strategy might be a step-by-step demonstration showing the computer and the data entry procedure. If the goal is to heighten awareness of a new health benefit, the strategy might be a simulated press conference with the most commonly expressed questions asked and answered. Obviously, your strategy should logically relate to achieving your goal. Your client should not wonder how your pure creativity is going to accomplish the goal. If the strategy does not make sense to the client at this stage, you are headed for big problems later on.

Content   The content need not be a verbatim script, but a general outline of what will happen and when. Being too specific is probably as inappropriate as being too vague. It is best to give yourself some creative wiggle room here. Often some of your original ideas will not pan out; leave room for slight changes to accomodate ideas that actually make it on to the video intact. But if you are too vague, the linkage between content, strategy and goal might not make sense to your client.

For most corporate video projects, a few pages specifying the treatment are sufficient. A complex fiction project with a 30- or 60-minute duration might require a 10- to 15-page treatment to help convey what the final product will look like. This type of treatment may include descriptions of the locations, characters and some camera direction as well.

Outline

Now all the facts, figures and visual ideas need to be organized so that they will form the skeleton for the body of your project. An outline should simply and succinctly list the points, facts, comments and visualizations that will tell your story in the appropriate order. You can easily reshuffle your ideas to form the best story at this stage. Allowing your outline to be reviewed by other production team members, other professionals or even the client may save hours of rewriting, re-editing or even reshooting. (See Figure 6.1.)

One convenient way to organize your outline is to use index cards. Utilize one idea, fact or visualization per index card, and include, when possible, a small sketch or photo to clarify the visual idea. Arrange your cards in a logical sequence, then try to tell your story by reading (and embellishing upon) each card in the sequence. A few attempts at this storytelling will probably reveal inconsistency, improper order and difficult or clumsy transitions that may be hiding in your future outline. Once your cards are in the proper order, construct an outline and allow others to give you some feedback.

Storyboard

The next step after the written outline is a storyboard or pictorial outline, which can be drawn up by the director, producer, advertising agency or even the clients. The storyboard is a roughed-out drawing of every scene to be produced in the video. Special pads of paper with blank TV screen outlines on them are usually used to maintain the proper aspect ratio for TV photography. (See Fig-

ure 6.2.) Under each picture or scene is the dialog or camera directions to be used. (See Figure 6.3.)

The storyboard allows all crew members to see exactly how the shots should look. This allows for all blocking, props, lighting, special equipment and special effects to be worked out while the video is still in pre-production. Costs and time can be more closely controlled using the storyboard, and the entire crew knows exactly how the finished product should look. Storyboards help eliminate the shocked comment that occurs upon showing the client the rough cut version: "That's not at all what we had in mind."

A good storyboard can save time in the long run and help head-off serious problems in the production of the piece. Even if no one involved in the production can draw, stick figures and rough drawings are better than none at all. Alfred Hitchcock never shot a frame of film until it was carefully drawn out in every detail on a storyboard.

Script

Now you are ready to write a script that will guide you in shooting the raw footage for your program. At this point your creativity and skill must be utilized. There are some guidelines to keep in mind:

1. *Visualize the items on your outline or expand the pictures from your storyboard.* Fill in the gaps between the panels of the storyboard; visualize the transitions. How do you get from one panel (or outline item) to the next? Think visually; then allow the audio portion of the script to enhance the video.

2. *Consider your writing style.* Do not write as if you are lecturing or writing a technical document or even a brochure. Make sure that your writing is conversational. It is best to try to create short sentences. This is the way most people talk to one another; therefore, it is appropriate in both dialogue or narration. Another suggestion is to avoid obscure or unfamiliar terminology unless the narrator explains the terms shortly before or after their use. Make sure that the dialogue or narration is appropriate for the speaker(s). You would not have the president of a corporation say, "Let's get your butts in gear," during a motivational video aimed at company workers. The statement, "Let's com-

Figure 6.1: Objectives and outline for a corporate video script. *Courtesy Allstate Insurance Co.*

NOTE TO REVIEWERS

This is the first draft of the video script for the video introducing the "Choice Program" and First Party Coverage to focus group participants. As reviewed and revised, the script will be used as the basis for recording and editing.

Program Purpose and Use

The primary purpose of this video is to help introduce the Choice Program to participants in focus group research at the Allstate Research Center.

We want the video to provide an easy-to-understand message that will enable the viewer to:

• Understand the coverages provided by the First Party Coverage option and what will happen in various claims situations

• Understand the broad benefits of the First Party Coverage option

• Be able to participate in a focus group discussion and provide their reactions to the First Party Coverage option.

Content

The major content points to be covered in the video are outlined below. The points are listed in the general order in which they will be presented in the video.

I. About this Tape
   A. Brief preview
   B. What's it it for you (the viewer) -- why you should watch this tape

II. Components of Auto Insurance
   A. Medical/Personal injury protection (PIP) -- injury to you or your passengers
   B. Bodily injury -- injury to another person in an accident
   C. Property damage -- damage to another's property
   D. Collision -- damage to your vehicle in an accident
   E. Uninsured motorist -- protection against injury or property damage loss caused by an uninsured motorist
   F. Under-insured motorist -- protection against injury or property damage loss caused by a motorist with insufficient coverage limits
   G. Comprehensive -- damage to your vehicle not the result of an accident

III. A Brief Explanation of How Third-Party and First-Party coverage Work
   A. Third-Party coverage (Tort)
   B. First-Party coverage (No-fault)

IV. An Overview of the First Party Coverage option
   A. Purpose -- to provide a "Choice" in auto insurance coverage
   B. Differentiation from tort
      1. No right to sue, except in certain cases
      2. Others can't sue you, except in certain cases
   C. Major benefits
   D. The Choice -- staying with or leaving the tort system

V. Details of First-Party Coverage
   A. Compulsory medical coverage -- First Party Injury
      1. Your own company pays for your medical expenses due to injury
      2. Limits
      3. Brings immunity to suits except for:
         a. drunk driving, criminal negligence, leaving the scene, intentional acts
         b. uncompensated economic injury damage, uncompensated non-auto economic property damage
         c. optional coverage can cover these exceptions
   B. Optional "Residual liability" coverage will handle certain special situations
      1. Uncompensated economic damages
      2. Tort immunity exceptions
      3. Driving out of state
   C. Other options to First-Party coverage
      1. Higher limits for the compulsory medical coverage
      2. Wage loss
      3. Loss of services
      4. Funeral benefits
      5. Coordination of benefits (brings a credit)
   D. Collision and Comprehensive -- Optional

VI. Scenarios -- What Happens If You Have First-Party Coverage And...
   A. You are in an accident caused by another first-party driver
   B. You cause an accident with a driver with third-party coverage
   C. A driver with third-party coverage causes an accident with you
   D. An uninsured motorist causes an accident with you
   E. Others

VII. Benefits of First-Party Coverage
   A. Freedom of choice
      1. Stay in or leave tort system
      2. Tailor coverage to your needs, resources, preferences
   B. Potentially lower cost for coverage
   C. More efficient compensation to accident victims
      1. Timeliness
      2. Fairness

VIII. Recap

IX. Conclusion

Figure 6.2: Blanks used for a storyboard by a corporate video operation. *Courtesy Motorola Gov't Electronics Group, Visual Media Productions.*

VISUAL MEDIA PRODUCTIONS

Ⓜ **MOTOROLA INC**

STORYBOARD

Project Number : ___ ___ ___ ___ ___ — ___ ___ ___ ___   Date : _____   Page _____ of _____

Project Name : _____   Contact Person : _____

Producer : _____   Director : _____   Writer : _____

VISUAL

AUDIO

VISUAL

AUDIO

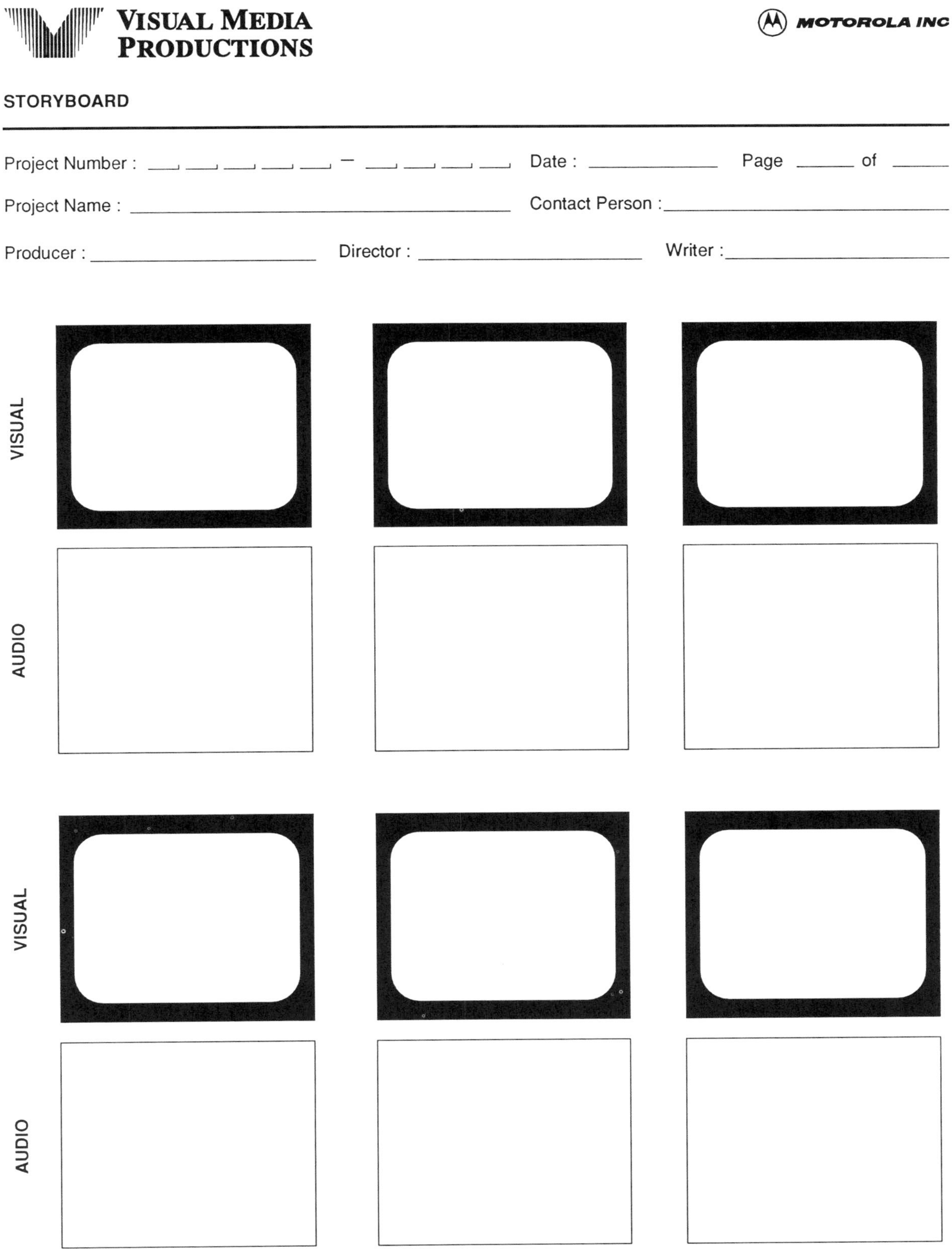

Figure 6.3: Completed storyboard for a local public service announcement.

Florida State
UNIVERSITY

NAME   LARRY CLARK

TIME   THIRTY SECONDS

Department of Communication
Video

Video Storyboard

Program/Project P.S.A. "THE RULES OF THE GAME"

Page __1__ of __2__

Date __JULY 1, 1987__

Shot   FADE UP- CU

"THE RULES OF THIS GAME ARE
SIMPLE..."

CUT- MCU

"___THE RULES OF THIS GAME
ARE SIMPLE..."

CUT- CU

"...EVERY TIME YOU DRIVE
DRUNK, YOU'RE TAKING A
CHANCE..."

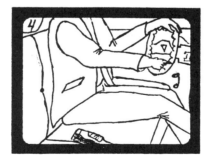

Shot   CUT- MCU

"...YOU RISK THE HUMILIATION
OF ARREST..."

CUT- CU

"...THE POSSIBILITY OF KILL-
ING OR INJURING YOURSELF..."

)(- SLOW ZOOM OUT

"...OR WORSE..."

MP 34

Figure 6.3: Completed storyboard for a local public service announcement. (cont.)

Florida State
U N I V E R S I T Y

Department of Communication
Video

Video Storyboard

Program/Project P.S.A. "THE RULES OF THE GAME"

Page __2__ of __2__
Date __JULY 1, 1987__

⑦	⑧ DON'T PUSH YOUR LUCK...	⑨ DON'T DRIVE DRUNK.
Shot CUT- XCU	)(	)(
"...THE RULES ARE SIMPLE: SOME GAMES JUST CAN'T BE WON..."		

Shot		

MP 34

Table 6.1: Terms used in scriptwriting.

Camera Shots	Common Abbreviations
Long shot, Wide shot	LS,WS
Medium shot	MS
Close-up Tight shot	CU, TS
Extreme close-up	XCU or ECU

Camera Movement	
Zoom or Zoom in	Z or ZI
Pan (left or right)	PL or PR
Dolly (in or out)	DI or DO
Tilt (up or down)	TU or TD

Transitions	
Cut, Take	---
Dissolve	Diss
Fade (in or out)	FI or FO

bine our energies and talents so we can get busy solving these problems together," would be more appropriate. A five-year-old would not normally say, "I seem to have developed an intense craving for an ice cream cone." More probably, a five-year-old would say, "Mommy, can I have some ice cream?" or "Gimme some ice cream!"

3. *Keep in mind that regardless of the specific goal of the video project, it must tell a story.* It should have a beginning, middle and end with an appropriate story line that attempts to meet your objectives. Make sure that your central visual theme is not obscured by an overly complex or convoluted story line.

4. *Include all necessary directions that explain comprehensively how to translate the written words and ideas into video information.* The style, clarity and completeness of the script should be such that

Figure 6.4: This storyboard (without audio) was drawn for a clay animation project designed to inform people about the importance of proper diet for cardio-vascular health. *Courtesy Arizona Heart Institute.*

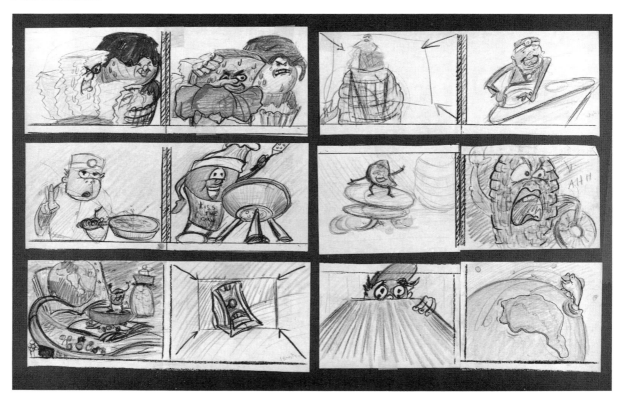

Figure 6.5: Scripts with revisions made after review. *Courtesy NAV-TV Services.*

Reviewer's Name   *L2/K9*
Title   *Autumn Prog Night*
Office   *2/CRBm*   Date   *1-24-92*

NED—LAND USERS (Navajo language version)

VIDEO	AUDIO
#1 Ext [Sunrise on the reservation over one of the sacred mountains, EAST or SOUTH]	Each dawn is a new beginning. The Mother Earth reaches out to meet the Father Sun.
#2 (Ext [Dramatic rock formation in Monument] ~~formation in Monument~~ *e*	Times seems to be at a standstill. The land of our home has lived through time. We have changed it very little.
#3 Ext (Sheep herd and shepherd]	Time stays with us - it is the center of our world, with its beauty all around us; from the east, south, west and north.
#4 Ext [Dramatic shot San Francisco Peaks]	*four* The land within the ✓ sacred ~~four~~ *e* *four sacred* mountains: *Names of the* ✓ *mountains should be spelled out.*
#5 Ext [Dramatic landscape at Shiprock and nearby mtns]	the land is sacred. The land is beautiful.
#6 Ext [CS face of Navajo woman]	The land is us. We love our land. We and our land are one.
#25 [DR WAYNE, NPHA 2, 6.36.25-6.42.03, COVER with chemistry experiment to indicate medical research - from NSP footage]	Issues such as AIDS have forced our schools to focus attention beyond more traditional learning. *and other serious diseases*
#26 [Back to DR WAYNE, NPHA 2, 9.22.19-9.24.19, hold just a second on DR WAYNE and dissolve to next shot]	What does all of this mean?
#27 [XLS rural school district from atop a hill, Jim's stock of Peach Springs USD] *Use CASA GRANDE FOOTAGE!*	NARRATOR There are more than a few voices proclaiming loud and fast that we have fallen behind other countries in the quality of services we provide in our schools.
#28 [Either blur the XLS of the school or slow fade to black]	Have we lost the ability to teach our young people?
#29 [Dissolve to sign on a classroom door - "This program has been discontinued due to lack of funding", TAPE O, 00.42.12-00.53.17]	To make matters worse, all this is happening at a time when the money to begin new programs - to deal with the expanded issues - is decreasing.
#30 [Young people walking down the street at night, footage]	The question is ~~deceptively~~ *e* (easy to understand) ~~e engaging~~. How do we keep our

81.3 (bracket grouping #25 and #26)

81.4 (bracket grouping #27 through #30)

Figure 6.6: A computer program designed to format and aid scriptwriting. *Photo courtesy Comprehensive Video Supply Co., Northvale, NJ.*

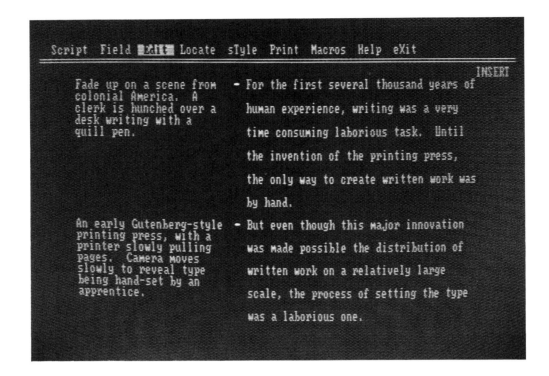

it allows a competent director who may not have been involved with the planning or scriptwriting to take the script and shoot the program as you intended it to be shot. (See Table 6.1 for some common production terms used in TV scriptwriting.)

5. *Expect revisions of your script.* No script remains intact in its first version throughout the production process. Your script should be considered a first draft. (See Figure 6.4.)

At this point, your script is ready for some fine tuning in the review process. (See Figure 6.5.)

Review   After the first draft is written, most scripts are subject to some sort of review process. For a practitioner of video art or a student of video, this review process is internal. The scriptwriter should re-read the script a few days after it is written and re-assess its merit. Does it depict the desired mood or concepts in the manner intended? Often some rewriting is necessary.

For scriptwriters in corporate video or any video made for a client, the client will generally want to read the first draft to see if it conveys the desired meaning. In many cases, this review process is not just helpful, it is mandatory. Production often cannot start without client approval of the script. Although it may seem tedious, this review and approval process is a safeguard for the EFP producer and scriptwriter. It often prevents a client from complaining about the scriptwriter's interpretation of his objectives.

This review process leads to a second draft and sometimes numerous successive drafts. When a draft is finally approved, it becomes a shooting script and acts as the guide for the actual production work.

Edit   After the raw footage has been shot, producers, directors and writers have another step in the script-writing process available to them that is often unavailable to those in studio TV. This step allows members of the EFP production team to view all tapes shot for the shooting script and decide if revisions to the original script are needed.

If changes are needed, the script can be rewritten to accommodate the editing process. Shot sequences may be changed, some shots or scenes may be deleted or some new shots may be added. One of the real advantages of EFP television over studio TV becomes especially apparent if new shots are needed: although equipment and personnel may need to be rescheduled, costly studio space will not have to be rescheduled. The additional EFP work can be done with as few as two or three crew members.

The final version of the script, the editing script, is completed at this point. It is the last step in the production process before the final edit of the program is completed. This step usually involves minor changes to fine-tune the most recent draft of the script and the raw footage into a completed program.

7 Pre-Production

Between scriptwriting and actual production of an EFP video comes the time for pre-production planning and preparation. This part of the production process should account for a majority of the total time spent on the project. Since careful and efficient planning at this stage can save time and money in the actual production phase, it is not unusual for video professionals to spend about 60% to 80% of their time in pre-production activities. The pre-production phase leads to a further divergence in methods between the ENG and EFP styles of portable video.

ENG

ENG style demands that events be covered as soon as they occur—leaving little or no time for careful planning. Preparations for upcoming stories are simply the experiences gained from the previous stories. Events occur on their own schedules, forcing the ENG photographer to cope with whatever difficulties are encountered without the benefit of a second take.

ENG situations call for a more bare bones style of TV photography. The number one goal is simply to bring back any video of the most arduous assignment. What you can do beyond this in the way of quality and content is what makes a news photographer great. Often all the equipment needed for the entire day must be carried by you at all times during that day; you must literally wear the gear. This limits the complexity of what you can do. It does not, however, limit the creativity of what you can do. Where EFP plans for every contingency and need, ENG plans for how much use can be derived from any one item of gear. The ability to travel quickly without an overload of equipment is essential due to the many deadlines in news gathering. A news photographer learns to anticipate how the story will unfold and what equipment will be useful on any given shoot mostly through experience. The trick to is to always have what you need before you need it and not have too much when you do not need it. The ability to improvise is the number one item on the list of things to bring.

Because of the nature of news stories, everything you may ever need should be in the van or car with you every day. A return trip to the station may be impossible and you may not even know what assignments you will have for that day. It becomes incumbent on the photographer, in many newsrooms, to find out what the next assignment is. Often the information given to the photographer is little more than a street address. Sometimes the assignment may require special considerations that the photographer really needs to know about. The first of these considerations is whether the story is to be done live or not. The planning for any event or story starts when the story is assigned. This may be days, hours or minutes before the shoot begins. More time available for planning gives news crews the opportunity to add more elements to their shooting plan and to raise the production values of the story. In the case of spot news you may have only the time it takes to drive to the location to formulate a plan as to how to shoot the scene, how much time to spend doing each task and how to get a live shot ready for the 5 p.m. news. A news photographer always has a plan waiting and ready.

EFP

EFP productions are usually shot from a carefully planned script or storyboard that gives the videographer control over much of what is shot. This preparation for EFP work is actually similar to the pre-production process in studio work, but with some important differences. As in studio pre-production, EFP pre-production includes crew and talent organization and selection; a large amount of scheduling, budgeting, graphics planning and preparation; and the procurement of clearance on copyrighted materials. Studio and EFP pre-production clearly differ, however, because of the added tasks of location selection, travel for talent and crew and transportation of equipment to the desired location for EFP production. (See Figure 7.1.)

PRODUCTION CREW

The responsibility for selecting the crew is commonly the domain of a person called the executive producer. This person first selects a producer who then helps the executive producer select the other major members of the production crew, including the director, videographer, audio engineer, lighting director, talent, grip and editor. The number of people assigned to each task depends upon the complexity of the project. A small project may require only one person in each area of responsibility or even one person who covers several areas. Larger projects require several people in each area.

News gathering crews are usually just one or two people: the photographer with or without a reporter. As market size or the demand for quality increases, a news crew can end up with the same staffing as a major EFP shoot. This is especially true in the area of documentary shooting. While technically a news-style product, documentaries are often done more like production work with large crews and several layers of creative and financial control.

Executive Producer

The production crew begins with the executive producer, who acts as a general supervisor of the project and often serves in this capacity on more than one project at a time. The executive producer initiates selection of the production crew after deciding upon project feasibility, given financial, equipment, personnel and time constraints. Very often the executive producer finds the money that funds the project.

A scriptwriter or project creator often seeks out a person to act as an executive producer who is able to find a funding source as well as the personnel and equipment to produce the script. Once the funding is located, the executive producer often decides generally how the money will be spent. Acting as a liaison between a client and the EFP team, the executive producer frequently selects (or at least suggests) the major members of the production team: the producer, director and talent.

The executive producer may also seek outlets for the exhibition of the project, if appropriate.

After initiating the project and selecting a producer, the executive producer often plays a minor role in the day-to-day operation of the project, which is delegated to the producer.

Producer

Usually selected by the executive producer, the producer is involved from the very beginning of an EFP project as the overall coordinator and schedule maker. Although the specifics of scheduling are often the responsibility of others on the team, the producer sets the parameters for the project (for example, the completion date). Having the best overall picture of the specific needs of the current production, the producer also knows the requirements for other projects that involve the production facility.

The pivotal person on the video production team, the producer makes the decisions regarding money, personnel selection and schedule.

For many projects done in-house at TV stations, production companies or corporations, the team may already be on staff and simply moves from project to project. Larger companies may have many people in pools of job categories selected on the basis of availability and not ability.

Figure 7.1: EFP preproduction checklist.

PREPRODUCTION CHECKLIST

Client work/general feasibility conversation
Proposal w/script
Specific feasibility decision
Projections of needs: costs, facilities, equipment, personnel
Budget compilation
Preparation of script for shooting
Analysis of script into component parts for final product:
     facilities and locations—studio, showroom, office, plant
     talent
     equipment
     graphics
     props, costumes, set design
     personnel for production
     number and length of shoots required during production
     post-production needs/scheduling
Location selection, survey, analysis, decision
Facilities decision and scheduling
Talent decision and scheduling:
     Is an audition necessary?
Equipment scheduling:
     Is equipment on - hand sufficient?
     Will renting/leasing be necessary?
Graphics, music, sound effects:
     Is artwork needed? Does it require outside work?
     Graphic design or computer graphics?
     Are there any computer/digital special effects?
     Is music required? Are composers/performers needed?
     Are sound effects needed?
     Order graphics, music, sound effects.
Clearance
     Will any copyrighted material be used?
Props, costume, set elements
     Do props need to be purchased or constructed?
Personnel
     How many shoots are there and how long will they be?
     Do you have enough qualified personnel to staff a crew for all shoots?
Post-production planning and scheduling
     Can editing be done in - house?
     Can the necessary editing time be scheduled either in - house or elsewhere?
Preparation for shooting
     Are rehearsals necessary?
     Can they be done on - location?
     Are crew or staff meetings necessary?

While this system works most of the time, it can lead to disaster. It is always better to have the production team hand-picked to get the best working relationships and the best end product.

Director

The director takes a script for a video project and translates it into a visual reality. The director is therefore an interpreter of the scriptwriter's words—a translator who takes written communication and transforms it into visual communication or makes a storyboard come to life. The director must coordinate activities just before and during production and coordinate the activities of the camera operator, talent and lighting director during rehearsals to create the effect called for by the script or storyboard.

Once the desired aesthetic effect is achieved, the director can begin the actual taping. Since most EFP productions differ from studio TV in that EFP usually involves one portable camera rather than several studio cameras, a good EFP director should know the **film style of shooting a scene**. The film style of direction does not require the one-take production with little or no post-production editing. Instead, in film style the director uses one camera to retake the scene from different camera angles and focal lengths to allow selection during post-production and the freedom to shoot scenes out of sequence for efficiency.

The director must also be able to work with people effectively. This may involve coaching, cajoling, coercing or otherwise persuading actors and other performers to get the desired performance from them. The director has to do this without alienating or demeaning the talent. One disgruntled talent can easily sour the efforts of an entire crew. Since field production involves smaller crews than studio work, each crew member's performance becomes essential to the success of the shoot. It is the director's responsibility to get the best possible work from the entire crew.

Videographer

The videographer in field TV has a larger responsibility than the videographer in studio TV primarily because the field director does not sit in front of a monitor bank in a sound-isolated control room and give directions as does the director in studio TV. In the field, the director may have a portable monitor (which may be small or washed out by the sun) but cannot always give direction during a shot because spoken commands may be picked up by live microphones.

The camera directions are given before a shot and then both director and videographer work together to make a shot look its best. A good videographer takes the director's verbal commands and gets the desired camera shots and finds additional shots through the variation of camera angle, focal length, selective focus or camera movement. This can make a scene more interesting after it is edited. If the director is working from a storyboard, the videographer gives suggestions as to how the camera can be placed and moved to match the desired effect and look.

Audio Engineer

The EFP audio engineer is responsible for accurately recording sounds on the location shoot. Unlike studio audio engineers who have the equipment storeroom within easy reach, the field sound engineer must anticipate all sound requirements of the location shoot and pack the necessary items to accommodate them. Once on location, the audio engineer must live with the equipment decisions already made.

While studio sound engineers often have large, easy-to-read VU meters and high-quality control room monitor speakers to assess sound quality, location audio engineers often cope with tiny VU meters located on a portable VCR and a set of headphones. Because of the popularity of the camcorder where the audio and video are recorded on a compound unit housed with the camera, the audio engineer may not even go on location on simple shoots. The camcorder is designed to be operated by one person: the videographer (or news photographer). The result can be that the videographer must also assume the duties of the audio engineer. This may be fine when the production is very basic but can be quite a burden on the videographer when the audio situation is complex. When more than one or two microphones are required, the person assuming audio responsibilities must set up the microphones with the use of a mixer and then provide one or two audio channels from the mixer to the camcorder for recording. Audio engineers sometimes record a separate sound track on an audio recorder to be added in post-production.

Location audio engineers are also subjected to a higher dose of RF interference than their studio counterparts. This interference (usually from a local AM radio station) can often ruin a sound recording by causing the VCR to act as a radio receiver. The stray signal may be recorded along with the audio. The radio station chatter may be welcome in your car on the way to the shoot but completely unwelcome in your location audio track since it is almost impossible to separate from your audio once recorded. The problem is often caused by a defective cable and can be a harsh reminder to those who take equipment (especially cables and connectors) for granted and do not test it or carry spares before leaving for location.

Lighting Director

The field lighting director is most useful when the location shoot is indoors. Since EFP shoots that take place in sunlight usually require fewer artificial lights, an extra crew member who just sets lighting instruments may be an unjustifiable luxury.

Location shoots require a crew member who can provide lighting that will satisfy the basic needs of the camera and the aesthetic requirements of the script. The lighting director should not only have a thorough knowledge of lighting techniques and instruments but also a familiarity with the specific demands of the lighting situation and the electrical power capabilities of the locations.

Often the photographer functions as the lighting director and simply uses an assistant to help set the lights. As the size or requisite speed of a shoot increases, the more a lighting director is needed. The photographer may need to start blocking and shooting one location while the lighting director and crew start lighting the next location to move the production along at a quicker pace.

Grip or Utility

In the film industry almost every member of the crew has a specific job title that has evolved over the years. Jobs like best boy, gaffer and key grip are lumped into one title for TV production: the grip. People from a TV studio background usually call them utilities. Unlike the film industry, these grips or utilities can cover quite a broad range of jobs on the production unless otherwise limited by a union agreement.

On any given crew, one or more members function as a grip whose responsibilities are to hold, or grip, reflectors or lights, a shotgun microphone, the VCR or any other piece of equipment that requires attention during the shoot. The grip is often an assistant or apprentice to one of the other crew members and should have a basic knowledge of the equipment, that is, knowing the equipment

by name and how to handle it. Because of the responsibility of holding equipment during the shoot, the grip should be steady and capable of moving equipment in and out of location as well as the vehicle used for transporting the equipment.

Talent

Selecting talent is a somewhat different chore from selecting other members of the team. While other crew members are most often employed by the same company as the producer, the talent may not be. In a half-dozen different shoots, it would not be unusual to have a different main talent for each one. This may not be the case, however, for industrial video for training and demonstration purposes or for internal public relations programs that have a regular host.

Talent may be selected by the executive producer or committee, producer or director. Talent can be locally acquired on location (that is, in another city) or imported with the rest of the crew. One mistake often made by beginners is to select nonprofessional actors as talent because of their voice or overall appearance. This can be dangerous.

Inexperienced talent often force numerous retakes—they may be unable to take directions to correct mistakes. Sometimes nonprofessionals look terrific in person or in rehearsal but cannot adapt to the real situation when taping. The advice here is to stick to experienced professionals whenever budget allows.

As in so many areas of today's TV production, the better professional is more likely to be in a union or guild. This is very much the case with talent. Any professional performer sooner or later is required to join either the Screen Actors Guild (SAG) or the American Federation of Television and Radio Artists (AFTRA). A requirement of membership is the commitment to never work without a union contract even in a non-union production. This means you will have to pay minimum professional rates (and maybe more) to have a union professional in your show.

Editor

The editor takes the original, or raw, footage that has been shot and, with the help of a script, reassembles the program into its proper order. Often the scenes are shot out of sequence and numerous takes are available for each scene. This allows the editor to use some creativity and professional skills to produce a finished master tape that is creative and visually pleasing. However, the master tape must also follow the accepted rules for keeping the flow of the program visually and chronologically correct, while yielding the meaning intended by the producer, director and scriptwriter.

A good editor enhances the ideas of the people who wrote and visually interpreted the script without changing either its meaning or its effect upon the viewer. When hiring an editor, look for two skills: a dexterity with the editing machinery and a strong sense for how to tell a story visually.

SCHEDULING AND COORDINATING

Scheduling an EFP project is often a slow and difficult process. Since many crew members in EFP work have other responsibilities and video equipment is constantly being used for a variety of projects, getting a full crew with all the necessary equipment sometimes seems like trying to carry all of the unfolded laundry without a laundry basket. If you stoop down to adjust a scheduled shoot time for a critical crew member, you may find that you have dropped something else, such as the availability of a special camera or even the talent. Occasionally an unforeseen delay, albeit a short one, can cause a serious problem in post-production, such as missing a scheduled visit to the editing suite of your choice.

Factors to Consider

When creating your schedule, first consider the general categories of items to be scheduled. You have people, equipment, materials, and facilities or locations. Prioritize these items based on your lack of control over them and schedule those items first over which you have little control. The logic here is that once you have locked into place those items that may have no flexibility, you can more easily schedule in the more flexible items. A couple of examples can help to illustrate.

First, your independent production company may have contracted to shoot a five-minute demonstration/sales tape for a company that manufactures a farm implement which attaches to a small tractor and removes weeds that grow between the rows of soybean fields. Obviously, the first thing to do is find out what a soybean is and where it is grown. If you are not from the Midwest, you may think that soybeans grow in health food stores. Hopefully, your client can not only orient you to soybeans and the new product but also suggest an

appropriate location such as the client's own test plots for the shoot.

Factors such as soil conditions, weed height, soybean height and weather may dictate whether you can actually go into the field for a demonstration. In other words, you must know the details and limitations of your location. After all these factors are considered, a window of time (for example, the last week of May) can be designated as the best period of time for the shoot to take place.

A second example probably represents a more common situation. An advertiser requests that your independent production company shoot a 30-second commercial featuring a new line of small kitchen appliances. Since the appliances require a precise setting and lighting situation, you decide that a studio is needed.

As is the case with most smaller production companies, you do not own a studio or a space large enough to house the necessary set and lights. In this case, you must find a studio affordable and technically acceptable. The studio must also be available at a time that will allow you enough post-production time to have the commercial completed before the first scheduled broadcast date. Once you have the studio scheduled, you can proceed to schedule other items.

These examples were chosen because location or facilities are often the least available and not within the producer's control. But any necessary item can have the least availability. Your talent may have only two days a month for shooting; the electronic cinematography camera that you need to rent may be in high demand and short supply; your whole team may have a sporadic schedule of shots for previously scheduled projects.

As a rule of thumb, you can expect to schedule the following categories of items (listed in descending order of scheduling difficulty).

1. Location or special facilities (studio, office building, yacht)
2. Special equipment (fog machine, fireworks, special spotlight)
3. Talent or crucial crew members (the famous spokesperson or star)
4. Post-production time/facilities/personnel
5. Graphics, props
6. Crew members for non-crucial assignments

Keep in mind that for any given shoot, any or all of these can be difficult to schedule.

Guidelines for Schedule-Making

There is no set formula to guide your schedule making, but here are a few hints that will come in handy when going about the chore:

1. *Be flexible.* Do not allow your own inflexibility to create scheduling problems. Even if you do not like starting a project on Friday, it may be the best starting day when you consider the schedules of others.
2. *Do not schedule too tightly.* Add time for reshooting or catch-up. If your shooting will be done outdoors, make sure you include some rain dates.
3. *Consult past schedules whenever possible.* How long did the same crew take for a similar project in the past?
4. *Have contingency plans.* What is the probability of equipment failure? Are certain pieces of equipment prone to failure in the field? Make sure that equipment failure, crew no-shows or talent problems do not prevent you from meeting your completion deadline.

LOCATION SELECTION AND SURVEY

In this phase of pre-production, the actual shooting location must be selected and investigated for specific information to facilitate the actual shoot. The script will probably guide you to a few choices for the location of your shoot. Many times the location is actually dictated by the script (for example, Disney World, a particular shopping center or the corporate president's office). In this case you can avoid the selection process and go right to the scouting procedure.

When the script gives only a general description of the location (for example, the backyard of a suburban home or a classroom), you have to select a few possible locations and scout them with a visit to see if they will satisfy your needs. Beyond the general look or aesthetics of the place, each location that you intend to use must meet some specific requirements. (See Figure 7.2.)

During this visit you may find it helpful to conduct a survey for later comparison with surveys taken at alternate locations. An excellent way to do this comparison is to use an instant camera such as the Polaroid. Using these still shots you can sit in the comfort of the office and discuss with other members of the team which site would be better suited to the production and what problems other members foresee. The following is a list of some of the questions you need to ask during the site survey or at least before the final decision is made.

1. *Is the location accessible?* A beautiful mountain meadow or an island in the middle of a lake may be aesthetically perfect, but if your crew can only reach it on foot, by canoe or by specially equipped, four-wheel drive vehicles you should be prepared to pay for that or look elsewhere.
2. *Can you get permission to use the site?* The owner might let you visit but not necessarily bring your 10-person crew, equipment, vehicles and the curious onlookers often attracted by the sight of a video camera. Permission in writing is the safest method. A check of local laws regarding shooting is necessary: a permit may be required.
3. *Can you maintain the appropriate traffic control?* Shooting on a street corner or sidestreet may seem easy at a 7 a.m. visit, but how busy would it be if you shot at 11 a.m.? Sidewalks or even hiking trails can be full of curious people or even not-so-curious people who demand the right-of-way. Make sure that the owner, park officials, city or highway police agree to let you divert traffic from your location. In many cities, permits are required to shoot on or near any public property. These permits may also require fees and proof of insurance coverage.
4. *What kind of lighting do you have?* Full sun can be as troublesome as no sun at all. You may need to add fill light to harsh shadows or shaded faces. If artificial light is preferred, can you somehow eliminate the unwanted light? Time of day may dictate your shooting schedule.
5. *What are the sound characteristics of the location?* Empty rooms without carpeting or draperies may cause echoes. Cluttered rooms with rugs and draperies can be devoid of natural ambience. In most cases, adding sound is no problem but taking away sound is nearly impossible. A too-noisy location is highly undesirable or may require highly specialized microphones. Again, try to find out what the location sound will be at the approximate time of day at which you will shoot.

Figure 7.2: Location scouting report used in corporate video. *Courtesy Motorola Government Electronics Group, Visual Media Productions.*

MOTOROLA INC.

VISUAL MEDIA PRODUCTIONS

LOCATION SCOUTING REPORT - Video

Project Number : ___ ___ ___ ___ ___ — ___ ___ ___ ___ Scouting Date : ________

Contact Person : ______________________ Phone : ________

▪ **ADDRESS OF LOCATION :** ______________________

Directions/Parking ? ______________________

FEEL FREE TO DRAW OUT DIRECTIONS

▪ **SPACE REQUIREMENTS :**

Number of Camerpersons : ________ Camera Positions : ______________________

Descibe Shot/Activity : ______________________

▪ **LIGHT REQUIREMENTS ;**

Level Required : ________ Source of Light : ________

Ceiling Height : ________ Ambient Light : ________

Reflective Surfaces : ________ Sun Location : ________

▪ **SOUND :**

Recording Sound : ________ ☐ Sync ☐ Wild Potential Interference : ________

Ambient Sound Present : ______________________ ☐ Use ☐ Avoid

▪ **POWER :**

Location of Outlets : ______________________ Capacity ? ________

Location of Circuit Breakers : ______________________ Tie In ? ☐ Yes ☐ No

Engineer/Maintenance Contact : ______________________ Phone : ________

6. *Is electrical power available at the location?* If there is none, you may only need to pack some batteries. But if artificial light is required, you will have to generate your own AC power. This may be accomplished with a gasoline-powered generator, but this is another piece of equipment that adds its own bulk and weight plus that of its fuel. Also keep in mind that video lights require *much* power and the generators produce noise as well as power.

7. *Is there an acceptable spot available for camera placement?* Many panoramic views available to the scout may be unavailable to a cumbersome video camera with attached tripod and cables. Make sure that there is a safe spot for your three-legged friend.

8. *Down the location allow convenient loading and unloading?* Are the doors and hallways wide enough, the floor even enough to allow your crew to roll in the cases of equipment? Where can you park the equipment van? Inconvenient access can add unnecessary and costly time to your shoot.

9. *Will the location be available at any time after the scheduled shoot?* It does not happen often, but even professionals can lose, destroy or record over raw footage before the edited master is completed. Clients or producers can change their minds about how the program should look and sometimes require a return to the location for a reshoot. Even if this is a rare necessity, it is a good idea to pick a location that allows a possible return for additional shooting.

10. *What crew conveniences are available?* Will the crew have to pack their own lunches? They may need adequate water, bathroom facilities, shade or a cool spot to rest. Full sun for a full day or no sun at all may lead to some very unhappy crew members. If talent has been hired to be on location, they may have special needs that require special facilities, such as a dressing room trailer parked at the site.

11. *Will the shoot be sent via microwave or satellite to another location?* Can the signal that you send to the other location be seen or are their buildings, mountains or interferences that may require special arrangements?

12. *Is safety and security an issue?* Can you physically watch all your equipment (and perhaps all your people) to guarantee safety throughout your stay? How cold or hot does it get at the location? Does your insurance include coverage for shooting at the location or under the circumstances?

GRAPHICS AND PROPS PREPARATION

The pre-production stage is the appropriate time to order the graphics and other necessary materials to have them ready before actual production begins. For most productions, this will include artwork for studio cards that do not have to be videotaped in a studio, photographic work for slides, film footage (for example, animation) or computer-generated animation or graphics. In large production houses, most of these things are done in-house by staff artists, photographers, cinematographers or computer specialists. Smaller production units often have to find specialists who can provide these materials as subcontractors.

This stage of the production process is the appropriate time to locate costumes, makeup accessories, set props and other items necessary for the production. If a set or props need to be constructed, initiate the process at this point.

CLEARANCE ON COPYRIGHT MATERIALS

If you expect your video project to really be yours after it is completed, it is best to make sure that *all* the material you use has been created by you or people who are working for you on the project. If you or one of your co-workers uses material owned by others, you may find yourself spending time with lawyers instead of looking for more video projects to produce.

The use of other people's material is copyright infringement; if you are caught doing it, you have created a legal problem for yourself. The problem arises very often when copyrighted music is used without permission. There are four simple approaches to avoiding this problem.

1. *If you need music for your program and the music you choose is copyrighted, contact the copyright holder (record company, music publishing company or individual artist) in writing and ask for per-*

mission to use the material. In your request, be as specific as you can as to your intentions. Name the material, the excerpt (if appropriate), the program it will be used in, the distribution or exhibition plans and any other relevant information. If you do this far enough in advance of your post-production time, you may get an approval for use of the materials or *clearance* as it is referred to in the publishing business.

2. *Use material that is in the public domain—material that has never been copyrighted or material whose copyright has expired.* Material that has not been copyrighted is probably available from your local amateur composer or music student. They may have excellent material already composed or may be able to compose music tailor-made for your project. Material composed long ago such as old folk tunes ("I've Been Workin' on the Railroad" or "Oh, Susanna") or classical music that could be performed especially for your project is generally available for use since the copyright has long since expired. (Bach and Beethoven are rarely offended when you use their material.)

3. *Purchase the material or subscribe to a library service that provides music or other material such as sound effects.* These services work in two ways. One way allows you to use the material as often as you need to use it; you buy this privilege when paying for the material and its use is at your discretion. A second type of service involves a needle-drop fee. Music library services provide you with the material, but you must pay when you use it. Hence, every time your needle drops on the record for actual use in a production, you owe the service a fee.

4. *Hire a musician or musical group that will use original compositions and perform them for you.* Once you pay for this service, you should own the privilege of using the material.

TRAVEL PLANNING

By definition, all EFP involves some type of travel. Some set procedures for travel will help you to cope with the trials and tribulations of constantly leaving your home base to get the work done. If the travel is local and requires only a reasonable amount of driving time, a minivan, station wagon or hatchback auto can possibly serve the needs of a small crew and a one-camera shoot.

Transporting Equipment

For out-of-town shoots, it is best to have plenty of space for backup equipment, extra personnel, extra tape and perhaps some test or repair equipment. If your shoot is three driving hours away from your studio or office, you certainly do not want to waste time sending the vehicle back for an extra battery, cable or mike.

A van or truck might also allow you to bring a power generator when needed. Sometimes renting the appropriate vehicle allows you to bring all the necessary equipment and personnel along and prevents the need to hire free-lance personnel or rent equipment at the location.

While EFP crews tend to carry their equipment in cases and use different vehicles for different shoots, an ENG crew usually has a dedicated vehicle with the equipment always stored in that vehicle. The typical news van has many built-in shelves and storage areas for the gear (including the camera) that allow quick and easy access. Most ENG gear is kept as ready-to-shoot as possible because of the ever-present possibility of spot news happening. In these situations, seconds can mean the difference in getting the shot or not. The camera system has to be in a constant state of readiness; just turn it on and shoot. This also means that the gear must be in a secured state while riding in the vehicle at all times. You cannot have equipment rolling around or falling over while you are driving. Careful thought has to be given as to how the gear will be carried. The goal is to get as much equipment in the van as possible, keep it readily accessible, and at the same time keep it safe under all kinds of driving conditions. (See Figure 7.3.)

Equipment Cube

Whether you drive a car, truck or other vehicle, you should know the volume and weight of your equipment before your shoot so that you can compare these figures with the available storage space and maximum load handling capability of your vehicle. This information is probably available in the owner's manuals for your equipment. Before renting a vehicle for a shoot, you should find out how much cubic space is needed for your equipment.

Figure 7.3: Equipment checklist.

EQUIPMENT CHECKLIST

CAMERA
- ☐ Set up and registration
- ☐ Charged batteries
- ☐ AC power supply
- ☐ Camera control unit
- ☐ Distribution amplifier/equalizer
- ☐ Composite/component adapter
- ☐ Wide angle lens/adapter
- ☐ Filters
- ☐ Waveform and vector scopes
- ☐ Tripod w/head
- ☐ High hat
- ☐ Tripod wheels/dolly
- ☐ Boom/crane
- ☐ Steadi-cam/Tyler mount
- ☐ Suction mount
- ☐ Gyro lens
- ☐ Tripod adapter plate
- ☐ Lens cleaner and tissue
- ☐ Shipping case
- ☐ Weather protection

LIGHTING
- ☐ Open-faced lights
- ☐ Fresnel lights
- ☐ HMI lights
- ☐ Reflectors
- ☐ Silks/scrims/butterflies/flags
- ☐ C-stands
- ☐ Extension cords
- ☐ Blue gels or dichroic filters
- ☐ Colored gels
- ☐ Black-out cloth
- ☐ Grip equipment
- ☐ Sand bags/water bags
- ☐ Spare lamps
- ☐ Gloves

RECORDER
- ☐ Record/play test

- ☐ Charged batteries
- ☐ AC power supply
- ☐ Playback machine
- ☐ Color monitor/outdoor hood
- ☐ Coaxial cable/barrels
- ☐ RF cable
- ☐ Multi-pin cable
- ☐ Tape stock
- ☐ Head cleaners
- ☐ Shipping/carrying case
- ☐ Audio monitoring headsets

AUDIO
- ☐ Omnidirectional/shotgun
- ☐ Hand-held/lavelier
- ☐ Fishpole/boom
- ☐ Wireless
- ☐ Filters
- ☐ Format adaptors
- ☐ Mixer/stereo
- ☐ Cables
- ☐ Wind protection
- ☐ Sound panels

ODDS AND ENDS
- ☐ Duct tape
- ☐ Rubber mats
- ☐ Plastic tarps/trash bags
- ☐ Rope
- ☐ Contact cement
- ☐ Tool kit
- ☐ Aluminum foil
- ☐ Spring clamps
- ☐ Colored tapes
- ☐ Magic markers/pens
- ☐ Self-stick labels
- ☐ Chairs
- ☐ Food/water
- ☐ Talent make-up
- ☐ Hair spray

ADDITIONAL ITEMS FOR THIS SHOOT

Figure 7.4: For any type of travel, your equipment should be well packed in protective cases; the number, size and weight of the cases should be carefully computed.

This can be done by simply stacking your equipment on the floor in a compact manner and measuring the height, width and depth of your cube. (Hint: try to arrange it neatly and compactly.) (See Figure 7.4.) First, multiply height by width by depth to find the volume. Then compare this amount to the volume that you would get by adding the measurement figures for the separate pieces of equipment as listed in the owner's manuals. The figures from the specifications should be slightly less because of the added dimensions of cases. Also, you will have non-square items in your equipment cube that will waste space.

This procedure may seem time consuming, but it only needs to be done correctly once. New pieces of equipment can usually be added to the list without going through the cube procedure. After you know the amount of cubic space you will need, it will be easier to select the appropriate vehicle for rental or purchase.

Air Travel

When the location is many miles away, air travel may be the only means of transportation. Because of the large expense involved you are faced with some tough decisions: Should you bring a full crew and pay their airfare, lodging and meals or hire free-lance professionals at the location? Should you bring your own equipment, pay for its transportation, risk its rough handling at airport loading and unloading or pay to rent equipment at the location?

Both questions are complex and depend upon the availability of qualified personnel and reasonably priced professional equipment that is dependable. Keep in mind that renting equipment often means changing equipment or brands and operating procedures may be different. Do this only if your personnel is experienced.

Whatever your decisions, make sure that you make your travel plans well in advance of your shoot date. Nothing is more aggravating than going through your travel decision-making process only to find that the vehicle you want to rent is not available or the flight you need is booked. Air travel reservations and tickets bought in advance of the shoot date often result in discount fares, which may allow you to bring the extra crew member or piece of equipment.

Travel Tips

Here are some travel pointers to consider before travelling:

1. *Never put your camera, camcorder or recorder in with the baggage or air freight.* Always hand-carry these items as carry-on luggage, and either stow them on the floor beneath your feet, in the overhead bin covered with airline blankets or strapped in an empty seat next to you. Many news companies actually buy a seat for the camera so it can be guaranteed its own space. The camera and recorder are the most important pieces of equipment you have and you cannot take a chance on them being dropped from the cargo bay door by a reckless handler or in Chicago when you went to Los Angeles. You must also be prepared to *shoot* tape at any time before, during or after the flight. You should have at least one battery, a tape and a mike with you at all times as well as the camera.

2. *Send all of your cases through as luggage.* Never ship any of your gear air freight unless you will not need it for awhile after you get where you are going. Air freight can take a day or more to get there.

3. *Keep all your cases at a reasonable size and weight.* Any cases larger than the biggest suitcase typically used by travelers or any case weighing more than 50 pounds will be rejected by the airline. This may mean more cases, but at least they will all be boarding the same flight as you.

4. *Expect to pay an excess baggage fee for most of your cases.* It is not unusual to have 15 or more cases with you for production shooting or extensive news shoots. It may cost more than sending them by freight but they will be there when you are. There often is no other option, especially for a traveling news crew.

5. *Call the airline in advance to tell them what you are bringing.* The airline may be able to help in getting the cases checked through and make better arrangements for your camera on the plane. They are used to dealing the with TV crews.

6. *Make sure everything is well packed and padded.* Remember those TV commercials with the gorilla throwing the suitcase around? It is not far from reality.

7. *Make a list with brand names, model numbers and serial numbers of everything you are taking.* Leave one copy at home, and keep one copy with you at all times.

8. *Remember that thieves know what expensive video equipment cases look like.* In a large airport an inattentive photographer can lose a case or two in a split second.

9. *Have a Skycap help you whenever you can.* This costs more money but secures the equipment from theft makes it easier to haul.

10. *Get a car or van that you can work out of the whole time you are on the shoot.* If the car is just big enough to hold the crew and gear with no room to spare, it may be quite an inconvenience to dig out equipment every time you need something. It may be better, though more costly, to rent a bigger vehicle to give yourself some room to work. At least you will not be unloading the entire car at every stop.

Foreign Travel

Traveling outside the United States can be fun and challenging but also a major headache for those unprepared. Each country has its own way of doing things; many do not have the rights of a free press. Doing business as usual could land you in jail and, in some repressive countries, can actually get you executed. These are not things to be taken lightly. Do extensive research regarding the countries you will be traveling in to see what media restrictions may be in place. Permits may be required to do any kind of professional photography, including news. Find someone who has shot in that country before, and gain from their experience.

Besides the political concerns that can be dangerous to your health, there are economic concerns. Most countries, including the United States, have import/export laws placing tariffs on certain high-quality photographic and electronic equipment. After going to certain countries and returning to this one, you will be asked to prove that the equipment you have is indeed yours and that you bought it here after paying the proper taxes. The best way to prove this is to have a **carnet,** a document recognized by the Customs Service that guarantees that the equipment is yours. You need a complete list of all your equipment with brands, serial numbers, purchase prices and model numbers. You should have many copies of this list with you as you travel. The carnet requires the posting of a bond for this list of gear (up to 10% of the equipment's value), but the document is recognized around the world. The next best solution is to simply have the gear registered with the Customs Service. This paper is for re-entry to the United States, but some countries also take it as proof of ownership. Always travel with as much documentation as possible. It is not unheard of to have gear confiscated or impounded for lack of documents. There are companies in almost every airport both here and abroad that offer a customs help service. These customs brokers are simply facilitators that, for a fee, can guide you through any customs clearance legally.

Press credentials are very useful in a foreign land. Officials at many entry points to a country are accustomed to seeing traveling news crews. Showing a press pass, even a home-town press pass, can prove effective. If your gear looks worn and has ID stickers of the station on it, few customs officials question its origin. If it is EFP gear that looks new, you will need documentation. A letter from the production company or from that country's consulate introducing you is better than nothing. Always have a return ticket with you even if it is for an incorrect date. Coming into a country with new or near new video gear and a one-way ticket can send up a very large red flag. You may find yourself trying to spring your gear from the impound cage for the next few days.

Always have a large amount of cash with you. It is amazing how many problems can be solved with the right amount of money in a foreign land. Credit cards and traveler's checks are fine in the hotel but not elsewhere. Bribery is not a nice word in this country, but is a way of life in many parts of the world. Gratuities may be a better word, but regardless of what you call it you had better be prepared for it. Never let anyone see how much money you have, and never keep it all in one place. A healthy dose of paranoia and some pre-planning can make your trip a smooth and successful one.

8 EFP Styles

EFP style encompasses many different types and applications of portable video. An easy definition of EFP is simply professional portable video *not* for broadcast journalism or ENG. While this definition tells us what it is not, it does not give us a sense of what EFP is or what style is necessary to produce good-quality EFP work. A better approach to understanding EFP style is to look at the various applications of portable video, the conditions under which productions are made and the audience for whom the video work is intended.

Unlike ENG where the audience is the general broadcast viewer, EFP often has a very specific audience. ENG concerns an event that is about to or has already occurred; EFP has a very specific purpose, such as a commercial or public service announcement, the promotion of a new product line or training about a new procedure.

In EFP, the key is planning. Careful pre-production and scripting help ensure that the final product is purposeful, effective and affordable. In a corporate setting the choice of EFP depends upon whether it is the best way to get a message across; that is, whether it is cheaper and/or better than other methods such as face-to-face communication. There is a sequence of planning in any EFP project that closely follows the sequence of events in writing a script. When a decision is made to embark upon a video project, the first questions that must be asked are "What do we hope to achieve by this project? What are the objectives?"

In corporate work the objective most often is to inform the audience of something such as a new or old product, a new benefit to employees, a reiteration of an existing policy or an introduction of a new corporate executive.

Another very common objective is to help create an attitude or stimulate motivation. A motivational tape may be created to inspire salespeople to promote and sell a new line of cosmetics or a new attachment to farm tractors. The project may include sales techniques, product information or a demonstration of how the product is used. The goal for this type of project is to inform, create or change an attitude and evoke a certain type of behavior. Corporate video is aimed at a *specific audience* to achieve a *specific purpose*. Rarely is it produced just for entertainment purposes.

Performance video, music video, nature and documentary video and video art are generally produced for entertainment purposes. These styles are often carefully pre-produced and scripted but do not always have very specific objectives beyond entertainment; the audience targeted is often more general. Outlets for exhibition are also more general; this type of video may be shown on broadcast, satellite or cable TV, in classrooms, theaters, festivals or contests. The audience often selects itself. The showing of the video is publicized in broadcast TV listings in the newspaper, in a flyer about a festival or even in a class syllabus. The audience decides if it wants to view it.

This chapter covers seven common categories of EFP style: (1) corporate and professional videos, (2) public service announcements and commercials, (3) performance videos, (4) sports videos, (5) music videos, (6) nature and documentary videos, and (7) video art.

CORPORATE AND PROFESSIONAL VIDEOS

The term "corporate video" has become a popular catch-all term for a number of types of EFP video. This category can include almost all professional non-broadcast users of portable video whose purposes are not entertainment. Some users of this EFP style are not necessarily members of corporations; in fact, many are not. Educational institutions, governmental agencies, labor unions, professional associations, clubs and civic organizations are common users of this type of video production.

Numerous types of video fit into the category of corporate video; the most common are news, information and public relations videos. Especially popular in large and/or decentralized organizations where face-to-face contact among members is difficult or unusual, these videos are used as a means of disseminating information efficiently and maintaining cohesiveness among members.

Corporate News Show

Corporate video often takes the form of a company news show. The show consists of several common elements: messages from or profiles of top management; company-wide news such as recent achievements in sales, profits, safety or growth; branch or regional news; and employee news. Although this communication is called news, it almost never includes hard news (for example, auto wrecks, burglary, or fires) and is never investigative in an adversarial way. This type of video is pure internal public relations. It is a way of making a large organization seem more personal and familiar. (See Figure 8.1.)

The host or reporter on an internal company news show conducts on-location interviews, reads news copy over video or gives lead-ins to packages of stories about the company and its employees. The shooting style is more like a magazine show (with features) than a news show. There is no sense of urgency and the videographer can usually control what is happening in front of the camera.

Figure 8.1: Three shots from a corporate-style news show created by the Florida Department of Law Enforcement. It shows employees working together toward common goals and gives information about the activities of the department.

Most of the rules mentioned for shooting general news and reporter stand-ups in previous chapters apply to this EFP style. The goal is to make the organization seem friendly and personal.

Your style should reflect this goal. You may use wide shots to quickly establish your location, but close-up shots help convey a friendly mood.

Instruction, Training and Demonstration

This general category includes instructional video production in classrooms designed to be viewed by persons other than those physically present in the classroom. This can mean a taped lecture for absent students or a taped production of an entire course for students viewing the videotape rather than attending live lectures. It also may mean **distant learning,** where TV is used for live, real-time interaction between two classrooms separated by distance. In corporate and other professional settings, training tapes have become so common that they are an expected part of employee orientation and training. Using video for training purposes is the single most common use of portable video in the corporate world. If properly produced, a good training video can save many hours of boring repetition by an instructor. It can also provide location shots and event shots that could not otherwise be viewed by the audience.

While instructional video for distant learning may not have a verbatim script, it most often has a very carefully prepared outline for the instructor to follow, with graphic material specially prepared in a form conducive to good video. For example, graphic material should conform to TV's 4 : 3 aspect ratio.

Instructional corporate video is used to convey very specific information to the intended audience. Its goal is to have the audience learn something specific, such as a procedure, a task or a safety rule. (See Figure 8.2.) This requires a very accurate and organized script and storyboard. Two shooting rules are standard.

Figure 8.2: This instructional video is being shot in a medical operating room. The surgeon who will be performing the surgery gives an introduction about the procedure about to be performed. *Courtesy Arizona Heart Institute.*

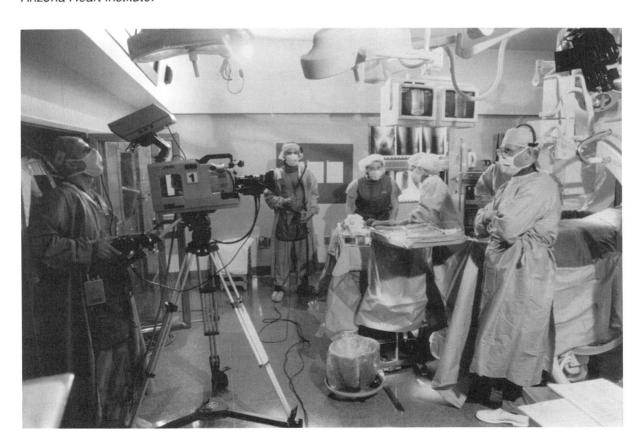

1. Each shot must be clear, accurate and supported by explanatory audio when appropriate.
2. Close-up shots are critical for demonstrating procedures and showing small equipment or controls on larger equipment.

Extreme close-ups may be necessary. When shooting XCUs, make sure they are rehearsed. Since XCUs require high magnification, slight movement by either the camera or the subject may give your shot an amateurish look. Also, shots at high magnification often have a shallow depth of field. Small movement of the object can cause a loss of focus. During a rehearsal of a shot, mark off the area that defines your sharp focus area, keep the camera still and the object in the focus area. Hand-holding of small objects for XCU shots is not recommended.

Teleconferencing   A significant growth area of corporate video or non-broadcast video is teleconferencing. Although teleconferencing re-

fers more to a method of distribution than a style of shooting, it has become an enormous part of corporate and non-broadcast TV in the 1990s. There are numerous reasons for this, but the most important are that teleconferencing can save much money by eliminating travel costs and that the technology needed is available at a reasonable cost. Executives of a given national organization in Boston and San Francisco can meet face to face through two-way TV, utilizing a satellite-distributed teleconference. A small university campus can reach out to employees of an engineering firm off campus with a graduate course in engineering through microwave distribution and audio call-in. Another university can distribute courses to its branch campus by using a two-way microwave TV system. (See Figure 8.3.) Students at both locations can ask the professor questions and get immediate answers. This process is often referred to as "distance learning."

The style of this type of video is a hybrid of studio and portable video. Most teleconferences

Figure 8.3: An instructional TV system connects a university with its branch campus located 200 miles away. In the photo at the top left, a student at the branch campus (shown in the large monitor at right) is able to ask the professor a question. In the photo at the top right, the director in the control room selects video from one of three remote-controlled cameras. In the bottom photo, the professor can see the students at the branch campus by looking at monitors in the back of the classroom.

occur in a room or location specially adapted for the purpose or in some type of TV studio. Teleconferences can be shot in various formats that can include elements of a news show, demonstration, motivational video panel discussion and lecture.

Sales, Promotion and Motivation

Public relations videos are shot with the intention of delivering information, but the desired effects are also behavioral and attitudinal. Corporations shoot these videos because they want their salespeople to know about the products and services that they must sell as well as instill in them the positive attitude and energy necessary to get the sales job done. Sales, promotion and motivational videos are characterized by high energy and dynamism. Enthusiasm is the key word.

As with the demonstration video, these videos require tight scripting to allow for the control necessary to keep the tempo of the video upbeat. Camera shots are dynamic, showing much movement. Sound tracks are crisp and lively—the music is upbeat. Lighting is usually bright with strong direction and modeling (not flat). Often, strong backlighting is used to separate the subject or the product from the background. Colors are often bright.

If editing is noticeable at all, it usually consists of quick cuts rather than slow dissolves to enhance the dynamic energy. Special effects are often employed to enhance the feeling that the product, service or concept has special merit. These effects can be as simple as a star effect from a star filter on a camera lens or a computer-generated special effect costing thousands of dollars.

PUBLIC SERVICE ANNOUNCEMENTS (PSAS) AND COMMERCIALS

Public service announcements (PSAs) and commercials for broadcast and cable TV probably include every conceivable style of shooting. Styles vary by market size—usually in relation to the budget, which is directly related to market size and type of product or issue to be discussed. Most videographers who shoot these short-format projects do so on a local level (for example, a local car dealership or the local United Way campaign).

Public Service Announcements

Public service announcements (PSAs) are short (usually 30-to-60 seconds) announcements cre-

ated and broadcast or cablecast for the benefit of the viewing audience. The sponsor is often a local non-profit agency, such as the library, humane society or police department. There are also many nationally distributed public service announcement campaigns produced by national groups such as the Advertising Council, American Dental Association, American Cancer Society, religious organizations and the U.S. Government. The national campaigns often discuss themes of national concern, such as drug abuse, literacy, environmental safety and health issues. Usually well financed and shot on film, these campaigns are distributed on videotape to broadcast and cable outlets throughout the country.

On a local level, state agencies and non-profit institutions often attempt to create and produce a campaign with donated help and small budgets. This need often provides students and beginning professionals an opportunity to produce creative work aired (sometimes repeatedly) on local or regional stations or cable systems. (See Figure 8.4.)

Commercials

In broadcasting, all TV stations except those with educational or Public Television affiliations rely on commercials to pay for their operation. All non-premium cable programming services such as ESPN, CNN or MTV also rely on paid commercials to keep them profitable. This presents an enormous opportunity for aspiring videographers to practice their skills. On the local level, tens of thousands of commercials are produced for airing.

Figure 8.4: This photo is from a student-produced public service announcement. This creatively produced, low-budget PSA had a simple message and was broadcast by a local TV station.

Formats It would be futile to describe the commercial style as it applies to EFP, since every style of video has probably been tried in a commercial. There are, however, a number of standard formats that have been used over the past forty years that encompass most of the TV commercials produced.

Celebrity Spokesperson A long time favorite of many commercial producers with large budgets, this type of commercial tries to associate a star with a particular product. Can you name the brand of athletic shoes Michael Jordan wears? How about Bo Jackson?

Slice of Life This is a very popular format for household products, such as detergents or mouthwash. Stubborn stains and bad breath present problems that can be solved by everyday people simply by purchasing the products named.

Stand-up Presentation This format is an attempt at interpersonal communication by an announcer; actually, it is usually a simple and direct sales talk. This can be shot anywhere and is often done in an auto sales lot. (See Figure 8.5.)

Hidden Camera Testimonials This format is the typical "yes, this coffee does taste great" spot where real people are the stars of the commercial.

Music Orientation Often a musical piece is composed to sell a product and becomes almost more important than any other selling points. The visuals serve to accentuate the music. Producers of these shots hope that the music becomes closely linked to the product. This is especially helpful if the video spots are used in combination with radio spots.

Visual Orientation Commercials are sometimes produced with very little, if any, emphasis placed on the audio. In this case, the audio merely supplements the video; the message is almost completely visual. National spots for autos often show the auto on the road and keep the factual information minimal. The Infiniti tried this approach in the early 1990s without even showing the auto. It was aesthetically pleasing, but dealers felt that showing the car was more important.

Comparative Demonstration This style often requires quite a bit of pre- and post-production. In

Figure 8.5: These stills are from typical stand-up presentation commercials. Note the direct eye contact with the camera that enhances interpersonal communication. *Courtesy of John Wade.*

a very short time frame, the producer tries to show how a product is used or compare two products' performance and/or cost. A typical example would be the grease-cutting ability of two dishwashing liquids. Props such as glass kitchen sinks are needed to show how the product works. Another popular version has a split screen with shots of the two products, for example, Honda versus Hyundai. The screens superimpose facts about price, horsepower, seating capacity or other simple, numerically oriented comparisons over the shots of the cars.

Animation   Animation is used to create a visual not possible in reality or to draw attention to the product. Toy and cereal manufacturers have long believed that animation attracts and holds children's attention better than many real announcers. Obviously, this is a time-consuming and expensive approach rarely used locally. The advances in personal computers and software designed for computer graphics and animation may change this in the near future.

In addition to the above general categories, there are numerous combinations of formats and exotic variations on them. A celebrity spokesperson may by joined by an animated spokesperson for a theme park. A slice-of-life commercial may include a family trying two different products for comparison. A stand-up presenter may introduce a strongly visually-oriented spot.

All the above approaches can be and often are accomplished in the field. Before high-quality, competitively priced ENG/EFP cameras were generally available, on-location local commercials for TV were usually shot on 16mm movie film or 35mm slide film. Low-budget commercials were shot on slides. Some (two to eight) slides from the shoot were loaded into the slide chain (telecine) at the studio and a sound track was added. Many commercials and PSAs are still done in this way, although the slides are often replaced with static video shots of the business doing the advertising.

It is easy to do better than that. Avoid static shots. Without overusing the zoom, add some movement to your shots with camera movement. If you have an on-camera announcer or subject, add interest to the shot by placing the subject in an unusual spot (for example, in a car lifted high above the ground with a crane, starting on a close-up shot, then zooming out to reveal the exact location). If you add music, try to make some of your edits coincide with the beat of the music to draw your viewers into the message.

When doing a commercial or PSA, keep your time frame in mind. You will probably have only 30 seconds to convey your idea and the needed information. This calls for careful scripting and storyboarding. Commercials and PSAs offer excellent ways of sharpening your creative skills, both with the camera and in scriptwriting. Do not settle for the ordinary, use these short-format projects as a challenge to your ability to interest audiences, and tell complete stories in a short time frame.

Budgets

Budgets for PSAs and commercials are usually quite small, limiting your alternatives for creativity and experimentation to those you do not have to buy. Forget about renting the helicopter for your aerial shot, but offer to trade-out with the local emergency health helicopter service—offer to shoot a public service spot or commercial for them in exchange for a free ride. If this does not work, try to get your bird's-eye view from the roof of the tallest adjacent building. Sometimes a wide angle shot from above gives the desired aerial shot effect. Conveying the notion of acres of gleaming new and used autos may be easier from 100 feet than from a helicopter at 300 feet.

Instead of flashy digital effects, retail commercials may force you to inject excitement and action with unusual camera angles and some dynamic editing. The point here is that network style and quality commercials require network-sized budgets. Ninety percent of video commercials are *low budget*; this is most likely what you will have to face, especially if you are a beginner.

PERFORMANCE VIDEOS

There are two major types of performance video that utilize EFP. The first is performance video for entertainment purposes done on location by one or more EFP cameras for later presentation to an audience. The other major type of performance video is shot for historical purposes; an event is captured on video and archived for future reference.

Entertainment

Many types of performances simply cannot be brought to the TV studio and still retain the mood or energy intended by the performers, directors or choreographers. Part of the reason for this is that the TV studio is rarely large enough to permit an audience. Many performers accustomed to having an audience present strongly prefer having the audience there for feedback and energy. Also, TV studios can rarely duplicate the space or specific lighting, floor or sound characteristics of a theatrical stage or auditorium. Because of these limitations many performers have been captured on videotape in EFP style. If a good post-production facility is available, a simple multiple-camera EFP shoot can yield a high-quality performance video

suitable for broadcasting or showing to an in-house audience.

Switchable Camera Field Shoot There are two common methods in practice for shooting on-location performance videos: (1) the switchable camera field shoot and (2) the isolated camera field shoot. The switchable camera field shoot uses multiple cameras with a field switcher that selects one camera to be the taking camera. (See Figure 8.6.) This system mimics the TV studio where a director makes real-time switching deci-

Figure 8.6: Three-camera remote shoot for performance video. Switching is live or real-time, yielding one finished tape at the end of the performance.

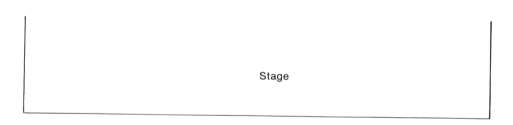

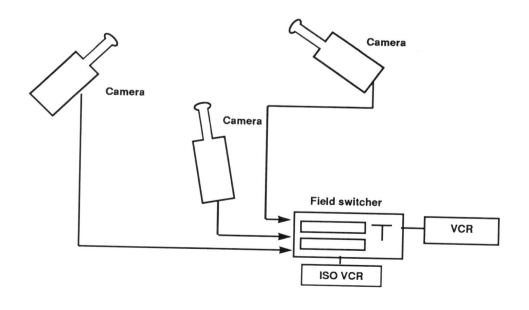

sions to select which camera does the actual recording. This system is convenient if the director is very familiar with the script of the performance and the look that the performance should have as a finished product.

Often this configuration of equipment has three cameras tied to one switcher and a videotape recorder connected to the program or outgoing line from the switcher. Since only one recording is made, the director decides on the spot which camera will be online. If the wrong decision is made or if the technical director pushes the wrong button, the videotape usually contains the bad decision or error with virtually no way of fixing it.

There are two ways to avoid the problem of having to live with your mistakes on a live-to-tape multi-camera switched recording. The easiest is to have one wild camera not hooked to the switcher that shoots cut-away shots during the show, such as audience reactions, extreme wide shots, extreme tight shots or any shot that could be considered non-synchronous. Later these can be inserted to cover any mistakes made by the director, technical director (TD) or subject on the master recording with a minimum of editing time and without a jump-cut or loss of continuity.

The second way is to have one of the switched cameras on an isolated line to its own VCR. Most switchers are capable of feeding an isolated (ISO) line from any of the cameras coming into the switcher. If the switcher cannot do this, then a separate deck can be hooked up to one of the cameras. This can be a small price to pay and minor hassle to ensure that the finished product meets the highest standards and does not look amateurish. The ISO camera is generally either the least-used camera or the widest, most stable camera of the group. Very few big-time experienced directors would work without a net (that is, an ISO camera) unless the production was live.

Whenever two or more cameras are brought together in the manner described above, they must be timed to avoid a glitch when the picture is cut from one of them to another. This method of timing is called **gen-lock**; there are two methods of doing this. Most professional multi-camera set-ups make use of a special camera cable on the back of the camera called a **triax adapter** that allows most camera functions to be done at a remote location wherever the cables come together—generally near the switcher. A video control person can **shade** the cameras (control the iris and manipulate the color so that each camera looks

as good as the other) as well as time them to each other. In lower-budget productions only a **coax** cable that attaches to the BNC connector on the side or back of the camera is used. Each camera must be matched manually before the shooting starts. To time them, a second coax cable must be run to each camera. This cable is attached to the gen-lock port on the camera and comes from the switcher, which is feeding a reference signal to each of the cameras that tells the cameras the clock they will use to synchronize the video scan rates. Without this timing function, nothing in a multi-camera set-up works.

Isolated Camera Field Shoot The alternative method for a multiple camera shoot uses the same number of cameras, usually three, but they are not tied to a switcher. Instead, each has its own independent videotape recorder. The director's job using this method is more one of guidance than final decision-making until the post-production stage. The director suggests certain shots to each camera operator, such as "Camera 1, look for Mr. X to enter from stage left, make sure you get a CU of his face as he sees Ms. Y." If Camera 1 misses the shot, the other two cameras may get it.

This method relies very strongly on post-production. After the shoot, there are three complete versions of the performance, one from each camera. One version is a master shot from the center camera; the other two versions are from the side cameras situated somewhat closer to the stage. (See Figure 8.7.)

Anytime two cameras are being used to shoot one scene or event that will be edited on a high-quality edit system, the cameras must be gen-locked. On a two-camera interview even without a switcher (each camera has its own deck), a gen-lock cable should be run between the cameras. One simple coax from the video out of one camera to the gen-lock port of the other will lock two cameras together; any number of cameras can be hooked together in series this way. This allows an edit machine to synchronize the two tapes in the edit process. Without it, even with common time code, the two tapes could be several seconds off over the course of a 20-minute interview. (See Figure 8.8.)

The post-production process consists of combining the three versions to get one high-quality version. The job is much easier if the three tapes have time code information to provide a permanent address for each frame of the video. This makes synchronization much easier. In editing

Figure 8.7: Three-camera remote shoot for performance video. Each camera is isolated and has its own VCR. Tapes from each camera will be mixed in post-production to yield a finished product.

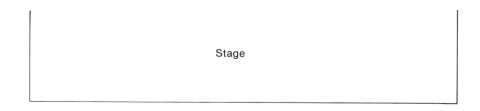

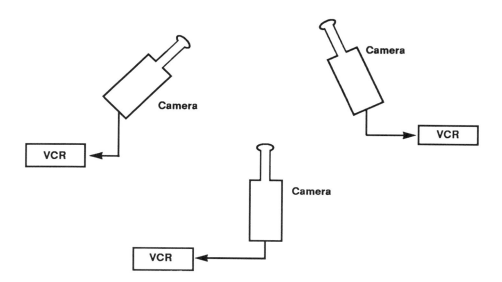

systems with three machines (two sources and a recorder to allow A/B roll editing where two sources of video permit transitions like dissolves and wipe rather than just cuts only), two versions (usually the center shot and one side shot) are synchronized on some action near the very beginning of the tape. Both tapes are then started. A switcher selects one of the two to feed the record machine at all times. The result is a mix of the center shot and one side shot.

This first tape is referred to as a two-camera submaster. The camera submaster is then used as a source tape with the third camera tape. These two tapes are synchronized and fed to the record machine. The editor switches between the two sources to yield a final tape. This tape should be a final mixture of the three camera views.

The major advantage of this method is that you can try many different combinations before you decide on the final version. One major disadvantage is that many extra hours (and possibly dollars) are spent in post-production. Another disadvantage is that parts of the final version of the tape are third-generation video, technically of lower quality than first or second generation.

The easiest way to synchronize the tapes of a multi-camera shoot is by using time code (providing the cameras are gen-locked). The method of doing this is called a **jam sync**. Any deck present or a separate time code generator can be used as the master. A coax cable from the master's time code out port can be run to the time code in port of any deck. Just like gen-sync, this process can be done in series so that a separate cable does not have to run from the master to every single machine but each machine needs to be connected to another. The time code master machine can be set to internal time code and all slaved machines need to be set to external time code on their control switches. Whatever the time code is set at on the master, each slave machine will record. If another deck is used as the master and the time code is in the record run position, it must be recording before it will send time code to the slave machines.

This set-up can make it easy to put a multi-camera show together in the edit room.

Historical Archive

One of the most sensible and efficient uses of video is the historical archive. Unique events, such

Figure 8.8: Two-camera remote shoot for performance video. Tapes can be mixed or each may be used unedited.

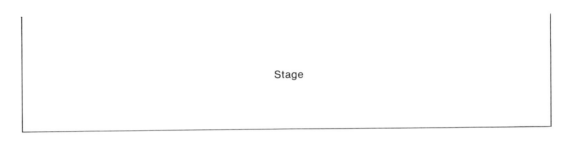
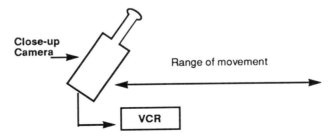
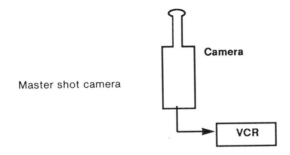

as celebrations, special performances and ground-breaking ceremonies are good reasons to use the inexpensive historical document that can be provided by good-quality videotape shot on location. The archive video is not the same as a performance-quality or entertainment video intended for later broadcast. It is a low-budget record of an occurrence worth keeping for future reference.

Choreographers and Directors   For the dance choreographer, archive video provides a representation of a creation as interpreted by the choreographer at a certain point in time and by the dancers available at that time. Video captures the movement and the staging for the choreographer to use during a later interpretation or reconstruction. (See Figure 8.9.)

In the same way, the theater director can obtain a record of a particular performance by the cast at a particular time, using the archive video. It provides a point of reference that a written script, review or summary could never provide. The director can obtain a ½-inch video cassette and show it just about anywhere on a home video deck.

Event Dictates Style   The style of the archive video is dictated by the event being recorded and the desires of the choreographer, director or interested group that will use the tape. Choreographers and directors often want to have the entire stage visible to show not just the performers, but also the relationship between the performers and the space in which they are performing. This requires that the videographer avoid the temptation of zoom-ing in on the action and framing it tightly. For both choreographers and directors, the expression of the performer on stage is not the only important aspect of the performance.

In dance, body positioning and articulation of the extremities should be included in all shots. Since dancers often move quickly, they can dance entirely out of the frame if the shot is too tight. Even cutting off the toes or hands in a shot of a dancer can lose what the choreographer needs to see. Directors often want to see entrances of characters while others are on stage. This also calls for a wide shot.

These types of requirements translate into a simple, static one-camera style. Use your tripod and set the camera on a wide master shot of the stage. Make sure that your shot is not so wide that it allows any stage lights to shine directly into your lens. If you are able to use two cameras, use the first camera for a master shot and the second for following action and close-ups of the main performers. You may want to edit these together into your final tape or simply provide two tapes.

This type of video may seem boring to you, or it may seem like unimaginative shooting. But keep in mind that the archive is *not* a commercial to be viewed on broadcast TV; rather it is a tool used by professionals and scholars to preserve an historically significant event or creative endeavor.

SPORTS VIDEO

There are two main kinds of sports EFP work: competition and features. Sports features are generally shot for use in pregame or highlight shows. EFP coverage of actual sports competition has two main purposes:

1.   Live coverage of the event for broadcast or cablecast.
2.   Coverage for replay at a later time, usually in a highlights show.

Live coverage of a sports event is a complex, expensive undertaking that requires numerous cameras, a truck or van with camera control, videotape, switching and other technical equipment, miles of camera cable and a group of hardworking professionals. (See Figures 8.10 and 8.11.) Each sport has a particular sequence of shots compiled from the various cameras to give the viewer a comprehensive and complete view of the event as it occurs.

Figure 8.9: An archive video was shot for the choreographer of this dance to provide a record of how the space on stage was utilized and how the dancers performed.

Figure 8.10: Cameras used for professional location video work are usually more like studio cameras. The large heavy lens and need for steady telephoto shots require a heavy support system. The camera operator can receive directions via an intercom system.

Features usually consist of four elements.

1. Interview with an athlete or participant (for example, the coach or auto racing pit crew member);
2. Shots of this person preparing for the sport or event (for example, lacing running shoes, changing a racing tire, taping a baseball bat);
3. Shots of an athletic performance, competition or game;
4. Shots of some type of previous success or future challenge.

These are all easy to shoot with one portable camera and can be easily edited together with a simple two-machine editing system. (See Figure 8.12).

Competition Coverage

The basic camera setup for a football game consists of six or more cameras. (See Figure 8.13.)

Figure 8.11: This sports interview could be shot for a pre-game show segment or as part of a highlight program. Two cameras are used to let the director in the remote production van choose a shot of the interviewer or the interviewees.

Figure 8.12: This vehicle is custom designed and equipped for remote video work. It houses all necessary cameras, decks, switches, cables, and so forth, and provides the control room and hardware needed to shoot a remote event such as football.

Cameras 1, 2 and 3 are located in the stands about one-half to two-thirds of the way up to the top of the stadium. These cameras are used to orient the viewer as to the field location and direction.

One of these three cameras will be used for the line of scrimmage, depending on the location of the ball. The camera closest to the line of scrimmage will be used to show the offensive team's huddle and one wide shot of their lineup at the line of scrimmage. Frame this shot so that about two-thirds to three-quarters of the screen is filled with the offensive team. (See Figure 8.14.) This allows

screen space for the quarterback to move into when he drops back to pass or hand off.

Just before the snap, the taking camera zooms in tighter on the quarterback. This camera will zoom in and follow the ball from the time the ball is snapped until the play is over. After the play has stopped and the players start to get back on their feet, the director will usually switch to the truck-top mounted camera that should have a close-up shot of the ball carrier and the tackler or key defensive person involved in the play. If the play was a good offensive play, the shot will follow the offensive ball carrier. On a good defensive play, the camera will follow the defensive player as he returns to his huddle.

At this point, the director can choose one of several alternatives:

1. A videotape replay, sometimes with slow motion from the on-air camera or any one of the ISO cameras;

2. A graphic superimposed over the real action as the players return to the huddle;

3. A special graphic or videotape of the key player—his statistics, or picture, or a short piece of videotape recorded before the game showing the player responding to a question;

4. A wide shot from the end zone camera or one of the other cameras (usually over a wide crowd shot), often used to frame statistics or a promo graphic that is superimposed over the shot;

5. A shot from the sideline camera of the coach, key players waiting to come into the game, an injured player or some other color shot of cheerleaders, fans, mascots or the typical "Hi Mom" or "We're Number 1" shot of a player on the sidelines;

6. As the end of the half or the game approaches, a shot of the clock or scoreboard.

If normal play is continuing, the sequence begins again with a wide shot from camera 1, 2 or 3.

Feature Coverage

Highlight shows are common to most professional and major college football teams. These shows consist of past matchups between the teams, a chronology of game footage with replays of key plays, coach interviews, player interviews and previews of upcoming opponents. You may not have the equipment, personnel or budget for live coverage of a football game, but one or two EFP cam-

Figure 8.13: Multi-camera remote professional sports shoot. Cameras 1, 2, 3 in seating areas on platform, one-half to two-thirds up. Camera 4 mounted on top of truck. Camera 5 in seating area on platform, used for reverse angle shots. Camera 6 in seating area behind either goalpost. Camera 7 roaming portable camera.

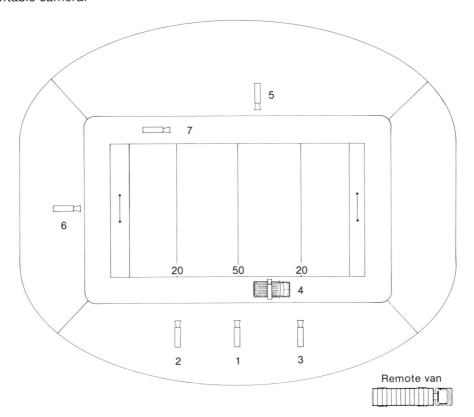

Figure 8.14: Line-of-scrimmage shot at beginning of football play. Note how the framing gives the quarterback room to move into for handoffs or passing.

eras with competent camera operators can do a decent job of covering the game for a highlights show.

If only one camera is available for a football game it should be the one placed at the 50-yard line, one-half to two-thirds of the way up to the top part of the stadium or even on top of the press box if there is one. Many fields provide a designated space for video cameras. This camera will have a good view of the line of scrimmage for a high percentage of the plays. If the ball is followed closely, a viewer should be able to follow the entire game from the video of that one camera. The trick is to always stay with the ball.

Keep the framing loose until you are sure where the ball is and the play has already developed. Then you can zoom in as the running back crosses the line of scrimmage or the wide receiver pulls in the long pass. Obviously, a camera with a high zoom ratio or range extender is best. The biggest mistake you can make is to zoom in to follow a running back who has been faked a handoff and does not have the ball.

A second camera would be best placed on a truck mount, but that requires additional personnel, a truck and lots of expensive cable. A platform about 10 feet above the field at the 50-yard line is a possible second choice. Most likely, the only alternative for a second camera is a hand-held one on the sidelines. This camera can provide very dramatic close-ups of the action but can also

be blocked by players, referees or even be run over by the play itself. This camera is most effective when it can shoot from the end zone and get close-ups of scoring plays. For midfield coverage, it is best to have the camera about 10 yards in front of the line of scrimmage. This is, however, far from ideal, since the field is often crowned with a center higher than the sidelines, yielding a low camera angle. This camera is most effective when it can shoot from the end zone and get close-ups of scoring plays. For midfield coverage, it is best to have the camera a few yards in front of the line of scrimmage.

Other sports have slightly different requirements and camera placements (for example, golf and tennis which are shot from the end of the green or court), but a few simple rules usually apply.

1. Get above and in the middle of the action (for example, mid-court in basketball or hockey).
2. Follow the ball (or puck or race car).
3. Frame loosely to avoid losing the object you are following.

MUSIC VIDEOS

The popularity of music videos is a recent phenomenon. Since the introduction of MTV (Music Television), the viewing world is now highly aware of the mixture of songs with visuals. This FM radio-to-TV product has stimulated enormous interest in music video style, as evidenced by the fact that shows featuring music videos seem to appear on almost every channel on the dial (possibly with the exception of the Cable News Network channel). This has caused great demand for this type of material and is a boost to the employment potential of all aspiring EFP professionals.

The notion of setting visuals to music has been around for a long time. A viewing of Walt Disney's 1940 classic *Fantasia* will convince you of that fact. The idea of having performers act to the music has also been around for some time. For example, *A Hard Day's Night* is a mid-sixties Beatles' film in which the Beatles have good-natured fun and sometimes lip-sync to their songs.

Most music videos are shot on film, then either transferred to video for editing or edited and then transferred to video for broadcast. Film, as mentioned in an earlier chapter, has a much better contrast ratio than video, and is better in very low light or very bright conditions. Many of the fancy digital effects in these videos are done on a video digital effects generator during the editing process.

Variety of Settings

Despite the drawbacks of video cameras for the big money music videos, the style of music video is perfect for the EFP videographer. Almost all of these videos have shots done on location outside of the studio. (Just imagine how dull they would be if all music videos only showed the musicians on a soundstage.) The fun in music videos comes from the unusual locations, camera angles, costumes and sophisticated transitions between the major elements. Music videos generally are composed of a combination of two elements: (1) the musicians in the studio or on stage performing a song, and (2) the musicians on location (somehow suggested by the song) either with instruments or in some dramatic vignette.

The variety of locations both for the performance and the vignette is virtually infinite, since almost anything is acceptable for a few minutes as accompaniment to a song. Sometimes animation is used to create new locations and effects. This really helps the beginners—sometimes a mundane location such as a supermarket or basement apartment can provide you with the look or mood that you want for your music video. The biggest factor in changing the mundane setting into something unusual is creative lighting.

Style and Technique

Since the person and personality of the performers are main interests of the music video, plan on shooting many more tight shots than long shots. You may use a brief long shot to give the viewer a sense of who is performing and where they are, but close-ups will probably be more interesting to the audience. You should also plan on low camera angles to accentuate the presence of the performers. You can shoot a music video in the style of the performance video. Using one camera on a master shot or using all three cameras, record a straight performance version of the song. If this is not a real performance and the performers are lip-synching, make sure you have the audio to which they are performing recorded on videotape. During subsequent takes in various locations, make sure that you play that same version of the song while they lip-sync to it. This allows you to go back to the master version and synchronize your

two audio tracks, then insert your video from your location shots.

If you are well organized in keeping track of your various versions, putting together a finished composite music video even from six versions at six different locations can be relatively easy. Just make sure that your reference audio is on every tape. If numerous locations are not possible or desirable, use the multiple-take style. When using this style, record multiple takes of the song (or portions of the song) while the performers vary their performance or while the focal length of the camera varies with each take. This style can yield a very respectable music video from an afternoon's shooting, and it is essential if you are doing single-camera work.

Music videos are an excellent opportunity for the beginning videographer to experiment with camera technique. Videographers and news photographers who usually have professional style restrictions placed on them can use music videos to loosen up and experiment with the camera. This even helps professionals become more familiar with the versatility and capability of their equipment.

NATURE AND DOCUMENTARY VIDEOS

Nature and documentary videos are perfectly suited for the portable film camera, just as they have been suited for the portable film camera for almost a century. This style requires a camera to be where the main characters (or animals or plants) are or where the main events are occurring. The camera views the events as they actually occur, and the characters as they appear, not as they are staged in front of the camera. This is not to say that no editing is done to restructure events. By the use of editing, nature programs such as *Wild Kingdom* have created many encounters between wild animals that never took place. Even documentaries will use editing to create events that occurred but were missed by the camera.

The point is that the videographer is meant to be a passive participant, not an active one. This is not necessarily intentional in nature programs, but wild animals rarely take cues from directors. Documentaries are meant to present a reality that will enlighten its viewers, not a reality as created by the videographer or director. This style requires an unobtrusive camera to avoid influencing the events that occur in front of the camera. Therefore, retakes of these events are almost impossible, the addition of a large amount of artificial light may be nearly impossible and getting every shot that you plan is certainly impossible.

Although the market for this type of video program is growing rapidly, the beginner should be aware of the fact that this type of work takes many long hours of shooting and editing. Because of this, the budget for this EFP style is necessarily large—at least in comparison to most commercials, performance videos and many applications of corporate video.

VIDEO ART

This EFP style is still a well-kept secret. The main reason for this is probably that the number of outlets for this style is quite small. Video art is not the style of on-location video to choose if you need to earn a living doing one style of video work.

Video art serves an important role in a democratic society. It allows diverse views to be expressed even if they are not the dominant ones in the culture. This diversity of viewpoint has a positive effect on a free society by stimulating people to think.

It is impossible to describe video art as a particular style. It is completely free form. It may resemble broadcast TV in length and form, while differing greatly in content. It can be a short piece that violates every known rule about pleasing an audience. Video art is the expression of the artist who looks at the same things that we do, yet sees something different. It is this difference in vision that makes video art an untapped source of creativity—video art has the capacity to show us a world at which we all look but do not see. (See Figure 8.15.)

The process of creating video art is different from other EFP work in several respects. First of

Figure 8.15: Mara Alper's experimental video *Silent Echoes* has been broadcast on PBS and the learning channel. *Photo by Mara Alper.*

all, it is usually not done at a client's request but because the video artist has the desire to express a topic or concept in a unique form. This means the time frame for creating the work is usually longer. It will generally be created in phases with arts funding often sought for production and post-production. Because the work is not being done for a client, the video artist has complete creative control.

Video art can combine EFP production, studio shoots and complex post-production techniques. It often entails use of advanced special effects equipment that allows the artist to manipulate the electronic signal. This can include digital processing of each pixel of information, varying the frequency of the signal, colorizing, solarizing, using multiple layers of wipes and dissolves, auditory processing and using feedback as a visual effect. Artists gain access to signal-processing equipment through media arts organizations located in diverse areas of the country, including non-metropolitan areas. In post-production, the editing rhythm is often a different tempo than conventional TV, either faster, slower or variable.

The video artist has unlimited possibilities. The only constraint is to make choices that stretch and enhance the existing conventions and allow the viewer to experience the world in an imaginative way.

Broadcasters show various types of entertainment, nature and documentary programs, commercials and sports. Corporations use and show the training tapes, sales tapes, and demonstration tapes. But where do the video artists show their work? In competitions, festivals and on a few scattered programs on cable or public TV.

Innovative approaches in video art find their way into the mainstream by influencing approaches used in TV advertising. Many commercials are really a form of applied video art. Other mainstream areas that use video art approaches are the promotional I.D.s used for stations and the opening graphics and title sequences for all programs. Visual artists comfortable with electronic graph-

ics equipment can apply their skill in these areas, as well as in helping create the overall design for these segments.

EFP equipment is affordable enough so that many college, art school and university students can gain access to it. But without seeing it themselves, students are often slow in wanting to try this EFP style. The instant gratification of seeing your work on a monitor immediately after it is shot should lure many people to the video art EFP style. Unfortunately, however, with the exception of the very largest cities in this country, video art is virtually unknown.

Perhaps film still attracts so many artistic persons because of its long history and acceptance as an art form. TV on the other hand, is often regarded as a medium of mediocrity as evidenced by the constant stream of prime-time fare that is usually tasteless, slick, insulting or all three. But broadcast TV is merely one method of delivering video; the networks are just some of the many programmers out to attract an audience. Other delivery systems for video exist and some of them do seek out video art.

Film has also enjoyed immense popularity as compared with video because of its high-resolution exhibition format. This difference in resolution quality may change when High Definition TV (HDTV) becomes a reality for commercial broadcast or cable TV. HDTV offers very high resolution, giving an image closer in quality to 35mm film.

In 1991 there were about 15 million camcorders in homes in the United States. This can only lead to what some call a democratization of portable video. Video can become a form of artistic expression for the masses, not just for the privileged minority that has access to professional video equipment. As portable video becomes more common and available in years to come, more creative individuals will attempt to use EFP equipment for art's sake. Perhaps then the Eisensteins, Griffiths, Chaplins and Fellinis of video art will begin to surface.

9 ENG Styles

The decisions you make in the field while shooting any story begin to give your video a look or a particular style. Because no two people see the same scene in the same way, your vision of what is possible with the camera is what becomes your style. Within the world of TV news, documentary work and reality-based programs, there are certain constants that help identify for the viewer the type of story. These constants act as an overlay to your individual style, not replacing it but limiting it to certain parameters.

In electronic news gathering, stories tend to fall into one of several categories: spot news, general news, feature news and sports news. Each of these areas has its own overlay style that defines a certain look. That look helps the viewer quickly understand the type and substance of the story.

SPOT NEWS

Spot news is the hardest ENG style to master. It is truly what shooting news is all about. Whether it is the Hindenburg crash, a raging war in the Middle East or the attempted assassination of the president, you, because of your presence, are recording history. The most mundane event can suddenly become a page in history that will live forever.

How well you do your job will also live forever. If you fail, generations to come will miss seeing a dramatic moment in history. Think for a moment how many events in history you remember by the pictures you saw; think how much less impact the events would have had they not been recorded on film or tape. If we never saw an atomic explosion, would we be as awed by its power? If we had not seen the war in Vietnam every night on the evening news, would we really grasp the death and suffering involved?

News photography lets the viewer see and hear things as if actually present. (See Figure 9.1.) An ENG photographer's job is to bring the event to the viewer so that the viewer can decide how to interpret what is happening.

It is not the videographer's job to tell someone that a war is immoral but rather to show what a war is like, what is taking place and the effect it has on those involved. Most ENG photographers will never be in a position to record a major part of history, but some will, often solely by the luck of being there at the right time. Therefore, each videographer must be prepared to rise to the occasion.

When shooting spot news, the videographer will be in one of three situations: (1) in the middle of what is happening; (2) in the middle of the aftermath; or (3) stuck on the perimeter while the event is happening or just after it happened.

Shooting in the Middle of the Action

One of the most famous examples of this situation is the assassination attempt on President Reagan in the early 1980s. The camera crews assigned to

Figure 9.1: An ENG photographer shooting a story on a city street.

shoot every move the president makes had no idea what was about to occur on that fateful morning. Within a few seconds, the calm scene was transformed into one of utter chaos. The photographers had to operate on instinct and training to capture that moment of history. Some did better than others at capturing the event. The best shooting came from an NBC cameraman, who held his shot wide until he could tell what was going on and then decided what was most important to show. He moved the camera and used the zoom lens to take viewers from one horrible section of the scene to the next, pausing just long enough to show what was happening before moving to the next area of action. No shaky, wild pans or zooms whip around to distort what the picture contains. The cameraman found and held the shot on each important element in the story in the order of importance.

You can imaging the amount of self-control it took to do his job under these circumstances. Not many people could have done it, but this is the situation you must always be ready for if you work in news. It does not have to be the president; it could be a simple court case or the shooting of a mail carrier on his route. Sometimes unexpected events happen when the cameras are there. A simple demonstration by a student group may escalate into a full-scale riot with you right at the center.

If you find yourself in the middle of a situation while it is happening, keep your lens at its widest setting and keep your videotape rolling. It sounds simple, but it is surprising how many good pieces of news have been lost because this rule was not followed. If the story is breaking around you, you must shoot it as you would see it. Don't zoom into one element and exclude the others that are still happening. Pan if you have to, or walk to a better vantage point, but save the zoom for later when things are more under control.

Keep Rolling Above all, keep rolling. From the moment the camera is turned on, roll tape and don't stop for any reason. (After things settle down or you gain control of the situation, you can be more selective about rolling tape.) White balance while rolling, run from your car or van while rolling and try to make every second of the tape airable. Even when you are running with the camera to get a better position, keep the camera on the action and as steady as possible.

Keep Lens Setting Wide   The previous point is one of the reasons to always stay wide—camera movement is less noticeable when the shot is wide and you have a smaller chance of missing something that is taking place. These are not events you will be able to get later on; once they are missed, they are gone forever. Use the camera as you use your eyes—let the viewer see as much as possible of what you see—let it all take place before you.

Hold the Shots   You must learn to count in your head while you shoot. In the middle of a breaking story, time will become very distorted. When you think you have a long enough shot of one particular element, you probably do not.

Ten is a great number to use. Unless you must change shots to capture something that is leaving the scene or happening right now, count to 10 before you change your shot. This allows the viewer time to perceive the shot and gives the editor the ability to cut out pans and walking shots to condense the event for presentation.

Get Static Shots   Keep the videotape rolling continuously to cover yourself in the event something more takes place while you are on the location that could be the best or most important element of the story. When the event is over, make sure you have plenty of static shots because they will probably be your best shots.

Check Gear Often   Don't panic in the middle of an action scene. Move to your first shot and count it out, go to the next shot and count it out, and keep that tape rolling. Check the tape often to make sure it is indeed rolling, and check your audio often to make sure the sound is there and not too low or overmodulated. Stay wide, keep rolling, time your shots by counting in your head and look for the most important elements to photograph. Stay with the action, and check all of your systems as often as possible.

Shooting in the Aftermath

The second example of a spot news situation is one in which the main action is over and all that remains is the aftermath. For example, you arrive at the scene of a gas explosion shortly after the firefighters have begun to aid the victims. This situation can also be very intense with quite a bit of pressure, but for the most part things are under control. While you should still follow many of the same principles as when shooting in the middle of the action, a situation like this usually gives a photographer more time to make shots.

It does not require rolling tape the entire time, but does demand fast decision making nonetheless. You are still trying to present the story as the viewer would see and hear it if present. Because the events are under more control than in the first situation, your shooting can be more controlled.

Look for Various Types of Shots   Look for a good opening wide shot, and try to stay wide for most of the action shots. Because things are not moving as quickly, you have the time to look for medium shots and, above all, close-ups. With the zoom lens, you can pursue the tight shots of faces that really tell the story of the individuals involved, without fear of losing other elements of the story.

Shooting in the aftermath is the most common type of spot news. It still requires much hustle to get all the elements, but nothing new is going to happen. All the fire equipment is in place, the medical personnel are attending the injured or the police have subdued the perpetrator.

Look for the Action   With your knowledge of sequencing and story-telling elements, you should know what shots to get and be out there getting them while staying out of the way. The key is to always look for the action: shoot what moves but keep with the story; do not get sidetracked with unimportant things. As when shooting in the middle of the action, this type of shooting is often off the shoulder.

Do not include extraneous shots in what you shoot; it only wastes time and tape. If the crowd of spectators is not part of the story, do not shoot them. If the story has enough action in it, then there is no need for a cutaway. By varying angles and focal lengths, the piece should fit together without the useless shot of people watching.

In many cases it will be obvious that the main element of the story is happening when you arrive. It may be as simple as flames shooting from a building's windows or as subtle as a single person lying on the ground surrounded by a few people. Generally, a quick look around at the people involved will give you a clue as to where the main action is. If firefighters are rushing to the back of a building, maybe you should too, if you can. The thing you must never forget is to focus on people. If there is a rescue unit at the scene of the fire, then look for the injured. Stop by the ambulance first, as it will soon be leaving for the hospital; the

Figure 9.2: When shooting spot news, the ENG videographer tries to get shots of the action that tell a story: (1) the visual intensity of the fire; (2) and (3) the human element—how the fire affects people; (4) the action taken by the firefighters to bring the fire under control.

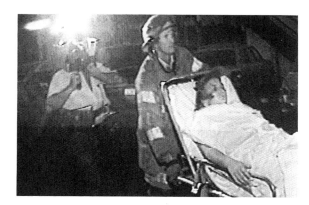
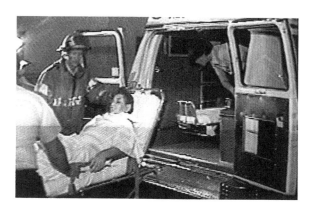

building will be there for quite a while. You may miss some of the best flames, but without the people the story would be lacking even more. A quick sound bite from a victim on the way to the hospital, describing a narrow escape, can sink the competition's shot of the flames you missed. Do not spend too much time on any one element. Keep moving. Look for those small but potentially powerful human elements that can take your story above and beyond the rest. Look for the elements that will not last long and get them as soon as you can. Decide which things will move and which will be there later when things are more calm or you have more time.

As the story is winding down, look for a good closing shot. The typical one for a fire story is that of a lone firefighter sitting on the curb, with smoldering ashes in the background, removing an air

mask and wiping away sweat. It may be a person reacting in grief at the site of the fire or the water to the hoses being turned off. It may also be symbolic, such as a tight shot of the police yellow or red line tape blowing in the wind. You want to leave the viewer with a sense that the story is over. It can also be the shot of the ambulance driving off, but it should say the end. If the story is only going to run as a 20-second voice-over there will be no air time to use such shots. For this type of presentation, you simply need the best 20 seconds of the event with the most action possible and that all important human element. (See Figure 9.2.)

Shooting on the Perimeter of the Action

In the third example of spot news, you are restricted from close access to the action. If you are held blocks away from a chemical leak or hostage situation, you must use the tripod and shoot at the longest focal length possible.

If the camera has a lens with a 2X extender (which doubles focal length), then use it to get the tightest shot possible of what is going on. You cannot shoot this type of shot off your shoulder because the video will be too shaky. Use the tripod if possible; if one is not available, rest the camera on the ground or on anything that will steady the picture.

Look for action even when you are on the perimeter. The action may be simple, such as people moving around police cars or fire engines, but any movement is better than none at all. In this situation more than any other, you need to shoot anything that moves: additional equipment arriving at the scene, officials talking on two-way radios or SWAT team members suiting up.

You may encounter a situation in which you will not get a shot of the real story but must tell the story with pictures of some sort. In this case, you come as close as you can to depicting the story with your shots. Sometimes this means just a shot of the police tape used at a crime scene to keep out unauthorized persons with a police officer standing next to it.

Never walk away from anything without enough video to cover a one-minute story (without shooting the same shot over and over). This is one case where a shot of onlookers could be useful; they still have nothing to do with the story, but they can help pad a piece that is already visually weak.

In most cases where you are restricted from the scene and held far from any direct action, you will usually be able to be at or near the command center set up by the controlling agency. This will become your major source of pictures for the story. You may get better shots later on but you cannot count on that. This is why you should shoot everything you can until you have exhausted the possibilities. Police officers looking at a map, conferring with each other or even just walking from one place to another will do. If the event goes on for quite a while, the station will ask for some tape to use in a live update. You had better have something to give them and more than one tape with you. This does not mean that you have to keep shooting the entire time the event goes on. Shoot until you have enough good pictures to cover about two minutes of narration. You should be able to do this in about 8 to 10 minutes of tape or less if you are making every shot really count. There is no point in getting volumes of generic video that will quickly look like the same shots over and over. Get the minimum necessary to cover two minutes; then save your energy, batteries and tape for better or different things that may come up later. The tripod is a must for this type of story as the sticks allow you to use the longest focal lengths and reach into any scene to pick out shots your shoulder-mount competition cannot get. They may also be the only shots you can get. After two to three hours of waiting, your shoulder will not be able to perform. If you use the sticks, you can always pull the camera off them quickly and run with it should the need arise.

Dealing with the Authorities

Before shooting any spot news, you should have a **press pass**, or ID card, issued by law enforcement agencies of cities, counties and states. This identifies you as a bona fide member of a news organization. Without this pass, shooting spot news can be a risky and sometimes impossible job. A press pass sometimes even gets you across police and fire lines to gain better access to the event. Sometimes the pass is worthless and at other times it can get you into more trouble than it keeps you out of. However, without it you do not stand a chance. The press pass involves some serious responsibilities. If the authorities let you in to or close to the scene, you can not interfere with what they are doing or disobey any special requests they have. Such requests may include not showing certain areas of a fire scene that is part of an arson investigation or showing the face of an undercover agent. If you violate the trust given you, your future dealings with that agency are jeopardized as well as those of other members of the press, not to mention the harm it may do the agency or the investigation.

It is not a good idea to try to outwit the authorities. It is quite impossible to shoot the rest of the story from the back seat of a police car. In some cases the risk involved in going around authority can be life threatening. You would not want to be in the line of fire of a deranged sniper. Police/media relations are always strained at best, but the only good course of action is to play by the rules. Often there will be a need to circumvent the authorities to get at the really good pictures of the story. These decisions can only be made on a case-by-case basis and must be made with the clear understanding that what you are doing is illegal and may harm you or someone else. Just like combat photographers, if you are willing to accept the ultimate responsibility, then you do as you think best. If you do get into trouble, your employer will most likely *not* help you out of it. Similar to getting a speeding ticket on the way to a story, you are on your own when dealing with the police.

Spot news requires instinct and a great deal of luck. You can increase the luck factor by always being prepared. If your equipment is organized and well maintained and you know what is required to make a good story, then when the big story comes your way the Emmy is yours. Shoot with both eyes open, always looking for the next shot or for what else may be about to happen. Keep your eyes moving but your camera steady. If you are not rolling tape, you will not get the shot.

GENERAL NEWS

This category of news stories is, as the label implies, very general. Most stories fall under this category. These are the stories about the city council, plans to build a new housing development for the elderly or a strike by local bus drivers. Most story-telling techniques apply directly to this form of news story. The main concept in general news stories is to communicate an idea or information to the viewer. The story must be very understandable with a good beginning, middle and end. It is on this type of story that reporter and photographer must work closely to produce the maximum impact on the viewer.

Presentation is of utmost importance. The subject matter might be the dullest in the world, but if the information is important (or if the boss demands it), the story must be done and done well. The idea is never to bore a viewer, never give a viewer the opportunity to say "so what" or "who cares" to what you are presenting or, worse yet, switch channels.

Get a Good First Shot

Always make the first shot of the story count. More than likely, it will be your best shot and it should be. Grab the viewer's attention immediately so that the viewer will watch the rest of the story. As a general rule, it is bad form to open a story with a talking head or a reporter stand-up. This opening looks too much like the people on the news set, that is, a person talking without showing you anything. If it starts to become the same as radio, why watch?

Sound is also important in the first shot. A natural sound clip is a good opening for almost any story; a dramatic sound bite can also be a good opening, but good ones do not occur too often.

Avoid Long Sound Bites

The worst thing about general news stories is the lengthy talking head shots that can make up the bulk of the video. While interviews are the bread and butter of TV news, they do not have to be the most boring part of the story. Like any thing in TV news, the talking head can be overused. The two basic styles most reporters use talking heads for are to make the story they have written more credible or to let the subjects tell their own story. The former is more of a traditional journalism style where the importance is placed on the reporter's ability to interpret and analyze and the latter is a style of simply allowing subjects to present their points at length with little input from the reporter. Both styles have their place, although letting subjects tell their own story is better suited to feature reports. In general, most subjects cannot speak well enough to adequately convey their point in the time allowed within the average news story. Many reporters still use this technique as simply an easy way to get out of doing most of the writing while still filling the time given to the story. Most reporters are far better writers than the subjects they are interviewing and should therefore be the primary giver of information in the story.

In either case, the talking head should be well shot. If the subject is to be on camera for a long time (maybe as much a two minutes in a three-minute story), then the interview shot had better be pleasing to look at for the entire time. By shooting each answer during the interview at a different focal length, maybe even doing some answers in a two-shot with the reporter, the parts used for the edited interview may look different enough to add some interest beyond nice framing to the long bites or groups of bites. It is sometimes possible to do parts of the same interview at different times and at different locations. If the same subject is to be heard many times or for an extensive time within the story, it may be possible to shoot in more than one location. One bite may have the subject behind a desk, another may be a walking conversation with the reporter, and still another may have the subject on a balcony overlooking the factory. It takes a little more time to do the interview, but the results are far better. Another way that can work in certain situations is simply different angles within the same basic set-up. By moving the camera to different points of view within the room for different sections of the interview, the edited piece can look like a multi-camera shoot. Work with the reporter or producer to find creative ways of avoiding long stretches of static talking heads.

Cover Long Sound Bites with Video

When a piece does have long stretches of talking heads or long sound bites, try to cover as much of them as possible with a **"B" roll** (shots of the context, objects of interest at the scene or cutaways). If you are going to use several bites or one long running bite from one subject, the audience only needs to see that individual for about 10 seconds. In that time, the voice is established with a name and a face and so the picture portion is free to go on to other parts of the story.

A 20-second sound bite with the builder of a new housing project could have the last 10 seconds or so covered by video of the topic (plans of the building, construction underway, and so forth.) Try also to make this video lead into the next audio, whether it is another talking head or reporter voice-over. Let the previous video overlap onto the next section.

The same can be done in reverse. If the reporter's track is about the housing construction and it leads into a sound bite from the builder, let the video of construction overlap the first 5 to 10 seconds of the builder's 20-second bite. The builder's face will appear and connect with the voice, but the length of the talking head has been reduced in favor of more interesting video.

If the builder is to appear twice fairly close together in a piece—for example, two bites separated by a reporter's comments—the second bite need not have the builder on camera at all; the entire bite can be covered by a "B" roll. This assumes that you have enough video to cover all the sound bites and that your video is appropriate to go over the audio.

Keep the Story Moving

Many times there will not be enough video (or any appropriate video) to use in or around talking heads. In these situations provide a large variety of two-shots, cutaways and setup shots to fill the time without shots running long or all looking same. An example of a setup shot is a zoom out from the plans on the wall to a two-shot of the builder and reporter talking, or shots of them walking around the site or office. A shot like this fills the time but keeps the video moving.

General news is sometimes referred to as **hard news.** It is the type of story that is serious and business-like in subject matter and approach. Your photography should also reflect the same characteristics. There is no staging of events or action. Your job is to simply and clearly represent the subject or event as accurately as possible while at the same time making it interesting or at least pleasing to watch. This type of story can be the greatest challenge to the news photographer, but it is the place where names are made in the industry. If you can make a city council story come alive and be as visually interesting as a feature without staging, then the rest of what you do in this business will be easy.

FEATURE NEWS

This category is perhaps the most free form of all. Feature stories are usually light-hearted looks at people or events or involved pieces on lighter or more personal subjects. They are not hard news by any means; rather, they are referred to as **soft news.** The stories in this category should entertain, touch or somehow please the viewer. Approach feature news with an emphasis on creativity; this type of story is a rare chance for both reporter and photographer to be as wild and imaginative as possible.

Music usually adds a lightness to feature stories and allows the editor to do some creative cutting. While there may be only one such story in a newscast, the feature piece can be the most memorable in the show. People like to feel good about things in what can be a very depressing news day. The feature gives viewers the chance to end the news time on a high note.

The feature may be a picture essay on a skydiving contest with no reporter or a simple story about children picking out pumpkins for Halloween. Almost any positive or good-news subject can be made into a good feature if a creative approach is used. Do not treat the feature as a nonstory and therefore a throwaway. The audience feels it is important and its purpose is to satisfy the need for relief after all the bad news.

It can take a whole day, a week or even a month to do a good feature story. The idea can be mapped out well in advance and shot a little at a time until the piece comes together. Features are very seldom timely so they can run at any time. This allows more work to be put into them. (However, you will not always be given enough time to spend on these stories. When you know time is limited, try to think out the story carefully so that the shooting and editing will make it look as though more time went into the story.)

Try Different Techniques

Feature news is a chance to use all the tricks of shooting and editing; the odd angle, dramatic camera move, unusual lighting, quick edits, wipes and other special effects. Features are the perfect place to use dissolves since you usually have the time to do the post-production. Nothing is too unusual for the feature story in the way of approach or technique. Try whatever you can to make your piece stand out and touch your audience. Good lighting, beautifully framed shots, slow zooms, dissolves and good images can come together in a feature story to touch even the most hardened news watcher. If you can feel with your camera and your editing, then the viewer will also see and feel. The audience should come away from the piece touched by what you have shown them.

You must be so immersed in the subject that you are part of the whole, not an observer or extra person. Do not let your self-consciousness detract from what you are trying to achieve. Be a part of, but not a participant in, what you are doing. Your presence should be unnoticed even though you may be only inches from what is happening.

Many feature stories take on the air of a Hollywood movie. They may be a parody of a harder story such as a tongue-in-cheek piece on a professional football league strike. The production of the story may become just as involved as any commercial shoot. The thing that separates pure journalism from this style of TV news is its goals. A general news story on the success of the Rubik's Cube (a popular puzzle toy) would discuss its inventor, sales and so forth. A feature on the Rubik's Cube may simply be about a character (perhaps the reporter) trying to solve the puzzle with no luck and then listing other uses for the toy, such as a door stop, and ending with the toy being run over by a streamroller. The first piece informs; the second entertains with little regard for information. Do not mislead the viewer. If the piece is to entertain, make sure it is obvious that is what is happening. Blending fact and fiction can be a dangerous game. Make sure that what you are doing has clearcut goals and that facts are never lumped in with staged material: keep them separated in the viewer's mind. A feature on a new private fishing lake may be mostly fact, but a shot of the reporter pulling a three-foot shark out of the

water may lead some viewers to think sharks are in the lake. Make sure there is only one possible interpretation of what you are doing in the story and that any jokes are clearly that.

SPORTS NEWS

Sports video falls into two categories: features and competition.

Features

The ENG photographer shoots the sports feature much like the news feature—with the maximum amount of creativity and involvement. If you are doing a piece on a boxer training for a fight, get in the ring and let the boxer spar right at the camera lens. This type of involvement can bring the subject up close for the viewer and give a perspective not available during a match.

You can do something similar for any sport. Use the fact that it is only practice to get the camera involved in places where it normally is not used. Gymnastics is a good sport for features; put the camera under the gymnasts, let them jump over the camera or put the camera right on the balance beam. Make these stories fun to do and fun to watch while trying to show the hard work taking place.

Competition

As an ENG photographer, you will videotape sports competition mainly for highlights or to capture a very short portion of the event, whereas competition coverage for EFP is often live coverage of the entire event. Almost all sporting events should be shot from a tripod. Choose a good vantage point where all the action is visible.

The public is used to seeing sports shot with many cameras on one event. Most of the time you will have only one camera but be required to do just as good a job and not miss any of the action. You must shoot the competition with that in mind. The best location for almost any sport is from above and as much to the center of the action as possible.

Basketball and Football For basketball, the ideal location is about one-third up the rows of seating and on the half-court line. Floor angles are nice, but if the action is at the far end of the court you stand a good chance of missing it or having your view blocked by the referee or other players. The high shot gets all the action clearly and allows you to zoom in or out to include as much of the action as you want.

If many plays are to be used as highlights it is impractical to use a cutaway between each of these plays. Good football plays usually end with a long run or pass or the score itself. The ending shot will look sufficiently different from the beginning of the next highlight and there is little worry of a jump cut. In basketball the field of action is much tighter and therefore everyone tends to be in the shot most of the time. For this sport it is a good idea to zoom in on the playmaker just after the point is scored. Besides emphasizing that player, this technique allows the editor to cut from that tight shot to the next highlight, which may be at the same end of the court. Even in football it is a good idea to zoom in to the key player as the play ends unless you are already on a tight shot of the ball carrier.

Sideline photography, usually done off your shoulder, is a way to add a closer, more dramatic feel to your highlight shots. The big risk with this position is not getting the shot because the referee, other players or even other photographers may be between you and the play. If you are covered by being able to take video from another source such as the company broadcasting the game, then anything you may miss on the sidelines can be obtained elsewhere. The biggest problem with ground-level shooting is the perspective of the camera. It is hard to tell relative distances between players, which makes some plays actually look rather undramatic. When you are learning how to shoot these two sports, it is better to master the high shot before moving to ground level.

Baseball   Baseball is difficult to shoot with only one camera. Action is taking place in two areas at the same time and it seems you should be following both the ball and the runners. Usually it is best to follow the ball until it is caught then you can pan quickly to the runners. Just following the ball will often give you all the action anyway, but if it is a long double and a runner is headed for home, it can be difficult to show both.

Do not take the easy way out and just go wide to show the whole field. A TV screen is too small for any of the real action to show up at all. If you miss the runner scoring, you can use a shot of the runner walking to the dugout as the run-scored shot. It you are above and directly behind home plate, you should see all the plays nicely.

Start on a two-shot of the pitcher and batter (top and bottom of the picture from the camera's position) and zoom in to follow the ball when it is hit. If you lose the ball, zoom out wide and pan in the direction it went until you regain sight of it. (You

will see the players running to where it is going.) If you make all of your moves as smoothly as possible, even when you lose sight of the ball, no one will notice any errors on your part.

Golf and Hockey   Golf balls and hockey pucks are difficult to follow: a golf ball is too small and a hockey puck moves too fast. Staying fairly wide in these sports is the best way to avoid missing the play entirely. As you become more used to the game, it will be easier to anticipate where the play is going and to keep your eye glued to the ball or puck.

Hockey is similar to basketball in how it is shot except that it moves much faster. A good sports photographer can shoot hockey fairly tight but most people cannot. It is best to be high up and at center ice to do the shooting and again zoom into the playmaker at the score. Golf is obviously a much slower game to shoot but can be the most strenuous to do because of all the walking between shots. It is best to be either directly behind or directly in front of the golfer. In front means way down the fairway, farther than is possible to hit the ball. From behind you can start wide and zoom in to follow the ball, from in front you can start tight on the golfer and widen out to keep the ball from leaving frame. Trying to **whip-pan** (pan the camera very fast with jerk-like movement) with the ball as it flies by you is not a good idea.

General Sports Tips   A good rule of thumb when shooting any sport you are not accustomed to is to stay wide at first and slowly shoot it tighter as you become more comfortable with the game. As shooting too tightly at first can leave you faked out causing you to miss the play, choose your focal length carefully. If too many plays are getting away from you, widen out until you have better control. Above all, make it smooth. Do not jerk the camera or hesitate in a zoom or pan; make every movement seem like it is purposeful whether it is or not.

Watch network TV's coverage of the sport that you are going to shoot. See how the experienced professionals do it; see the kind of shots they get and how they follow the ball. Try to take what they are doing and adapt it to a one-camera shoot. The cuts that are done live on the network may have to be done in editing for you, but if you get the right elements on tape, you can make it look pretty close to network coverage. The main thing is to follow the ball or stay with the leader. It takes practice and much concentration, but it is the only way to get professional results.

10 Technical Editing Basics

One of the true advantages that videotape enjoys over film is the ease of editing. Film requires developing time, viewing time, and cutting and splicing time—a slow process often involving several different people and companies. Videotape can be taken directly to an editing system and quickly edited by one person. Since videotape requires no developing time and the editing process requires no physical cutting or gluing, the time required to shoot and edit a videotape story is much shorter and the process easier than for a story done on film.

The videotape editing process is basically a process of information transfer. Information such as video pictures, sound and control signals is transferred from a source or player machine to an edit machine or recorder. The source machine has the unedited, or raw, videotape footage; the edit machine or recorder eventually has the edited story, or edited master, recorded on its tape. Almost all editing systems in TV stations, corporate video centers and independent production houses are set up so that the information flows from left to right.

In the early days of videotape, some videotape editing was accomplished in a way similar to film and audiotape (reel-to-reel) editing—the cut-and-splice method. Information recorded out of sequence was physically cut up and reassembled in the desired order. This process is still common in film, somewhat unusual in audio, but totally nonexistent in videotape. The cut-and-splice method

is no longer used with videotape because it is very slow and inexact, making clean video edits almost impossible. As soon as videocassettes entered the marketplace, physical splice-editing of videotape went the way of hand-crank starters on automobiles.

In multicamera studio TV work, one technique of shooting is referred to as **live on tape**. This refers to shooting the entire scene or show without having to stop and make edits or do what is called **pull-ups** where the show is edited at a later time. This process is the same as live TV. A 30-minute show is completed 30 minutes after the show begins; no editing is required. The most obvious reason for this is economic: saving studio time and eliminating editing time. In ENG the need for immediacy in a newscast and the ability to have a late-breaking news story air quickly require a live-on-tape technique.

More commonly, however, the expectation is that the field footage is shot for the edit. In other words, editing is an expected and necessary part of the production process. Scenes are often shot out of order for convenience. Multiple takes of the same scene or shot are done to allow the director and editor to select the shot that best captures what they intend to communicate. In studio TV the director usually has multiple cameras to choose from to yield various camera angles and focal length. The director is expected to be able to choose which camera provides the best shot while the

179

show is being aired or recorded so that editing is unnecessary. In portable video, the director and editor often have plenty of time to think about and make these decisions.

In corporate video production centers, the first skill that managers look for in their entry-level hires is editing. A person skilled in editing should be knowledgeable not only about the process of editing itself, but also about framing, composition, visual pacing and flow. A skilled editor knows how to put it all together and is therefore a crucial member of the production team. (See Figure 10.1.)

VIDEOTAPE FORMATS

A thorough knowledge of the information contained on videotape is a necessity in understanding the process of electronic editing or information transfer. There are various ways of recording information (audio, video and synchronization) onto videotape, which results in a number of different formats. The formats vary in a number of ways:

1. Tape width
2. Types of information
3. Physical and electronic methods of actually placing the information onto the tape

Some formats share the same tape width, but with the exception of Sony's standard and SP tape types their U-Matic and Beta formats, no two formats mentioned here are compatible, that is, one format's tape cannot be played on another format's machine.

Reel-to-Reel Format

Before cassettes came into use, videotape was wrapped on reels similar to those used for film projection. This system required a supply reel and a take-up reel.

Two-Inch Quadruplex Quadruplex tape was the broadcast industry standard for many years. Quadruplex is a high-quality format that uses four heads and records four tracks of information (hence the name quadruplex) onto 2-inch magnetic tape. (See Figure 10.2.) The four tracks of information include:

1. the control track (which gives synchronization information)
2. the video track
3. the audio track
4. the cue track (used for additional audio or a time code signal for addressing or location purposes)

The Quadruplex format has been replaced by the smaller 1-inch Type C and newer ½-inch formats. Because these formats are narrower and less bulky, broadcasters save both storage space and money.

One-Inch Type C The 1-inch Type C format works on a smaller machine and surpasses the quality of the quadruplex, or 2-inch, format. Video information is recorded onto the tape somewhat differently on the 1-inch format than on the quad format. (See Figure 10.3.) Type C is very popular because it allows special effects, such as slow motion, accelerated motion and freeze frame.

The 1-inch Type C format has become the broadcast industry standard for most studio production. Most often used by networks to record programs that will be rebroadcast by their affiliates, this format is used only occasionally in the field because of its size and the expense of the portable recording machines. Large-scale portable shoots such as those for professional sports often have large production vehicles that can house a number of 1-inch machines. In addition to using one VCR per camera for recording, there often are one or more machines used for instant replay.

One-Inch Type B One-inch Type B is a high-quality format similar to Type C, but it does not allow variable speed motion because of the way the video is encoded onto tape. This format also does not allow an image to be shown during fast-forward or fast-reverse modes, making the editing process slower. For these reasons, this format has not been used very widely and is not marketed currently.

Videocassette Format

Cassettes were successfully adapted for use with videotape in the early 1970s. The videocassette allows the tape supply and take-up reels to be housed inside a plastic case. Since videocassettes are self-threading, physical handling of the tape is not necessary. When housed in a videocassette, the videotape is better protected from heat, moisture and dust than on reel-to-reel tape.

Professional Generally superior in performance to those used by consumers, professional videocassette formats are used by professional broadcasters, networks (both cable and broadcast), independent production houses and high-end corporate video users. These formats provide more lines of resolution and better color reproduction than most consumer formats and have less signal loss during editing and duplication.

Figure 10.1: The top picture shows a simple ¾-inch U-Matic edit system with a remote edit control panel; the bottom picture shows an A/B roll editing system with two player VCRs that send the signal through a TBC and switcher and then to a recorder. The switcher receives video from the two player VCRs, an effects generator and a character generator.

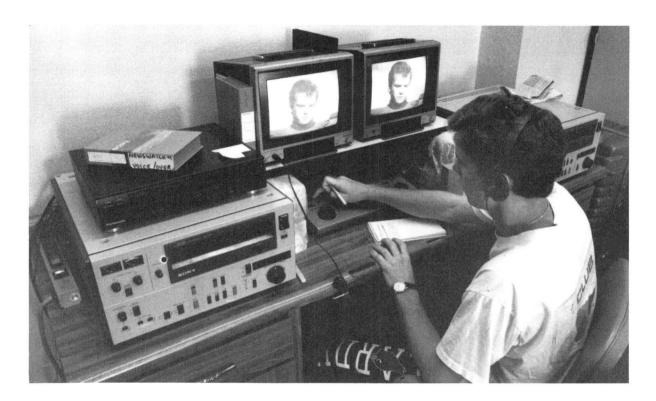

Figure 10.2: Video and audio track pattern on a section of 2-inch quadruplex videotape.

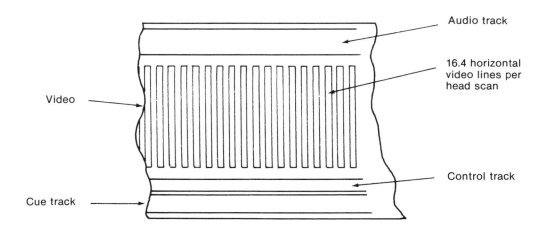

Three-quarter-Inch U-Matic and SP U-Matic
From the late 1970s through most of the 1980s, the ¾-inch videocassette was the standard for most broadcast news operations, educational, institutional and corporate video production units. Unlike reel-to-reel formats which have to be manually threaded, all the videotape is automatically threaded on a videocassette and is in the general U-Matic format. (See Figure 10.4.) Within U-Matic there are two different subformats. Regular U-Matic has been commonly used since the mid-1970s. An improved version of the U-Matic format called SP U-Matic, introduced in 1986, has better resolution (330 lines compared to 280) and

less ringing of both the luminance (brightness) and chrominance (color) signals. In addition, the format also features a noise reduction system for its audio channels, time code that is part of the video signal and less generational loss. A third-generation SP tape will look almost as good as a first-generation regular U-Matic recording. SP U-Matic will rapidly replace regular U-Matic format because the manufacturer has phased regular U-Matic out of production. However, a large number of regular U-Matic machines purchased before 1987 will continue to be in operation for some time. A regular U-Matic cassette plays in an SP U-Matic machine and vice versa, but the full benefit

Figure 10.3: Video and audio track pattern on a section of Type C videotape.

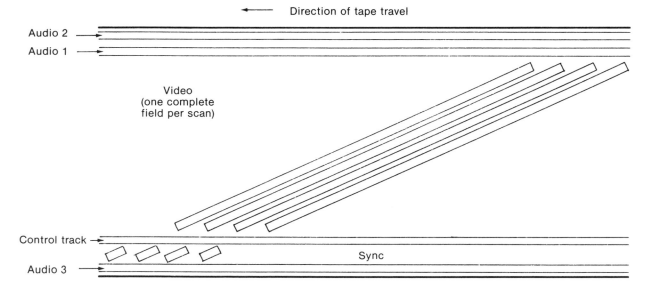

Figure 10.4: Video and audio track pattern on a section of ¾-inch U-Matic cassette tape.

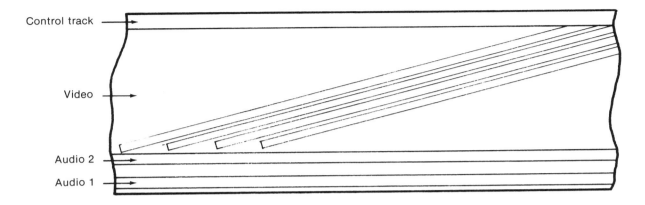

Control track

Video

Audio 2

Audio 1

of this improvement will not be realized unless the specially formulated SP tape is used and played back in an SP machine. There are U-Matic machines available for editing systems with a feature called dynamic tracking that provides noise-free freeze frames and slow-motion video in forward and reverse—features that were previously available only the more expensive machines in the 2-inch, 1-inch and professional ½-inch formats. However, for the dynamic tracking feature to work, the machine must be connected to a time base corrector.

The ¾-inch formats are slant-tracked or helical, as are the 1-inch formats. As in the quadruplex format, four different tracks of information are encoded onto this type of videotape.

Half-Inch Betacam, Betacam SP and MII In many professional production operations, especially broadcast and high-quality independent production, the format of choice is professional ½-inch Betacam, Betacam SP or MII. Regular Betacam is no longer manufactured although it is still extensively used. Most of the professional operations still have ¾-inch machines available for the occasional tape that is shot on ¾-inch and must be bumped up, or duped, to a different format.

Betacam, Betacam SP and MII use ½-inch videotape cassettes designed for Betamax and VHS, but they are professional formats. The process of encoding information on Betacam and MII is radically different from the consumer formats. This style of encoding information is called component video. Component video recording utilizes different tracks on the videotape to record the luminance (brightness) and chrominance (color) information. The procedure used by the other formats

is **composite video**, where the luminance and chrominance information (along with the appropriate synchronization signals) are combined on one track per video field. In component video, two tracks are required per video field. These tracks, the Y track for luminance and the C track for chrominance, are combined for replay to yield one video field. (See Figure 10.5.)

The advantage of using component video recording is that the higher-frequency information in the luminance and chrominance signals is not lost when combined as they are in composite recording. The quality of component video is very similar to 1-inch C format video, but the advantages of smaller and less expensive videocassettes, recorders and players make these two formats the ones preferred by the majority of professionals who demand the highest quality when shooting portable video. Of the two formats, Betacam (now Betacam SP) enjoys enormous popularity with the

Figure 10.5: Video and audio track pattern on a section of ½-inch Betacam SP videotape.

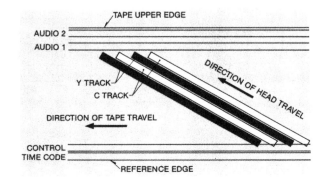

high-end portable video users, most notably with the major market and network ENG operations.

Digital Video   The videotape formats discussed to this point have utilized an analog procedure to encode and decode video and audio information that does have some drawbacks. The analog process is a process that reads a video signal and then approximates it in reproduction. This becomes especially apparent in duplication. In the process of duplicating a signal from one tape to another, a small amount of information is lost. After several repetitions of this process, a tape that is several generations old has noticeably less sharpness and may have smeary and inaccurate color. The amount of signal lost depends on the format; professional formats such as 1-inch C lose less information per generation than other formats such as U-Matic and the home video formats. Because of the nature of the way the signal is encoded onto tape, digital video recording allows for no signal degradation from generation to generation as long as the signal transfer is done properly. This means a tape can be reproduced 20 times or go through 20 generations before any signal degradation occurs. Digital video also has superior video and audio signals as compared with all other formats. Specifically, the video signal has a very high signal-to-noise ratio and avoids the moire pattern problem (a herringbone distortion when striped patterns appear) common to all analog formats. The audio is exceptionally good—similar in quality to audio compact disc. There are four audio channels available for recording and editing. In addition, digital video enjoys a signal free of dropout. (See Figures 10.6 and 10.7.)

Consumer   Consumer videocassette formats were developed to be easy to use, inexpensive and of good quality. Consumer formats generally have fewer lines of resolution and poorer color reproduction than professional formats.

Betamax and VHS   Betamax, the first home video format, has become essentially obsolete. Although there are many machines in homes throughout the country, video stores that rent Betamax tapes are becoming quite scarce. Camcorders and editing systems for Betamax are no longer in production. The format is technically equivalent to the VHS format, also ½-inch, but has less recording time per cassette. The VHS format has flourished significantly in the last ten years and enjoys enormous popularity. Camcorders and editing systems abound in the marketplace. In fact, editing systems have become quite good for

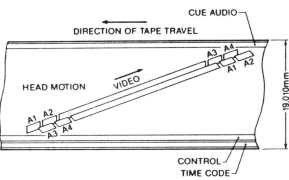

Figure 10.6: Video and audio track pattern on a section of digital videotape, $A_1 \rightarrow A_4$ refers to the four audio tracks.

VHS tape and are common in educational, governmental, institutional and independent video production facilities. Perhaps the greatest growth has been in home video where large numbers of consumers have purchased camcorders and are now starting to purchase editing equipment.

VHS-C   VHS-C, or compact VHS, records information onto the tape similarly to VHS, but the cassette is compact, or smaller. The smaller size cassette allows the camcorders to be smaller. Tabletop and edit machines are not readily available and have only recently been marketed for this derivative of the VHS format. Standard VHS machines can be used for playback with the use of a special adapter.

S-VHS   S-VHS, referred to as Super VHS, is another derivative of standard VHS, but is not compatible with standard VHS VCRs. The benefit of the format is increased resolution and elimination of some of the color interference of VHS recording. The resolution is greater than 400 lines (as compared with 260 for standard VHS) thus allowing the picture to have a professional appearance. A larger bandwidth for more video signal information makes this high resolution possible but it requires a special output cable that separates the luminance or brightness information (y) from the chrominance or color information (c). This cable features a special connector referred to as an S connector.

8mm and HI8   In the late 1980s, a videotape format was introduced that utilized a tape width even narrower than the ½-inch formats. The videotape for this format was only 8mm wide, or roughly ⅓-inch wide. Despite this diminutive size, the quality of the format is comparable to the

Figure 10.7: Digital video recorders for (1) studio and (2) portable applications. *Courtesy Sony Corp.*

Figure 10.8: Video and audio track pattern on a section of 8mm videotape. *Courtesy Sony Corp.*

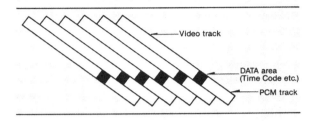

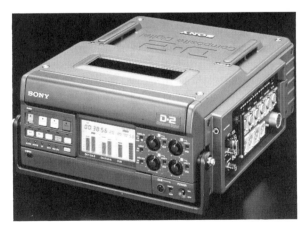

existing consumer formats of VHS and Betamax. In addition to good-quality video, this format offered two different kinds of audio recording. Two standard linear audio tracks are available that are comparable to that of other formats. In addition, a **pulse code modulation** (PCM) system is utilized that yields two tracks of near digital-quality audio. This type of audio recording yields a larger dynamic range and frequency response superior to

existing analog audio-recording methods. (See Figure 10.8.)

This 8mm format, despite being designed for non-broadcast use, comes with the capability of encoding time code on the tape. This time code, though incompatible with the time code on professional formats, significantly helps make the editing process more exact by putting a permanent address on each frame of video.

Just as VHS was improved with S-VHS, 8mm received a significant upgrade with the advent of HI8. By increasing the bandwidth for the luminance signal, a horizontal resolution of over 400 TV lines is possible in this format. The video signal-to-noise ratio (S/N ratio) is also improved, yielding a clearer picture with less interference. Like S-VHS, it requires a special output cable—an S connector—to separate the luminance from the chrominance information. Another feature of the format is that it can reproduce images in the slow-motion or still-frame mode without distortion or interference.

Because of its extremely compact size, the 8mm format allows for a very compact editing system. In fact, the all-in-one editing system offered by the manufacturer resembles a dual-drive computer more closely than a standard two-machine, two-monitor editing system. (See Figure 10.9.) The HI8 system also features a playback machine designed to interface directly with existing ¾-inch SP U-Matic systems, making this the first high-performance consumer/industrial format to merge directly with professional systems. (See Figure 10.10.)

TYPES OF EDITS

There are two types of edits that can be done on editing systems: the assemble edit and the insert

Figure 10.9: This Sony EVO-9700 HI8 edit system is small enough to fit on a desktop. *Courtesy Sony Corp.*

edit. Choosing between these two types of edits is often the first decision that you will make when beginning to edit your story or project.

Assemble Edit

An assemble edit transfers all information from the source machine to the edit machine. Specifically, it transfers the control track, video track and both audio tracks to the edit machine. In other words, it duplicates the information from the source tape onto the edit tape. When placing an entire program or long segment onto a new videotape, an assemble edit is usually appropriate. This process is similar to a straight dubbing, or duping, process that can be accomplished using two tape machines and no editing controller. Pressing "play" on the source machine and "record" and "play" on the edit machine will achieve the same thing as an assemble edit.

Assemble edits have two disadvantages.

1. This edit is all or nothing. All information is transferred; there are no options such as adding extra audio or video to the edit master. Everything must be laid down in one edit.
2. At the end of every assemble edit, a few frames of snow or glitch appear on the tape. This is a result of transferring the control track. The erase head of the recorder precedes the record head by several frames. It erases everything on the tape in an assemble edit and thus leaves a hole at the end of every edit.

This presents no problem if you are duplicating an entire program, but if you are trying to place a video segment into an already existing story or piece on your edited master tape, you will then have an annoying (and technically unacceptable) glitch in your final edited master. You can avoid this problem when editing a piece consecutively, one segment at a time. After each segment is recorded on the edit machine, you must back up the tape and start your next segment before the glitch. (See Figure 10.11.)

Figure 10.10: This HI8 player/recorder will interface with ¾-inch U-Matic or SP U-Matic. This allows direct editing to ¾-inch. *Courtesy Sony Corp.*

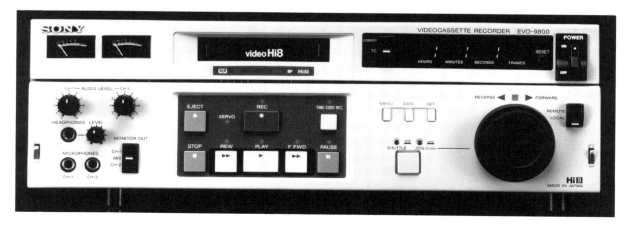

Figure 10.11: When assemble editing one segment at a time, backspace to a point before the glitch and start the next segment there.

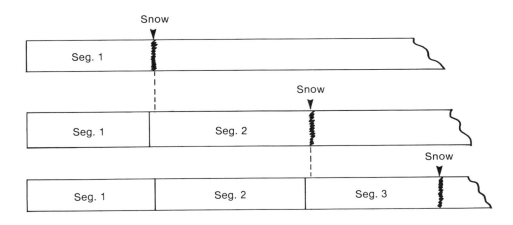

Insert Edit

The insert edit allows you to select either the video track, audio one track, audio two track or any combination of them to be transferred to the edit master. This selection process is accomplished by a simple button-pushing procedure before the edit begins. (See Figure 10.12.)

An insert edit does not cause a glitch at the end of the edit because it does not transfer control track information. Since insert edits do not transfer control track, no erasures are made on the control track of the edit master tape. Therefore, you can insert pieces of video, audio one, audio two or any combination into an existing piece without causing video or audio breakup or noise. (See Figure 10.13.)

One disadvantage of insert editing is that the tape you use for the edit master must have a good control track before you attempt an insert edit. If you use a tape that already has any type of video recorded on it, there is no problem as long as the control track has no breaks in it. If you use a new tape as the edit master (as is common when you have an important story or program to edit onto the tape), you must put a control track on it.

The most common procedure for doing this is called **black bursting** the tape. This is a procedure that requires you to record your videotape with a steady black-only signal (that is, with no other picture information). This can be accomplished using a signal generator that generates video black (a steady black picture) or by connecting your tape deck to a camera and recording the tape with the camera on, but with the lens capped.

Some editors choose an alternative to the black-only signal and use a color bar pattern from a signal generator or camera instead of black. This method prevents the possibility of unedited spaces within the edit master slipping past a hurried editor's eye. Black frames remain in the edit master when a black-bursted tape has some missed spaces on it due to inaccurate editing. If the tape is color bar bursted, these unedited spaces show the bright color bars and are easy to spot and cover with additional edits.

TECHNICAL CONCEPTS

You can gain a better understanding of the editing process by familiarizing yourself with some key terms and concepts that explain the videotaping process. Since electronic editing is basically a process of information transfer and videotape recording, a solid understanding of videotape recording fundamentals should provide a good context for understanding the videotape editing process.

Scanning

When a light image is focused on the light-sensitive front plate of a pickup device in a video camera, a single electron beam scans this sensitive area by starting in the upper left corner and going straight across to the right until it gets to the end of the light-sensitive area. Once it reaches the right edge, the beam shuts off momentarily and repositions itself on the beginning of the third line. The beam then turns back on and "scans" the third line

Figure 10.12: The edit control buttons on a Sony BVW-75 Beta SP studio recorder.

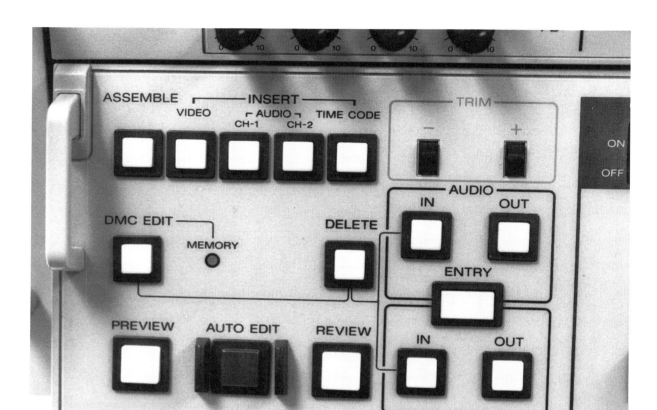

to the end. The beam then shuts off and repositions itself at the beginning of the fifth line. (See Figure 10.14.)

This process continues to the middle of line 525, where the beam shuts off and repositions itself at the top of the light-sensitive area and begins its movement on the left edge of the second line. It repeats the above process, except that it scans or reads all of the even-numbered lines, finishing at the end of line 524. In total, it scans 262.5 odd-numbered lines, and 262.5 even-numbered lines. This entire scanning process occurs 30 times per second, fast enough to allow our eyes and brains to believe that we are seeing a solid, constant image.

The complete scanning of either the odd or the even lines forms a half-picture known as a **field**. Two fields, when combined or interlaced, form a **frame** or complete picture.

This scanning process is also accomplished in the picture tube of a TV set or monitor. An electron beam of varying strength strikes the phosphors (luminescent dots or stripes) on the inside of the front surface of the picture tube, causing them to glow with varying intensity. With all this rapid activity going on in the pickup tube of the camera and picture tube of the TV set, it is easy to understand why synchronization is so important. Scanning rates for video must be identical in the camera and monitor to reproduce a good-quality image.

Fields, Frames and Segments

A field is a half-picture that combines with a second half-picture to form a frame. In some formats (for example, the 1-inch Type C), a frame is encoded onto tape in one continuous line and is called a **non-segmented format**. Other formats (for example, the ¼-inch U-Matic) that encode each frame on a separate line are **segmented formats**. The non-segmented format allows for some special effects like noise-free slow motion or freeze-frame without using a time base corrector, while segmented formats do not.

Figure 10.13: When insert editing, you can insert a new segment into an existing program without causing a glitch (a few frames of snow).

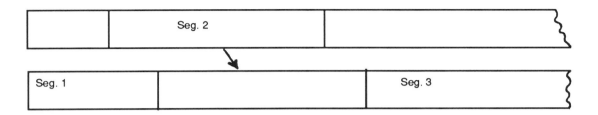

Fields have a definite order to them: they are recorded and played back in sequence—the first field and the the second in order to make one frame. Editing systems must be able to distinguish between the first and second fields when edits are made. If this distinction is not made and an edit is done between fields one and two (in the middle of a frame), it will cause a glitch, picture breakup or simply a bad edit. Editing systems have a special circuit built in called a **frame servo,** which prevents these bad edits (also known as **wrong field edits**) from occurring.

Figure 10.14: The electron beam must scan each frame of video twice, once for each field. Field 1 starts at the upper left and ends in the middle of the frame at the bottom. Field 2 starts at mid-frame at the top and ends at the lower right. This process occurs 30 times per second.

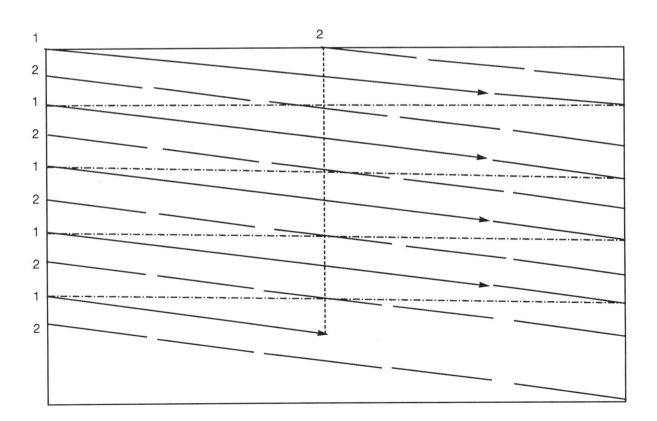

Tracking

When a videotape is recorded on a VCR, it is recorded at a particular speed with the information placed onto the tape at particular locations. The word "particular" here indicates that each VCR has its own speed and location of information on tape. Thus each VCR is slightly different from the next. This slight difference between VCRs is called tracking, and VCRs generally have a control that allows the playback machine to track very closely to the way the original recorder has placed the information onto the tape.

When you begin an editing session, you should set the tracking control (measured by a small meter) on your source or playback machine to optimize your tracking. If your playback machine tracks much differently than the machine originally used for recording, a poor-quality picture with snow, wrong colors, distortion and/or bad audio will result.

Control Track Editing

All formats of videotape include one track of information called the control track. This track is crucial to the editing process because editing systems rely on the control track for synchronization. The control track is analogous to the sprocket holes in film. The control track indicates the location of the video information.

If your control track is damaged or partially missing, your videocassette deck will not locate the video information and you may have a total loss of video on the screen. The editing system will only make edits when it can read the control track of your source machine. You can think of your control track as the clothes rod in your closet; without a good strong clothes rod, you can put your clothes in the closet, but they will probably fall down. If you edit with a poorly recorded or missing control track, you may think that you are making an edit, but your video will fall out of sight.

Time Code Editing

Almost all the newest professional editing machines make extensive use of time code in the editing process. Time code numbers are available to the producer or editor to keep track of which shots they want to use as the tape is being shot from the VCR or while viewing the tape on a machine with a time code reader. The editor can quickly find any shot on the tape if the time code for the start of that shot is known. Modern edit machines can edit either by control track reference or by time code reference. Both appear as numbers in the timer display on the edit machine and a switch tells you which you are using.

For control track editing, the timer can be set at any number and changed at any time during the edit process (but not during an actual edit). Time code display will always show the number that is recorded on the tape. Professional editors always edit with the machines in time code mode because the edits are more accurate (there is less chance that a control track error might cause the edit to miss by several frames) and easier if the editor is working from script notes or even making notes for further work to be done on the piece. This means that the black-burst edit master tape must have time code on it also. These tapes are generally blackened on a machine similar to the edit VCR (if not the same machine) and the time code would be put there automatically. It does not matter what the time code numbers are on the recorder; they are just there as a permanent reference to locate frames within the tape and as a reference for the edit controller. In EFP edit masters where only one finished piece will be put on a single tape, many editors like to black-burst the tape starting with 00:59:00:00 and begin the first shot of the piece at 01:00:00:00, leaving the first minute of the tape for color bars, test tone and countdown.

Time Base Correction

Although most video recorders marketed today for professional ENG and EFP are high quality and manufactured to very strict standards, there are often slight variations in their performance. In other words, there are slight differences in each helical scan videotape recorder. Even if two recorders are capable of identical performances when new, subtle differences become apparent over time because of different wear.

These subtle differences cause slight timing variation or error when tapes are recorded on one VCR and played back on another. Differences are usually attributable to physical or mechanical problems which, although minor, cause an unstable signal. When these signals are played through a monitor, they are usually not noticeable. If they are meant for broadcasting, however, they may be too unstable to meet the technical standards set by the FCC for an acceptable broadcast signal.

The answer to this problem is a time base corrector, which takes the output of a helical scan

VCR and corrects the signal by making the necessary adjustments, line by line, to that signal. Time base correctors often have a second device installed within them which allows for manipulation of the video level or gain, the black level, the color phase or tint, and the chroma level or amount of color information of the signal. This device, known as a **processing amplifier**, or proc-amp, is often built right into the same housing as the time base corrector.

Many editors in independent production houses or corporate video departments have these units installed in their editing systems (after the source machine, before the editor). The processing amplifier cannot be used without a waveform monitor and a vectorscope. Without these two monitors, you cannot see the effects of any adjustments you make on the processing amplifier. Machines designed to be used as edit players in SP Beta and MII formats have built-in time base correctors, eliminating the need to add these devices to their edit systems.

EDITING MACHINES

Most editing machines follow the same approach to performing an edit. Besides the basic FAST FORWARD, REWIND, PLAY, STOP, PAUSE and RECORD, there is a variable speed control on the tape called SHUTTLE/JOG/SEARCH that allows the operator to cue the videotape to the precise frame at which to start an edit. There will also be some means of entering the edit points chosen by the operator into the edit console memory. Usually, the ENTER button is used in conjunction with the IN and OUT buttons to give that message to the recorder. (See Figure 10.15.)

Most recorders allow the editor to shift the edit mode from assemble to insert as well as preview the edit, without actually performing it, with the use of the PREVIEW button. To make slight corrections in the edit points that are already entered in the console, there are usually two buttons, (+) and (−), for edit point shifting or trimming. When an edit console is in the insert edit mode, you must choose whether you will insert video, channel one audio or channel two audio. You can choose one or more in any combination. (See Figure 10.16.)

Video Controls

Besides the controls for performing edits, there are also other controls on some tape machines relating to input and output. In general there are three controls for video and two for audio. The

skew knob (which controls the tension in a videotape) is generally not used by the operator unless there is some major problem with the tape in the machine. **Video level control** (which measures the amplitude of the video signal) is usually not used by the operator unless a waveform monitor is hooked up to the output of the tape machine. Without the scope, the video level knob should be left centered in the notch, or automatic, position.

The operator has to adjust tracking control on the machine used as the player. Leave the **tracking knob** on the recorder in the notch (usually the 12-o'clock position) during the editing. Adjust the tracking knob on the player while the tape is being played. Each time a different tape is played in the playback machine, adjust the tracking knob so that you can achieve optimum tracking.

To set the tracking for the tape to be used in the player, play any portion of the tape and rotate the tracking knob until the needle on the meter reads as high as it can in the positive direction. The knob can stay in that position as long as you are using that tape. If you should switch to another tape in the player, then the tracking will have to be readjusted. New machines now have automatic tracking.

Audio Controls

The audio controls follow basic standard practices. There is usually an **audio limiter switch,** ON or OFF. Unless the machine will be unattended and levels cannot be preset, do not use the audio limiter. Most limiters are too slow to react and recover from extreme levels and can produce uneven audio levels or dropout (clipped) audio.

Most newer tape machines have separate **record** and **playback controls**. In general, for both playback and recording levels, the controls should be set for the loudest peaks of the audio signal. A peak should deflect the needle on the VU meter to at or near 0. The VU meter measures volume units; its scale goes from a minus 10 to a plus 5. A good range for maximum needle deflection is between minus 7 and minus 2. (See Figure 10.17.)

The best way to calibrate audio levels is to use a standard or known source, preferably an oscillating tone from an audio mixer or other source. From this source, the audio level should be set at 0 dB. Feed this signal through the player and onto the recorder. The playback levels on the player should be adjusted to read 0 dB on the scale and the record level on the recorder should be set at 0 dB.

Figure 10.15: This is the front panel of BTS's version of the Sony BVW-75 edit machine. The built-in TBC has its control behind the lower portion of the front panel, which can be accessed by pulling the panel forward.

To maintain the calibration of the audio setup, do all audio mixing in only one area, in most cases, at the playback source. Leave the record levels untouched for the entire editing process. Many edit setups will have a separate audio mixer between the player and the recorder to give better control over the audio or to allow the mixing in of audio sources other than those on the tape machines. Again, calibration of all audio controls before editing is very important.

Most edit-capable machines also have **mix select switches** of some type. These can route the audio input and output. They indicate which channel of audio is coming from a machine and to which channel it is going and indicate which channel is being fed to the audio monitor. The way one machine is wired to the other can also determine how the routing of the audio can be controlled. If you familiarize yourself with your audio setup, you should be able to mix or isolate any channel

Figure 10.16: Standard editing system.

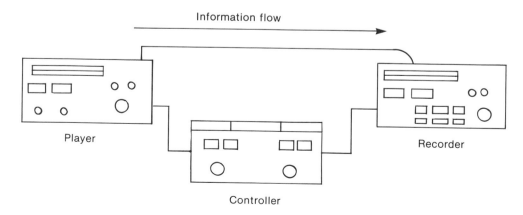

Figure 10.17: Audio VU meters with volume controls and a video meter with tracking and level controls for a Sony 5850.

and record it onto any channel of the recorder. On the recorder leave the audio output to the monitor in mix and the playback levels set in the calibrated positions so there will not be any surprises in the audio of the finished product.

On the machines that can record metal oxide tapes, such as SP Beta and MII, there are four channels of audio. For the most part you will only be using the two linear channels (one and two) for all your audio needs. As you progress into more professional situations and stereo audio recording, you can make better use of the other two channels. This book limits discussion to only the linear channels.

Video Connections

Cable hookups between machines are a key to understanding the operation of any editing setup. (See Figure 10.18.) The most important cable be-

tween the player and recorder is the edit control cable. If a separate edit console is required, then this cable goes from each of the decks to the console. The edit control cable is a multi-pin cable that allows the two machines to talk to each other via the edit controls. Both the player and the recorder have several video inputs and outputs. (See Figure 10.19.)

In most TV stations and production houses, editing packages are on a video routing system. The video cable from the routing system goes into the VIDEO IN connector on the recorder. If the edit machines are on house sync, then a video line with that sync goes into the SYNC IN connector.

Video Routing System   A video routing system is like a cable TV system. Multiple channels of audio and video (not a combined RF signal) from a central distribution center are sent to each editing setup (or edit bay). An **RF signal**

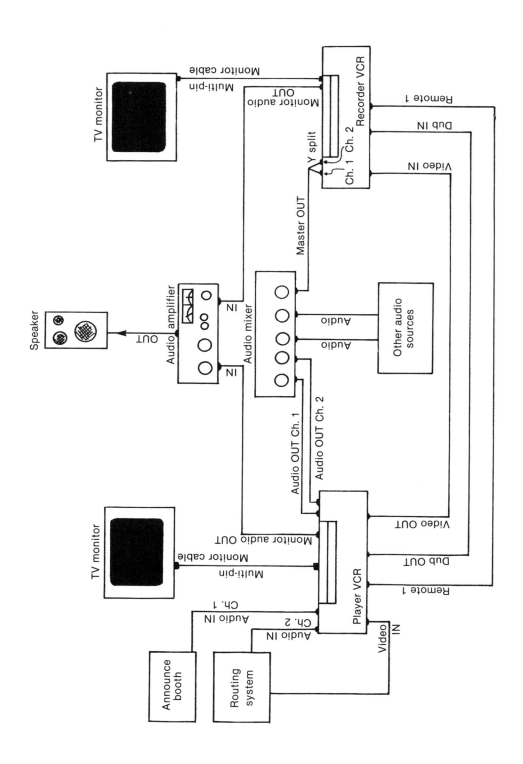

Figure 10.18: Cables for a professional two-machine editing setup.

Figure 10.19: The back panel of a Sony BVW-75. On this machine the synchronization inputs/outputs are called "REF.VIDEO" and can be switched from external to automatic select.

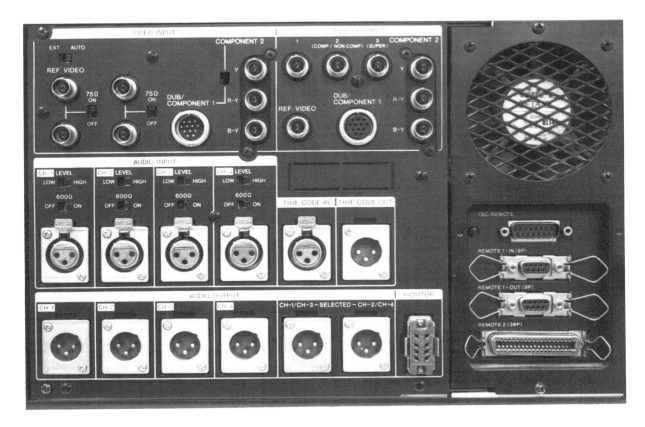

combines audio and video and transmits at a frequency similar to radio or home cable TV.) Almost any video output in the building can be put on the routing system. Such things as color bars, black video, character generators, switch outputs, studio cameras, satellite reception, other tape machines and even broadcast signals from other TV stations can be on the routing system.

By dialing the number of what you want to see, you can feed the video of the router to the player of that edit bay. The player machine can pass it on just like video and audio from a tape. Most of the time the machine should be fed black video from the routing system.

Synchronization

A synchronization pulse or reference signal is the time reference that allows the electronics of two or more tape machines or cameras to work together. While a VCR or camera has internal synchronization if two machines are hooked together (such as multiple cameras feeding into one switcher or two VCRs in an edit bay), only one sync source can be

used. Any two machines designed to edit always allow the player machine to be the source of synchronization for the recorder as part of their edit functions.

Cameras, like edit machines, do not sync to each other without being connected to each other. They must be fed a reference that can be common to all of them; this is called **gen-lock**. Edit machines and cameras can be fed an external reference sync from the main sync generator in the station or studio. This **house sync**, as it is referred to, is more reliable and enables the machines to perform at their peak. An editing system works without either a routing system or external sync, but both are a great advantage.

On the player, there will be two VIDEO OUT connectors, one to be cabled to the recorder's VIDEO IN and the other to the monitor's VIDEO IN. If you are using a monitor that can interface with the player via a multi-pin monitor cable, then the simple video-only cable is not necessary.

As with the player, if the recorder is running on house sync, then the sync cable will go into the recorder's SYNC IN connector and the switch at both the SYNC IN connectors should be in the EXTERNAL SYNC position. If the edit bay is freestanding (not on house sync), the switch is in the INTERNAL SYNC position. Newer edit machines not only have internal sync but also an internal black generator.

Audio Connections

The audio connections can be much more complicated than the video. For the player, if the edit unit is on a routing system that delivers sound to various locations, then the audio from that system goes into the AUDIO IN connector. On some machines it may be necessary to have a Y cable made to get the audio onto both channels of the audio input. The output of the machine should be from channel one, channel two and monitor AUDIO OUT. If you are using a multi-pin monitor cable then you will not need the monitor AUDIO OUT.

From here the audio lines can go to an audio mixing board or straight to the recorder. If the lines go to a separate mixer, the two channels can be mixed at the mixer or can be Y-cabled to only one input and mixed at the player output at the player output controls on its front panel. The single audio line from the mixer output can be split into a Y to feed both channels of the recorder's AUDIO IN because all mixing is done at either the player or the mixer.

Even though there probably is different audio on the two channels of the finished product, they should be premixed to the proper volumes respective of each other. In other words, the two channels on the recorder are for receiving premixed audio, and their playback and record levels should never be changed from their calibrated position. The two channels of audio play together with no need to monitor the volume of one versus the other. Each audio input should have a switch for line- or mike-level input/output. Set the switches for the signal level you are using.

VIDEO INPUT Switch

Another control for older VCRS is the VIDEO INPUT. The switch usually has two inputs, line and dub. For the player, the switch is usually in the LINE position. When the player is hooked up to a routing system, the LINE position allows it to be fed whatever is coming off the router; for editing, the player should be fed black video. If there is no

router, the machine is not receiving any source and the position of the switch is unimportant for the player.

The recorder's switch should always be in the DUB or EDIT position. This switch commands the recorder to look to the other machine for its reference control (very necessary information for the editing process) and for its video source. If you are using a multi-pin cable with your monitors and your machine has a VIDEO INPUT switch for TV, that position feeds the machine whatever is on the TV tuner of its monitor. In other words, you can record off air anything that the TV set can pick up.

The VIDEO INPUT switch on newer component VCRs is somewhat different from the one on the older U-Matic machines. There are often three positions for the switch: Y/R-B, composite and CTDM. In general the player machine is in the composite position, and the recorder is in the Y/R-B (component) position. The set-up may vary from format to format and as to how the machines are tied into the house system or type of edit controller. Like any complicated piece of machinery, it is best to read the operator's book thoroughly and check to see exactly how the machines are hooked up. With so many formats and composite/component translations, it is easy to become confused especially when machines of different formats are connected together as part of an edit system. In most TV stations and many production houses an edit station will have several formats interconnected to be able to make use of the vast tape libraries that contain a broad range of tape types.

Understanding the Editing System

It is not possible for this book to cover all the combinations of formats, manufacturers and wiring hook-ups. The following sections concern the basic functions of edit machines in general. While machines may vary by brand and format, the process of making a simple edit remains almost identical.

Performing an Insert Edit

Here is a sample edit on a Sony BVU-75 editing system. The tape you are editing onto should be black burst or have some type of video signal layed down on it. You can burst the entire tape or just enough of it to give plenty of room for the length of your finished product. This gives the record tape a control track that allows you to do insert editing right from the start of your project.

Assume you already have a countdown or leader on your record tape and you are ready to lay the first shot down. With the raw material in the player and the edit tape in the recorder, both machines should be in STOP. The control panel of the recorder controls both machines by using the PLAYER/RECORDER switch to designate which machine is being commanded. (See Figure 10.20.)

The PB-PB/EE (playback-playback/edit entry) switch allows you to play the audio and video through the recorder while the recorder is not in the RECORD mode but merely in STOP. PB lets the machine act as a normal VCR. PB/EE feeds video and audio through the meters to the record heads and to the recorder's while the machine is in STOP. This allows you to use only one video and audio monitor for both machines if necessary, without having to eject the tape in the recorder or put the recorder in record mode to look at the output of the player.

With the PB-PB/EE switch in the PB/EE position on the recorder, change the control designator to PLAYER and push the SEARCH button. This allows you to move the tape by means of the SEARCH knob in either direction up to 10 times

the normal speed. Using the SEARCH knob, shuttle the tape to the point you would like to have as the beginning of the shot. By pushing the ENTER and the IN buttons at the same time you have given the edit control memory the in-point.

Switch the designator to RECORDER, and do the same procedure to line up the spot on the record tape where you wish the edit to begin. Give the recorder its in-time. While still on the RECORDER designator, push the button marked PREVIEW and view what the edit will actually look like. The machines will go through the editing process but will not actually transfer the video.

The edit will continue to run until you give it a STOP command. There are two ways of doing this: by pushing the STOP button on the recorder which will leave no memory of an out-point in the edit control, or by pressing ENTER OUT on the recorder which will be placed in the memory.

If this preview edit appears satisfactory, press the EDIT button and the machines will perform the edit by the in-points you have given them. If an out-point has been entered (you need to enter an out-point only on the recorder), then the edit will run only to that point. When the edit is finished the

Figure 10.20: The PLAYER/RECORDER control.

recorder and player will cue up their tapes on the last frame of that edit and erase all previous in- and out-points.

If you stop an edit by simply pressing STOP on the recorder, the edit will instantly stop but the machines will still have the memory of the in- and out-points last given because you have interrupted the edit. The machine thinks it must redo the edit from the beginning. The only ways to erase those times are to put in an out-point and let the edit run its course, enter new points for both machines or reset the timers on both machines which will erase the memory of any in-points or out-points previously given.

If you should wish to change an edit point slightly, either an in- or an out-point, you can use the TRIM button on the control panel. Use the machine designator to shift control to the machine which needs the edit point changes. By holding down the IN button, press the + or the − button once for every fame of video you wish the edit point to be moved forward or backward. The same can be done for the out-points and this can be done for either machine.

Once you master what the buttons do and how to use them to their best advantage (and you will find many shortcuts), you can edit swiftly and accurately. Study the user's booklet that comes with the machine you are using.

11 Creative Editing Basics

Once you know how to operate an editing machine, the next step is starting the creative editing process. Each shot of the video must be thought of as a sentence or phrase. Just as there is proper grammar in language, a grammar of sorts exists in the assemblage of shots on the way to forming stories. Often the pieces you put together are nothing more than laundry lists of shots that go with some prewritten script.

Everything in an edited piece should have purpose and relationship. Every shot is there for a reason, every sound is there for a reason. Every shot should be related to the shot before it and after it, every sound related to the video over it. Everything should work together to tell the story. Sequence the shots to establish ideas; the product should be greater than the sum of its parts.

Each shot must be in its position for a reason; the story line must be advanced by the constant progression of pictures or images. Editing is not just the butting together of shots, but it is the creation of a story with a beginning, a middle and an ending all working to communicate an idea or show an event.

SEQUENCING THE SHOTS

Ideally, every grouping of shots, or sequence, should have an overall statement or idea that is more than the sum of its parts. The viewer should come away with more than just the experience of seeing a collection of shots. There should be an understanding of the idea just expressed. The idea may be as simple as a blood shortage at the Red Cross, but a random collection of shots on this subject adds nothing to a viewer's perception of the shortage. On the other hand, a well-thought-out ordering of the proper shots can convey much added information and understanding for the viewer.

Instead of random shots of the interior of the blood center, a careful selection can show the viewer what the script is conveying. A good three-shot segment on the blood shortage might consist of (1) an opening shot of a room half-full of donors giving blood; (2) a shot of a blood bag being filled at the end of a tube; (3) a closing shot of a technician stacking filled bags in a nearly empty cooler. This series shows people giving blood, but it also demonstrates that very little blood is on hand to give to hospitals.

Basic Sequence

A basic sequence is made up of a wide shot, a medium shot, a tight shot and a cutaway. This is the minimum sequence but the idea usually stays intact within many variations. This basic sequence translates to this:

1. Establish what the viewer is looking at.
2. Develop that idea by giving more detailed information.

199

3. Emphasize the details.
4. Add any related but nonessential information, if necessary, to break the thought and prepare for the next sequence.

Preparing for the next one, in most cases, simply means allowing an unnoticed bridge of time in the telling of a story.

Sample Script

Consider the following script which a writer might hand you to cut a story with.

Here at the ACME trade school, former workers of the now closed auto factory are being retrained for a new career in the field of micro-electronics. Assembly line workers have traded their wrenches for textbooks in the battle to stay competitive in the fast changing job market.
Each member of the class hopes the new skills learned here will help land a job in the expanding high-tech work force. Locally, almost 300 new jobs were created in the last year, but none of the former Cal-plant workers were able to land any of those jobs. (Take sound-bite of student.)

There can be two story lines here; the written story as it appears, and a visual story that can add even more information to what is being said.
Read the script over to determine:

1. the amount of time you have to cover;
2. what specific subjects must be shown;
3. what information can be added to enhance the story.

The first paragraph of the script is about 14 seconds long. You can use approximately four shots to cover that paragraph—a classroom, individual students and textbooks. You will be adding a visual sense to the size of the class, the type of elements currently being studied, and so forth.

Each story for a TV newscast should start off with about two seconds of video and natural sound if possible. Since the news is live, timing errors can be made on roll cues, which can result in the first second or two being cut off before it goes out over the air. It is better to lose some natural sound than part of the reporter's audio track, which is essential to understanding the story.

First Sequence   In our example here, a good opening shot is a wide shot of the whole room

from one of the corners. The first two seconds are the sound of the teacher telling the class about the subject of the day. As the teacher's audio quickly fades down to the background level, the reporter's audio comes in. This same shot will continue to run as the reporter begins the story.

A logical place to make the first edits is at the end of the word "factory" in the first sentence because the subject has been established. We are dissecting the first sentence visually in a fashion similar to how a grammar teacher would dissect it in an English class. The cut is here because the subject of this visual sentence has been illustrated by the wide shot.

The next shot is a medium shot of a group of students listening to the teacher. It cuts best at the end of the first sentence. Just as the body of a paragraph is used to expand on the idea expressed in its topic sentence, the medium shot gives a more detailed view of the situation illustrated in the wide shot.

The next shot is a tight shot of one of the students ending on the word "for" in the second sentence and then a cut to a tight shot of a textbook and a student's hands taking notes on the paper next to it. This shot goes until the end of the paragraph. If you have the right shots with which to work, you should be able to see how the combination of shots works to punctuate the script and round out the information the story is conveying. This is one sequence.

Second Sequence   Like the script, we begin a new sequence (paragraph) at this point. Again the paragraph is about 14 seconds long. This time, however, there are few specifics to show other than the students. This is a good place to use the video to advance the story in a different but parallel course. This new paragraph gives us a chance to explore another direction of the classroom setting. To enhance the feeling of positive emotion on the part of the students, we will show them in their efforts to learn.

The opening shot of this sequence is a wide shot of the instructor helping a student who is soldering circuit boards. This shot ends at the word "here" in the first sentence. The next shot is a very different angle of that same student working. The student's position and movements should be the same as in the wide shot with the teacher in order to avoid a jump cut. This shot ends at the word "force" at the end of the first sentence.

Even though the script begins a new sentence, our visual sentence is not done. The next shot is a close-up of the student's hands working on the circuit board ending on the word "year" in the second sentence. A tight shot of the concentration in the same student's face is the next shot and ends on the words "workers were."

The last shot of the sequence and the paragraph would be a shot of the board the student is working on. This time, however, it is an extreme close-up of the soldering, showing the smoke rise from the hot solder. From this shot you can cut to anything including the same student for the sound bite if that is necessary.

Think about these shots, cut on these words, and see how they fit with the script without matching it word for picture. We have captured the feel of the script but added more to it by showing more of how these students are going about learning a new career. By focusing on one student in particular, it is easier to build a sequence and help the viewer follow what the students are doing. Use the visuals to punch-up a story, give emphasis to what is being said without stating the same thing and, above all, to give more information.

The pacing just discussed is just one possible way to cover this script. As you work with the shots in the edit room, you may find that some will look better when allowed to run longer and others when used very briefly. No two editors will cut the story the same way. In effect, there is no one right way of doing it. The only common denominator is that it should feel right when viewed as a whole.

Match-Action Cutting

Within sequences of this type there is a method called match-action cutting that can really make a sequence come alive. If the video was shot with this in mind, or if you as editor are clever enough to see it in the raw material given you, match-action editing can help liven up a story. The idea is to make it appear as though more than one camera is taping a scene and it is being edited live on tape (as if switching between two cameras the way a director does in a studio).

To perform match-action editing in ENG or EFP, the photographer must separate the action into the different parts and then shoot each part separately. A good example is a factory assembly line. A sheet of metal is taken from a stack, put into a drill press, drilled, removed and put on a new stack. Each part of the process is broken down into different shots, each from a different angle and with at least some variation in focal length.

The shots are edited together so that the viewer follows the sheet of metal through the drilling process but from many vantage points instead of just one. The edits must be precise so that the action from one shot to the next is smooth. If things are taking place quickly, each edit must be very accurate or it will look like a jump cut. The assembly line example is an easy one because the same thing takes place over and over. It is harder to get the shots necessary for match-action editing when you have no control over the situation and things are not following a set pattern.

A good photographer always looks for things that can be built into a matched sequence. It may take some thinking and patience but a better looking product is always worth it. If you are shooting in an office and one of the subjects answers the phone, talks and then hangs up, perhaps another call will need to be answered. For this shot, choose a different angle and/or focal length. For example, you could match-cut a tight shot of the phone ringing to a wider shot as the person picks up the receiver. A good editor sees the sequence and cuts it together to put life and interest in an otherwise dull office sequence.

Match-action cuts exist in most things you shoot—look for them. Even in interviews, the establishing two-shot can have the interviewee in the exact same position saying something similar to the beginning of the sound bite. The edit from the two-shot to the talking head shot can be made into a match-action edit. It looks sharp but it has to be done correctly. Watch the movies and see how they use matched action and then look for examples of it in TV news.

MAINTAINING CONTINUITY

Even in news shooting, like movie making, the visual story is often done in bits and pieces to be assembled later. The continuity of the finished product determines how well the viewer will be able to follow the story. There are several aspects to maintaining good continuity when it comes to choosing camera angles and shot choices in the edit process. (See Figure 11.1.)

The 180° Line Rule

The main element of continuity is the 180° line rule. A simple example of this is an interview on TV news or any two-person conversation in production or theatrical settings. In the theater, the audience or viewer stays on one side of the sub-

Figure 11.1: This series of photos represents the shots needed to maintain continuity in a simple action sequence. The actions of the subject are broken down into their individual parts and shot separately. Action shots such as walking or chopping can be combined in matched-action editing. Close-up shots can be used as transitions by allowing the subject to enter or exit the frame. Each of these shots can be done at various focal lengths (wide, medium or tight) to allow the same action several times but never the same shot twice. This variety of shots as raw material also allows for contracting or expanding the edited length from a quick 10-second piece to a leisurely 2-minute sequence.

jects. When you are shooting a similar situation, the camera replaces the audience and therefore should always stay on one side. Draw a line between the two people involved in the interview or conversation. All camera angles should be taken from one of the two 180° semicircles defined by that line. You choose which side of the line to shoot from, but you must stay on only one side.

This line is sometimes called the **line of interest**. A person looking in a direction determines a line of interest or two people in an interview determine a common line (nose to nose). All your camera angles should be looking either up or down that line.

For ENG and EFP photography, the line should be established in most shooting situations: meet-

ings, speeches, concerts, protests, marches, parades, sports, and so forth. If the subject does not determine the line, draw one where you will have the best background or lighting conditions and stick with it. Your wide shot not only establishes what you are looking at but also the relationships among the objects in the picture. These relationships must be maintained. The line rule keeps the relationships constant throughout your sequence of shots no matter how many shots you use.

A speaker delivering a speech shot from the left side of the room (as you face the speaker) will be facing screen-right. (See Figure 11.2.) Through the rest of the piece the speaker will always face right. Therefore, a line of interest is drawn between the speaker and audience. The audience

Figure 11.2: Camera placement and several sample shots for covering a typical speech.

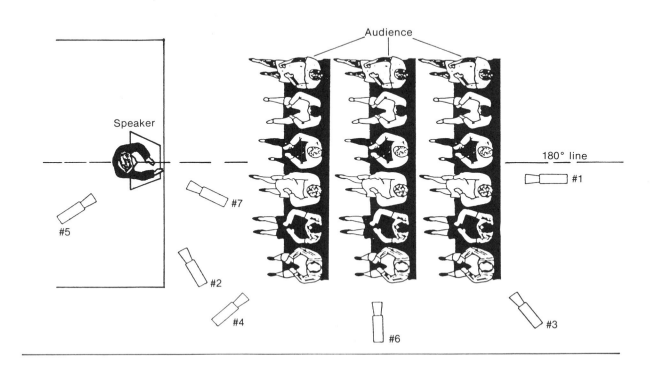

will always be facing screen-left. If you shoot all your shots with this in mind, any combination of shots can be edited together and the audience will always appear to be facing the speaker and vice versa. The viewer is never at a loss to identify the relationships among the subjects.

Crossing-the-Line Editing

These points work well when the shots are done correctly and in a controlled situation. What if the shot was not done correctly or the situation was uncontrolled and no line was ever established? The editor still must maintain continuity for a good, understandable flow of shots. By letting the line float but always keeping it in mind, the editor can move the camera angle anywhere.

The key to continuity is movement or direction, both actual and implied: the actual movement of a basketball team on the court or the implied direction of two people in an interview. As long as it has movement or direction any shot you start with defines your first continuity line, your line of interest. A good rule of thumb to get to the other side of that line in editing is to "turn on" one of these types of shots: (1) a shot straight down the line of interest; (2) a close-up shot; or (3) a wide shot that cuts to another wide shot with a different 180° line.

In the example of the speaker and the meeting, a shot straight down the line of interest would come from the center-back of the room and have no movement or direction. This type of shot destroys the line and gives you freedom to re-establish a different one. If you choose to turn using a close-up, shoot a tight shot of the speaker facing left, then cut to a wide shot from the other side of the room so that the speaker is now facing right. You have crossed the line but not confused the viewer. This switch from tight shot to wide shot with a new line gives the viewer a new point of reference to use for the shots to follow. If you want to turn using two wide shots, you can shoot one from the right rear of the room and cut to a wide shot from the middle of the left side of the room. It is possible to turn and not confuse the viewer, using wide shots, because all the elements of the scene are present in both shots while still being very different.

For this crossing-the-line editing to work, the line cannot be crossed very often or the continuity is lost. As always, when you sit down to edit, look at all the shots available to you, not only for content but also for continuity. You should be able to separate shots into sequences by continuity: grouping shots with common 180° lines and identifying turn shots to cross those lines if necessary.

Continuity Within Sequences

Each visual sequence like a written paragraph must stick to one subject. To allow the viewer to fully understand that subject, each shot in the sequence must flow easily to the next shot. Each aspect of continuity must be maintained within the sequence.

Movement   Each sequence of shots must maintain continuity. Continuity can be changed at the end of a sequence but not in the middle of one. Within a sequence, every subject that has movement or direction must maintain that direction. If the subject's direction or movement is to the right at the beginning, it should always be to the right throughout the sequence. Watch a good action movie and look for the direction of the subjects (cars, people, backgrounds). Look for the 180° line and study how it is used. The continuity is usually very good in action movies. Also watch for how they use turn shots to change the 180° line.

Details   Continuity also refers to other elements in the picture besides movement. Not only must directional and spatial relationships be maintained, but also the details within the sequences. An obvious example is the clothes a subject is wearing. If the subject has on a green shirt in one shot and a blue shirt in the next but there is no implied change in time or place, then there is an obvious break in continuity.

Background   Objects in the background cannot move from one shot to the next because there will be a disruption in the sense of reality (for example, furniture in a room must stay in the same arrangement). Continuity means that elements such as these must remain the same within the framework of the story line. For ENG and EFP, many elements are not controllable, but you still must avoid the very obvious breaks in continuity.

Lighting   The lighting within a sequence must also remain the same, particularly outside. Shots taken on a cloudy day cannot be intercut with shots in full sunlight. A dusk-to-night outdoor concert should not show the group playing at full darkness intercut with shots of the audience in sunset lighting. The time difference is too great and noticeable to even the least discriminating viewer. TV viewers are all professionals at TV watching—they have been doing it almost all of their lives.

ESTABLISHING A STORY LINE

Most finished products in ENG and EFP tell some sort of story. As a photographer or editor, it is your job to make that story come alive and make it understandable within the confines of the script and the time limit. Many news pieces and commercials have no real visual story line, just a sequence of shots that show a particular subject. But whenever an event occurs or time obviously passes during a shoot, it can be put into story form.

In TV, the script determines most, but not all, story lines. Whenever you shoot or edit, your goal must be to establish a good story line, even in the presence of a bad script. A basic story line is very simple. Just like a story in literature, there should be a beginning, a middle and an end.

Beginning

Each story must start somewhere, so why not at the beginning? What happened first? Where? How? Generally, you can think of the beginning as the wide shot, the shot that establishes the content of the story and the relationships among the elements. Most things happen along a time line; you would not show the outcome of the race and then show some of the racers still running or even starting. Things should be shown in the order that they occur.

There should be a sense of positive time flow within the editing, as if we are seeing a capsulized version of what took place. The beginning should initiate the story and make the viewer want to see more of it. Aim to spark a viewer's attention or at least enhance it by the opening sequence of the story line. The question "What's next?" should always be present. Try not to lose the viewer's attention; the viewer should always be anticipating the next element of the story.

A good way of securing a viewer's attention is to establish a sequence of action to follow. A story about a school building that is going to close need not be a collection of building shots. Instead, you can open the story with a shot of kids entering the building. By doing this, you have the wide shot of the building, but the added element of kids entering the building within that shot has now started a story line. Very simply, you have posed the questions: Where are the kids going in the building? What are they going to do? These are questions that you as editor and photographer can answer visually.

In this example, these questions would not be pressing in the minds of viewers but suggesting a story line. Try to present a situation that needs further information or investigation to satisfy the viewer. Show the subject doing something or moving so that the activity or direction can be explored more fully. A beginning must always appear to be headed somewhere. Invite the viewer to follow your lead. Make the viewer consciously or subconsciously ask "What's next?" "Why?" or "How?" and then proceed to answer the question. The beginning has to be the grabber. If you lose the viewer's interest at the beginning, then the viewer will never make it through the middle.

Middle

The middle is the guts of the story, the development of the idea started in the beginning. Once the race has begun, how is everyone doing? As the wide shot is to the beginning of the story, the medium shot is to the middle. The elements established at the start are now explored in greater detail and examined as to how they can further the story.

In our school closing story line, showing the reasons for this closure would make up the middle. Possible medium shots are half-full classrooms or students sitting amidst dilapidated surroundings. The middle is obviously the longest segment of any story because developing a point of view can be time-consuming. Therefore, you must have very descriptive shots to build the best possible sequences to keep the story moving.

End

Every story should come to some sort of conclusion. Whether it actually comes to an end or the sun simply sets in the last shot, the story must finish in some way. In the race analogy the end is simple: the winner crosses the finish line and receives the trophy. In the school closing story line, the end may be the kids leaving the building and the doors closing. The rule of thumb for the end is that something concludes, finishes or at least moves away from the camera.

A story about taxis could be ended on a shot of a cab pulling away from the camera and driving off down the street—the old riding off into the sunset idea. Even if there is no real conclusion or end, the appearance of one is desirable. It can be called negative motion (that is, away from the camera), but it works as a way of saying "That's it."

Hopefully, the idea started at the beginning has now been brought to an end. The end may be displaying a finished sculpture, sealing up a box, closing a door, the crowd applauding, a skyline shot of the city, or anything that says "The End." The more thought put into how the story will end, the better the chance the viewer will come away with a feeling that the story is complete.

Visualizing Paragraphs

There is no set length or number of shots that make up any segment. The beginning may be just one shot or many. The total length of the story usually determines how long each segment will be. A 90-second story probably will not have a 30-second opening sequence. Sequences are like visual paragraphs. Each part of the story can have one or more paragraphs. Once you have established a story line in your head or on paper, break it down into the beginning, middle and end. Take each part, and look for the visual paragraphs that make up each part. By organizing yourself before you shoot and edit, these visual paragraphs should come together in a flowing, descriptive story with a beginning, a middle and an end.

In many TV scripts, it is impossible to establish much in the way of a visual story line. Many pieces end up being laundry lists of shots or wallpaper jobs. The script has no real visual interpretation, except for the very literal. A story about banks that are in financial trouble may be made up of exterior shots of the banks named in the story. The videographer and editor have little creative input. If the writer and photographer can work together as much as possible, some of these situations can be avoided or worked out but not always.

The point is to always strive for good TV—the mesh of good audio and good pictures to communicate the maximum information to the viewer. In following the script, strive for the best sequencing and story line. You have a good chance of communicating something if you can visually hold the viewer's interest. Sometimes pretty pictures are the best solution to the story line problem if you cannot obtain sequencing within the confines of the script. In this case, each shot should be able to stand alone as a complete idea or picture.

Shooting Without a Script

The biggest difference between ENG and EFP is the order in which the product is assembled. For EFP you are shooting to a script and it is easy to get what you need to cover that script. You go out knowing what pictures you need. For ENG you are shooting for a script that has not been written

yet. It is hard to second-guess how the final story will be structured, what parts will be included or left out, and what specifics will be written about. You must shoot to maximize the editor's latitude when the piece is edited. At the same time, you cannot provide too much material because there will not be enough time to go through it all within the usual TV news deadlines.

Sometimes you must shoot for two or three different story lines because the outcome or direction is unclear as the story develops before you. At a certain location, the story may be the crowd at the beach, the heat, the traffic, the troublemakers or people being turned away because the park is full. All these elements, or only a few, can be included in one story, or you may concentrate on just one. The final script determines the kind and amount of material that should be shot, but the final script does not materialize until long after the shooting is over. How do you cover all the possibilities and still come up with good sequences and story lines but not over-shoot?

Many times the writer/producer will not be present when you shoot the video. However, if you follow the basic guidelines regarding what kind of shots to get and keep in mind what it takes to edit a good story, you should have the material for any good basic story. If you look at each situation as a mini-story (beginning, middle and end) and shoot each situation as though it will be sequenced together (wide shot, medium shot, tight shot and cutaway), then you have covered all the bases.

By getting the minimum number of essential shots, the photographer has covered the story and given the editor the basis for cutting to almost any script. Get the basic four-shot sequences first, just in case that is all you get. Extra shots or artistic shots can be taken only after the basics are on tape and time permits. If the editor is in a hurry, there must be places on the tape where the basic shots can be found without much searching through shots that may be good but of lesser interest or importance to a basic story line.

PACING

The last element in the relationship among shots in editing is the pacing, or timing, of the shots. The timing of each shot helps determine the mood of the piece. As a general rule, a shot less than two seconds long will not be consciously perceived by the viewer unless it is a very graphic or aesthetically simple shot. A shot longer than seven seconds with no movement is usually longer than the attention span of the viewer. A zoom, pan, tilt or action in the picture can allow a shot to run almost any length depending on the mood you are trying to capture.

Editing for Dynamics

If all the shots are static with no camera moves, then the pace of the edits will generally be quicker than if there are some camera moves or action shots. If you are cutting several static shots together, try not to make the edits on a predictable beat. Vary the time between edits to give the piece some dynamics of its own. Let wide shots stay up longer than tight shots. It is easy to see what is in a tight shot, but a wide shot usually contains more information that takes longer to perceive.

Zooms and pans must be allowed to run their course. Cutting in the middle of camera movement is most often uncomfortable to the viewer. By their nature, these types of shots should be going somewhere and cutting out early makes them unfulfilling to the viewer. Anticipation is created with no real payoff.

If movement is needed but the whole shot is too long, it is better to start in the middle of the movement than to end in the middle. Let the shot finish. It is usually easier to see where the shot was coming from than to not know where it is going. It sometimes works to use just the middle of the movement, no start or finish, as long as you can tell what it is you are looking at.

A camera move shot has a certain mood to it that may not fit with the rest of the piece. It is usually used to add dynamics in dramatic or emotional editing. Camera moves can add much complexity to your piece, which you may not want. That is why most new photographers are asked not to use zooms and pans until all other basics have been mastered.

Avoiding Predictability

While staying within the sequencing, story line and continuity guidelines, try to vary the pace of the shots enough to avoid any predictability. The worst case is when the viewer can tell when the next edit is about to occur. The viewer should always be expecting more information (until the end of the piece) but should never be able to guess how or when it will come. As long as this anticipation is satisfied and the viewer cannot predict the next edit, the edit pace is correct.

A fast-moving story requires faster edits. A slow-moving story requires more time between edits. A good action piece can have quite a few short shots if they are advancing or enhancing the action. In a fast-paced sequence, the shots may be shorter than three seconds, but they must still be aesthetically clean enough so that there is not too much information and the viewer can perceive what is in the shot. This usually means using many close-ups and extreme close-ups.

Editing to Music

Cutting to music is a good example of following a preset pace. Most of the time it does not look good to cut on the simple beat of the music because it is too predictable. You will have a better flowing piece if you cut on a beat, but not on every beat. Use the edits to emphasize or punctuate the music, so that the cuts are not simply a tapping foot, blindly following the lead of the music.

Picking out one instrument to follow with the edits can give the piece a nice tie-in with the music—on the beat but never predictable. Sometimes switching from one instrument to another for different parts of the song can add to the interest of the pacing. With the current abundance of rock videos, there are many examples of good editing to music. Take a close look. If you turn down the sound and watch the edits, you can get a feel for the dynamics of the editing without the music.

Varying Editing Speed

By changing the pacing of edits you can change the whole mood of the piece. Switching from long-running shots to quick edits can heighten tension, action, excitement or anticipation. Slowing down the pace can give a more relaxed feeling, an easier flow, or an emotional touch such as a feeling of relaxation, serenity or sadness. Sit back and watch how your piece plays after you complete each segment. Do not just watch how the shots fit together, but watch how the piece feels as it moves along. Is it too fast, too slow, does it convey the wrong mood, does it flow as one unit or is it simply a slide show?

Ask another editor to take a look at your piece. Sometimes you can be too close to your own work to give it an objective critique. Bad pacing can make a piece drag on forever or seem as choppy as rough seas. Good pacing can make a piece fly by while generating much information or touching the hearts of the viewers by its warm flow of images.

POST-PRODUCTION

Up to this point, we have been addressing what used to be called butt-splice editing. Now it is simply called a cut when one shot changes to another on the frame line; it is a machine-to-machine edit. By adding a video switcher with an effects panel, however, it is possible to add another dimension to your editing. The most common effect is the mix or dissolve, but such effects as wipes, squeezes and digital processing are now available on most switchers. To do this type of editing in most offline setups (in which the edit machines do not go through a switcher), shots must be edited onto work tapes called the A and B reels.

In the early days of TV, most news stories were cut on A/B reels (or rolls). The A reel had all of the sound on it: talking heads, sound bites, stand-ups, etc. The B reel had all the cover footage to be used over the reporter's voice track, which sometimes came from a third source like an audiocassette. The piece would then be assembled live on the air. It required the technical director to switch from one film machine to the other and back at the proper times so that there was always a picture on the air. Needless to say, the process often became mixed up. If the piece was not timed out correctly by the editor when it was put together, or the director called for the wrong reel, things could look pretty bad.

The same principles are used to create effects with video today, but they are not done live on the air. The piece must be divided into parts determined by each special effect. A part goes from one special effect to the next special effect. The opening part is the first thing on reel A. The second part is on reel B, and so on, back and forth. (See Figure 11.3.)

For offline editing the A and B reels are done just as they are in film. In this case, the two cassettes are cut so that when both are cued up on the same number on their countdown leaders and rolled at the same time in two machines feeding the video switcher, the technical director can switch back and forth using the desired effects according to the script. While this occurs, the output of the switcher is being recorded. This recording then becomes the edit master.

There has to be enough overlap between segments on the two reels to allow the effect to be done. If there are several effects in a piece, the construction of the two reels can get very complex. It is wise (if not essential) to keep a video log

as to where each effect is to be made. Make the notations as to the exact running time from the head of each tape. Note that the head of the B reel will still be at the end of the countdown even though no video is present.

Film-style editing of the A and B reels is common in small stations and edit facilities where three-machine edit controllers are not available. With the higher quality of today's formats, the generational loss due to making these submaster reels is very small. It can cut the time and cost of doing effects with limited loss of quality. Another way to get simpler effects in the edit process is to have an edit controller that can operate three or more machines. This is still an offline edit system, but the controller can incorporate a video switcher with all its effects. (See Figure 11.4.) This type of system eliminates the need for building the different reels but not necessarily making dubs. When you do an effect, the two shots involved in the effect must be on separate playback machines. This may mean that shots on the same field tape must be dubbed to a work tape in order to use them together, thus losing a generation for one of the two shots.

As of this writing, there are hundreds of different special effects that can be used in video post-production. For the offline processes discussed above, there are two basic effects most often used for transitions: the dissolve and the wipe. While there are many variations of these two effects, the net result is about the same. As the video industry continues to progress by leaps and bounds, the effects available to the editor will continue to increase, even on simple offline systems.

Dissolve

Special effects can allow an editor to explore a whole new area of pacing and mood creation. The dissolve or mix can be a boon or bust to the finished piece. The dissolve is an excellent way of showing the lapse in time from one shot to the next. To go from the city in daylight to the city at night with a straight edit (or cut) would be rather abrupt, but a dissolve can make the transition smooth and even artistic.

In many pieces, this way of showing the passage of time can aid in the telling of the story since fewer shots are needed to make the transition. You can take a subject from one location to another with a simple dissolve instead of transition shots. In a long piece it is a good idea to use both transition shots and dissolves for variety.

Figure 11.3: A/B reels.

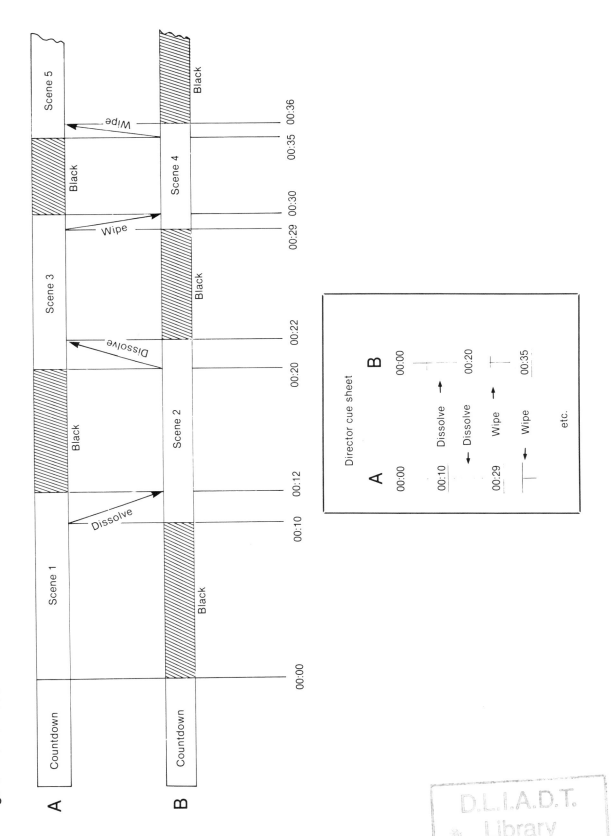

Figure 11.4: An editor operates the controls of a multi-machine edit system. Player or source machines are mounted in the rack to the left. The edit controller, video switcher for special effects and keys, and the audio mixer are mounted in the console. The record machine is in the rack to the right. *Photo by John Lebya.*

When a piece calls for a slow edit pace, a dissolve adds to the relaxed feeling and the flow from one shot to the next. Going from static shot to static shot, the dissolve takes the hard edge off the edit and gives that desirable fluid transition. For the artistic piece, the fall colors story or the day in the life of a nursing home, the dissolve can add to the beauty of the shots or give that feeling of sensitive compassion.

The basic rules of editing should still apply, however. You do not dissolve between two shots very similar in composition. You still try to give variety to the shot selection and follow basic sequencing patterns. For a solo dancer on a stage, dissolves are desirable but each shot should be as different as possible from the next. If the dancer is framed screen right in a wide shot, the next shot should be a medium shot with the dancer in the left part of the picture. In other words, do not overlap similar images.

Let the mood and pacing of the piece determine how long a dissolve should last. A duration of 30 to 40 frames seems to look best for most uses. The slower the pace, the slower the dissolve. You must keep in mind, however, that making all edits into dissolves can make the piece boring and predictable. Try to have a good practical or artistic reason for each dissolve and every other effect you use.

Wipe

Wipes come in a great variety; the standard left-to-right straight edge is the most common. With digital effects, wipes can be as wild as you can imagine and the effects just as varied. Most of the fancy ones, like spinning stars or heart shapes, have little place in ENG but have some application in EFP or magazine shows. The straight line wipe is used in live newscasts to go from one story to the next without having to cut back to the set for the transition.

You very seldom see a wipe used in a produced news story. The use of a wipe for ENG stories is similar to its use in the newscast itself: to go from one thing to something totally separate. If several pages of written information are to be put on the screen, a wipe is used to go from one page to the next, such as in election night tallies. Digital wipes, such as **page** or **cube wipes**, are very popular for this type of transition. The different types of wipes are often used in entertainment programs and commercials to give the production variety and a jazzy look.

OnLine Edit

As the complexity of editing increases, the more likely it is to be done online. Online editing makes use of a computer to control the machines involved in the edit as well as the video switcher. Where off-line editing can be done using control track edits, the online process can only be done using time code. The time code numbers are used to tell the computer where everything starts and stops. This type of editing is probably the most complicated system in the entire video process. The people who operate this type of equipment are often very experienced, always in demand and can command large salaries.

A computer is necessary for all the very precise and fancy work done today. For day-to-day news, however, it is too time consuming and quite expensive. Even on a computer, it can take a week to edit a one-minute commercial, but a one-minute news story often has to be done in less than 20 minutes.

EDITING SOUND

For the most part, sound editing has never been as complicated for TV as it has been for the movies. The poor quality of most TV speakers and the conditions under which most people watch TV have reduced the need for good sound, although

this is changing. Picture quality and technique have come a long way but sound quality and mixing have lagged behind. This is evident in many TV news markets in which audio is still sometimes completely absent from ENG tape.

Accurate Representation of the Event

There should be two sources of audio in ENG: the audio of the talent (news anchor or recorded reporter) and the sound accompanying the pictures. Because most TV news is loosely based on journalistic standards, the addition of any other audio is frowned upon. The addition of music is the only exception, although in some cases it is not desirable. Adding sound can be misleading, deceptive and sometimes downright dishonest.

The best you can do in ENG is to move the sound around from one shot to another, but the sound must accurately represent what you would hear if you were there. An example is a shot of a mine with a whistle blowing; the next shot is of miners filing out to go home. The sound of the whistle may not have been recorded at the same time as that shot of the mine, but it did blow while the crew was taping and it did signal the end of a shift. The sound was used correctly.

An example of sound used incorrectly is a shot of people at an accident scene and the photographer running up to the injured on the ground while a siren is heard. The siren in this case was taken from a story shot last week and used to add a feeling of breaking news to the piece. The photographer had actually arrived late. In this case, the siren should not have been used at all. It made the story into something it was not. If you did not get the sound at the location, you should not manufacture sound to make it appear as though it came from the location. If it makes the pictures seem different from what they really were, then the sound should not be added. Sound needs to accurately depict what happened.

Adding Sound for Effect

If you photograph an explosion from a mile away, it takes the sound of the explosion a second or two to reach the camera. Do you move the sound? For EFP the answer is simple because any sound is fair game if it enhances the idea you are trying to get across. You would have to get far out of line to violate the "truth-in-advertising" law.

For ENG the question is harder to answer. Years of Hollywood conditioning have made audiences expect to hear the sound at the same time they see the explosion. In real life, however, the sound and picture do not match. What do you do?

You can assume that sound and picture are in sync at the point of origin (the explosion site). The audio can be synced back up in editing if the shot contains the explosion as the only audio source. If, however, there are people in the foreground reacting to the explosion as it happens, their audio and therefore the audio from the explosion cannot be moved. Moving the explosion's audio would distort the people's reaction to it.

There is, nevertheless, room for creativity when it comes to audio in ENG. You can add sound where it is obvious to the viewer that the sound is added for effect. Shots of an abandoned school house with the sounds of a school bell and children playing can give a powerful emotional touch to the scene. It is obvious that no children have been there in decades, but the audio implies the rich history of the once thriving school.

Imagine a reporter doing a standup in front of a roaring water pump with a mike that does not pick up the sound of the pump because of its placement. You see the pump but not do not hear it. By adding the background sound of the pump in editing, the shot seems to come together better. All the pieces fit and work together for the overall effect. These are just a few examples of adding sound to enhance ENG work, but you must use sound carefully. It is a fine line that separates enhancement from deception.

Avoid Abrupt Edits

In general, avoid abrupt starting and stopping when editing audio. Even when audio must come in very quickly, a fast twist of the volume knob is better than a flip of a switch. Audio cutoff at either end tends to pop and can be annoying to the viewer. Background audio can come and go at the edit points by turning the volume control up or down. The volume of background audio is already low and often sound bites must start abruptly to cut off an unwanted word. For the most part, though, it is better to mix the audio in and out if it is to be heard in full. Every picture has a sound unless it is graphics or a freeze-frame. There is background noise for just about everything.

Natural Sound

A good news story opens with a picture that begins to tell the story or captures the viewer's attention. A reporter standup open is often boring and gives the viewer little to look forward to. It looks like more news anchor and not more news. With an opening shot, there should be some good natural sound.

Use with Opening Video   A story on flooding may open with a shot of water flowing over a dam. The roar of the water is heard for a few seconds before the reporter's voice comes in. It breaks the constant flow of talking and can spark someone's interest to look at the TV instead of only listening to it.

This is not radio, but TV. Not only must the pictures be good, but the sound must also be good enough to make someone want to watch the pictures. Good use of natural sound can draw the viewer into the story and give the pictures that you-are-there feeling. This means you must open a story with the best picture you can as well as the best sound.

Use as a Transition   There should be audio under the reporter's track for the entire piece. You can use the natural sound of the pictures to break up paragraphs in the track, get into or out of sound bites (talking heads) and bridge a gap from one part of a story to another. To move from talking about people buying new homes to discussing the number of new homes being built requires a shot such as an electric saw (sound up full) cutting a board in front of new construction. After a couple of seconds of the saw, the reporter continues the story, now talking about all the new construction. Time limits can make this type of editing difficult, but if the story is well thought-out and the reporter and photographer work together on producing it, the end product will show the effort.

Use with Music and Reporter   Every edit system has at least two channels of audio with which to work. One channel is usually designated for the reporter's audio and the other channel for all natural sound and sound bites. When you use music, however, it becomes difficult to incorporate natural sound (natsound). The music has to have a channel of its own if it is to last the entire story. This leaves only one channel for the reporter's track and any natsound, which translates into no natsound when the reporter's audio is up full. It is possible, however, to carefully mix in the natsound and fade it in and out to obtain a good blend of natsound and reporter audio on the same channel.

Laydowns and Laybacks

The method of combining more than two tracks of audio for a video program or segment is known as laydowns and laybacks. In our example above, the editor would decide which two audio sources were most important for determining the pacing and shot selection for the story. The story would be edited with just those two sources all the way to its conclusion.

For this discussion, assume it is reporter's voice track and the natural sound of the pictures. Wanting to add a music track under the entire piece, the editor would first take one or both the audio tracks of the finished piece and do a laydown onto a work tape of some sort. This work tape would then be synced back up with the original story and laid back to its previous track(s) while mixing in the music from a second playback source. The obvious requirement here is that the layback be in sync with the story it was lifted from. While this process can be done on any edit system, it is usually done on an online system using a multi-track audio recorder tied to the edit computer by a time code reference. The online computer can keep the layback in sync no matter how long the piece is. If you are trying to do this process without the aid of the computer, it is best not to try it on long-running pieces and to pick a track for laydown that has the least amount of lip-sync sound on it. Then, if you are off a few frames by the end of the layback, it may not be noticeable.

Editing Methods

Unlike working with a computer where sentences can be added or subtracted at will, once a shot or a sound is laid down on tape in video editing, that is where it stays. Adding a longer or shorter video or audio shot in the middle of a finished piece necessitates the re-editing of the rest of the story to make up for the time difference. Before you start to edit, you must have an idea of where you are going to avoid this problem.

Advance Planning   The best way to avoid audio problems is to plan the editing well in advance. With script in hand, decide what shots you want to use and where you will use any natural sound. If your planning is good and you can stick with your decisions, edit all the sound-up-full parts first, then lay in the rest of the cover video. This means lay down your first shot with its sound up full, fade it down at the right point, lay in the

reporter's track, lay in the shot with natsound full, then the sound bite, and so on.

When you have completed this, go back and fill in all the black areas with the proper shots and their audio to complete the story. Now, this method only works if you never change your mind after you have begun to edit, if your planning is well done and all the sequences fit. With the audio already down, you have no room to change anything as you begin to lay in your video.

Section by Section   The other method, which is just as fast, is to edit one section at a time. This allows you to fine-tune each part of the story as you go, gives you the freedom to change parts of the story as you come to them and, in the case of a real time bind, allows you to skip over parts of the story and go straight to the end to finish in some form so it can be on the air in its scheduled time slot.

Sometimes a visual sequence needs just one more second of space to have it look right. If you are editing section by section, you can make these changes without affecting anything after that part. It is very important to plan ahead. Know where you are going and what you have to work with. If you edit section by section, you keep your creative options open. Even if you are working under deadline pressure, section-by-section editing can greatly enhance the quality of the piece.

Music Editing   When using music, it must be laid down first if any of the video is to be edited to the music. If nothing is to be in sync with the music, then it is best left until last so it is easier to mix it with other audio. Again, planning is the key. To cut to music, time out the script as to where and for how long the music and other audio is to be up full. These times must be set in advance.

Start by laying in the music and mixing it to up full or just background sound levels. You must do this according to the prearranged times decided before the editing began. Next, lay in all the other audio that is to be up full (reporter's track or sound bites) in the proper place with the video. Finally, insert the rest of the shots editing to the music and any natsound if appropriate or needed. If planned properly, this method lets you edit to the music without affecting the placement of the rest of the audio so that the finished piece has all the elements timed perfectly.

12 Live TV from the Field

One of the greatest advantages that video has over film for TV is the use of portable cameras to produce live coverage from just about anywhere. It is one of the reasons that TV news has soared to such a high level of popularity. Just as an earlier generation had Edward R. Murrow giving live accounts of the bombings of London during World War II, today's generation has watched U.S. forces under missile attack live on CNN. There can be no greater drama and no greater use of the medium than to see history being made live on the screen. The fact that countless millions of people everywhere in the world can view this makes an even greater impact on world society. Marshall McLuhan's fantasy forecast that the world would become one giant global village because of TV has now become reality. The Gulf War, the crackdown in Tiananmen Square, the dismantling of the Berlin Wall or the meetings of world leaders are all examples of the power of live TV to captivate viewers all over the world.

Even on local news stations, the use of live TV has led to the same mesmerizing effect on viewers during events of great importance or curiosity. An earthquake in San Francisco, a plane crash on the Potomac, a shootout in Watts or a baby girl stranded at the bottom of a well have all riveted local audiences as living dramas unfold before them just as for the people actually present.

Live TV is a power of enormous proportion and social responsibility. The use of live TV during the Gulf War was criticized both for elevating the reporter's personal experience above that of overall events and for revealing too much information of possible use to the enemy. The only certainty was that everyone was watching. A single reporter panicking or giving misinformation during a major story could have had a profound effect around the world. On another level, local TV news has reduced live TV to just another gimmick to attract viewers. Despite its drawbacks and misuses, live TV is the pinnacle of broadcast journalism when news breaks out anywhere in the world.

Live TV can also be of considerable importance to the business world through teleconferences. Just as local news stations use live cameras to hype ratings, companies and educators can use live TV to add a new sense of timeliness to the information they are trying to convey.

This chapter discusses the tools of live TV, its typical formats and uses, some tricks of the trade and some common problems.

GETTING THE PICTURE OUT

The starting point of live TV transmission is the camera. Any broadcast quality video camera with a composite National Television Standards Committee (**NTSC**) output can feed a transmitter. Often the output of the camera is fed through a distribution amplifier (**DA**) to maintain proper video levels. A low video signal may not transmit

215

well and will come across muddy with increased noise or poor color. A high, or hot, video signal may transmit as a washed-out picture, possibly causing a breakup in the transmission or noise in the audio portion. The most common faults in these two examples are either an improperly exposed camera or signal loss due to a long cable run from the camera to the transmitter. If these problems are not too extreme, the DA can correct them by its gain and equalizing functions. To operate, the DA must be connected to a waveform monitor to display the effects of any adjustments.

There are three basic ways of transmitting a live picture from the field: (1) telephone lines, (2) microwaves and (3) satellites.

Telephone Lines

The local telephone company can set up a video feed point from just about anywhere using a balanced line (different from a regular phone line). Because of the time necessary to set up this type of transmission, it is rarely used except for events such as election returns where there is plenty of lead time for installation. The most common transmission medium is the microwave system. (See Figure 12.1.)

Microwaves

Microwave equipment is relatively small and usually owned by the TV station using it. The most common placement of a microwave system is in a van (sometimes called a live truck, RF truck or feeder) that has an antenna at the top of a telescoping mast that may go as high as 50 feet. The truck usually has a reel of multi-line cable (two video and four audio lines in one cable) that can stretch about 300 feet. A normal video cable allows up to a 1000-foot run before the loss of signal becomes too great for the DA to compensate.

Microwave transmitters work in a spectrum of radio frequencies measured in Gigahertz (GHz) and have specific channels assigned by the Federal Communications Commission (FCC). The standard ENG channels have always been 2, 7 and 13 GHz. Each channel can be subdivided further into parts simply called A, B, C, D and Center with the option of the microwaves going clockwise or counterclockwise. These variations allow many stations in the same market or many transmitters at one station to be transmitting at the same time. With the increased use of this technology, more channels have been opened up to include 2.5, 6, 6.5, 10, 12 and 40 GHz. Generally, the

lower the channel number, the easier it is to transmit over long distances. It is not impossible for a microwave link to go 50 miles if there are no obstructions. Microwaves need a clear line of sight from transmitter to receiver to work. This is why the antenna (either a dish or golden rods) is on a mast and the receiver is usually on a mountain top or the tallest building; it can then go from there to the station by a secondary microwave link or hard line. Because the microwave beam is very narrow, it is essential that the transmitter and receiver antennas be pointed precisely at each other. When they are many miles apart, this is not an easy task. Experienced people at each end can accomplish this in a very short period of time, sometimes in seconds if the operators are very good.

While the truck-mounted microwaves are usually on channels 2 or 7, a portable system called a mini-mike uses channels 13, 18 and 40 GHz. This shoebox-size transmitter can be placed in a backpack for the camera operator to wear; it can also be mounted on a small tripod near the camera to take the place of what might be a hard or impossible cable run back to the live truck. Because the range of this small transmitter is limited, a mini-mike is primarily used in sports coverage or to replace a cable where mobility is the critical factor (for example, from a high floor of a skyscraper). The receiver would be at the live van where the signal would be retransmitted to the station.

Satellites

The late 1980s saw a revolution in the cost and availability of satellite time. With so many satellites in orbit, almost anyone who had an **uplink** (a ground-to-satellite transmitter link) could buy time. (See Figure 12.2.) Because of such factors as CNN's 24-hour news channel, covering breaking stories live to the whole country became a must. While microwaves are limited to about 50 miles and line of sight (although they can be relayed or hopped to greater distances), a portable satellite uplink mounted on a truck can go anywhere where there is a road and sky. (See Figure 12.3.) Today almost every TV market in the top 80 markets has at least one satellite truck and most stations in the top 30 markets and larger have one. There is even a large rental business of independently owned trucks that serve broadcast and nonbroadcast users all over the country.

No one can forget the dramatic and historic pictures of CNN's Peter Arnett broadcasting live from Baghdad during the Gulf War. He was using

Figure 12.1: This microwave van has its telescoping mast extended. The large (4.6 meters across) dish at right is used for satellite transmitting and receiving. This dish is not mobile and is mounted on the ground.

an up-link system called a **fly-away** that is small enough to be folded down and shipped as airline baggage. Powered by batteries a fly-away system can be used in any remote area without any utilities. The batteries can be recharged by solar devices if necessary. Live TV can literally be done from any spot on the face of the earth as soon as the crew arrives and sets up. Travel time is the only limit to getting it on the air. (See Figure 12.4.)

COMMUNICATIONS

None of this is possible without a top-rate communications package. This usually means a good two-way radio system or a cell phone or both. As mentioned earlier, it is critical that the transmitter and receiver of both microwave and satellite systems be pointed directly at each other. Being off by as much as one degree can mean the difference

in getting the signal or not. Microwave systems are one-way transmissions. There is no way in the field to tell if you are lined up with the receiver without someone at the receiving point telling you. Microwave receivers are generally controlled remotely from the TV station by an ENG coordinator who watches a digital readout of the incoming signals' strength and can pan the receiver to get the strongest reading and then have the transmitter operator pan the antenna until the strongest signal is found. The truck operator usually has a map with the receive site(s) on it and can aim the antenna fairly accurately with a compass or a good guess. The fine tuning should be an easy process with good communications.

Satellite set-ups are much more technical but can be done without talking to anyone. Because a satellite also sends a return signal, it is possible for the operator to see the quality of the signal as it is returned and tell how well in line the two are. The

Figure 12.2: This portable satellite transmitter (uplink) allows live ENG video to be sent from almost anywhere in the world to a network or news service receiver (down link). *Courtesy CNN. All Rights Reserved.*

concern here is knowing which satellite, which channel and what time to set up. Since people from all over the country may be trying to use the same satellite, there has to be a coordinator who tells each up-link what to do and when. Unlike a microwave system, this coordinator is usually at the headquarters of the satellite company, which may be on the other side of the country. Having a cell phone is sometimes the only answer but having some type of phone is mandatory.

The receiver dish must be lined up with the satellite in use and tuned to the channel of video and audio; these are two separate systems within the transmission. The exact times of transmission must be confirmed. Satellite time can be bought on the spot or can be arranged in advance to ensure availability. Satellite time is purchased in multiples of five minutes and cannot be extended. If you buy five minutes of time for 12:00:00 p.m.,

at 12:05:02 p.m. you are off the air; the satellite owner pulls the plug. For ENG work this means you either buy more time than you think you need or have someone on the phone constantly with the satellite company to okay purchasing more time if it looks like the shot is going to run long. It is also possible that the next time block has already been sold and is unavailable to you. For major news events a network may buy up all the time available and share the time with others, using a local coordinator at a single feed point. The coordinating network feeds their material first and all others literally line up on a first-come, first-served basis to feed their material. Because of the time factors involved with satellites most taped material is edited before sending and live shots are inked in to specific times so local producers must slide everything else in their program to accommodate the satellite. This is one reason most satellite trucks have edit systems inside them.

The use of satellite trucks for EFP is generally much less hectic. These situations are usually planned well in advance and the satellite time booked with much spare time to work out any bugs or in case things run long.

INTERRUPTED FEED BACK (IFB)

Interrupted feed back (IFB) is just as essential as the communications needed to set up the transmissions. The on-camera talent needs to be able to hear the cue that they are on the air.

Portable TV

The most primitive way of doing this in live news is to have a portable TV set tuned to your station; the talent can simply see when they are on the air. An earphone run from the TV set lets them hear the introduction and any questions that may follow. The camera operator usually has the same two-way radio used to set up the microwave signal with an earphone to listen for any instructions from the station. If the regular speaker in the TV is used, it may cause an audio feedback (a high-pitched screech) when the reporter's mike is live that would ruin the shot. Using this type of IFB set-up does not have the interrupt part of the system since the audio is right off the TV. Any instructions from the show director, producer or assignment desk must be relayed to the reporter by the photographer listening to the two-way radio. It is a good idea to be sure everyone understands the

Figure 12.3: Satellite News Gathering (SNG) trucks make it possible to feed live pictures/reports or videotape from virtually anywhere to anywhere.

basic hand signals of TV production in case things need to be communicated while on air.

Mix-Minus

The more common form of IFB is a separate off-air audio feed called **mix-minus**. This feed is from the on-air audio board with the audio from the remote or live shot taken out or subtracted. It can be annoying for the talent to hear their own voices coming back in their ears while they are talking. Because of the time delays involved in the signal transmission, particularly with a two-second satellite delay, the talent hear their voices as strange echos. A mix-minus feed is usually patched into a telephone line and/or a two-way radio. Some TV stations have a radio channel dedicated to broadcasting nothing but off-air or program audio 24 hours a day. In this way an IFB system is always in place. Other stations with multiple channels on

their two-ways may simply give one channel over to IFB for the short time needed to do the shot and use it for other traffic the rest of the time. This mix-minus system allows the producer or other needed participants to interrupt the program audio and give special instructions, cues, a countdown to hit a sound bite or whatever over the radio or phone IFB. Just like the dedicated radio channel for IFB, many stations have dedicated phone lines that when called automatically hook up to the mix-minus feed. In large markets where there can be as many as six or seven different live shots back to back, the radio and phone systems can be quite complex.

FORM AND STYLE

Essentially, live shots are just like stand-ups. They are generally short and done in a controlled man-

Figure 12.4: Peter Arnett's CNN coverage of the Gulf War from Baghdad, Iraq, was a riveting example of how important live TV coverage of a news event can be. *Courtesy of CNN. All Rights Reserved.*

ner. The biggest difference is that they occur at a very specific point in time and there can be no second take.

Spot News

In this age of instant information, the ability to go live from any major breaking story is essential. The most common may be a major fire, earthquake, plane crash, or shooting. Most stations have extensive plans for how to cover big stories such as these but they all follow some basic rules. If more than one crew is being sent to the event, the first crew is responsible for shooting tape to document the event and the second or next crew on the scene is to set up for the live shot. If only one crew is available, it will quickly shoot enough tape to air about one minute of edited video and then return to the van to set up the live shot. The pressure to do two things at the same time can be intense; the desire to cover the story has to be weighed against the need to get the story out first to beat the competition. This is one of the great moral dilemmas in TV journalism. The ultimate success or failure to balance these two concerns rides on the location of the live van at the scene. If the photographer can anticipate the situation on arrival and know whether any particular parking spot will allow for a signal to be set up, then the story can be shown live or taped from the same location. The ideal situation is to set up where you can see the event or disaster area and leave the camera on the tripod rolling tape while you set up the signal and run the cables. Even though this is a two-person job, most stations only staff a live truck with one photographer/engineer. Once hooked up, the camera feeds the event live to the studio where it can be recorded as well as taken live at the producer's call.

If the van is parked under power lines or thick trees or a tall building is between it and the only receiver available, then the station could be at a serious disadvantage. In extreme cases, jobs could be lost over the failure to get a signal out. The greatest pressure in all of TV comes during setting up a live shot from a major spot news story. Without a clear battle plan as to how to pull it off, the story can turn into a nightmare. On the other hand if you can get it set up in record time and get good pictures as well, then you will most certainly be a hero.

The other concern in the location of the van is proximity to the story. You need to ask yourself questions such as these.

- If I have only 300 feet of cable, can I get the camera to a good vantage point?
- Am I blocking a roadway or emergency vehicle route?
- Am I too close and likely to be caught in a dangerous situation (such as a brush fire) and have to move quickly?
- Are the authorities going to let me stay here?

The wrong answer to any of these questions can ruin your shoot; always have a backup plan.

What the producer wants to see is the event or location itself. Sometimes this may mean being on a hilltop overlooking the site. At other times you may have to settle for just seeing the SWAT team suiting up because the street is closed and access is denied. The main thing, as in tape coverage, is to see action. If you cannot show the actual story, show the next best thing. Most of the time the live shot will be a subject in front of the camera. You should be able to zoom past the subject into anything happening in the background as the reporter talks about it. Be prepared to ride both the iris (try never to use auto-iris) and the focus. The lighting will probably be of little concern as long as the subject is visible. If the lighting is particularly bad, it may be necessary to place the subject in better lighting with a worse background and simply pan to the action.

The use of the tripod is generally determined by proximity to the action. If you are in the middle of things, it is probably best to hand-hold the camera. If you are at a distance, then you should use sticks. Handholding the camera can add to the drama of a live shot. The reporter can be talking to eyewitnesses or authorities; the freedom to move around can make the background

interesting regardless of where the guest stands. Keep in mind that hand-held shots look best at wider focal lengths. The biggest problem with moving is the cables. If you out-distance the cable, it can pull the camera off your shoulder. Make sure you know how much cable is available and if anyone is likely to be standing on it at any time. A good trick is to coil about three feet of cable at the camera end and tuck it in your back pocket or through your belt. Then if the cable gets stuck during a move, it will pull out of that safety coil and not yank on the back of the camera. The reporter should do the same with the mike cable. Doing spot news live is the ultimate in news coverage. Every bit of talent, experience and training comes to bear in this situation.

Scheduled Events

Most live shots for news are done at events planned well in advance. Parades, city council meetings and demonstrations are typical live situations. In fact, many organizers purposely schedule their events to coincide with the news time to get live coverage. In situations like these, there is usually sufficient time to set up in a more relaxed manner or even site-survey the location well in advance for the best location. With more set-up time it is possible to get just the shot you want. You may have to run extra cable or use a 13 GHz short hop back to the van but you have the time to do it.

For these types of live situations, the basic rules for doing a simple stand-up apply. Find a location where there will be some action in the background but not action that would interfere with what you are doing. The shot should convey the event easily and quickly to the viewer. Some identifiable aspect of the event should be present in the background.

Two aspects of these types of live shots need special consideration: graphics and guests. Most TV stations tend to add a lot of written information on the screen during a live shot. Not only is the bottom third of the picture taken up with the location, reporter's name and station call letters or slogans, but the upper corners of the picture may be filled with words reminding the viewer that the picture is live. The photographer needs to be aware of where this information appears and when it is in the picture. You may spend much time lining up a background only to have it covered by a graphic. This can be particularly troublesome when the reporter has a guest. In a two-shot their heads tend to be at the two upper corners of the picture; if the "live" graphic is also there it will cover one the subjects' faces. Your shots must be designed around the graphics as well as the scene.

The best technique for taping guests during a live shot is to have them on camera only when they are introduced or talking. One way to set up such a shot is to block it before you go live by having the guest and reporter stand side by side at comfortable distance. The reporter should already be in the best place for the background. The guest should be one large step to the side away from the reporter and one step back away from the camera. The guest should maintain this position throughout the live shot. This allows the photographer to start the shot on a single shot of the reporter without being zoomed in too closely. As the reporter introduces the guest, the camera can widen out to reveal the guest; the reporter then turns on the foot closest to the guest and faces him/her. This puts the two in a more traditional position for an interview so that the camera can zoom into the guest as a single shot without the reporter and not have a one eye or profile view of the guest. As the interview is wrapping up, the camera can zoom back out to a two-shot and the reporter can pivot back to face the camera. The camera can now zoom into the reporter; the guest is free to leave.

Live for the Sake of Live

Many times in local news photographers and reporters are asked to do live shots from places where nothing is going on. It may be an empty field, a house where a shooting happened the night before or just a street corner. Many stations feel it is necessary to use the live technology just to show the viewer that they have it. Even though it serves no journalistic purpose, it can be seen as a good excuse to train for the more important times and to experiment with different styles and techniques. You should always be looking for ways to make live shots look like they are live. For live-for-the-sake-of-live shots this may not be easy. Try to include some action indicative of the time of day such as a setting sun, rush hour traffic or maybe totally empty streets if it is for the late news.

The weather and sports segments are other examples of this type of live TV. With these two segments, it is possible to be more creative and possibly practice hand holding the camera during live shots. The sports segment may come from a pre-game warm-up where the sports anchor walks around among the players asking how their spirits are. The weather segment may be from a cultural fair where the weatherperson walks to a few booths

to sample food before giving the weather. It may not be news but it is a chance to hone some skills that can come in handy at another time.

EFP

Not many non-news productions are done live. With a few notable exceptions in the entertainment field, only teleconferencing is done live, usually from a studio. But, just as many news techniques slowly find their way into other forms of TV, live TV will eventually be used more and more in non-broadcast outlets. Instead of stodgy studio teleconferences, perhaps individual managers will do their segments live from the plant floor or inside a research lab. Viewers from all over the country could ask questions of the manager and key workers as they work. Live TV for corporate, business and educational use has just begun. In the coming decade there is bound to be more of it. Already video arraignments are taking place in courthouses so that prisoners do not have to leave jail to go downtown, and classes are being sent live to remote classrooms so that two campuses can be served by one teacher. These are just two examples of two-way interactive live TV. As fiber optic cable systems come on line with two-way capability, perhaps individuals will be doing live TV for friends, family or business. The possibilities are endless.

WHAT CAN GO WRONG?

At almost every step of the process of portable video production, problems can occur and cause delays resulting in missed shots, time wasted and money lost. When something goes wrong on a live shot from the field, a newscast can become chaotic.

Know the System

Live TV has the most pressure of any form of this business. It is also the time when the most things usually go wrong: the station does not have your picture or audio, the talent cannot hear the cues or the signal is full of breakup. The easiest way to deal with any of these problems is to know how the system works. If you work with a live truck (microwave or satellite), you must know the elements that make up the system and the order that they come in; you should be able to trace the signal from the camera to the antenna though every tiny part of the truck. If the receiver gets the color bars from the truck but not the picture from the camera, then you know the problem is not with the transmitter. You should have a checklist for the entire system within the van. The color bar generator/switcher, waveform monitor, tone generator/audio mixer, transmitter, power amp and TV monitor are all clues to where any problem may be. If color bars are okay at the other end and your waveform says that the video is correct, then any problem may be at the other end and not with you. The last resort is to bypass everything in the truck and put the video and audio directly into the transmitter. (Transmitters usually require line-level audio.) By eliminating possibilities, you can narrow any problem down to the piece of equipment or section of the truck.

Power in the Truck

All live trucks have a gas-powered generator to supply electricity to the video/audio racks and the transmitter. Larger generators can also provide enough power for lights as well; many are as strong as 20 amps for outside use (called **tech power**). A back-up system and sometimes the main system of power in small vans is an inverter that runs off the truck's engine. This small device converts the DC power from the engine's alternator and turns it into AC power for use in the rack. Most large vans actually run all equipment off a battery system that is continually charged by the generator. In case of generator failure this battery system can allow you to keep transmitting for a short period of time if the power load is kept to a minimum. Make sure you understand the power system in the truck and know what to do if any one element fails.

Lighting

If the live shot is indoors, the lighting will be similar to that used for most stand-ups. Time will of course be a factor in how fancy you will be able to get and how many lights you can set up. One consideration in doing live shots is matching the studio style of lighting. While in some cases you might do a stand-up in available light to make it fit with the rest of the story, a live shot should match more to the studio than to the story it may be introducing. That means a high-key flat style with little shadow or modeling detail. This does not mean good lighting but it is typical at most TV stations. You must also take into account any guests that may be interviewed and the light level of the background. It would look silly to have the reporter brightly lit and the background almost black by comparison, although that is often the case when only one light is used. Try always to set

the light up on a stand and not on top of the camera, unless the camera must be panned beyond the range of the stand light.

Outdoor live shots may look easy when being set up, but the sun can move to the wrong place in the sky, such as directly behind the talent or below the horizon. You must always be conscious of what time of day the live shot will go unless it is spot news. It may be daylight when you are setting up for the high-tide story, but at 5:30 p.m. when the live shot happens it may be pitch dark because it is no longer Daylight Savings Time. If you have not set up some powerful background lights to show the surf, the live shot could come off looking like the parking lot at the station. Live shots should always have backgrounds and at night this can be very difficult. You cannot light up the outdoors. A good 1000-watt focusing spot light can be used to punch up a detail in the background just enough to be visible over the talent's shoulder. Most of the time you would want to light the talent so the camera would be wide open to get the proper exposure. This would give the biggest advantage to getting something in the background to show up at night. Keep in mind the power limits of your generator if you do not have a reliable source of electricity. It is possible to blow an overloaded circuit anywhere. If you use battery lights, make sure they are not going to go dead in the middle of your shot.

Cables

The minimum cable to do a live shot is one video and one audio line. Many photographers keep a 100-foot bundle of **twin-lead**, or **Siamese** (an audio and video line in cable), to use whenever they are in a very big hurry. They can simply throw it out on the ground, hook up the camera and mike and be ready to go. More complex shots would make use of the multi-line cable that contains two video lines and four audio lines. This heavy cable, usually stored on a power reel, makes use of the full capabilities in the van. One video line is for the camera signal to the truck, another for an off-air TV signal from the truck's antenna to be used with the talent's monitor. One audio line is for the talent's mike to the truck, two lines are for IFB to the talent and camera operator being fed from the van and one spare audio line can be used for a separate guest mike. A good live van should be able to send any audio down the cable from the inside the van, including the two-way radio. Always make sure you have a backup cable in case any one of the primary cables fails. It is better to go live from next to the truck than to not go live at all because of a broken cable.

Batteries

Everything needed to go live should be able to be powered by battery. The rack and transmitter should function off the tech battery in the van for at least an hour without recharge in case the generator fails. The camera will most likely be powered by battery unless the shot is required for a very long time and AC is available. It can be very embarrassing if your battery fails while you are on the air. Always change to a fresh fully charged battery several minutes before the live shot. The off-air TV monitor should also be battery-powered, and a battery-powered light should be available in case the power fails for any AC lights you may be using.

Live TV is the perfect case for knowing the condition and performance level of each of your batteries. A misjudgment here could cost the station dramatic coverage of a big story. Always have a backup battery handy. Some companies make a battery belt that uses two camera batteries in series, allowing one to be taken off the belt and replaced with a fresh one while not disrupting power to the camera. This type of battery system would be a good investment for any live van.

Crowds

Nothing can ruin a live shot faster than the talent being swallowed up by an overly anxious crowd of onlookers. Not only is this bad TV, but it can be dangerous as well. A live shot from an area of large crowds of young people can quickly get out of control. It is not unusual for such a group to turn violent, assaulting the reporter and crew. The type of people and the size of the crowd must be taken into consideration when setting up the shot. A nice quite plaza at 3 p.m. might seem like a good place to do a simple live shot, except that at 5 p.m. the plaza is jammed with workers heading home. You may want that look but sometimes you do not; it can get dangerous without some form of crowd control. Many stations like to assign St. Patrick's Day live shots from inside bars. The most dangerous crowds are the crowds that are drunken. Do not let the station's desire for flashy live graphics push you into a situation that can cost you a camera or an injury. If the crowd cannot be controlled to your liking, then find a situation that will protect you. At times this may mean doing the live shot from the roof of the van or from behind a homemade barricade. Look at the traffic patterns of the area you are setting up in. Don't try to do a live shot from the busiest hallway in the building. Leave room for people to walk around you and stand and watch behind you and not behind the reporter. Nothing looks worse than some idiot making faces behind the talent who is talking about what a horrible tragedy has taken place. Sometimes it may be necessary to tape off an area with duct tape to keep people out (some people will walk right between you and the reporter as if you were not there). If the situation is really bad, like a spring break story, if may even be necessary to have the police there to protect you.

Permission

Another nightmare that is quite common is to set up for a live shot and then find out the owner of the property is demanding you get out. This can happen at any time you are not on public property if you have not secured permission beforehand. In spot news the situation is usually too chaotic for anyone to care, but if the shot does not come until after things have settled down, you may be in for a fight with an upset property owner. Police can do the same thing to you. You may set up in an area open to the press only to find that same area closed just before you are to go live. Pleading with them to give you just a few more minutes sometimes works but you should not rely on this technique to come through. Be prepared to move and have an alternative site picked out.

Timing

There cannot be enough emphasis on the fact that you have no control over when your shot will be taken live. Whether it is the satellite time that has been booked or the producer's sense of flow within the show, it is someone else who will say, "You're hot." If you were hoping for a certain background, it may disappear just as the director comes to you. Unless you have total control of the picture's contents, you must live with the fact that things change. The only way to cover yourself is to be flexible. Never totally rely on any one thing to be there. It can be as simple as a fire truck pulling in behind the reporter and blocking the view of the fire or as annoying as all of the people leaving the room 30 seconds before you go live. The only safe approach to live TV is to assume everything will go wrong because it usually does. If you consider all the factors mentioned, plan for the contingencies, and always stay two steps ahead of yourself, you should be able to surmount any obstacle to doing live TV.

13 Budgeting and Pricing

Whether you are in broadcasting, in-house corporate video or independent production, one of the first and most basic principles of video is that it is a business. Your work can be aesthetically superb, but if you do not know how much it cost to produce or if you cannot price it to make a profit, you may soon be out of a job or a business.

Most managers see the use of video as an added cost, while most videographers and producers see it as a sound investment. This difference of perspective is common throughout the industry. The best argument for using video is that it tells the necessary story and generates the desired effect more convincingly than other methods. In broadcast news operations, video can deliver the news stories from the field faster and cheaper than film. In the corporate world, video can deliver a message about a new benefit, procedure or product more quickly and effectively than other methods. For example, a corporation that has a new health benefit option that cuts health costs to employees may want the president of the corporation to deliver the message to encourage employees to choose the option and to enhance an image of a caring and concerned chief executive. The options available for delivery of the message are (1) a brochure with a picture and message from the president, (2) a visit from the president to all branches of the corporation to personally deliver the message or (3) a video of the president's message delivered to all branches of the corporation.

A simple cost analysis may reveal that the brochure is the least expensive of the options. But a good video manager may easily make the case that brochures are often read once, if at all, and then thrown away by most employees. A face-to-face video from the president may be viewed several times, especially when the specific details of the new health plan are explained. The video can be used for other public relations purposes, and the costs are relatively low. The president only has to deliver the message on one good take that can be seen by the entire corporation. Obviously, the expenses incurred by the travel of the president and any assistants would probably exceed the cost of the video. Also, this would take the president away from other important tasks.

The size of the budget may not necessarily be the best indicator of the quality of the resulting video project. Creativity and skill can often substitute for dollars in a budget. This is especially true in corporate video where entertainment value is secondary to effectiveness.

Constructing an elegant set would enhance the aesthetics of a scene but may not help the audience remember the purpose of the video. The same is true of elaborate paintbox graphics and digital effects. These may be both beautiful and exciting but may not contribute directly to the effectiveness of the video project. This logic may apply to many aspects of the production. Big-name talent may be recognizable, but are they credible to the particular audience? Vanna White may look great in your video, but is she credible when demonstrating and discussing a new optical disk computer? How about Cher—would she be better? A local public school teacher with knowledge and confidence about using computers may be more convincing and certainly less expensive for getting the audience to focus on the goals of the video.

Large-area lighting that requires numerous lights and people to set them may not be much better than a lighting strategy that relies on close-up lighting with a three-to-five light kit.

Big budgets can give you more flexibility because you have the option of high-priced talent, fancy post-production work or a large crew. But solving a problem with video is similar to other problem-solving situations: throwing money at the problem may help but it is expensive and does not guarantee anything. For any video production, creativity and skill can often compensate for a low budget.

ENG VERSUS EFP

Large differences between ENG and EFP emerge in the pricing and costs of portable video. Generally speaking, strict adherence to a budget is necessary in EFP work but only marginally important in ENG work. A big-budget EFP project usually results in a high-quality video piece, while the quality of ENG stories may have no direct relationship to the amount of money spent shooting them. EFP work usually begins when a budget is approved, but ENG work begins whenever an event worth covering is imminent or an issue worth showing and discussing surfaces.

ENG

A majority of ENG work is shot and edited by news department employees in broadcast TV stations. The footage is owned by the station and is almost always shown during the station's own newscasts. Usually, these stories are not marketed to any other users.

A story or event coverage is sometimes sold to another broadcaster (for example, another TV station) or news programmer (for example, Cable News Network). The sale may occur on a per-piece basis or may be part of a contractual agreement for numerous stories on one or more topics over a period of time. Pictures may also be traded for other services or pictures.

Prices for this type of ENG product may fluctuate wildly. The key determinants of price are the importance (news value) of the piece (which may depend on the importance of the event), the length of time it will be available and how many other ENG photographers obtained similar footage. The price range may begin as low as $25 for a short piece of moderate interest and increase to thousands of dollars for dramatic footage in high demand.

Many ENG stories sold by TV stations are sold to that station's network or, if the station has no network affiliation, to a news service or state or regional cooperative. These stories are sometimes made available to other members of the group or network via some type of closed circuit, satellite distribution system or feed.

Cable News Network (CNN) has become the world leader in acquiring and distributing video news from every corner of the globe. Because of all CNN's arrangements with various TV stations and foreign networks, they are a 24-hour per day trading service for news pictures.

Freelance ENG photographers, sometimes called "stringers," shoot news stories and cover events for a variety of buyers. These professionals, like their counterparts in EFP who do freelance work or have independent production companies, are often found in larger markets or locations that tend to generate many news stories, such as state capitals.

Since most ENG stories are not shot to be sold, most pieces are not budgeted as in EFP work. News budgets are not broken down by story. A news director for a TV station looks at ENG costs by a time unit (such as a typical broadcast week or month) and considers the salaries of the photographer, editor and reporter, knowing that maintenance and overhead expenses are met by other departments. News departments do create emergency funds in case of big and expensive stories to keep the station on a relatively stable and predictable budget.

EFP

Whether you are the manager of an in-house video production unit in a corporation or a manager/owner of a small independent production house, knowing the worth of your video product is the key to staying in business. Knowing the worth of your product helps you to charge your clients reasonable prices while allowing you to make a fair profit. The profit allows you to reinvest in your future through the purchase of new production or business equipment or to provide special benefits such as bonuses to employees for high-quality work.

Costs in EFP production are somewhat different from those in studio TV. In EFP work, the setting does not come to you; you must go the setting. This often generates large expenses for transportation of equipment and personnel. Because of the extensive handling that portable equipment receives, all equipment requires more frequent maintenance.

Tape costs in EFP are higher than in studio production. Film-style shooting of EFP requires many takes of each scene, resulting in a minimum of two to three times more tape than studio work. Most ½- and ¾-inch tape shot on portable video-cassette recorders must be shot on 20-minute small-format cassettes. These cassettes are smaller and hold less videotape than the 60-minute standard ½- and ¾-inch cassettes used in studio machines.

An hour of videotape recording in the small format costs about $40 for three 20-minute cassettes. One hour of studio videotaping on a 60-minute cassette costs about $25 for oxide or $50 for metal. On the other hand, studio costs are higher because of overhead expenses, such as rent or mortgage payments and regular utilities expenses.

IN-HOUSE VERSUS INDEPENDENT PRODUCTION UNITS

When video services are needed, an individual can do the work or hire a professional. When a corporate entity has repeated need for video services, it may decide to start its own video production unit or contract with an outside production business often referred to as an independent production house.

In-House

The purpose of establishing an in-house corporate video production center is to provide the corporation with a much-needed service for less money than contracting outside the firm. Almost always the size of this unit grows or shrinks in way that corresponds to the corporate need for the service and the health of the business environment. The corporate video production unit receives money in two general ways: (1) by charging the in-house customers for services rendered (sometimes referred to as a chargeback) or (2) by a direct flat-rate budget based on projected expenses.

The first method simulates an independent production unit in the marketplace. In-house clients go to the video manager and agree upon services to be rendered by the video unit and the cost of those services. The payment is made through some type of interdepartmental transfer. Often when this type of system exists, the video manager competes with other media or even with outside production units.

This keeps the pricing structure of the in-house unit very realistic. A good production team can do well in this system by keeping busy and providing excellent services at good prices. This system forces the video unit to earn its salary, that is, the only financial support it receives is obtained directly through the amount of work it does.

A second method for financing an in-house video production unit is through some type of annual budget. The production unit is automatically funded on a year-to-year basis without actually charging the in-house client on a per-piece basis. Variations on these two basic funding systems are common. Video units may receive some type of annual budget and may charge certain in-house clients for some kinds of services. In-house units that usually work on a chargeback basis may perform some services or provide services to in-house clients without charge.

Regardless of what type of financial system the company utilizes, it is essential to know the costs of providing necessary services to your clients. Since managers of corporate video units that receive annual funding are expected to provide the production service on the given budget, the manager should know how much work can be done with a given finite budget in order to avoid operating at a deficit. Unrealistic prices by a video unit on a chargeback system either result in a noticeable deficit or a surplus that might anger the in-house clients.

Independent

Independent production units generally have more freedom in their pricing. The only limitations are the goals set by the owners and managers and the need to make enough money to stay in business. Often the marketplace exerts a great deal of influence on the price. The general rule is that the price is what the market will bear. This is directly related to competition. Numerous competitors lead to lower prices.

This is not to say that quality and reliability are not pricing factors. High-quality work and a high degree of reliability are certainly worth a higher price, but competition limits your pricing range and flexibility. Too much competition often leads to underpricing and cutting corners to get the job done. Too little competition might prevent your prices from having credibility. Without any competition, your client has no point of reference on prices. Keep in mind that few clients actually understand and appreciate all the time, equipment and labor required to produce a professional-quality EFP video project.

CREATING AN ACCURATE BUDGET

The secret to creating an accurate budget is understanding all the possible sources of costs for the production. Most production units have some type of guide or budget sheet that lists possible costs for productions based on those done in the past by that unit. As new sources of cost are incurred, these new sources are added to the list.

These costs can be broken down into categories to help the organization of the process. Various strategies and systems exist. For many, especially smaller operations and most in-house corporate video units, the categorization follows a more generic approach that would be typical of any business that sells a product. The categories typically found in this system include materials cost, services cost, labor cost and overhead cost.

A tradition handed down from the movie industry regarding budgets consists of two very general categories: creative and executive talent and production, post-production and related expenses. This system uses the terms "above the line" and "below the line."

Line Costs

Budgets for large-scale productions in both the film and broadcast industries have traditionally delineated costs in a specific way. The first classification consists of costs encountered in securing the story rights and script, the producer and producer's immediate staff, the talent, the director and the costs for travel and fringes of these people. These costs are referred to as **above-the-line costs**.

All other costs directly incurred by the production are categorized together (though listed separately) and referred to as **below-the-line costs**. These are for materials, services, labor, and so forth—costs not included in the above-the-line category. The below-the-line costs are sometimes categorized by the stage in the production process (for example, pre-production, post-production) in which they are incurred.

The above-the-line costs and below-the-line costs are combined with the indirect or overhead costs to give a grand total. Although this budgeting procedure works for major studios, it is not as functional for smaller operations that have not had as much budget and budget-tracking experience.

Materials   Some materials for video projects, such as lamps, set or scenery construction and materials used for graphics preparation (slides or graphic cards) are expected to provide only one usage. For every project that requires a script, there is also a certain amount of paper and office forms used. Other materials may have some leftovers or reusables, but it is not safe to expect this to occur. Include the full cost of these materials in your budget.

The video and audiotape used in the project may or may not have later use. Some of it will not be recycled, for example, the edited master will remain in use only for the project for which it was purchased for a long time or at least until the client is thoroughly satisfied with the finished program.

Typical materials costs include the following.

- Videotape
- Audiotape
- Film stock (slides, still, movie)
- Set construction (lumber, paint, nails)
- Graphics materials (markers, paper, paint, photocopies)
- Tools (purchased for a specific project)
- Props (furniture, equipment for a specific project)
- Miscellaneous (gaffers tape, special adapters)

However, some of the raw footage shot on location may come in very handy for future productions that require a specific shot or cutaway from that location or type of location. It is sometimes amazing how creative and resourceful video people can be if reusing video or audiotape can save a return trip to a location. If you keep these things in mind, you can be more accurate when assessing materials cost for videotape.

Services   This cost category includes the services purchased specifically for the project that are not provided by in-house personnel or equipment. When you must rent a vehicle, do a special effect at another facility or cater meals at a location, categorize these as services costs. A slightly different type of cost, that falls under this general category is the type incurred when you must use copyrighted materials and pay a fee for that privilege.

Typical services costs include the following.

- Rental of equipment/vehicles
- Rental of locations
- Rental of facilities (for example, post-production)
- License fees (music, stock photo/slides or video)
- Catering for meals
- Outside contracts (security, construction)
- Production of graphics materials or special effects
- Photo processing
- Duplication (videotape or audiotape)

Labor The general definition of labor costs is the total cost of all hours (or days) spent by all employees involved in a project. Assigning exact costs for this category is most accurately done after the project is completed. However, you must try to predict exactly how many hours or days a director will or can spend on a given project. The price for the project is often needed well ahead of the project's competition—usually before the project is even begun.

Typical labor costs include the following.

- Executive producer
- Producer
- Director
- Writer(s)
- Researcher(s)
- Assistants
- Camera operators
- Videotape recorder operators
- Engineer(s)
- Lighting director
- Art director
- Grip(s)
- Production assistants
- Editor
- Office staff

This calls for accurate predicting if your production is to be successful. Predictions are most accurate when two types of information are available: (1) the number of hours spent by your director on a similar project and (2) the number of hours generally spent by other directors on similar projects or amount of work.

Very simply, once you have predicted the amount of time, multiply this figure by the director's unit rate. The unit rate is determined for any convenient length of time, for example, hour, day or week, by dividing the director's total pay for a known period by the appropriate number of units.

For example, your director earns $2000 per month. What are the unit rates for each (a) day or (b) hour he works? The following equation will give the daily unit rate (we assume here that each month has 20 work days):

$$
\begin{aligned}
\text{Daily unit rate} \quad &= \text{total monthly salary} \div \\
&\quad \text{number of work days per month} \\
&= \$2000 \text{ per month} \div 20 \text{ work} \\
&\quad \text{days per month} \\
&= \$100
\end{aligned}
$$

To find the hourly unit rate use this equation.

$$
\begin{aligned}
\text{Hourly unit rate} \quad &= \text{daily unit rate} \div \text{number of} \\
&\quad \text{work hours per day} \\
&= \$100 \text{ per day} \div 8 \text{ work hours per} \\
&\quad \text{day} \\
&= \$12.50
\end{aligned}
$$

The hourly or daily rate should be multiplied by the projected number of hours that will be spent by the director on this particular project. This procedure needs to be repeated for all persons involved in the production.

For most union or personal service contracts there is a base-pay unit, usually set at one full day. Along with this rate for union and non-union people are overtime and other compensation agreed to be employee and employer. In some cases, flat rates can be negotiated.

When the labor costs for all production personnel are added together, you then have a general idea of what the actual costs will be. This first sum is merely the dollar amount that will be going directly to the employees. What must be added to this direct payment is the amount that your company pays for employee benefits such as life insurance, hospitalization, retirement or bonuses.

These fringe benefits can add from 30% to over 100% to your direct labor costs. These added costs are almost always associated with full-time employees. Failure to include these costs will cause you to underestimate your overall costs which may result in underpricing your product and lead to some red ink.

Overhead Expenses

Overhead expenses are those expenses generally associated with being in business. Typical overhead expenses include the following:

- Salaries (nonproduction)
- Benefits
- Office/Studio space rental
- Utilities (heat, light, water, telephone)
- Dues (professional organizations)
- Subscriptions (magazines)
- Reference/library materials (books, sound library, graphics clip art)
- Equipment depreciation (office/production equipment)
- Maintenance (janitorial, groundskeeping)
- Miscellaneous (donations)

Certain kinds of labor costs may also be associated with overhead. Salaries of others not directly involved in the project (for example, a secretary) can be included in labor costs if the employee spends an easily definable amount of time on the particular project being priced. Often this is not the case and the project is merely assigned a portion of this type of office salary in the overhead cost.

Equipment depreciation costs may also be included in a general category of overhead expenses. Without going into great detail or accounting theory, depreciation can be thought of as the value that your equipment loses as a result of use and aging. For example, if an EFP-style VCR costs $6000 and is expected to last three years, the cost of owning and using the VCR can be calculated as $2000 per year.

There are numerous ways to deal with these costs, but for use in pricing your product follow a simple procedure in which you ascertain a unit rate of overhead costs in the same way you obtain a unit rate for labor costs. Total the previous year's overhead costs and then divide that total by the number of working or operating days:

$$\frac{\text{Total Previous Year's Overhead Costs}}{\text{Number of Operating Days}}$$

The result is a daily overhead cost. This daily cost, or fraction thereof, should be added to other costs.

Keep in mind that this cost may fluctuate from year to year. If you are aware of definite fluctuations in overhead that would change the overhead unit rate in your current year, you should adjust the figures accordingly. Salary raises or bonuses for office or executive employees, increases in utility use or rates or changes in tax rates can influence current overhead expenses.

If you think that changes like those mentioned have occurred, you can adjust the unit rate by first adjusting last year's total overhead expenses by the amount of the expected changes.

Another method is to arrive at your overhead cost more often than once per year. A quarterly assessment of overhead costs will sometimes help to keep your unit rate closer to reality.

When the four general cost categories (materials, services, labor and overhead) are added together, you have a total cost for the project. This is also the price at which you or your company can break even with no financial loss or gain. But if your price is set to break even, chances are that your department or company will lose money. As unforeseen expenses always crop up, it is good business policy to add something to your total cost to provide for a rainy day.

If you include another factor—profit—in your pricing formula, you will help guarantee that you will be able to meet any cost overruns and perhaps save some money to buy more or better equipment in the future.

BUDGET TRACKING

The best way to give accurate prices for your video work is to have accurate information regarding what the actual costs are. You can do this by keeping accurate records of expenditures for the projects your company produces. This recordkeeping or bookkeeping process is called **budget tracking**.

This procedure allows you to compare the projected budget for a video service with the actual cost. By making this comparison, you not only can assess your ability to cover your incurred costs and attain your desired profit amount, you also gain valuable data for pricing future projects. If you track your budgets after you make them, you can easily evaluate your ability to predict costs. This procedure is a relatively easy one to establish.

First, whenever you give a budget estimate for a project, make sure that it includes a dollar amount for all possible items within each of the cost categories (see Table 13.1). Set up this budget breakdown so that each cost item has a line with at least

Table 13.1: Budget Tracking.

Cost Category	Budgeted	Actual
Materials		
Videotape	$450	$275
Set	150	175
Paint and lumber	85	80
Total materials	$685	$530
Services		
Van rental	$150	$150
Special effects	250	350
Costume rental	75	75
. . .	. . .	. . .
Total services	. . .	. . .

two columns: one for the budgeted or predicted cost and a second for the actual cost.

A third column might also be included for cost overruns—when actual costs are more the estimated costs. Or the third column may be used for budget surpluses—when the actual costs are less than predicted costs. This third column is derived by subtracting the actual cost from the predicted cost. The sum of the positive and negative numbers in the third column will give you a report on your pricing accuracy: a positive number shows that you have safely assessed your costs and have some money left over to contribute to profit; a negative number means that you have underestimated costs and you may have to use money initially earmarked for profit to pay for the costs of producing the project.

Computer Assistance

Just as computers and computer programs are helping so many business managers to organize, track, project and plan in their areas of responsibility, these new technologies are helping EFP producers with the planning and business aspects of portable video production. (See Figure 13.1.) Computer programs created by video professionals allow producers and their staffs to generate budget figures in standardized categories in very short periods of time whereas the tedious paper-and-pencil mode formerly took days. This type of program

also allows the individual producer to create special tailor-made budget categories.

This type of software can also perform budget tracking. After a final budget for a project is entered, expenses are entered as they are incurred, either at some regular interval or at the end of the production. This type of program allows you to quickly recall the amount budgeted for a particular category of expense, the number of expense entries in that category and the remaining balance. The program also allows you to update the budget when hourly or unit rates change.

EFP PRICING FORMULA

Every production situation brings a unique problem to the person who must accurately assess costs and set prices. This section presents a general formula for the identification and categorization of costs associated with EFP video projects.

A combination of five factors makes up the components necessary to set the price for an EFP video project. The first four factors are materials, services, labor and overhead costs. These can be combined into one major category of cost:

$$\begin{array}{r} \text{Materials Cost} \\ \text{Services Cost} \\ \text{Labor Cost} \\ \underline{+\text{Overhead Cost}} \\ \text{Total Cost} \end{array}$$

These four, when combined and added to the fifth factor, profit, yield the formula for price:

$$\begin{array}{r} \text{Total Cost} \\ \underline{+\text{ Profit}} \\ \text{Price} \end{array}$$

or

$$\begin{array}{r} \text{Materials Cost} \\ \text{Services Cost} \\ \text{Labor Cost} \\ \text{Overhead Cost} \\ \underline{+\textbf{Profit}} \\ \text{Price} \end{array}$$

The fifth factor, profit, is considered separately because the amount of profit is often under the control of the price setter. Profit is the amount of money you want to make over and above all of your costs for the project. Profit may be used for reinvestment in equipment, facilities, real estate, bonuses or simply to build the company's cash

Figure 13.1: Sample computer program for video producers. *Courtesy of Comprehensive Video Supply Corp.*

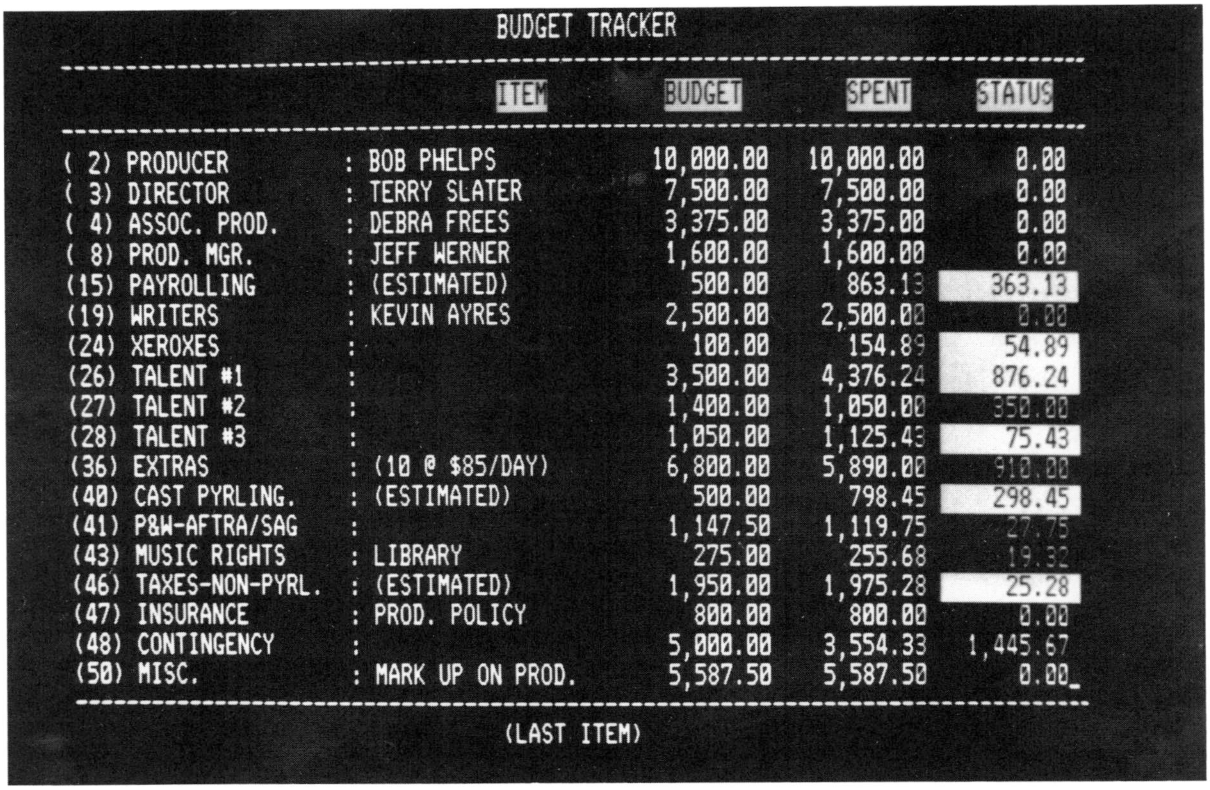

```
                            BUDGET TRACKER
------------------------------------------------------------------------
                        ITEM        BUDGET       SPENT      STATUS
------------------------------------------------------------------------
( 2) PRODUCER      : BOB PHELPS    10,000.00   10,000.00       0.00
( 3) DIRECTOR      : TERRY SLATER   7,500.00    7,500.00       0.00
( 4) ASSOC. PROD.  : DEBRA FREES    3,375.00    3,375.00       0.00
( 8) PROD. MGR.    : JEFF WERNER    1,600.00    1,600.00       0.00
(15) PAYROLLING    : (ESTIMATED)      500.00      863.13     363.13
(19) WRITERS       : KEVIN AYRES    2,500.00    2,500.00       0.00
(24) XEROXES       :                 100.00      154.89      54.89
(26) TALENT #1     :               3,500.00    4,376.24     876.24
(27) TALENT #2     :               1,400.00    1,050.00     350.00
(28) TALENT #3     :               1,050.00    1,125.43      75.43
(36) EXTRAS        : (10 @ $85/DAY) 6,800.00    5,890.00     910.00
(40) CAST PYRLING. : (ESTIMATED)      500.00      798.45     298.45
(41) P&W-AFTRA/SAG :               1,147.50    1,119.75      27.75
(43) MUSIC RIGHTS  : LIBRARY          275.00      255.68      19.32
(46) TAXES-NON-PYRL.: (ESTIMATED)   1,950.00    1,975.28      25.28
(47) INSURANCE     : PROD. POLICY     800.00      800.00       0.00
(48) CONTINGENCY   :               5,000.00    3,554.33   1,445.67
(50) MISC.         : MARK UP ON PROD. 5,587.50   5,587.50      0.00
------------------------------------------------------------------------
                           (LAST ITEM)
```

reserves. A closer look at these factors gives a better understanding of the role each plays in price setting.

The fifth factor in the pricing formula is often the one most difficult to quantify. How much money do you want to make on a project? Enough to buy dinner? Enough to buy 10 cases of tape? Enough for a new video camera? Enough to pay off your mortgage? Obviously, the amount of profit is related to the total cost of the project. No one expects to make $800 profit on a project that involves only $200 of real cost.

A good manager would not settle for a $50 profit on an $8000 job. The base profit percentage in the production business is about 20%. In other words, you can usually add 20% of the total cost as the profit factor in your pricing formula (or multiply total costs by 1.2).

Some projects may justify a higher profit figure. Low-priced jobs usually have a minimum dollar amount included for profit. Some projects may be risky, require crucial deadlines or present difficult or unpleasant conditions. If any of these conditions are present, a 25% to 50% profit margin may be quite reasonable.

There may be projects that you feel you should do for reasons other than direct economic gain. These are the jobs that may enhance your credibility, give you desired publicity, give your creative desires a boost or simply give you a shot at working for a highly desired clientele. Foregoing profit even in these cases may not be necessary, but it may assure you of getting the job because you are the lowest bidder.

In some instances, you may want to take on a video project at a loss, even if the client is not a highly desired one. For example, the price structure in a voluntary loss situation may look like this:

Materials cost	$100
Services cost	50
Labor cost	100
Overhead cost	50
Total cost	$300

The above figures are the costs for a small video project (for example, a public service announcement or commercial). If the client pays only $275, you are left with a negative profit of $25. For what reason would you undertake this project?

A quick look at the cost of being in business can shed some light. Some costs, such as labor and overhead, are incurred whether you have a project to do or not. Your overhead costs are fixed, and your labor costs might come from full-time employees who get paid whether they have a project to do or whether they are reading magazines in the office. If you do not have a project, you still have some costs:

Labor cost	$100
Overhead cost	+50
Total cost	$150

If you do not take on this project, you still have to pay $150 in costs. By taking on the project you cover most of your costs and lose only $25 instead of $150. Besides, it is better to have your employees gaining experience in video production instead of in magazine reading.

This policy of accepting negative-profit jobs is risky. If client X finds out that client Y paid less for a similar job, the integrity of your rate structure may suffer and you may have to continually justify your prices to clients. Except for highly unusual circumstances, it is best to take on jobs at your normal profit rate.

14 Copyright and Legal Issues

One of the attractive aspects of portable video is that a large number of people see your work. In fact, if you are in a city, many people may even see it while you are shooting. While this exposure is a blessing for videomakers in added recognition, the high profile can also be a blessing through higher ratings, more sales, a larger corporate budget, and so on. But with the two rewards of exposure and money can come some very substantial legal problems. For those who plan to produce video programs or segments, a cursory knowledge of how to protect yourself from legal entanglements and your material from being stolen or misused are as necessary as any video techniques.

There are two major areas of the law most videographers encounter: the right of privacy and the right of ownership (or copyright). The former is the most common problem in ENG and the latter in EFP, although both can certainly create more trouble than you would suspect. The safest thing to do before shooting anything, whether news or not, is to be sure not only of your rights but of the rights of everyone or everything that appears in your video or had anything to do with it. This sounds complex but the level of complexity is somewhat a function of the amount of money involved. A student project only seen by a class or school can do many things that a multimillion dollar network TV show could never dream of doing without having every legal "i" dotted.

PRIVACY

One of the basic rights of all Americans is the right to privacy. Many areas within our laws are interpreted by measuring them against this right. The greatest concern for video producers, regarding privacy, comes in two areas: using peoples' images and their names. Any time a person writes about anyone else or picks up a camera and photographs anyone else, the right of that person's privacy has to be considered. There are a number of ways a person can have their privacy limited and there are a number of people who seem to have no privacy at all. Broadcast, cable and industrial video producers need to be constantly aware of this right in order to avoid what can be major legal problems after a program or segment is shown.

News Productions

Broadcast journalism has a great many freedoms under the law that other types of video production do not enjoy. How the end product is used is very crucial to the rights of the makers as well as the subjects. Because news is a public service and the right of a free press is guaranteed under the Constitution of the United States, there are very few ways to stop someone from covering an event or showing a particular picture or scene on a newscast. However, if the news staff does not understand the subtleties of interpreting the right to privacy, the results can range from loss of prestige to high-priced civil suits. Being wrong can be costly to you and to your employer.

Public's Right to Know The courts have made it very clear that the public's right to know is one of our most secure freedoms. The right to know generally applies to anything that could be considered interesting to the public, is in the public eye or affects any portion of the populace. The public's right to know allows the news to show the victim of a car crash, the president on vacation or the unsanitary conditions inside a poorly run meat-packing plant. This does not mean a news broadcast has the right to libel or slander someone or otherwise misrepresent the pictures shown or the words read. However, it is very difficult to prove claims of such wrongdoing against a news organization.

In the late 1980s Las Vegas singer Wayne Newton sued NBC News for linking him to known organized crime figures, thereby damaging his public image. It was alleged that NBC's combination of words and pictures created a defamatory impression. Newton won a record judgment in a local court, but a higher court deemed the award to be too high. If the news organization had a legitimate reason for doing a story on a particular person (such as Mr. Newton because he is in the public eye), that person's complaint would have to show the information used was not only totally false but also that the news reporter knew it was false. A reporter's ability to protect the identity of sources can make it hard to prove how much a reporter really knows about what was written. This legal loophole applies to any news media and explains why supermarket tabloids get away with saying the most outrageous things. The small chance of proving malicious intent and falsity is usually not worth the time, trouble, added publicity or money needed to sue the paper. What separates this type of journalism from the mainstream is ethics. Any news organization seeking the respect of the public should try to uphold not only the letter of the law but the spirit of the law as well.

The public's right to know permits great freedom in a story but also requires great responsibility. Suppose that your videotape of a well-known politician showing affection to a member of the same sex implies that he is gay. You may have the right to show it but if he has not made public his sexual preference, is it ethical to show it? Would his being gay mean anything about his ability to be a good public servant? The public may find it interesting but it may also cost him his office. There is an ongoing debate as to how far the media can go in this type of reporting. It may be legal but you must always weigh the benefits of what you do against the harm it may cause. Often it rests on you, and you alone, to decide.

Public Property A common misconception on the part of the public upon seeing a TV camera is what the right of privacy means. For example, a store owner may see a news photographer taking pictures and order the photographer to stop. If the photographer does not, the store owner may call the police even though there are no legal grounds for doing so as long as the photographer is on public property. If the photographer is not harassing the owner or creating a public disturbance, any action against the photographer by the owner could end with the owner going to court, not the photographer. As long as a photographer is on public property, practically the only reasons that can prevent videotaping are public safety or risk to national security.

While most people think they have the right to reject any coverage of themselves or their property, they often have no legal basis for that belief. The factors that determine the right of privacy in video are the location of the camera and the context in which the pictures are used. Generally, if a photographer is on public property or even on private property with the permission of the owner or management, anything the camera can see fair game regardless of where it is in relationship to the photographer. Even when former President Reagan vacationed at his Santa Barbara ranch, the public saw fuzzy pictures of him riding horses. The news media had permission to be on adjoining property and with special telephoto lenses, they could see and photograph Reagan.

Exercising the right to take pictures can be overdone. When pop singer Madonna was married, the press hired helicopters to survey and photograph her outdoor wedding. The resulting air show with its noise spoiled the wedding and became almost as big a story as the event. Unfortunately, celebrity status brings attention. It was reported that during his wedding, *Miami Vice's* Don Johnson fired at helicopters observing the event. Everyone would agree that the helicopters were an invasion of privacy but any news show or newspaper would pay to have the pictures because the public really wanted to see those weddings. This does not make it ethical but the public's right to know is a powerful force and, in this case, it did make it legal.

Context Being in the news media does not, however, give you the right to misrepresent what you see or imply criminal wrongdoing without reasonable proof. The context in which the scene is used must reflect the reality of the situation at the time of taping. While most problems of misrepresentation or accusation come during editing or because of narration used over the pictures, the photographer should still be aware of any potential problems.

This is a typical situation in which you could find yourself when shooting news. Suppose the assignment is to shoot people smoking in a public restaurant for a story on a proposed change in smoking laws. The owner of the Dinner Bell Cafe has agreed to let you shoot there. With the owner's permission, you do not need the consent of each individual patron. However, it is considered polite and ethical to seek permission of any customer that your camera approaches or anyone who needs to be lit by your sungun or stand light. If you can make the same shot using your zoom lens and existing lighting, then you need not ask them. Let's suppose that you shoot the cafe when it is lit well enough for you to shoot with natural light and you do most of it on a tripod from the sides of the room so that many of the diners do not even notice your presence. The video airs on the news and one of the shots depicts an easily recognizable couple who are having an affair and are discovered only after appearing on the news. The two sue the station for airing their pictures.

Is the station liable? No. The station cannot be held responsible. The couple may sue the restaurant but they have no legal grounds for suing the broadcaster. If the story was about people having affairs and they showed this couple, it would be quite different. Even if it were true, it would be an unjustified invasion of privacy unless the story was actually about that particular couple. This is the reason why videotapes of people apparently committing crimes show their faces covered by a video effect so that they are unrecognizable. These people have not yet been charged with any crimes. The safest way of dealing with questionable situations is to apply a good measure of caution. Do not say or imply anything bad about some one unless you are prepared to defend that accusation in court or know for certain on advice from an attorney that you are within your rights.

Public Figures The really gray area of the privacy issue concerns people who can be considered public figures: politicians, movie stars, business leaders and so on. The media hid outside presidential candidate Gary Hart's condo during his campaign. They could not have done that to just anyone. Hart put himself in the public spotlight and yielded most of his right to privacy to the public's right to know. There is still a large debate as to whether that media stake-out was ethical but it was legal. The unfortunate part of this area of the law is that not all public figures attain this status by choice. Some are the innocent bystanders caught up in events not of their making. The victims of crimes and disasters, relatives of the famous and even witnesses to events can suddenly find themselves the center of media attention and powerless to do anything about it.

Trespassing In the pursuit of an important story or shot, many news photographers have found themselves breaking other laws. The most common law broken is trespass. A property owner is powerless to stop a news crew from taping while the crew remains on public property but this does not apply to private property where not only can they be removed but also arrested. Trespassing charges are seldom filled against news crews for two main reasons. First, property owners usually do not want the added publicity or hassle; second, courts are generally sympathetic to the media if the story is in the public interest. The public's right to know is an area of the law with a wide latitude for abuse by the media. The news technique made famous by *Sixty Minutes* where the photographer and reporter barge into a private place and thrust the camera into the accused face is a prime example. The reporters fire accusations at the accused who screams for them to leave while covering his or her face. It produces very dramatic pictures and can make any subject look guilty. *Sixty Minutes* does this successfully because the producers are *very* sure of the person's guilt or inability to prove innocence. However, this *is* trespassing.

Most trespassing by news crews goes unnoticed until after the fact. It may be as simple as a photographer hopping a farmer's fence to get a better shot of a beautiful sunset or as serious as sneaking into a building to show that foreign workers removing asbestos are not provided protective clothing and masks. The former is done out of the innocence of the story; the latter, out of the public's right to know that people are being unfairly exploited and their lives put at risk. In both cases, the photographer may have ended up in jail. The charges may later be dropped or the fine, if any, inconsequential. No matter what the reason for the trespass, you may experience at least some trouble.

In the majority of cases, the trespassing photographer would be ordered to leave and that would be the end of it. There will be cases, however, when just the opposite can happen. The photographer shooting the sunset could be held at gunpoint by an angry farmer tired of too many vandals. The farmer can make the photographer wait until the sheriff shows up. When you are an uninvited interloper, you increase the chances of being in the wrong place at the wrong time.

A law that makes it an acceptable risk for so many news crews to trespass is the one against robbery. If you are caught taking pictures on nonpublic property, the property owner can order you to leave or even detain you until the police arrive but cannot take your camera, videotape or any other of your possessions because this is your property. Taking it against your will or by threat is defined as robbery. It does not matter that you are on someone else's property; your things, including the images recorded on the tape, belong to you or to your employers with you as their representative. Unfortunately, just as the law often allows you extra leeway in cases of trespass, it also tends to allow leeway to angry property owners who may destroy your tape or damage your equipment. You may be told that pursuing any charges against the property owner is inadvisable because there is virtually nothing to gain from it. You can easily appear to be the bad guy breaking the law or harassing the property owner. You must weigh the worth of what you are trying to do against the risks you are taking. The laws do not bend in your direction only.

Hidden Cameras   A common technique for taking news pictures on private property where there is no way that the owner would allow a crew access is using a hidden camera. With the new small tape formats like VHS, S-VHS, 8mm, and H8 that are at or near broadcast quality, videotape recorders can be hidden with ease in a handbag, briefcase or even under clothing. With the use of fiber optic lenses, miniature color cameras can be placed almost anywhere. For this type of set-up, a wide-angle lens is often no larger than a button and can easily look just like one. Fiber optics allows the camera to be placed some distance from the lens in the same way that a microphone is run by cable to a recorder.

The use of a hidden camera is as old as photojournalism. News organizations as well as law enforcement agencies have set up sting operations using a camera concealed behind a false wall or shooting through a two-way mirror to capture subjects doing everything from selling phony health insurance to the elderly to selling cocaine to well-known public figures like the famous John DeLorean case. While such uses often lead to grand jury investigations or even arrests, this does not mean that the accused will be found guilty. DeLorean was acquitted of the charges against him despite the videotape evidence. The jury thought he had been pressured into buying the cocaine by government agents. If it had been a news crew doing the taping and DeLorean suing them, it could have cost the news organization millions of dollars to be wrong. You must make sure the law is on your side before you engage in or make public your investigative activities.

The most common situation involves going onto private property to show illegal or questionable activity where the visible presence of a camera would cause the activity to stop. The photographer usually uses the disguise of an interested party to the activity, for example, a spectator at a pit bull dog fight or a buyer of child pornography. Making use of a wide-angle lens, the hidden camera can merely be pointed in the direction of the activity to show an overall view of what is happening. This type of photography can be quite dangerous. Before engaging in any risky form of photojournalism, you should consider what the worst possible outcome might be and how you can minimize your risks. In some cases, it could cost you your life.

Because this technique pushes the limits of the right to privacy, the laws concerning the use of a hidden camera can vary from state to state. Check with your state's attorney general's office before using a hidden camera on private property; check with your lawyer before airing any part of it. Not only the context in which the video is used but also the way in which it was obtained can determine liability in any criminal or civil complaint. At least one state in the Midwest has made it illegal to use such a camera to videotape on farms in reaction to the use of hidden cameras by the news media and by animal rights' groups that were protesting the treatment of livestock. Disguised protest group members and TV journalists in that state were visiting "puppy mills" to expose the horrible conditions under which the dogs were bred and raised. The resulting public outcry did not lead the state to clamp down on the offending "mills" but rather on the bearers of the bad news. The law will surely be tested in the courts, but it does point out the complexity of interpreting the right of privacy verses the public's right to know.

Names and Numbers   Another aspect of privacy involves information. Credit card numbers, tax returns, addresses, social security numbers, bank account and telephone numbers cannot be made public by the news media. Showing an audience this type of information without good cause can be a serious violation of the right to privacy, even for people who fit the category of public figure.

The U.S. Post Office has one hard and fast rule: you may not show the names and addresses of any letters or packages in a photo because it is not public information any more than the parcel's contents; it is meant only for the sender and the addressee to know. This situation would also exist in a department store if you were shooting a story on consumer credit. You cannot show someone's credit card number on the screen. In both situations, there are ways to get all the shots needed, including extreme close-ups, without violating anyone's rights.

It may be part of a story to show the destination of mail. By carefully arranging the letters in a pile, you can have successive letters stacked so that only the city line of the address can be seen. Without the name and street, the city cannot be linked to any one individual. The same can be done with credit cards. By asking the customer to hold the care with a finger covering the name and part of the card's number, a viewer would have no way of getting the name and credit number to misuse.

Anything you shoot names and numbers, you must pay special attention to the rights of the people associated with them. Sometimes the most innocent situation can lead to a nasty legal conflict. If you are in a real estate office doing a story on home buying and you shoot a close-up on some bid papers, you may inadvertently show the name of the bidder. If other business associates see the story and confrontation results in a deal falling through, you may be sued for invasion of privacy. Permission was never given to make the deal public and the bidder was not a public figure.

No matter what the situation is, you must always consider how much personal information you may be revealing about someone, especially if that person has nothing directly to do with your story. The safest thing to do is never show anyone's name or any of their personal identification numbers unless you have their permission or that information is already public knowledge, such as the address of a criminal charged in a serious crime. Because someone's name and number are listed in the phone book does not give you the right to use this information unless that particular person is the subject of public interest.

Police Orders   Many times a police officer will try to stop the videotaping of crime or accident scenes and threatens a photographer with arrest. The photographer usually complies with this request to maintain good media/police relations but also attempts to find a way to circumvent the officer's orders. Usually the photographer will simply back away and use a telephoto lens to continue shooting. Nonetheless, the threat of arrest is real although the officer knows charges are unlikely to be filed against the photographer; the police usually release the photographer after a short time. The official reason for detaining the photographer can simply be interfering with a peace officer. This offense can be hard to prosecute but gives the police legal grounds to lock a photographer in the back of a squad car. The reality is that most police know that keeping the photographer locked up until the event is over accomplishes what they want: no pictures. If you are threatened with arrest, believe the officer whether he is right or wrong about your rights.

There will be times when the police and the media seem to be at cross-purposes and you must take extra care to make sure you are not pointlessly exercising your rights at the expense of good police work. One of the reasons police often do not want pictures at the scene of a crime is to prevent valuable evidence from becoming common knowledge. Only the criminal, the police investigators and the prosecutor should know the details of the crime scene until the trial. This eliminates the innocent but disturbed suspects who confess to the offense or false witnesses who come forward to throw off suspicion from someone else. If the police are sure that only the real criminal would know certain details about the crime scene, then the fakers can easily be spotted.

The greatest problems arise when the police do not make clear their reasons for denying pictures. The public's right to know can be on a collision course with the ability of the police to do their job. If the news organization has well-established good relations with local law enforcement, many problems will not arise. One part of the constitutional responsibility of a free press is to question authority. This aspect of journalism can put you on a collision course with the police. In the absence of a good working relationship, the news media can hamper an investigation by its aggressive coverage. Knowing where the line is between your rights and the duty of the police to protect the public can be almost impossible. You must decide in a split second whether the shot is worth the chance of getting arrested. Sometimes you have to lose a battle to win the war.

Part of your duty to serve the public's right to know is to be able to actually do just that. The police or any other agency or organization may try to stop your coverage for any number of reasons. It is your job as a journalist to decide if their reasons are valid (not showing a rape victim) or are simply self-serving (no bad publicity) or an attempt to cover-up wrongdoing (the police using excessive force). If you are locked in a squad car, you will not be able to make any decisions or take any pictures for that matter. Your most important goal to keep shooting video without getting arrested. You can be a very powerful person with your camera; with that power comes a great deal of pressure to direct what you do or do not do. Without your camera, you are powerless. Many people will want to censor what you are shooting.

Avoiding Problems   Almost all TV stations have lawyers who pour over a picture or script that might lead to legal problems before the material is aired. Of course there will always be times when a lawyer is not available for this purpose. A news organization may have to rely on the judgment of the producer or other news management. If you, as a news photographer, know that something you are taping is a potential legal problem, try to head off as much as you can in the field while still covering the story. If some people really do not want their pictures taken and they are not directly part of the story, don't shoot them. Avoid problems that serve no purpose in covering the story. If you know that the video you are shooting in our cafe example earlier is for a story on couples having affairs, then you should provide plenty of shots of couples where the audience would have no way of identifying them. Shoot only their clasped hands, shoot them out of focus, use a potted plant in the foreground to block the view of their faces, shoot them from behind, do not let the particular cafe be recognizable in the shots, and so on. This makes the job of the editor easier and adds another layer of safety to keep you and the station out of trouble.

On the other hand, you should not censor yourself so heavily that you cannot get the job done or get all the pictures you need. You will have to rely a certain amount on the other people involved with putting the material on the air. You may not always be the best person to make the decision on what to show or how to show it. Unless you know for a fact that you cannot show something or were given explicit instructions on how to shoot it, do

the shooting with several options in mind. Trust the editors and the news management to make the best use of the pictures. After all, the pictures are not public until they are aired. You can shoot anything but you cannot always air everything shot. If you at least avoid the obvious problems (like showing the faces of undercover police officers), other problems can be dealt with in post-production by not using the shot or by applying special effects.

Non-News Productions

Any video product that does not fall under the category of news does not enjoy the same latitude regarding privacy. Without the backing of the Fourth Amendment to the Constitution, violating someone's right to privacy can quickly lead to the courtroom. The way the courts interpret privacy laws is much stricter for non-news production than for news. Even if the method of shooting and the presentation is the same as news, if the videographer is not with a functioning news organization there are no "free press" rights.

Profit and Publicity   Most non-news production is done not to serve the public but to serve the producer or subject of the video. Because one or both of these parties are benefitting from the video, they are not allowed to do so at the expense of someone else's rights. Non-news production normally brings to mind commercials or entertainment and informational programs, but it also includes areas like public service announcements, charity promotions and business presentations. While a community service organization may be nonprofit and its 30-second video spot shot free, the organization still benefits from the publicity. People see the spot and donate money to that charity. The cause may be very important and have the best community needs in mind, but the organization is not allowed to invade the privacy of anyone. It is easy to see that showing without permission the face of a down-and-out person on skid row in a commercial for a trade school is violating a right to privacy for simple monetary gain. It may not be as easy to see that a skid-row charity using the same face in a public service announcement without permission still violates this same right. (See Figure 14.1.)

Content   Even with permission you cannot use a person's image in any way you please. It is not acceptable to misrepresent what you are doing. If you ask permission to photograph someone and give either a direct answer or implication of how the pictures will be used and then use the

Figure 14.1: Two examples of model release forms. If a videographer or producer has a model complete a release form, the chances of being sued for unauthorized use are greatly reduced. These forms are used extensively in non-news production. *Courtesy Comprehensive Video Supply Corp., Northvale, NJ.*

MODEL RELEASE

I hereby assign rights to the videotape and sound recording made of me this date, _____, by, _____ and I hereby authorize the reproduction, sale, copyright, exhibition, broadcast and/or distribution of said videotape without limitation for the purpose of

_____

I certify that I am over 21 years old.

Signed _____

Dated _____

MODEL RELEASE

For and in consideration of my engagement as a model by _____, hereafter referred to as the videographer, on terms or fee hereinafter stated, I hereby give the videographer, his legal representatives and assigns, those for whom the videographer is acting, and those acting with his permission, or his employees, the right and permission to copyright and/or use, reuse and/or broadcast and republish videotape recordings of me, or in which I may be distorted in character, or form, in conjunction with my own or fictitious name, on reproductions thereof in color, or black and white made through any media by the videographer at his studio or elsewhere, for any purpose whatsoever, including the use of any printed matter in conjunction therewith.

I hereby waive any right to inspect or approve the finished videotape, sound track, or advertising copy or printed matter that may be used in conjunction therewith or to the eventual use that it might be applied.

I hereby release, discharge and agree to save harmless the videographer, his representatives, assigns, employees or any person or persons, corporation or corporations, acting under his permission or authority, or any person, persons, corporation or corporations, for whom he might be acting, including any firm publishing and/or distributing the finished product, in whole or in part, from and against any liability as a result of any distortion, blurring, or alteration, optical illusion, or use in composite form, either intentionally or otherwise, that may occur or be produced in the taking, processing or reproduction of the finished product, its publication, distribution, or broadcast of the same even should the same subject me to ridicule, scandal, reproach, scorn, or indignity.

I hereby certify that I am over twenty one years of age, and competent to contract in my own name in so far as the above is concerned.

I am compensated as follows

I have read the foregoing release, authorization and agreement, before affixing my signature below, and warrant that I fully understand the contents thereof.

DATED _____

_____L.S.   _____L.S.
WITNESS   NAME

_____   _____
ADDRESS   ADDRESS

I hereby certify that I am the parent and/or guardian of _____ an infant under the age of twenty one years, and in consideration of value received, the receipt of which is hereby acknowledged, I hereby consent that any videotapes which have been, or are about to be made by the videographer may be used by him for the purposes set forth in original release hereinabove, signed by the infant model, with the same force and effect as if executed by me.

_____L.S.
PARENT OR GUARDIAN

_____
ADDRESS

Videographer 1 - Fill in terms of employment.
         2 - Strike out words that do not apply.

pictures in a totally different manner, for example, one that shows the person in a negative way, you could still be in for a big law suit. Also unlike news, the plaintiffs in cases like this tend to be more aggressive because the producers were doing it for money and not for journalistic reasons. A news organization may be able to show that the misuse of the picture came about by error due to the rush to meet a deadline and the material was not double-checked. A production company does not have the problem of on-air deadlines only hours from shooting because it has the time to make sure that everything is right and legal.

Intended Audience The greater the number of people who see your product, the more you need to make sure that every little legal detail is properly handled. In the case of a student video, the rights of some subjects may be overlooked because only a very small number of people will ever see the video. A student is generally allowed to gather video in the same way as a news crew even without a press pass. Context can be overlooked because no one outside the class will see the video. It is similar to art students copying a great painting for a class project; any use of that copy outside the classroom would be illegal. If a student video is to be judged in a contest, the student had better start worrying about the rights of the people in the video.

Most corporate videos are not too concerned with the right of privacy in their video presentations if the intended audience is only the workers within the company. Just as in the student video example, the size of the audience is small enough that any infractions of the law will more than likely go unnoticed. The key word here is unnoticed. As a corporate video producer you may tape in public areas and never get permission to use people's pictures in your presentation because they and anyone who knows them will probably never see the end product. Of course, there is a remote possibility that someone portrayed in a negative fashion will find out and sue.

The feeling that if your audience is small enough you need not worry at all about anyone else's rights can lead to real trouble. Most of the time this belief will work. The one time that it does not could cost the company or you a fortune. The key to this issue is that a person's image is recognizable in a video when permission for its use has not been given. If the shot is wide enough or done from behind or lasts such a short time that the subject cannot be recognized, then a charge of invasion of privacy will be hard to justify. Unless

you know for certain that no one you are shooting will complain or even find out how their pictures are used, you had better secure an okay from all parties involved in any recognizable on-screen appearance.

COPYRIGHTS

A TV news photographer can shoot almost anything and air it. But an editor cannot take just any source of video and insert it into a news story. One TV station cannot simply tape another's newscast and use video from it as its own. Nor can segments of any other program or movie be used in its news stories unless it is used by permission of, or by purchase from, its owner.

Violations

The biggest copyright violation is the use of movie clips in news stories. Without the permission of the owner of the movie (the studio or producer), you cannot use any part of a movie in your news story. If the studio has sent you a video press kit made up of the trailer and several clips from that film, you can use the pictures in any news story where they would be appropriate. The same rule applys to any other TV show or program.

Often TV stations in smaller markets will break the copyright rules because no one from the movie or TV industry will see the story. This is similar to making copies of your favorite movie and giving them to your friends. It seems innocent but it is illegal. The FBI warning at the head of each tape applies to newspeople as well as to the public. If you want people to respect your right of ownership for what you produce, you must respect their rights. If you are caught using parts of movies or TV shows without permission, the owner can charge you a rental or licensing fee that may be as high as several thousand dollars a minute for what you used plus residual payments to those who worked on the show.

There is a way around this rule that the news media often use. The ability of a news photographer to videotape a still picture in a book or magazine without permission can also be applied to pictures appearing on a TV screen. The story you are doing may be about the host of a particular TV program. Because the story is not going to portray this person in a good light, the producers of the show will not give permission for you to use tape of the show. If seeing the person in question hosting the show is a direct part of the story, then the photographer can set up a camera in front of a TV set showing the program and simply shoot the screen. Shooting the screen full frame lowers the quality of the displayed picture much more than if you simply recorded a direct feed of that program. You can help justify this lower quality to the viewer and also show the program owner how you acquired the video by shooting the screen slightly wider so the audience can see the edges of the TV set from which you are taping. Check with your legal department or employer before doing this to make sure this method is okay in your particular circumstances.

In 1989 a United jumbo jet crashed at the Sioux City, Iowa, airport. Only one TV photographer was there to capture the horrible event on tape. Within hours every TV news outlet in the world was running the tape. How did others get access to it? The news director of the Iowa station said they stole it. The issue went to the courts.

The age of satellite transmission has not only made it easier to get images from one place to another but it has also made it easier for more people to have access to these images. Unless a signal is scrambled, anyone with a satellite dish and the proper tuner can tap into any channel on the satellite. Because so many different organizations use the few satellites available for occasional use, scrambling has not been a practical method of protecting news material. Entertainment outlets such as HBO or pay-per-view shows control one particular channel on the satellite for extended periods of time or even own a particular channel. They can easily have their signals scrambled to protect against piracy.

Piracy

News organizations have traditionally shown a low concern for piracy because the ease of accessibility and speed of delivery are always more important. News organizations in the past have generally respected each other's rights of ownership even when they share the same satellite channel. It is not unusual to see NBC, ABC, CBS and CNN stories all being fed one after another on a single channel from the satellite. Sometimes only their mutual cooperation allows any network to get material from a distant location in a timely manner. Unfortunately, the expanding number of news organizations has made the competition to get exclusive pictures more important than ever. The expanding market for the pictures has also made the ability to keep them exclusive harder and harder.

A picture taken by an NBC affiliate can be sent via satellite to NBC network in New York, which can in turn send the picture to all NBC affiliates across the country on their regular news feed by satellite. One of the affiliates that receives the feed may have a contract to provide pictures to CNN News and uses the shot in a story sent to CNN. CNN puts the story on its feed to all its subscribers. One such station happens to be a CBS affiliate, which repackages the story and sends it to CBS network in New York. In the evening the shot appears on both NBC and CBS. If the special group-owned stations' news services contain affiliates of all three networks, the picture may end up on every news show in America. The lighting speed of satellite delivery makes each of these transfers possible and explains how one picture can make it to every TV channel in the country in a few short hours and not openly break any copyright laws (individual agreements notwithstanding).

The case of the Sioux City plane video is more complex. It was alleged that the video never made the more legal rounds and was simply stolen off the original feed to the Iowa station's network. If it was taken at that point by anyone else, it would be a case of copyright violation. However, once the pictures start to travel from one station or from one company (a broadcasting company can own stations with different affiliations) to another through network or smaller news services' feeds like the Conas Network, the copyright laws can be stretched to the limit.

Exclusivity

The way business is generally done in TV news, it can be almost impossible to keep a particular picture exclusively in your organization if the picture is of great interest to the public. On the other hand if proper legal precautions are taken and the pictures are tightly controlled, you may be able to maintain exclusivity. It can be easier to control pictures not produced by members of your station or company. Previous agreements can make pictures shot by staff members available to other members of the group or company automatically. An independent producer or freelance photographer may offer you exclusive pictures, and as part of the agreement to let you air them, the pictures come with tight restrictions on their use. The famous Zapruder film showing the assassination of President Kennedy is not the property of the public or any news organization. It requires special permission from the owners to air it and you must comply with many restrictions in its use. As in any legal contract, you are bound by the agreement you have signed and it can take precedent over other agreements. The agreement may say that only your station and not other parts of your network or group can air the video.

Bugs

One way producers keep track of their video and avoid any unauthorized use of it is by marking the video as theirs. Similar to a putting a brand on cows, videomakers can literally do the same. In TV terms it is called a bug: a small logo or abbreviation much like the rancher's brand is superimposed in one corner of the picture when the video is dubbed or transmitted. While it is widely used in news throughout the world, it is most common in sporting event highlights. Instead of recording hours and hours of sports, a local station may simply contract with an authorized highlight producer. Several times a day this company will feed by satellite condensed highlights of all the important sporting events of the day. All the video will have a bug in the corner of the screen to identify the origin of the pictures. If the bug should appear on another station or anywhere else that has no agreement with the producer, then legal action may be taken to stop this activity.

Courtesies

The easiest way to get other people's material is to simply ask for it. For pictures that are not controversial or have little competitive advantage, most stations or producers allow their use if the owner of the video gets an on-screen credit. This is somewhat like the bug only larger. Usually across the bottom of the screen, it will say "tape courtesy of (producer's name)" whether it be CBS News or Paramount Pictures or John Doe. You must obtain permission to use this method of protection.

The use of the "courtesy" is usually granted by verbal agreement and not written up or signed. If you or your company has a reputation for honesty in this type of agreement, then getting permission is usually quite easy. But when the video is very important, it is more difficult to get permission for use in this way.

There is a point where the escalation of fighting within the media to keep exclusive rights to something does slow down. A news organization that should happen to get video of a dramatic or history-making event when others did not may indeed share the pictures with or even without a credit because they feel the public, not just their viewers,

must see it. A private party might not feel that sense of duty to inform the public and reserve the rights to the pictures as in the case of the Zapruder film.

Pool

There are situations where only one camera is allowed to enter a restricted area or there is only enough room for one camera. In the course of daily news coverage and during large national stories, this situation arises time and time again. The solution is to form a pool. One camera goes but its video is shared among all interested organizations. If you had ever seen the president of the United States outside the White House, you would have noticed a small band of press people who have a slightly closer position than the larger group of press. This small group is the White House Pool. The four TV cameras are from NBC, CBS, ABC and CNN, but the video from each of them is made available to anyone who wants it. Since every TV news photographer covering the President would want this front-row advantage, it would be a madhouse of pushing and shoving without the pool arrangement.

The most common use of pools in the TV news industry is the courtroom. As in the example of the president above, it would be too disruptive to have many cameras in a courtroom. Usually one person or group in every market coordinates the pools to make sure the burden of having to do the extra work involved (wiring a courtroom for sound, providing a multiple outlet box or making dubs) gets handled fairly. Often the pool photographer cannot be in position in the hallway to get the crucial just-out-of-court statements by the defendants. In these cases, it is common practice for a non-pool photographer to let the pool organization use the hallway interviews.

There can be situations in the field that may require the photographers present to form an impromptu pool on the spot without the time or ability to check with management before doing so. An example might be a group of photographers at the command post of firefighters battling a raging forest fire. The commander is going via helicopter to see if the fire lines are holding in a remote village cut off from the usable roads; one seat is offered for a photographer from the group. In this situation, the photographers present would decide among themselves who is the best to go. The video will be dubbed either at the site later or at the station. The group can enter into an agreement on the ownership of the tape independent of any outside input.

This ability gives the photographer in the field the power to negotiate access to restricted or dangerous areas. By setting up a pool so that the tape can be shared and no other cameras need to access the site, it makes handling the media for the emergency services people so much easier. If the media can be satisfied with one photographer, then it becomes an easy solution to a growing problem: throngs of photographers all wanting pictures, or worse yet, trying to sneak their way into a very dangerous situation. Once a deal is made, all parties must abide by the agreement or the possibility of it working out again in the future will be jeopardized. The emergency agency cannot let anyone else into the area and whoever is pool must make the video readily available to virtually anyone who asks.

Certain restrictions apply if the organization allowing the pool is made fully aware of them and understands them. The pool may be restricted to only those present at the time of departure or to those there by the time of arrival back from shooting. In this case, a news organization that showed up several hours late or simply did not send anyone to the site would not have a right to the tape. Usually any media outlet that was trying to cover the event, whether present at the time the pool was formed or not, gets a share of the tape.

Public Domain Materials

Many portable video producers have the need to obtain video or audio but cannot obtain it through their own shooting and have no musicians on staff to compose or perform it. There is an answer to this general and widespread problem. An abundance of film footage may be used when its copyright has expired. Many films are sold on videocassette in discount or grocery stores for less than $10. Often these films no longer have copyright protection and a video producer may use this footage as desired. Buying these videocassettes from the grocery store may be convenient, but the quality derived from the VHS copy may not be acceptable. There are companies that can, for a reasonable fee, supply a copy of the material you need in the format of your choice.

Music or sound-track material is similarly obtained. Excerpts from some old radio shows are often available at a very reasonable price and tape format is less of a problem. You should note that

sound quality is always an important criterion for the decision to use this type of material.

If you have a musician or vocalist available, you may choose to have a fresh version of a song produced for you. This may yield a high-quality sound track, but the producer must either obtain permission from the publisher or use music that is not copyright-protected. Material in this category, both audio and video, is referred to as "in the public domain," meaning that it is owned by the public in genera or includes traditional songs that may never have been copyrighted. For example, your musicians could perform songs like "Turkey in the Straw" or "She'll Be Comin' Round the Mountain" without fear of copyright problems. Classical music has this benefit as well, but not other artists' performance of classical works because their performances is their property even if the music is not.

If you choose to use copyrighted music, you may find that the copyright holder has an organization that will provide assistance in obtaining clearance and collecting fees. For much of the popular music recorded in the last 30 years, this organization would be either BMI (Broadcast Music Inc.) or ASCAP (American Society of Composers, Authors and Publishers).

Protecting Your Work

A common violation of copyright laws occurs when copyrighted material is copied and used improperly. This law concerns all VCR owners. Broadcast material recorded off the air or from cable TV can be re-used for some length of time for personal or educational use. After this period of time has elapsed, you must re-record the program from its broadcast in order to have a legal copy to use.

After putting many hours and dollars into an original creation, it would be quite annoying to have your work stolen by unscrupulous video producers who decided that it was easier to use your video rather than produce their own. This is difficult to prevent; a copy of your video can easily be duplicated. But you may be able to be compensated for this theft. As mentioned earlier, copyright law provides legal protection against unauthorized use of your work. Intentional theft of your copyrighted work can be penalized with very stiff fines of up to $100,000. There may also be criminal penalties (for example, a jail term) as well. Accidental use of copyrighted material carries penalties of $500 to $20,000 per incidence of such use.

Obtaining Protection

Protection of your creative work is guaranteed by law. This protection is easy to obtain through the U.S. Copyright Office in Washington, D.C. You can call 202-707-9100 and ask that an application form be sent to you. This form, along with a $10 fee, registers your copyright. The office will send you a certificate as proof of the registration. If the work you wish to protect is to be exhibited to the public (for example, broadcast or shown to a large, public audience) or if your script is to be published, send two copies of the work along with your application. Unpublished work requires only one copy of the product. (See Figure 14.2.)

Alerting Others of Protection

Perhaps the most effective way to discourage others from unauthorized use of your work is to indicate that you hold a copyright on the work. This is simple and straightforward. If you want to copyright a videotape, simply put the word "copyright" with your name and the year on the label. The Copyright Office recommends that you include this information in the video itself. The abbreviation "Copr." or the symbol "C" can also be used.

For written work, the notice of copyright should appear on each page.

The copyright notice protects you in the United States. To protect your work in other countries, add the words, "All Rights Reserved."

Scope

What aspects of your creative project can be copyrighted? The complete project can certainly receive this protection. Some components of the project can be protected as well. The entire script and the music and/or audio track are also subject to copyright protection. Any portion of these aspects of the work is protected as well. But it is important to note that the idea for the video project cannot be copyrighted. Others may use your basic idea and produce another project. In fact, they can obtain their own copyright protection for their work. In other words, your ideas can be stolen, but the specific way you have expressed them cannot, at least not legally. Another video producer can take your idea but must express it differently in the final project. If the methods are too similar, you may be able to sue the infringer for monetary damages.

INSURANCE

No matter how many precautions you take, something always goes wrong. Most of the time the problem is simple like a broken cable or a deck that will not thread the tape. The delays and breakdowns may cost the news photographer a shot or cost the production photographer much money. Sometimes people can be injured by a falling light or their business can suffer losses due to a water pipe you broke. You can violate someone's rights even without turning on a camera. In the case of physical injury, your troubles may skyrocket. As an employee, you may not have to worry about the ultimate outcome of such events because your employer is covered by insurance. If you are a freelancer or working as an independent contractor, then you should protect yourself with insurance.

Comprehensive Liability

Everyone doing business needs some type of protection in case of accidents. When you are in an automobile, you may though no real fault of your own cause someone to be injured or even killed. This is why you need car insurance. You also need insurance at work for the same reason. Working for a TV station or corporation, you usually can rely on them to have such insurance. A news photographer who causes an accident (such as setting up a light that eventually falls on someone) would be able to turn to the company for protection against a law suit. A freelance photographer hoping to sell a video would be responsible and held liable for the injuries.

Anyone making videos on their own for news, production and other uses needs to consider what being held liable means if they are without insurance. Suppose you agree to shoot a public service announcement for a charity at a very wealthy person's mansion. A light falls, starting a fire that gets out of control and burns the house to the ground along with its priceless art collection. If the owner does not sue, then the insurance company will. Without insurance you may loose everything you own and end up in personal bankruptcy court for a simple one-hour shoot.

In the early 1990, the average coverage for an independent videomaker is one million dollars in liability insurance. This amount covers most common claims filed as a result of property or bodily injury or death. This sounds like a great deal of money, but if you look back at the burned-down mansion example you can see that even this

Figure 14.2: Form PA is used to obtain coyright protection.

FORM PA
UNITED STATES COPYRIGHT OFFICE

REGISTRATION NUMBER

PA   PAU

EFFECTIVE DATE OF REGISTRATION

Month   Day   Year

DO NOT WRITE ABOVE THIS LINE. IF YOU NEED MORE SPACE, USE A SEPARATE CONTINUATION SHEET.

1 **TITLE OF THIS WORK ▼**

PREVIOUS OR ALTERNATIVE TITLES ▼

NATURE OF THIS WORK ▼ See instructions

2

NAME OF AUTHOR ▼

DATES OF BIRTH AND DEATH
Year Born ▼   Year Died ▼

Was this contribution to the work a "work made for hire"?
☐ Yes
☐ No

AUTHOR'S NATIONALITY OR DOMICILE Name of Country
OR { Citizen of ▶
Domiciled in ▶

WAS THIS AUTHOR'S CONTRIBUTION TO THE WORK
Anonymous? ☐ Yes ☐ No
Pseudonymous? ☐ Yes ☐ No
If the answer to either of these questions is "Yes," see detailed instructions

NATURE OF AUTHORSHIP Briefly describe nature of the material created by this author in which copyright is claimed. ▼

NOTE
Under the law the "author" of a work made for hire is generally the employer not the employee (see instructions) For any part of this work that was "made for hire" check "Yes" in the space provided give the employer (or other person for whom the work was prepared) as "Author" of that part, and leave the space for dates of birth and death blank

NAME OF AUTHOR ▼

DATES OF BIRTH AND DEATH
Year Born ▼   Year Died ▼

Was this contribution to the work a "work made for hire"?
☐ Yes
☐ No

AUTHOR'S NATIONALITY OR DOMICILE Name of country
OR { Citizen of ▶
Domiciled in ▶

WAS THIS AUTHOR'S CONTRIBUTION TO THE WORK
Anonymous? ☐ Yes ☐ No
Pseudonymous? ☐ Yes ☐ No
If the answer to either of these questions is "Yes," see detailed instructions

NATURE OF AUTHORSHIP Briefly describe nature of the material created by this author in which copyright is claimed. ▼

NAME OF AUTHOR ▼

DATES OF BIRTH AND DEATH
Year Born ▼   Year Died ▼

Was this contribution to the work a "work made for hire"?
☐ Yes
☐ No

AUTHOR'S NATIONALITY OR DOMICILE Name of Country
OR { Citizen of ▶
Domiciled in ▶

WAS THIS AUTHOR'S CONTRIBUTION TO THE WORK
Anonymous? ☐ Yes ☐ No
Pseudonymous? ☐ Yes ☐ No
If the answer to either of these questions is "Yes," see detailed instructions

NATURE OF AUTHORSHIP Briefly describe nature of the material created by this author in which copyright is claimed. ▼

3

YEAR IN WHICH CREATION OF THIS WORK WAS COMPLETED This information must be given in all cases.
◀ Year

DATE AND NATION OF FIRST PUBLICATION OF THIS PARTICULAR WORK
Complete this information Month ▶ _____ Day ▶ _____ Year ▶ _____
ONLY if this work has been published.
◀ Nation

4

See instructions before completing this space

COPYRIGHT CLAIMANT(S) Name and address must be given even if the claimant is the same as the author given in space 2. ▼

TRANSFER If the claimant(s) named here in space 4 are different from the author(s) named in space 2, give a brief statement of how the claimant(s) obtained ownership of the copyright. ▼

APPLICATION RECEIVED

ONE DEPOSIT RECEIVED

TWO DEPOSITS RECEIVED

REMITTANCE NUMBER AND DATE

DO NOT WRITE HERE OFFICE USE ONLY

MORE ON BACK ▶
• Complete all applicable spaces (numbers 5-9) on the reverse side of this page
• See detailed instructions   • Sign the form at line 8

DO NOT WRITE HERE
Page 1 of _____ pages

Figure 14.2: Form PA is used to obtain copyright protection. (cont.)

EXAMINED BY

FORM PA

CHECKED BY

☐ CORRESPONDENCE
   Yes

FOR
COPYRIGHT
OFFICE
USE
ONLY

DO NOT WRITE ABOVE THIS LINE. IF YOU NEED MORE SPACE, USE A SEPARATE CONTINUATION SHEET.

PREVIOUS REGISTRATION Has registration for this work, or for an earlier version of this work, already been made in the Copyright Office?
☐ **Yes** ☐ **No** If your answer is "Yes," why is another registration being sought? (Check appropriate box) ▼

☐ This is the first published edition of a work previously registered in unpublished form.

☐ This is the first application submitted by this author as copyright claimant.

☐ This is a changed version of the work, as shown by space 6 on this application.

If your answer is "Yes," give: **Previous Registration Number** ▼   **Year of Registration** ▼

5

DERIVATIVE WORK OR COMPILATION Complete both space 6a & 6b for a derivative work; complete only 6b for a compilation.
a. Preexisting Material Identify any preexisting work or works that this work is based on or incorporates. ▼

b. Material Added to This Work Give a brief, general statement of the material that has been added to this work and in which copyright is claimed. ▼

6

See instructions
before completing
this space

DEPOSIT ACCOUNT If the registration fee is to be charged to a Deposit Account established in the Copyright Office, give name and number of Account.
Name ▼   **Account Number** ▼

7

CORRESPONDENCE Give name and address to which correspondence about this application should be sent.   Name/Address/Apt/City/State/Zip ▼

Area Code & Telephone Number ▶

Be sure to
give your
daytime phone
◀ number

CERTIFICATION* I, the undersigned, hereby certify that I am the
Check only one ▼

☐ author

☐ other copyright claimant

☐ owner of exclusive right(s)

☐ authorized agent of
   Name of author or other copyright claimant, or owner of exclusive right(s) ▲

8

of the work identified in this application and that the statements made
by me in this application are correct to the best of my knowledge.

Typed or printed name and date ▼ If this application gives a date of publication in space 3, do not sign and submit it before that date.

_____ date ▶ _____

☞ Handwritten signature (X) ▼

**MAIL
CERTIFI-
CATE TO**

Name ▼

Number/Street/Apartment Number ▼

**Certificate
will be
mailed in
window
envelope**

City/State/ZIP ▼

YOU MUST:
• Complete all necessary spaces
• Sign your application in space 8
**SEND ALL 3 ELEMENTS
IN THE SAME PACKAGE:**
1. Application form
2. Non-refundable $10 filing fee
   in check or money order
   payable to *Register of Copyrights*
3. Deposit material
MAIL TO:
Register of Copyrights
Library of Congress
Washington, D.C. 20559

9

* 17 U.S.C. § 506(e) Any person who knowingly makes a false representation of a material fact in the application for copyright registration provided for by section 409, or in any written statement filed in
connection with the application, shall be fined not more than $2,500.

June 1989—200,000   ☆ U.S. GOVERNMENT PRINTING OFFICE: 1989—241-428/80,026 may not be enough. More than likely it would be more than enough for any problems you would normally encounter. One million dollars' worth of coverage may cost several thousand dollars a year in premiums, but if you want to stay in business it is a necessary cost.

Comprehensive liability insurance is required if you want to do any taping on public property that requires a permit. Many rental companies require it before renting you any equipment. Even production companies asking you to work as an independent contractor want you to have liability coverage. Everyone who has anything to do with you, your equipment or the location in which you are shooting will want some assurance that they will be protected in case anything should happen and you are found at full or partial fault. Not having liability insurance can cause prospective video clients to take their business elsewhere.

Equipment Loss or Damage

When you work for yourself, people routinely want to know if you have appropriate loss or damage coverage and the means to cover any damages you might cause to the equipment you are using. The bank may still own part of your gear and the rental house does own the gear. If your $30,000 camera should fall from a tripod and topple over a second-story balcony, then you would want some means of replacing it without a second mortgage on your house. If you rented the camera from a rental company, the company would also want to know about your coverage.

If you are using equipment owned or rented by your employer, then you need not worry about who pays if something happens but only about preventing something from happening. People working for themselves more than likely would own their own equipment or rent or borrow it. A freelance photographer can invest anywhere from $10,000 to $100,000 for a set of broadcast-quality gear. Having insurance can mean the difference between losing everything, including your ability to make a living and going right on to the next shoot.

Rental Floaters

A good insurance policy not only covers anything you own but also any equipment you need to rent. This additional rental coverage, known as a floater, covers you in case anything should happen to the rental gear while it is in your possession. Each floater is issued for a certain dollar maximum; it is priced according to how high the coverage is. If you are renting a VCR, then a $15,000 floater would probably be enough. The amount must be high enough to replace at current cost all the equipment rented at any one time. The floater also needs to be made out to the company or person from whom you are renting the equipment before you take the gear. You will need a floater for each company or person from whom you rent. Most insurance companies charge a fee for each company named and a copy is sent to that company. A floater is usually good for one year no matter how many or how few times you need it.

Rental houses can offer insurance on the spot to qualified renters who do not have a floater. The cost of this type of insurance is usually 10% of the rental fee. You can also get an uninsured renter's policy if you rent equipment you own to other people. This type of coverage would be added to your own equipment loss policy and would not only cover you in case the person damaged your gear but also in case of that person's inadequate coverage.

Restrictions

In almost every policy there are exceptions to what is covered and when it is covered. Some policies may not cover your equipment if it is stolen from inside a vehicle. Others may not cover injuries that happen from operating or riding in a boat or airplane. By reading the fine print, you can discover any number of things that a particular policy does not cover. You may find that the video tape in the machine is not covered but the recorder is.

Other Coverages

You can get insurance for just about anything concerning a video production that is non-news. Some may sound silly but as the cost of the production increases, a small expense for some protection in an uncertain world may not be a bad idea. The average coverage required for the video business is aimed at protecting the people around from getting hurt either physically or financially. Many exceptions to the coverage are things that can hurt you if you are the producer of the project. For a price you can get things like cast insurance for your production. This covers any additional expenses incurred because the person you appearing in your program or segment cannot finish the project due to sickness or injury.

You can insure the videotape for the cost of producing it so that if it is stolen everyone can still get paid. You can even insure the camera against failure in case you miss the shot because a chip goes bad. Other coverages include sets or props you may use as well as the wardrobe of the people appearing on camera. If you are working with any union or guild contracts, they may require special coverages. While most of these extra coverages are out of the budget range for small video productions, anyone dealing with large amounts of money for an ever increasingly complex production should consider them. This type of coverage usually is required when people have invested money in your project and want some guarantees of at least seeing the project finished in case something goes wrong. There are several special coverages that all videomakers might consider as their budgets grow.

Errors and Omissions

A special type of coverage called Errors and Omissions (E & O) can protect you from an oversight in the use of copyrighted material. You may think you have received licensed permission but find out after the production airs that the person who gave you the rights did not own them. This coverage protects you from this and also covers plagiarism, unfair competition, libel, breach of contract and invasion of privacy. Any complete production that you plan to sell or syndicate for public viewing often requires this type of insurance before anyone will buy it or show it.

Workers' Compensation

Should you be in charge of a production large enough that you are hiring people to work for you, many state and federal laws determine how much protection you must give employees. Workers' compensation insurance is required in most states for anyone having employees or independent contractors. This coverage provides medical, disability or death benefits to any cast or crew member who becomes injured in the course of their employment. This coverage is needed in addition to normal liability insurance.

Completion Guaranty Bond

This coverage is used to guaranty that the video project you have agreed to do will get the funding necessary for completion. When independent producers finances a project with a bank, a company or a group of investors, they will often ask for this type of policy to protect their investment from poor budget planning on your part or some other

reason. The bondholder is saying that the program will be made for it to at least have a chance to make money or otherwise satisfy those concerned.

Producers' Insurance Policies (PIPs)

Almost all the above-mentioned coverages can be combined into one blanket policy, referred to as Producers' Insurance Policies (PIPs), that comes with different combinations of coverages to fit almost any type of production. You can often design your own package to fit the exact needs of your production. By working with an insurance company experienced in the film and video industries, you can tailor the coverage to suit your budget as well as your risk.

The cost of any insurance coverage is dependent on several factors. The higher the budget, the higher the insurance costs. The ceiling of the policy also determines the price: a $10,000 floater costs less than a $50,000 one. The amount of the deductible can change your premiums. Some deductibles are rather high but the annual premium is significantly lower. Most small independent photographers and/or producers have year-round policies that cover all the work they do in that year (within the limits of the policy). You can often determine the cost of insurance before you actually have to buy any special coverage for a particular production. The premiums are usually based on the cost of the project and run between 2% to 4% of the total budget. With extra coverages, a long shooting schedule or any hazards, the cost can be as much as 10% of the project's budget. Often, for small productions, it ends up being 10% of the budget because the premiums cannot go below certain minimum amounts. It is possible for the insurance to be the major cost of the shoot if you are doing things on a shoestring.

The more you have to interact with the public or any public agencies, the more you are going to have to know about insurance. Even if you do not have the coverage, knowing what you are not covered for can be a great help. Having insurance takes the risk out of what you are doing. Many people, especially at the low end of the budget scale, go without any coverage. They have chosen to assume all the risk themselves. Most of the time they play the odds and win. You should always step back and ask yourself what would happen if something should go wrong. It may be a risk you are no longer ready to take.

15 New Trends and Technologies

Video and associated technologies are rapidly changing. What was state of the art two years ago in any particular area is not state of the art today. The top-of-the-line video camera purchased in 1986 is not nearly as good as a middle-of-the-line camera that can be purchased in 1992. If there is no major quality difference between the two cameras, there is most certainly a price difference. Each year cameras are available with more features and better picture quality for prices similar to last year's models.

While it is not essential to keep up with each and every innovation or product change that surfaces from the myriad companies that sell equipment to the video production industry, keeping track of trends is worth doing for several reasons.

1. New equipment may be available to enhance the performance of the equipment that you have.
2. You may be asked to make a purchase recommendation for a major piece of equipment and selecting a soon-to-be obsolete format or technology (for example, buying a camera with pickup tubes) may make you look less than knowledgeable. Generally, newer equipment is not only higher quality but often more economical to use, less expensive to maintain and more durable than older equipment. While it is true that a young ENG photographer

may have little or no input into major buying decisions at a broadcast TV station, corporate video specialists may be responsible for a capital equipment budget soon after taking a job.

Keeping current with new trends and technologies in the video and related fields (for example, desktop video and computers that can be used with video and multi-image) will help you make better recommendations for future purchases and prepare you for needed technique changes when appropriate. Knowing that a good portable video projection system is now available at a reasonable price may convince you to shoot video instead of film for exhibition to several large audiences at a convention. Several years ago, before liquid-crystal display video projectors were marketed, film might have been the better choice.

DIGITAL TECHNOLOGY IN PORTABLE VIDEO

Digital recording, manipulation and re-recording of audio and video signals are part of a revolution that has been occurring for some time. Digital recording is a highly accurate, totally reproducible method that allows amazing special effects and no signal loss from generation to generation.

Although the biggest changes have not yet arrived, digital applications are changing the way portable video work is produced. This is especially true for EFP, where post-production can utilize digital effects to enhance a program to get more attention and appear more professional.

Digital audio is a reality as shown by compact discs, digital audiotape and audio portions of videotape recording (for example, 8mm format) that can be done with an inexpensive camcorder. Audio editing for video has changed considerably. Sound libraries that formerly consisted of numerous LP records (where some of the most used tracks wore out after numerous uses) now consist of a smaller number of compact discs that take up less space, are supposedly impervious to wear and supply amazing sound.

Digital video has generally been limited (except at the most upscale production facilities) to special effects generators that take existing analog video recordings and manipulate them in countless ways. These special effects generators, often incorporated into switchers and time-base correctors are now becoming available to a broad portion of the portable video market. In fact, digital effects switchers are now available that sell for less than $2000, making them affordable to the home video market. Another interesting digital innovation now available is the digital zoom feature on some consumer camcorders. While most camcorder lenses magnify up to 8 times, the digital zoom introduced recently is capable of magnification up to 100 times. At present, the quality of the video from this magnification may not be good enough for professional applications, but an improved digital zoom may soon be a standard feature on ENG/EFP cameras.

Digital video recording is available in the D2 format and will soon be available in D3. Though highly accurate and having the other benefits of digital recording, it also has the disadvantages of many new professional formats when first introduced: bulky equipment, high cost and lack of compatibility with existing equipment. These problems seem to go away with time because more manufacturers introduce new equipment featuring the format and creating more competitive pricing. This may also lead to digital camcorders for professionals and eventually digital camcorders for home video enthusiasts. When this revolution hits the lower end of the marketplace, camcorders for industrial, educational or home use may no longer use videocassettes. In fact, these camcorders may not even use videotape but some kind of magnetic hard drive or compact disc drive for storage of

video and audio images. This type of change is not expected in the immediate future, but there are many innovations just beginning to appear in the professional video marketplace.

CAMERAS

The biggest changes in cameras for the foreseeable future concern both quality and size. The **Charged Coupled Device (CCD)** will continue to be the means of converting light into electronic energy. The IS chip introduced by Sony in the early 1990s has already been improved both in resolution and sensitivity. With more than 750 lines of resolution and a capability of shooting in fractions of a footcandle, the latest cameras already outperform the rest of the TV system. Until the high-definition video question is resolved, there will be a limit to how good a camera needs to be. More and more of the inner workings of the camera will be going to the digital process in preparation for the upcoming digital tape formats; without these tape formats in use, a truly digital camera is of little good.

Because of the political issues surrounding High Density TV (HDTV), the next most likely area for real change in cameras is size. Already there are color cameras the size of lipstick tubes that have a fairly high degree of quality. Since there is a point where a camera can be too small and thus impossible to hold steady on the long shots so necessary in TV photography, the bulk of the camera/recorder unit may simply be filled with other bells and whistles to enhance the number of possible functions. The days of the camera head separate from the recorder are all but gone in non-studio work already. As the VCR becomes an integral part of the camera itself, the "camcorder" will replace the terms camera and recorder. In the future the two will be designed as one package and work as one unit.

A new video camera cannot be bought in the early 1990s without some type of solid-state imaging device. In other words, tube cameras are no longer marketed. Solid-state cameras have achieved the needed resolution to equal or surpass pickup-tube cameras. In addition, they are smaller, lighter and do not have some of the drawbacks of tube cameras, such as comet-tailing, lag and burn-in. In fact, the size and weight of camcorders has decreased so much that the problem is no longer too much bulk or weight but perhaps too little. Small-format camcorders are often too small to rest on your shoulder and must be held in front of your face for shooting. While this allows very small people to shoot video for long periods of time without much fatigue, this sometimes makes getting a steady shot difficult, especially at a long focal length.

It should be no surprise that camcorders are incorporating many new features to attract buyers. Since size, weight and even resolution have become of similar quality among cameras (especially those available to consumers), other aspects of camcorders have been added to help differentiate between cameras. A recent consumer camcorder made by Canon not only features hi-fi stereo recording but also offers direct-to-video music and graphics capabilities through the use of small chip-like cards on the camcorder. Camcorders often have a built-in character generator, a fade-to-black/ white control, auto focus and auto iris, variable high-speed shutter and an infrared remote control. They are also capable of delivering a video picture with as little as ½ lux (5.57 footcandles).

VIDEOTAPE RECORDERS

Video manufactures are racing to bring new all-digital tape formats to the market. Sony has developed the D1 and D2 formats for high-quality studio recording and editing with other versions on the way. These two formats make full use of the already existing digital effects machines and digital audio sources to give post-production an incredible range of possibilities. While Sony does make a portable version of this format, it is not light nor easy to use nor dockable. It should not be long before a truly portable version of this format is on the back of a camera.

Already on the consumer market is a digital camcorder that can do lap dissolves in the camera; this process used to require two playback machines and a record machine. The digital effects built into this camcorder can take the last scene shot and combine it into the next one in a dissolve. These are the kind of tricks and effects that will be quickly incorporated into professional equipment.

NONLINEAR EDITORS

Editing technology for the everyday user has not changed much except that the machines involved have generally become better and more reliable. The most common editing bay still features two VCRs, two monitors and an edit controller. More

and more editing systems have become open ended to allow the video input from a large variety of machines with different formats. It is not uncommon to see a ¾-inch editing system with two source machines, one a ¾-inch SP U-Matic format, the other perhaps Hi8, Beta SP or MII. This allows video to be acquired in one format and edited to another without having to dub or bump the first generation video to a second generation for it to be used on the editing system.

More production facilities are upgrading their editing bays from cuts-only systems to A/B roll-editing systems that allow more sophisticated transitions. The technology to do this has been around for some time, but the demand for more sophisticated transitions between shots and edits of multicamera field shoots has grown considerably.

The vast majority of editing systems sold until now have been **linear editing systems**. These systems search tape for the desired in- and out-points by using an accelerated search mode in either forward or reverse. This is a fairly slow way of building a program. In addition, changes made to the beginning of a program after it is edited cause all edits after that point to require significant change. A new editing system utilizing a nonlinear technique may change the way editing is done in the near future.

The concept of nonlinear editing can best be understood after the concept of linear editing is understood. **Linear editing** is accomplished by building a program or project, scene by scene in a straight line. The editor begins with the first scene or shot, then adds the second, then the third, and so forth until the last scene is edited and the program is complete. A 30-second commercial may have 15 different edits. This purpose is somewhat like a scriptwriter typing a 15-page script by starting on page 1 and continuing to page 15.

But what if the writer has a change of mind and decides to change the bottom half of page 6 and the top of page 7? Everything from page 6 on would have to be retyped if the new material is longer or shorter than the previous material. In editing, the editor builds a program or project scene by scene or shot by shot. If something in the middle of the 30-second commercial has been left out, everything from that point on must be rerecorded and all edit points must be manually readjusted.

Nonlinear editing (sometimes referred to as **disc-based editing** or **random-access editing**) is similar to having a word processor for use in the scriptwriting example above. If you have to add or change something in the middle of your script, you simply insert it and the program adjusts everything after it to accommodate your addition. Nonlinear editing accomplishes the same feat. If you change a shot or scene in the middle of a program or project, you do not lose all your editing points past that point; the editor remembers them and adjusts the program to accommodate your change. There have been some nonlinear editors available for some time, but recently some nonlinear digital editors have reached the marketplace. These new systems work by first transferring source material from tape to an optical drive that records the image on an optical disc. The images are stored as low-resolution images with digitized audio information. The editor can then view scenes without search time because there is no tape that must be fast-forwarded, rewound or searched, either forward or backward. Access to each shot is instantaneous. The editing is accomplished by using simple graphics menu options, similar to doing work on a MacIntosh, Amiga or an IBM-type computer with a Windows program. Currently, editors of this type are quite expensive: about $40,000. As they become more popular and more manufacturers have versions of this type of product, the price will drop. Even at this high price, there is a very strong logic in using a nonlinear or disc-based editor because the editor can save much during the editing process. (See Figure 15.1.)

The other change to look for in editing is the size of the equipment. As in so many home units, the player side of the edit set-up may simply be the camcorder. The record side may not be much larger either. Because of all the built-in digital functions, you may soon be able to do a version of A/B roll-editing with two machines that together can fit in a small suitcase. For news use this would mean being able to edit anywhere, including the hallway floor at the courthouse or the back seat of the car as the reporter drives to the next location.

EXHIBITION MONITORS

TV monitors have ostensibly changed little in recent years. They are still large and heavy and also utilize a glass vacuum tube for a direct view of the video picture. Projection sets, both front- and rear-projection types, are basically unchanged in concept but much improved in performance. There are some very useful and accurate portable video

Figure 15.1: Non-linear editing has become available in a number of system configurations. This system uses a PC laptop as the heart of the system. *Courtesy Editing Machines Corp.*

projectors that through the use of liquid-crystal display technology can project a good-quality picture in variable size from 10 to 100 inches in diameter onto any screen with very little distortion and good resolution.

Direct-view monitors have become much more accurate in recent years, especially as measured by the horizontal lines of resolution. Monitors are now designed for home use that can reproduce well over 400 lines of resolution. These monitors have been developed because consumers can now record in several videotape formats (S-VHS, ED-Beta, Hi8) that can play back a signal with that much resolution. To do this these monitors have added new signal inputs that allow for the separation of the luminance and chrominance portions of the video signal. A recent innovation in direct-view TV sets is the **improved definition TV** set (IDTV). This set uses microprocessors and digital techniques to scan two video fields together as one video frame. This yields a picture with more apparent resolution, especially on still pictures. Although some of these sets offer a significant improvement over standard sets, others have annoying traits that yield a blurring in scenes with motion. IDTV works with the existing National TV Standards Committee (NTSC) TV system and is often seen as an intermediate step between standard 525-line TV and the high-definition TV (HDTV) system that we expect for the future.

HIGH-DEFINITION TV (HDTV)

High-definition television (HDTV) gets its name from the fact that it can offer about twice as much visual information per frame as the standard NTSC television in use today. This large amount of visual information gives a picture that is very high in resolution and puts the picture quality in a class occupied currently by 35mm-motion picture film. High definition TV also has a different aspect ratio. While current technology allows for a 4:3 width-to-height ratio, HDTV will probably have an aspect ratio of about 5:3, similar to the ratio seen in a movie theater. Much has been said about this new system for TV recording and transmission for many years. Unfortunately this change is still years away from everyday use for several reasons. Technical difficulties (such as noncompatibility with existing TV sets and the need for more bandwidth), political questions (such as which of the competing systems should be adopted as the standard) and economic realities (the majority of broadcast TV stations could not afford the change) will keep this highly desirable new technology experimental for some time.

DESKTOP VIDEO

Desktop video is a natural progression of the development of personal computers and video equipment. The two areas seem to merge together in many ways, since the most used output of personal computers is video that can be easily manipulated with the ever increasing number of powerful software programs available. This merger began to take shape almost 20 years ago when the need for words and graphics representations for video increased. Character generators were developed that functioned as video typewriters, allowing the operator to type in the necessary information (weather, sports scores, election results, and so forth) and have that information superimposed over video from tape or a camera. More complex machines were developed that could generate and manipulate pictures, such as weather maps or sophisticated charts and graphs. These applications led to the development of highly sophisticated and therefore costly video graphics systems specifically designed for the video industry. These systems, with price tags of over $100,000, often go beyond character generation to applications such as animation and graphics generation.

Recently products have been developed that make this type of work feasible in corporate video and other forms of portable video. Personal computers can be designed for or adapted to use in video systems with the addition of special cards and software packages. A full discussion of this technology and the myriad of applications is not warranted here, but some general comments are worth noting. Desktop video systems can provide affordable special effects, editing, character generation, graphics creation and manipulation, and even animation for video projects. The systems available are often based on computers available to all, such as the Amiga, Macintosh, IBM or IBM-compatible. The hardware and software needed for desktop video vary greatly in price but need not be extravagant. With the appropriate **genlock** (videotape synchronizer), the computer equipped for desktop video can supply its output to a VCR, switcher or even camcorder to be used as another video input for the EFP or ENG video producer's creativity.

Another bonus with desktop video is that some systems have the capability to be complete editing systems that utilize a home computer as the editor (sometimes with nonlinear editing) and also have the capability to produce graphics.

A desktop product has recently appeared that truly signals the merger between video and computer technologies and a big change in the way lower-budget video can be produced. This product, when added to an existing personal computer or when used as a stand-alone unit, performs numerous functions that once were possible only with very expensive systems. The system has the capability of serving the function of a four-input switcher that can perform cuts, fades and wipes among inputs and internal video sources; a digital video effects generator; a character generator; a drawing/paint device; a 3-D animator, a luminance keyer (similar to a chromakey device), a color processor and a still store/frame grabber to freeze images without distortion or video noise. (See Figure 15.2.)

This product takes the place of several pieces of broadcast quality equipment that would have a retail price of about $60,000. Because this is a relatively new product, it is difficult to predict what will be the exact outcome of its introduction. The price of the product puts it in a range that makes it available to almost all corporate and

Figure 15.2: This multifunction device performs numerous post-production operations. It uses existing computer and video technology and is relatively low-priced, making it available for work on small-budget video projects. *Courtesy NewTek Inc.*

independent video production users and some serious amateurs and hobbyists. It is probably safe to say that this and other products of this kind will spawn a new generation of video artists who were previously barred from entry into the field because of prohibitive equipment and software expenses.

It may be worth mentioning at this point that not all of these new technologies are as benign as they might seem. As digital effects become more and more sophisticated with the addition of the modern high-speed computer, the more reality and science become blended into a seamless picture. While this is great fun for commercial and entertainment video makers, it can lead to real moral and ethical problems for the news and documentary photographers. If you can make it happen in the computer, why not? A subtle manipulation in a picture can be made to look so real that it could fool anyone. People can be placed in a scene that they never attended with the look of total reality. If just one case of this type of manipulation occurs in the future, it may cost the entire news industry its credibility with the public just as its attempt to use re-creations in newscasts did in 1990. The practice was halted almost immediately but the damage it caused was real and lasting.

Glossary

above the line: personnel costs and expenses involved with securing a script and rights, producer and staff, talent (performers) and the director.

ampere: A measure of the amount or volume of electrical current.

ampere hours: A way of rating a battery as to how much electrical current it can generate over a period of time.

angle: Location of a camera relative to the camera's subject.

ASA: A rating of the ability of photographic film to record light; the higher the rating, the less light is needed to record an image.

aspect ratio: The relationship of the width of a TV screen to its height; for standard NTSC television, it is 4:3.

assemble: A type of edit that transfers all information from the source machine to the editing recorder; it is similar to a *dud*.

audio limiter switch: This control prevents the recorded audio signal from becoming distorted because of too much signal strength.

auto-iris: A feature on video cameras that allows the exposure to be automatically set by the camera.

available light: The natural light in a scene; light that exists before additional light sources are added.

background light: A light placed on the same side as the *key light* but pointed at the background. It is usually the fourth light in a lighting kit.

backlight: A directional light used in three-point lighting. It is placed in line with the camera, but aimed at the back of the subject's head and shoulders.

balanced audio input: An input into an electronic device that accepts signals with two conductors of equal voltage. It is used in professional work to ensure a better signal.

bandwidth: The difference between the upper and lower frequency limits of an audio or video component.

barndoor: A rectangular piece of dark metal attached to a light to modify the direction of the beam, often used around a light in a set of four.

bass/roll-off/switch: A microphone switch that prevents the microphone from reproducing low-frequency sounds below a certain set level.

batt check: A control that when depressed or engaged gives an indication of the quality of the battery in use.

behavioral effects: Changes in the things people say and do as a result of viewing a video program. See *cognitive effects* and *emotional effects*.

Betacam: A professional $\frac{1}{2}$-inch component video format most popular with professional ENG operations in the 1980s.

Betacam SP: The improved Betacam format; SP stands for "superior performance."

bite: A piece of video (often a person being interviewed) with audio. Also called a sound bite.

black bursting: Recording a tape with a pure black signal (a control track, but no viewable picture), usually used for insert editing.

blocking: The talent and camera movements specified by the director for each scene.

BNC connector: A connector with a twist lock or positive grip feature used with single conductor video cable.

boom: A pole (often extension type) mounted on some type of tripod base used as a microphone mount that can bring the mike close to the subject without being in the picture. See *fishpole*.

bottomers: A flag used below a light source to shade the lower portion of the scene.

bounced light: A diffuse, indirect light that reflects onto a desired subject. See *reflector*.

brick battery: A powerful rectangular battery usually used to supply DC current to a videocamera.

broad light: A rectangular-shaped video light that casts bright light over a large area.

budget tracking: A recordkeeping process in which one records actual expenditures from a production and compares them with the projected expenses.

bug: A small logo or abbreviation that identifies the source of the video being shown, usually located in one corner of the picture.

burn-in: Image retention by a pickup tube caused by shooting a very bright object or by aiming the camera at a static scene for a long period of time.

butted: Two scenes edited together without the benefit of an electronic transition such as a *dissolve*, sometimes called a straight cut.

camcorder: A one-piece, combination video camera and recorder.

camera control unit (CCU): An electronic device used to properly set up and maintain the quality of a video camera's image.

cannon connector: A high-quality multi-pin connector with a positive lock feature used for audio input and output. See also *XLR connector*.

capacitor: An electrical device used in condenser microphones that stores an electrical charge.

cardioid: A microphone pickup pattern that resembles a heart shape. A mike with this pattern is also known as unidirectional and is most sensitive to sounds in front of it.

centrifugal force: The force that tends to pull a thing outward when it is rotating rapidly around a center; this force may affect the operation of some videocassette recorders if they are physically moving while recording.

chargeback: The amount paid by one unit of a corporation to an in-house production unit for services rendered on a piece-by-piece basis.

charge coupled device (CCD): An imaging device made of solid-state microelectronics that changes light into an electrical signal. It is used in place of a vacuum *pickup tube*.

chrominance: The combination of the red, green and blue information in video.

cinema vérité: A portable shooting style developed in France in the 1950s that popularized handheld work.

clearance: Permission granted by a copyright holder to allow use of copyrighted material.

clogged heads: A condition that occurs when minute dirt or magnetic particles from the videotape attach themselves to the video head of a VCR and cause poor-quality recording or playback.

close-up lenses: Lenses designed to allow focusing on an object located a very short distance from the front of the lens.

close-up shot: A shot in which the subject is framed tightly, for example, when a person is framed from the neck up. Also called a tight shot.

coax: Wire that carries audio and/or video signals; the wire has one central conductor and a braided shield for grounding that surrounds it.

cognitive effects: Changes in knowledge as a result of viewing a videotape for training purposes. See *behavioral effects* and *emotional effects*.

color: *Chrominance*—the control on a TV set that varies the amount or intensity of the chroma information.

color enhancement filters: A piece of glass or a gel that functions to brighten (or increase the saturation of) the colors of the subject being shot.

color gels: Cellophane material placed in front of lights to alter the color of light that reaches a subject or object to be shot.

color temperature: A measure of the tint of light, helpful in color balancing between shots. A light with high color temperature is blue; a light with a lower color temperature is red.

color temperature blue (CTB): Color correction gel that when placed in front of a light raises the color temperature of that light toward the blue (daylight) end of the scale.

color temperature orange (CTO): Color correction gel that lowers the color temperature of a light source toward the red (tungsten) end of the scale.

comet tailing: The smearing of light that occurs when a bright image source is moved across a darkened background.

compensator group: Two lenses in a typical zoom (compound) lens.

component recording: A recent development in videotape recording in which the color information is recorded separately from the brightness and synchronization information.

compression: The reduction of size or value of a signal.

condenser: The transducing element in a microphone that generates electrical signals as a result of changes in capacitance between the diaphragm and the backplate.

contrast ratio: The relationship between the brightest portion and the darkest portion of a picture, for example, 20:1.

convertible or systems mike: A microphone that can be modified in shape, pickup pattern or sensitivity to accommodate various audio situations.

cookie: A metal sheet with a pattern cut out that is used to project light patterns on floors, cycloramas and so on. Also called a cucalorus.

corporate video: Video for nonbroadcast purposes used mainly by private enterprise, government, nonprofit organizations and associations.

crab dolly: A movable camera mount that can be steered and is designed to allow the camera operator to sit on the device to operate the camera.

cut: A signal or command to stop cameras and tape during a production. See *take*.

cut-away: Shot related to, but slightly away from, the action being recorded, often used to cover unsatisfactory parts of a scene or interview.

cutter: A narrow *flag*.

daylight blue: When a blue gel is placed in front of a standard video light, it gives off light similar to sunlight or daylight.

depth of field: The area in front of the camera where all objects appear in focus.

dew: Moisture that may form or condense inside a camcorder or VCR due to environmental conditions; when dew is sensed inside of a VCR, a sensor may light, warning the user that the VCR or camcorder will not work.

diaphragm: A moving part of a microphone. See *element*.

diffuser: A piece of material (glass, fiberglass, cloth) that reduces the intensity or amount of light from a source and makes it less harsh; it may also be placed in front of a camera lens.

digital effects: Special effects for transitions such as picture compression, tumble or page peel accomplished by the digital encoding of the video picture to be manipulated.

digital video recording: A method of recording a video signal that changes the signal into bits of data stored as numbers (0 and 1).

diopter: A single lens designed to magnify an image.

director: The person who translates a written script into a video program.

dissolve: A transition in video where one video source is faded out while another is faded in. See *fade*.

distant learning: Instructional TV that utilizes two-way communication over a distance, often accomplished by microwave or satellite transmission.

doorway dolly: A small platform on wheels used to carry a camera on a tripod and small enough to fit through an average doorway.

double fog filter: Lowers the contrast of the overall scene but only looks like fog over the very brightest areas.

draw: The shadow on a subject created by directional light.

dual redundancy: Two small (tie-clip) microphones placed on a single clip to provide a backup mike if one fails while recording.

dub: A copy (dupe, duplicate) or the process of copying a video- or audiotape. See *assemble*.

dynamic: A description of a shot or edit that shows movement, power, strength or energy.

edit: To put together, rearrange or eliminate segments of video or audio information on tape.

EFP: Electronic field production—portable video for non-news applications.

element: A basic moving part of a microphone that generates the basic electrical signal.

emotional effects: A desirable effect of a video project where the audience experiences feelings as a result of viewing the video.

ENG: Electronic news gathering—portable electronic journalism.

extender: A device used on a zoom lens that can double the focal length of the lens.

external time code: Time code sent to a VCR that is generated outside the VCR.

eye light: A small light used in dramatic shots to illuminate the subject's upper facial area.

fade: Gradual change from a video source to a black screen or vice versa. See *dissolve*.

faders: Sliding rheostats used to adjust the volume in audio, the intensity in lights or the mixing of two video signals.

fast lens: A lens that is capable of gathering a large amount of light; a lens capable of an f-stop of 1.4 would be a fast lens to one that was only capable of an f-stop of 4.0.

fat side: The side of the face including the ear that receives fill rather than *key light.* Also called the long side. See *short side.*

feeders: Microwave-equipped trucks used in *ENG* to relay video back to the station.

field: One-half of a complete TV picture, that is 262.5 scanning lines. See *frame.*

fill light: Light used to soften the shadows caused by the *key* or main directional light.

film style: A type of portable production that utilizes a single camera and often uses many takes of a scene for later editing.

filter: Cellophane, glass, spun glass or similar material used in lenses, cameras, or in front of lights that somehow modulates or changes the light passing through it.

fishpole: A handheld extension pole used to get a microphone close to a subject. See *boom.*

flag: A solid or opaque light modulator used to direct light.

flat: An upright square or rectangular frame covered with cloth or other material that can be painted for a scenic effect.

flat lighting: A type of lighting that does not yield shadows, often created with non-directional lighting.

flat rate: A nonvariable payment made on a regular basis, for example, a regular payment made to an in-house media production unit for services rendered.

floater: An insurance policy that provides coverage for rented production equipment.

flooded: When an adjustable or focusable spotlight is in the least focused position; when a scene is lit with a large quantity of nondirectional light.

floodlight: A video light that produces a diffuse wide beam of light.

focal length: The distance from the optical center of a lens to the point at which the light rays converge on the face of the image sensor.

focal plane: The point where the light rays that pass through a zoom lens converge and are in focus; when in proper focus this point falls on the image sensor.

focusing group: The front three lens elements in a compound zoom lens.

footcandle: A measure of the amount of light used in countries that have not adopted the metric system.

frame: One complete picture in video, equal to two *fields,* that is, 525 scanning lines. See *field.*

fringe benefits: Items used to pay employees other than salary or wage dollars, for example, health insurance.

f-stop: A designation of the size of the iris opening in a video lens.

gaffer grip: A device used to hold equipment in place.

gaffer tape: A wide, strong tape used to hold various pieces of equipment or wire in place.

gel: A cellophane-type material placed in front of a video light that changes the color of the light.

gel frames: A frame used to hold gel in place in front of a video light.

gen-lock: A device that allows the synchronization of two video signals.

graphic card: A card (especially prepared for use in a video production) that conforms to the aspect ratio and other restrictions of TV.

grip: A person who helps carry and place equipment.

gyro: A stabilizing device on the lens to reduce the shakiness of telephoto shots or pictures taken from aircraft or other unstable locations.

hard news: A news story that is factual, timely and deals with important issues in society, for example, crime or politics.

head light: Slang term for a camera-mounted light.

head room: The amount of space from the top of the subject's head in a shot to the top of the frame.

hertz (Hz): A unit of measurement for frequency equal to one cycle per second.

HI8: A videotape format that uses 8mm tape and features high-resolution and high-quality audio reproduction.

high-definition/high-density TV: A recently developed TV format that yields a higher-resolution picture due to an increased number of scanning lines per *frame.*

high-intensity discharge (HID): A type of mercury or sodium vapor arc discharge lamp that uses a low amount of electricity but generates a large amount of light.

high-key lighting: Lighting that is bright, often used in sitcoms when an upbeat mood is desired.

hot: A video picture with too much light; any signal whose level is too high.

house sound: Sound that is available from the audio board of the "house" (theater, concert hall).

house sync: A synchronization signal created by a sync generator for the purpose of having all equipment in a production facility work together.

hyperfocal distance: A measurement from the lens to the closest point that an object will be in focus when the lens focus ring is set at infinity.

impedance: The opposition or restriction to the flow of current, usually measured in ohms.

incandescent: Lamps that give off light when they glow from electrical current passing through a filament located inside a vacuum.

insert: A type of *edit* in which video, audio or both are put into an existing video piece.

internal optical system: In almost all video cameras available now, a prism block that separates the white light into red, green and blue light before the light strikes the image sensors.

internal time code: An electrical signal generated by a VCR that labels each frame of videotape it records.

inverse square law: The rule that the amount of light that falls on an object decreases by the square of the inverse of the distance from the light to the object. If the distance from the light to the subject is doubled, the amount of light falling on the object is one-fourth the original amount of light.

iris: The adjustable diaphragm inside a lens that varies the amount of light that enters the camera— the aperture.

jam sync: Synchronization signals sent into camcorders and VCRs from one central source.

jump cut: An uncomfortable *edit* juxtaposing two shots that do not go together smoothly, for example, an *XCU* to a *wide shot*.

key light: A directional video light used to focus attention and give proper shadow and contrast to a subject.

lag: The after-image seen as a result of the aging of a *pickup tube* or low-light conditions.

lamp: A bulb for a video light.

lead-in: A reporter's introduction to a story or shot.

LED (light emitting diode): A small light (usually red, yellow or green) used as an indicator light.

lens flare: When a strong light shines directly into a lens, an optical distortion can be seen, often appearing as a series of pentagons. This problem can be avoided by changing the camera angle or deflecting the direct light.

lighting grid: In a TV studio, a cross-hatch system of bars mounted below the ceiling that allows the mounting of video lights.

lighting panel: The electronic device in a TV control room or studio that allows connection for, and control of, the lighting system.

line: (1) One of 525 scanning lines in a video picture; (2) In audio work, a level of signal that has been amplified and is higher in level than a signal from a microphone; (3) In a TV control room, the signal path that leads out from the switcher to the transmitter or videotape recorder— the on-air signal.

line level: A signal level in audio that is amplified and therefore stronger than a microphone level signal.

line of interest: Sometimes called the stage line or the 180-degree line, it is a line drawn through a scene to maintain continuity-of-screen direction when editing together shots taken from different angles to the subject by keeping the camera always on the same side of that line. Two people talking to each other create a line of interest drawn from one person to the other that extends to infinity in both directions.

lip-sync: The accurate or synchronized combination of sound and picture, especially matching words with a talking person.

live: In *ENG* work, a shot from the field that is microwaved back to the TV station and broadcast as it is being photographed.

live on tape: A method of recording a program on videotape where the program is performed as if it were done live, all in one take, with no editing.

low-key lighting: Lighting that is low-level and used to create a serious or even somber mood, used in dramatic programs.

luminance: The brightness information in a TV signal and picture.

M II: A professional 1/2-inch component video-tape format used in portable video, especially ENG.

macrofocus: Videotaping that is done at a very short distance from the camera lens, usually for the purpose of showing fine detail in the shot.

macro ring/macro lever: The device on the barrel of the lens that engages the macrofocusing capability of the lens.

male: A type of plug with prongs or pins designed to fit into a corresponding socket.

matched action: A technique in which one camera is used to shoot the same action from different angles and the raw footage is edited to give the appearance of multiple cameras shooting the action at one time.

matte box: A rectangular bellows-shaped hood that fits over the front of the lens to aid in shading the lens and as a holder for large filters that do not attach to the lens.

medium shot: A relative description of a video shot, usually framing a subject from head to toe.

microphone: A device for translating sound energy into electrical energy for amplifying or recording purposes.

mike level: 150 ohms, the standard impedance level of a professional microphone.

miniboom: A small crane-like arm used for camera mounting.

mix: The combination of two or more signals.

mix select switches: Levers on a VCR that control which channels of audio are to be monitored.

modeling effect: The effect of creating depth and texture by using directional light shadows; the effect is created on subjects and objects illuminated by artificial lighting.

modular camera: A newly developed portable video camera that allows a variety of on-board videocassette recorders to be attached or others to be connected by cable.

modules: A rectangular light made up of rows of individual PAR lights.

moire: The rainbow distortion seen on videotaped subjects with a very small, repeated geometric pattern such as a tie with very thin evenly spaced stripes.

moving-coil: A type of microphone transducer that has a coil suspended in a magnetic field. A *diaphragm* reacts to sound pressure and displaces the coil in the field to create an electrical current, often referred to as a dynamic microphone.

multi-pin cable connector: A cable plug designed to connect a single cable containing many smaller individual wires that must always stay insulated from one another.

needle drop fee: A cost incurred when using a copyrighted musical piece for production purposes.

neutral density gel (ND): A gray gelatin filter in varying densities which cuts down the amount of light without affecting any other characteristics of the light source.

nickel-cadmium cell: A rechargeable battery unit made from nickel and cadmium often referred to as a "nicad."

non-segmented videotape: A type of videotape recording format in which information for one entire *frame* is recorded by one head without being broken into two parts, allowing for easier special effects such as slow motion or still frame.

NTSC (National Television Standards Committee): The U.S. government group formed in 1953 to set standards for TV's video signal.

off-axis: A sound source coming from some place other than where the mike is pointed.

omnidirectional: A microphone that receives sound equally well regardless of the direction the mike is pointed from the source.

on-axis: Sound coming from directly in front of the microphone.

overhead expenses: Costs incurred as a result of being in business, such as rent and utilities, not directly related to a video production.

PAL (Phase Alteration by Line): The video signal standard set by Germany, England and Holland in 1966.

parabolic: An inward curved reflector that focuses the light or sound it receives to a single point in front of it.

Parabolic Aluminized Reflector (PAR): A sealed-beam light with the bulb built into a reflector at its focal point, such as the headlights of a car.

party colors: A slang term for colored gels that change a light source to a single color of light such as deep red, forest green, and so on.

photons: Units of energy that make up light waves.

pickup tube: An imaging device of vacuum tube construction used in video cameras to change light into an electronic signal.

pinned: A position on an adjustable video light that yields its narrowest beam; the maximum reading that a needle-type meter can show.

pixels: The extremely small light-sensitive surfaces that make up the image-recording area of a charged couple device (CCD); the more pixels, the sharper the image will be.

plumb bubble bullseye: A circular container with a single bubble in a liquid; when the bubble is in a ring painted on top of the container, the device (tripod, camera, and so on) is level to the horizontal plane.

plumicon tube: A vacuum tube designed to produce a video picture using a lead oxide coating on its light-sensitive surface.

polar pattern: A diagram of a microphone's sensitivity or pickup capability, shown as a top view.

polarizing filter: A glass filter over the lens that reduces glare and reflections by preventing certain angles of reflected light from passing through it.

portable: Refers to production equipment that can be easily transported to an on-location shoot, implies that it can be run on direct current or battery power.

Porta-pack: The first portable video system developed by Sony that used a reel-to-reel VCR and a black-and-white camera.

post-production: The last stage in the process of creating a video project; the stage in which editing is accomplished.

pre-production: The first or planning stage in the process of creating a video project.

presence boost: An audio filter that emphasizes frequencies in the upper midrange around 5 kHz to enhance voices.

press pass: A photo identification card issued by law enforcement agencies to bonafide members of the news media.

primary additive colors: Red, green and blue. A TV camera reduces a picture to varying amounts of these three colors to make up the chroma segment of a video signal.

prime lens: A fixed focal length lens.

prime lens group: The series of lenses at the rear of any type of lens that focuses the image onto the recording surface.

prism block: A device in a video camera that consists of several prisms that split the incoming light into its red, green and blue components and guide the light to the appropriate *pickup tube*.

processing amplifier: A device to boost a video signal with control over the strength and black level of that signal (similar to brightness and contrast controls).

producer: The person in charge of a production.

production: The middle stage in the process of creating a video project when images and/or sound are recorded.

prop: An abbreviation for property used on the set of a video shoot or scene.

public domain: A property on which no one holds the creative rights and no royalties can be collected.

pull-ups: Subtractions or changes done to an edited piece of video causing a change in the total length of the piece.

quality light: Light from a very large source that produces very soft-edged shadows.

quality of light: A measure of both the color temperature and the harshness or softness of the light source.

real-time switching: The changing of video sources done *live* or when a program is recorded live on tape.

record and playback controls: The buttons to put the VCR in either the record or playback mode.

reflector: Hard or soft surface covered with a highly reflective material to redirect light to fall on a desired area.

registration: The alignment of the three color *pickup tubes* in a video camera to give one full-color image.

Rembrandt lighting: The style of lighting made famous by the Dutch painter and characterized by the use of alternating areas of light and shadow in his scenes.

remote: An on-location shoot that relays a signal to another location such as a broadcast station.

retrozoom: A multi-element glass lens that attaches on a zoom lens to decrease the focal length throughout the zoom range.

resolution: A measure of sharpness or clarity in a video picture.

RF interference: Noise in a video signal caused by unwanted broadcast signals (often from AM radio signals).

rim light: The dimmer portion of light at the outer edges of a video light's light pattern.

roaming: Having the automatic iris constantly changing due to a small element in the scene fluctuating in brightness.

"rocker"-style switch. A long switch operated with a finger at each end and the axis of the switch in between; as the switch is rocked downward in the front the servo runs forward, as the switch is rocked down at its rear the servo reverses direction.

routing system: A system that allows the video and/or audio signal to be channeled or directed.

rule of "three to one" or rule of thirds: When lining up a shot it is aesthetically more pleasing to have the major elements in the frame fall on lines created by dividing the screen in thirds both horizontally and vertically.

saticon: A type of *pickup tube* used in industrial-quality and some professional-quality video cameras.

saturation: The amount of overall color in a picture.

scoop: A type of artificial light that provides generally diffuse light for fill purposes.

scrim: A piece of spun glass material placed over a light to diffuse it; also a large curtain used as a backdrop. See *diffuser* and *filter*.

SECAM: (Sequential Couleur a Memoire): The 1962 TV signal standard developed and used in France.

segmented video: A videotape format in which two (or more) video head passes are necessary to record a *frame* of video.

servo: A small electric motor used to turn a set of gears.

shade: To prevent light from falling on a certain area.

shaky camera: Having too much movement of the camera while recording.

shoot: The actual production work of a video project.

short side: The part of the face that should be pointed toward the *key light*. See *fat side*.

shower curtain: A slang term for a heavy plastic diffusion material used over a light source.

siders: Flags that are used to the side of a light source.

single-element wide-angle lens: A glass lens that fits on a zoom lens to reduce the focal length to one specific focal length so the zoom elements cannot be used with it in place.

signal-to-noise ratio: A ratio that compares picture strength to noise strength. The higher the ratio, the better the picture.

skew knob: On older-style VCRs this control would manually adjust the tension of the videotape across the playback heads.

sliding element: A group of lenses within a complete lens that is able to move closer to or further from the other lens groups.

slow lens: A lens whose iris does not open very wide and thus does not let very much light pass through it.

smearing: An undesirable aspect of a video picture with too much gain; smearing appears as colors trailing or flaring off objects in the *frame*.

snap zoom: A very fast-changing zoom, accomplished by manually rotating the zoom control with a quick wrist motion.

soft frost: A type of diffusion gel used over a light source to soften the harshness of the light.

soft light: A large diffuse light source that bounces light off its own reflective surface to illuminate a subject with nondirectional light.

softnet filter: A very fine net material within a glass filter used over the lens to soften the look of a scene.

soft news: News stories that are more entertaining in nature and not as informational.

special effects filters: Glass filters on the lens that manipulate the image's color, focus or position.

speed: A photographic term for describing how sensitive a material or surface is to light.

split-field effect: A filter on the lens that changes the plane of focus for only one-half the picture.

spotlight: A directional, often adjustable, type of artificial light source for video.

stand-up: A shot in which a standing reporter introduces or sometimes wraps up a story.

star filter: A glass filter in front of the lens with a screen material in it that makes highlights such as lightbulbs appear pointed like stars.

sticks: Slang term for a tripod.

stopped down: To have the iris at a very small opening or even completely closed.

storyboard: A two-dimensional pictorial representation of a script which represents the visual theme and important shots.

studio arcs: Large carbon arc lights used in movie production.

studio pedestal mount: A professional, heavy-duty mounting system for studio cameras; it often has a counterbalance system for smooth camera movement.

subtractive primary colors: Magenta, cyan and yellow used in paint mixing and color photo printing to obtain all the other colors but not used in video recording.

sungun: A small battery-powered light, usually camera-mounted.

switcher: A device to combine or switch video signals and special effects from a variety of sources into one video output.

sync generator: An electronic device used in a video studio that gives timing pulses to the cameras, VCRs and all other equipment that need to be time coordinated.

take: An individual shot or scene, usually one of several; an instantaneous change from one video source to another. See *cut.*

talent: The person(s) who are performing in front of the camera.

talking head: A shot of a person speaking, usually a static head and shoulder or head-only shot.

teasers: Large black flats used to prevent light from falling on certain areas.

telecine: A device that transfers film or slides to video, consists of a film projector, slide projector, video camera and multiplexer; a device to direct projection into a video camera lens. Also called film chain or film island.

teleconverter: A multi-element glass filter that fits onto a zoom lens to increase its focal length while still being able to zoom.

tilt: Angling the camera either up or down.

time base corrector (TBC): An electronic device that corrects for speed and mechanical errors in a videotape machine, giving the videotape a broadcast standard horizontal sync.

toppers: *Flags* used above a light source.

tracing paper: Slang for a heavy paper-like diffusion material used in front of a light source.

tracking: The speed and angle at which the videotape passes the video heads, often adjustable during playback to maximize picture quality.

tracking knob: A manual adjustment when playing back a videotape to align the video heads of a VCR with the video tracks layed down on the tape.

transition shot: A shot used to combine two video segments that otherwise might not smoothly connect.

treatment: A preliminary synopsis or storyline which describes plot, characters, setting, and so on, for a forthcoming script.

tungsten-halogen lamp: The standard light source for film and video production using a tungsten filament inside a sealed glass globe that gives off light at 3200 degrees Kelvin.

two-X range: The range of focal lengths created on a zoom lens after the 2X extender is used.

U-Matic format: The first color video cassette format developed by Sony for use in the field and often referred to as ¾-inch because of the tape's width.

U-Matic SP format: An improved version of the original U-Matic format using metal particle tape for better sharpness and color; SP means superior performance.

umbrella: A device shaped like a regular rain umbrella that is mounted on a portable video light.

The reflective undersurface of this umbrella reflects a diffuse light on a subject.

unit rate: The amount of cost incurred in a particular time frame, for example, the cost per day of owning a portable camera.

UV: Ultra violet.

vanishing point: A point on the horizon or outside the *frame* where parallel lines in a shot seem to converge.

variator group: The lens grouping within a zoom lens that changes image size by moving toward or away from the main lens groups.

vertical interval time code: The series of numbers stored in the vertical interval of a video signal that mark each frame of that video so those frames can be cataloged for later reference.

video digital effects: A sophisticated video manipulation that allows the video picture to be compressed, flipped, tumbled, and so on.

video level control: A device that can adjust the amplification of a video signal either up or down.

video processors: Electronic circuits that control the amount and quality of all the components of a video signal.

video switcher: An electronic device that allows an individual to select among many video inputs.

viewfinder: A small black-and-white TV monitor with an eyepiece used by the camera operator to see what the camera sees.

vignetting: Dark areas in the corners of a picture caused by lens problems or the lens not being properly lined up with the camera's internal optics system.

voice coil: A small wire coil used in a microphone to transduce sound into electric energy so that it can be recorded.

VU meter: A device to measure volume units of audio on a tape machine or sound mixer/amplifier.

wide angle lens: A lens with large field of view and focal lengths starting around 5.5mm for video lenses.

wide shot: A camera shot with a short focal length that includes a large amount of the area in front of the camera. Also called a long shot.

wrong-field edits: When the edit machine mistakenly cuts from a position or negative field of one shot to the like field of the next shot breaking the required pattern of alternating fields.

XCU: An extreme close-up video shot.

XLR connector: The standard three-contact plugs used in all professional sound work, sometimes called canon connectors.

zebra bars: The diagonal white lines superimposed over parts of the picture that have a certain level of video signal and can only be seen in the viewfinder. Many cameras have the zebra bars set at 70 units of video, which aids the operator in determining proper exposure.

zip light: A small soft light of either 500 or 1000 watts.

zoom control: The device that operates the zoom servo to determine the direction and speed of the zoom.

zoom lens: A lens capable of changing focal lengths without affecting the plane of focus, thus allowing continuous change in image size from widest to narrowest field of view with no other adjustments needed.

zoom ratio: This ratio compares the longest focal length to the shortest, such as 120mm to 10mm or 140mm to 10mm; often expressed in ratio form, for example, 12:1 or 14:1. Also called the zoom range.

Bibliography

BOOKS

Aesthetics

Arijon, Daniel. *Grammar of the Film Language.* Boston, MA: Focal Press, 1976.

Zettl, Herbert. *Sight, Sound, Motion: Applied Media Aesthetics.* 2nd ed. Belmont, CA: Wadsworth Publishing Co., 1990.

Audio

Alten, Stanley R. *Audio in Media,* 3rd ed. Belmont, CA: Wadsworth Publishing Co., 1990.

Bartlett, Bruce. *Introduction to Professional Recording Techniques.* Indianapolis, IN: Howard Sams & Co., 1987.

Clifford, Martin. *Microphones,* 2nd ed. Blue Ridge Summit: PA, Tab Books, 1982.

Huber, Miles. *Microphone Manual: Design and Application.* Indianapolis, IN: Howard Sams & Co., 1988.

Budgeting/Business

Marsh, Ken. *Independent Video.* San Francisco, CA: Straight Arrow Books, 1974.

Van Deusen, Richard E. *Practical AV/Video Budgeting.* White Plains, NY: Knowledge Industry Publications, Inc., 1984.

Wiese, Michael. *Film & Video Budgets.* Westport, CT: Michael Wiese Film Productions, 1984.

Corporate Video

Hausman, Carl. *Institutional Video.* Belmont, CA: Wadsworth Publishing Co., 1991.

Gayeski, Diane. *Corporate and Instructional Video,* 2nd ed. Englewood Cliffs, NJ: Prentice Hall, 1991.

Dizazzo, Ray. *Corporate Television.* Boston, MA: Focal Press, 1990.

Directing

Blumenthal, Howard J. *Television Producing and Directing.* New York, NY: Barnes and Noble Books, 1987.

Hickman, Harold R. *Television Direction.* Santa Rosa, CA: Cole Publishing Co., 1991.

Kennedy, Thomas. *Directing Video.* White Plains, NY: Knowledge Industry Publications, Inc., 1989.

Editing

Anderson, Gary. *Video Editing and Post Production: A Professional Guide,* 2nd ed. White Plains, NY: Knowledge Industry Publications, Inc., 1988.

Browne, Steven E. *Videotape Editing.* Boston, MA: Focal Press, 1989.

Reisz, Karel and Millar, Gavin. *The Technique of Film Editing.* Boston, MA: Focal Press, 1986.

Schneider, Arthur. *Electronic Post-Production and Videotape Editing.* Boston, MA: Focal Press, 1989.

Legal

Blue, Martha. *Making It Legal.* Flagstaff, AZ: Northland Publishing Co., 1988.

Miller, Philip. *Media Law for Producers.* White Plains, NY: Knowledge Industry Publications, Inc., 1990.

Lighting

Carlson, Verne and Carlson, Sylvia. *Professional Lighting Handbook*. Boston, MA: Focal Press, 1985.

LeTourneau, Tom. *Lighting Techniques for Video Production*. White Plains, NY: Knowledge Industry Publications, Inc., 1987.

Malkiewicz, Kris. *Film Lighting*. New York, NY: Prentice Hall, 1986.

Millerson, Gerald. *The Technique of Lighting for Television and Motion Pictures,* 2nd ed. Boston, MA: Focal Press. 1982.

Ritsko, Alan J. *Lighting for Location Motion Pictures*. New York, NY: Van Nostrand Reinhold Co., Inc., 1979.

News

Hausman, Carl. *Crafting the News for Electronic Media*. Belmont, CA: Wadsworth Publishing Co., 1992.

Yoakam Richard D. and Cremer, Charles F. *ENG: Television News and the New Technology,* 2nd ed. New York, NY: Random House, 1989.

Production

Compesi, Ronald, and Sherriffs, Ronald. *Small Format Television Production,* 2nd ed. Boston, MA: Allyn and Bacon, 1990.

Mathias, Harry and Patterson, Richard. *Electronic Cinematography*. Belmont, CA: Wadsworth Publishing Co., 1985.

Millerson, Gerald. *Video Production Handbook*. Boston, MA: Focal Press, 1987.

Schroeppel, Tom. *The Bare Bones Camera Course for Film and Video,* 2nd ed. Miami, FL: Tom Schroeppel, 1982.

————————. *Video Goals: Getting Results with Pictures and Sound*. Miami, FL: Tom Schroeppel, 1987.

Smith, David. *Video Communication*. Belmont, CA: Wadsworth Publishing Co., 1991.

Utz, Peter. *Today's Video*. Englewood Cliffs, NJ: Prentice Hall, Inc., 1987.

Whittaker, Ron. *Video Field Production*. Mountain View, CA: Mayfield Publishing Co., 1989.

Zettl, Herbert. *Television Production Handbook,* 5th ed. Belmont, CA: Wadsworth Publishing Co., 1991.

Writing

Garvey, Daniel and Rivers, William. *Broadcast Writing Workbook,* New York, NY: Longman Inc., 1982.

Meeske, Miland, and Norris, R.C. *Copywriting for the Electronic Media,* 2nd ed. Belmont, CA: Wadsworth Publishing Co., 1992.

PERIODICALS

AV Video. Montage Publishing, Inc., 701 Westchester Ave., White Plains, NY 10604.

Videography. P.S.N. Publications, 2 Park Ave., Suite 1820, New York, NY 10016.

Videomaker. Videomaker, Inc., 290 Airpark Blvd., Chico, CA 95926.

Video Systems. Intertec Publishing Corp., 9221 Quivira Rd., Overland Park, KS 66215.

Index

Above-the-line costs, 228
American Federation of Television and Radio Artists (AFTRA), 139
American Society of Composers, Authors and Publishers (ASCAP), 245
Ampere hours (amps, or Ah), 40, 83
Animation, 255
Archive videos, 155, 159-160
Arnett, Peter, 220
ASA rating, 28
Aspect ratio, 17-18
Audio, background, 62
Audio engineers, 136, 138-139

B roll, 175
Barndoors, 76, 78-79, 100-101
Baseball, 177
Basketball, 176-177
Balancing pictures, 96-98, 100
Batteries, 39-42, 224
Behavioral changes, 122
Below-the-line costs, 228
Betacam, *See* Videotape formats
Black bursting, 187, 196
Booms, 43-44, 51, 53-54, 57
Bottomers, 78
Bounce cards, 92
Broadcast Music Inc. (BMI), 245
Broads, 75-76
Budgeting, 225-233
Burn-in, 252
Butting, 111

Cables, 157-158, 223-224
Camcorders, 1, 9-10, 13, 34, 64, 94, 138, 146, 167, 252
Camera operators, 138
Cameras, 13
    chip, 83, 85-86, 93
    controls of, 30-31
    film, 6-7
    lipstick-size, 44-45, 252
    portable, 9-11
    solid-state, 252
    Sony BVP-70
    Studio 9-10
    tube, 29, 86, 252
    videotape, 27-33, 252

Capacitors, 48
Carnet, 147
C-clamps, 77-78
Central visual theme, 122-123
Character generators, 255
Charge Coupled Devices (CCDs), *See* Chips
Chips, 29, 252
Chroma, 29, 84
Chromakey device, 255
Cinéma vérité, 120
Close-up lenses, 24
Cognitive effects, 122
Color bars, 32
Color elimination gels, 82, 95
Color temperature, 91
Comet-tailing, 252
Commericals, 122, 149-150, 153-155
Compact discs, 252
Component video, 183-184
Composite video, 183
Compression, 104
Concave lenses, 16
Confidence playback, 37
Connectors, 36-37, 58-59, 157
Contrast ratio, 84-86, 95
Control track reference, 190
Convex lenses, 16
Cookie, 80
Copyrights, 143-144, 235, 242-298
Corporate and professional videos, 149-153
Cranes, 43
Cucalorus, 80
Cutters, 78
Cuts, 130, 255

DeLorean, John, 238
Depth of field, 16-17
Diffusers, 80, 92
Digital applications, 208, 251-252, 255-256
Diopters, *See* Close-up lenses
Directors, 136, 138-139
Dissolves, 130, 208, 210
Distant learning, 151-152
Distribution amplifiers, 215-216
Documentaries, 136
Dollies, 43, 130
Dots, 78
Draw, 89-90

Dubs, 208
Duvetyn curtains, 93

Editing
    A/B roll, 158, 208-209, 253-254
    butt-splice, 208
    control track, 190
    creative, 199-213
    crossing-the-line, 204
    cut-and-splice, 179
    methods of, 213
    music, 213
    off-line, 208, 211
    online, 211
    reel-to-reel, 179
    sound, 211-213
    technical, 179-198
    time code, 190
    types of, 181-183
    wrong field, 189
Editing machines, 186, 191-198, 210
Editors, 136, 139-140
    nonlinear, 249-250, 255
Edit systems
    assemble, 185-187
    digital, 254
    disc-based, 253-254
    insert, 185-187, 196-198
    linear, 253
    multi-machine, 210
    nonlinear, 253-254
    random-access, 253-254
Electronic field production (EFP), 1-11
    budgeting, 226-227
    live, 222
    pre-production, 135-148
    pricing, 226-227, 231-233
    scriptwriting, 121-123
    styles, 149-167
Electronic news gathering (ENG), 1-11, 149
    budgeting, 226
    channels, 216
    pre-production, 135-136
    pricing, 226
    scriptwriting, 121-122
    styles, 169-177
Elements, lens, 16
Emotional effects, 122
Entertainment videos, 122
Equipment checklist, 145
Equipment cubes, 144, 146
Executive producers, 136, 139

Faders, 79
Fades, 130, 255
Farkas, Ray, 64, 101, 119-120

Fast lenses, 84
Feature news, 169, 175-176
Federal Communications Commission (FCC), 216
Fiber optics, 222, 238
Fields, 29, 188-189
Filament bulbs, 73
Film cameras, 6-7
Filters, 9, 23-26, 28-29, 86, 93-94
Filter wheels, 28-29
Fingers, 78
Flags, 78, 82
Flares, 23
Fly-away, 217
Floodlights, 75-76
Foam cores, 92-93
Focal length, 16, 104-105, 114, 119
Focus, 16-17
Football, 176-177
Footcandles (FCs), 85
Form PA, 247-248
Formats, 122-123
Frames, 29, 188
Frame servo, 189
Framing, 97-98
F-stops, 18-19

Gel frames, 80, 82
General news, 169, 174-175
Gen-lock port, 157, 158, 255
Gigahertz (GHz), 216
Gobos, See Flags
Golf, 177
Graininess, 30
Grips, 77-78, 82, 136, 139

Hart, Gary, 237
Head room, 37
Headphones, 65
High Definition TV (HDTV), 167, 252, 255
High-gain circuit, 84
Hockey, 177
Home videos, 2-3, 9
House sound, 64
Hyperfocal distance, 17

Ikegani HL-55, 31
Improved Definition TV Set (IDTV), 254
In-house production units, 227
Independent production units, 227-228
Institute of Radio Engineers (IRE), 32
Instructional videos, 122, 149-153
Insurance, 246, 249-250
Interchangeable lenses, 26-27
Interrupted feed back (IFB), 218-219
Iris, 18-19
IS chip, 252

Isolated camera field shoot, 157-159
Jam sync, 158
Johnson, Don, 236
Jump cut, 109, 111-112

Lag, 252
Lamps, 74-75, 77
Laybacks, 212-213
Laydowns, 212-213
Lenses, video, 13, 15-27
Light
    as an aesthetic force, 94-96
    background, 90-91, 98, 100
    backlight, 86, 90, 93, 98, 100-102
    battery-powered, 94
    bounced, 92-93
    broad, 93
    camcorder, 94
    camera-mounted, 92-94
    caroon arc, 73
    color temperature of, 28
    daylight, 102
    diffused, 86
    direct, 92
    eye, 91, 100
    fill, 86, 90, 92, 95, 98, 100-101
    flooded, 86, 90
    fluorescent, 73
    fresnel, 93, 101
    high-intensity discharge (HID), 74
    hydrargyum medium arc-length iodide (HMI), 73-74, 77
    incandescent, 93
    key, 86, 89-90, 92-93, 95, 97-98, 100-101
    kicker, 91, 100
    metal halide, 74
    overhead, 94
    parabolic aluminized reflector (PAR), 73
    physical properties of, 67-72
    portable, 93-94
    placement, 98-99
    practicle, 93
    primed, 93
    quartz, 72
        halogen, 72
        tubular, 72
    sealed beam, 73
    sources of, 72
    special effects, 95, 100
    studio arc, 73
    theory of, 13-15
    tungsten, 72-73, 80, 82, 93, 102
    unmodulated, 91
    window, 93
Light-emitting diode (LED), 84
Light filters, 82

    chocolate, 82
    cosmetic rouge, 82
Light housings, 75-77
Light modulators, 78-82
Light mounts, 77-78
Light waves, 13-15
    length of, 14-15
Lighting, 67-102
    base, 83-84
    cameo, 100
    chiaroscuro, 100-101
    color, 101-102
    equipment, 74-83
    flat, 94
    grid for, 77
    mood, 100
    placement, 88
    portrait, 94-96
    quality, 84-85
    Rembrandt, 100
    soft, 91-92
    source, 94-95
    techniques of, 86-102
    three-point, 86-91, 93, 95
    zones of, 87, 101
Lighting directors, 136, 138-139
Line costs, 228-229
Line of interest, 202-204
Location scouting report, 142
Luminance, 29
Lux, 84

Macrofocus, 17-18
Madonna, 236
Match-action cutting, 201-202
Matte box, 24
Microphones
    adapters for, 59
    bidirectional, 50
    boom, 54, 62
    boundary, 55-56
    cables and connectors for, 58-60
    camera-mounted, 62
    carbon, 47
    cardioid, 50, 55, 60
    ceramic, 47
    clasps for, 58, 62-63
    condenser, 47-49, 51, 55, 60, 65
    contact, 57
    convertible, 55
    directional, 49-51
    directional sensitivity of, 48-51
    dish, 57
    dynamic, 47-48, 50-51, 53, 55, 60, 62
    filters for, 57-58, 60
    fishpole, 54, 62

frequency response of, 49, 51
hand, 53, 55, 58, 60-61
headset, 55, 58, 65
    micro-, 61
hypercardioid, 50
impedance of, 51-52
integral, 53
lavaliere, 52, 54-55, 58, 62-63
level of, 52
line level of, 52
low-impedance, 59
mini-, 52, 54-55, 58, 62-63
miniboom, 55
mounts, 53, 57, 62
moving coil, 47-48
Mylar, 47
omnidirectional, 49-50, 53, 55, 57, 60, 62
pads for, 60
parabolic, 57
performance, 54-55
pickup patterns of, 49
placement, 62
radio frequency (RF), 56, 138
ribbon, 48, 50, 53
sound sensitivity of, 49, 51
shotgun, 50-54, 58, 62
studio, 53
style of, 52-54
supercardioid, 50
system, 55
tie-clip, 54
ultradirectional, 50-51, 62
unidirectional, 50, 55, 60
velocity, 48
windscreens for, 57-58
wireless, 33, 56-57, 63-64
Microwave transmitters, 32, 152, 216-217
Mix, 208
Mix-minus, 219
Mixing sound, 64-65
Model release forms, 241
Modeling effect, 89-90, 94
Monitoring sound, 64-66
Music, 149-150, 164-165, 207

Nanometers (nm), 14-15
National TV Standards Committee (NTSC), 29, 37, 215, 254-255
Nature and documentary videos, 149-150, 165-166
Net, 157
News production and privacy, 235-240
Newton, Wayne, 236
Neutral density (ND) gel, 79, 95
Non-news production and privacy, 240-242

Nook lights, 76

Off-axis sounds, 49, 62
On-axis sounds, 49, 62
100° line rule, 201-202, 204
Outline, 122, 125
Overhead expenses, 230

Pacing, 206-207
Pans, 23, 130, 207
Parabolic Aluminized Reflector (PAR) light, 73
Party gels, 82
Performance videos, 149-150, 155-160
Permissions, 224
Phantom power, 48, 64-65
Phase Alteration by Line (PAL), 29-30
Photons, 13-14
Picture noise, 30
Pixels, 29
Polar response chart, 49
Pop-and-blast mike filters, 57-58
Post-production, 208-211
Pre-production, 135-148
Pricing, 225-233
Prime lenses, 16
Privacy, 235-242
Porta-pack video system, 8
Press pass, 173-174
Processing amplifier (proc-amp), 191
Producers, 136, 139
Production crew, 136-140
Project creators, 136
Props preparation, 143
Public service announcements (PSAs), 128-129, 149-150, 153-155, 240
Pull-ups, 179
Pulse code modulation (PCM), 185
Puppy mills, 238

RCA-type connectors, 59
Reflectors, 79, 81
Reporter standups, 174
Retrozoom, 24
RF signal, 193, 195
Roaming, 19
Rule of thirds, 111

Satellite transmitters, 32, 152, 216-219, 243
Scanning, 187-189
Scoops, 75-76
Scope, 32-33
Screen Actors Guild (SAG), 139
Scrim, 79
Scriptwriters, 136
Scriptwriting, 121-133

Sealed-beam light, 73
Sequential Couleur à Memoire (SECAM) system, 29-30
Servo, 19, 38
Shade, 157
Shots
    basic, 103-120
    closeup, 108-109, 111-113, 130
    closing, 199
    cutaway, 109, 111-112, 199
    dolly, 118-119
    extreme closeup (XCU), 109, 112-113, 130
    flat, 107
    focal length, 104-109
    interview, 113, 115-116
    live, 219-221
    long, 130
    medium, 108-109, 111, 130, 199
    opening, 199
    pan, 118-119
    reporter stand-up, 115-117, 219-220
    sequencing of, 199-201
    tight, 114, 130, 199
    transition, 113, 119, 212
    types of, 103-119
    wide, 105-108, 111-114, 130, 199, 202
    zoom, 113-114, 117-119
Siders, 78
Silk, 82
Slow lenses, 84
Soft news. *See* Feature news
Sound engineers. *See* Audio engineers
Special effects generators, 252
Speed, 18-19
Spotlights, 76-77
Spot news, 119, 169-174, 220-221
Sports news, 169, 176-177
Sports videos, 150, 160-164
Squeezes, 208
Steadicam, 44-45
Stereo sound, 64, 66
Sticks, 78
Story line, 205-206
Storyboards, 122, 125, 127-130
Stringers, 226
Studio, indoor, 9-11
Sungun, 3, 92
Switchable camera field shoot, 156-157
Switchers, 157-158, 208, 210, 252, 255

Takes, 130
Talent, 136, 138-139
Talking heads, 98, 111, 113, 115, 119, 174-175, 212
Targets, 78
Tech power, 223
Telecine, 155

Teleconferencing, 152-153
Teleconverter, 24
Telephone line transmitters, 216
Telephoto lenses, 16, 104-105
Telescoping mast, 217
Tilts, 23, 116, 130, 207
Time Base Correctors (TBCs), 37-39, 84, 190-191, 252
Time code reference, 190
    linear, 35
    vertical interval (VITC), 35-36
Toppers, 78
Tracking, 190
Training videos. *See* Instructional videos
Triax adapter, 157
Tripods, 42-43
TV monitors, 32, 35, 223, 254-255
Tyler mount, 45

Umbrella lighting, 79, 81, 91-92, 96-97
U.S. Copyright Office, 246
U.S. Post Office, 238
Utility, *See* Grips

Vanishing point, 107-108
Variable capacitance, 48
Vectorscope, 32, 34
Video art, 149, 166-167
Videographers, 136, 138
Videotape formats, 9, 35, 38, 180-185, 191, 193, 196, 252-254
    VHS, 184-185
    VHS-C, 184
Videotape recorders, 13, 33-39, 183, 253
Vignetting, 24
Volts, 83
VU meter, 37, 138, 191, 193

Watts, 83
Waveform monitors, 32-33, 223
Whip pan, 177
White balance, 30-31, 73, 94
White light, 15
Wide-angle lenses, 16, 24, 104-106, 238
Wide shots, 207
Wipes, 208, 211, 255
Wire mesh screens, 81

Zapruder, 243-244
Zebra bars, 31-32
Zeppelin mike windscreen, 58
Zip lights, 76
Zoom lenses, 16, 18-24, 104-105
Zoom shots, 130, 207

About the Authors

Norman J. Medoff has been active in media management, media consulting, media audience research, media production and media education for more than 20 years. He and his students have produced numerous programs for commercial, public and corporate TV. He has given workshops on video production to audiences across the country.

Medoff received his Ph.D in Mass Communication from Indiana University. In addition to being a college professor since 1979, he has served as head of Media Production and Chairman of the Department of Communication at Florida State University and director of the Media Center at the University of Colorado at Colorado Springs.

Currently, Dr. Medoff is director and professor at the School of Communication at Northern Arizona University.

Tom Tanquary has worked as a video photographer in TV news and production since 1976. Starting as a film processing operator in a small TV market, Mr. Tanquary has worked his way up to his current position as documentary photographer for PBS affiliate KCET in Los Angeles.

Mr. Tanquary also gained experience in a number of newsroom jobs including reporter, producer, writer, editor, studio camera operator and assignment editor. During the eight years he spent at KNBC in Los Angeles, his work regularly appeared on *NBC Nightly News, The Today Show* and several network and syndicated entertainment programs. He has also directed segments for ABC's *Home Show*.

Mr. Tanquary's photography has won an Emmy award, two Emmy nominations and numerous state and local awards. Also honored by the National Press Photographers Association as Southwestern Photographer of the Year, he is a member of the Directors Guild of America (DGA), the National Association of Broadcast Employees and Technicians (NABET) Local 53, and the International Alliance of Theatrical and Stage Employees (IAISE) Locals 659 and 695.

274